CARL WIMAR

CARL WIMAR

CHRONICLER OF THE MISSOURI RIVER FRONTIER

◆

Rick Stewart, Joseph D. Ketner II, and Angela L. Miller

Amon Carter Museum, Fort Worth

Distributed by Harry N. Abrams, Inc., New York

Published on the occasion of the exhibition:

January 26–March 24, 1991
Washington University Gallery of Art
Saint Louis, Missouri

May 4–August 4, 1991
Amon Carter Museum
Fort Worth, Texas

Distributed by Harry N. Abrams, Incorporated, New York.
A Times Mirror Company

ISBN 0-8109-3958-4
LC 90-84701

Printed in Hong Kong by South China Printing Company

FRONTISPIECE
Carl Wimar. Ambrotype by Enoch Long, 1858. Missouri Historical Society, Saint Louis.

The Amon Carter Museum was established in 1961 under the will of Fort Worth publisher Amon G. Carter (1879–1955). Initially comprising Carter's collection of paintings and sculpture by Frederic Remington and Charles M. Russell, the Museum has since broadened the scope of its collection to include American paintings, prints, drawings, and sculpture of the nineteenth and early twentieth centuries, and American photography from its beginnings to the present day. Through its collections, special exhibitions, public programs, and publications, the Museum serves as a center for the study and appreciation of American art.

Contents

Foreword   ix

Acknowledgments   x

Plates   1

Introduction   25

  I. The Indian Painter in Düsseldorf
     Joseph D. Ketner II   30

 II. An Artist on the Great Missouri
     Rick Stewart   80

III. A Muralist of Civic Ambitions
     Angela L. Miller   188

Appendix: Checklist of Art Works by
Carl Wimar   227

Selected Bibliography   241

Index   247

Foreword

A scholarly examination of Carl Wimar's work is long overdue. Some years ago, Joseph D. Ketner II, formerly Curator and now Director of the Gallery of Art at Washington University in Saint Louis, realized this and set out to uncover the artist's accomplishments and clarify his contribution to the history of American art. Ketner, assisted by Gallery staff, worked at the exacting task of locating and recording every possible example of Wimar's work in public and private collections. As the research progressed, Gerald Bolas, then Director of the Gallery of Art, invited the staff of the Amon Carter Museum to consider a collaborative project. A full-scale exhibition was proposed, the first comprehensive presentation of Wimar's work since the Saint Louis Art Museum exhibition in 1946. Rick Stewart, Curator of Western Painting and Sculpture at the Amon Carter Museum, had long been interested in Wimar's art and enthusiastically agreed to head the project, serving as co-curator with Ketner and as editor of this publication.

From the beginning, Ketner and Stewart planned to write about Wimar's artistic achievement in the context of American culture along the Missouri frontier in the decade before the Civil War. Angela Miller, Assistant Professor of Art History at Washington University, agreed to provide a discussion of the artist's efforts to give visual form to the region's aspirations as a center for the rapidly developing trans-Mississippi West. In the present study, which reproduces many of the artist's works for the first time, Carl Wimar emerges as one of the most important early artists to record the confluence of reality and myth that has characterized practically all subsequent depictions of the American frontier.

This volume would not have been possible without the spirit of collaboration that has existed between the two organizing museums and their sister institutions in the city of Saint Louis. Heartfelt thanks go to the directors and staffs of the Saint Louis Art Museum, the Missouri Historical Society, the Saint Louis Mercantile Library, and the Jefferson National Expansion Memorial for their unfailing assistance at every stage of the project. The resulting exhibition and publication are due to a common desire to see the work of Carl Wimar receive the scholarly attention it deserves.

Jan Keene Muhlert
Director
Amon Carter Museum

Acknowledgments

The efforts to compile a catalogue and mount a scholarly exhibition of Carl Wimar's work began at the Washington University Gallery of Art, where student interns, as an exercise in primary research, compiled a comprehensive catalogue and bibliography on Wimar. Since its inception in 1985 many students have contributed their efforts to this project, including Janet Bickers, Catherine David, Melissa Neves, Steven Nowack (now at the Toledo Museum of Art), Alicia Miller, Diane Mullin, Ayssa Karp Sadoff, and Anna Vemer.

A majority of Wimar's works survive in the collections of the Gallery of Art's sister institutions, the Missouri Historical Society and the Saint Louis Art Museum. Without their generous and continuous support, this project would not have been possible. At the Missouri Historical Society, Robert R. Archibald, Director, and Karen Goering, Acting Director, deserve our gratitude for making the resources of that important institution available to us. The authors especially wish to thank Katherine Corbett, Anne Hamilton, and Peter Michel in the archival collections, and Magdalyn M. Sebastian, Registrar; Duane R. Sneddeker, Curator of Photographs and Prints; Jill Sherman, Pictorial History Collections; and Ken Wynn for their untiring assistance throughout the project. At the Saint Louis Art Museum, James D. Burke, Director; Sidney M. Goldstein, Associate Director; and Michael E. Shapiro, Chief Curator, were responsible for key support in the loan of a number of significant paintings and works on paper. Betsy Wright, previously Assistant Curator of Prints and Photographs and now Curator of Contemporary Art, deserves special mention for her continuous and valuable assistance with many research requests, and Patricia Woods efficiently and speedily answered our many requests for photographs. At the Saint Louis Mercantile Library, John Neal Hoover, Acting Librarian, and Mark J. Cedeck, of the John W. Barriger III National Railroad Library, enthusiastically supported our efforts and made the library's valuable resources available for study. The National Park Service staff at the Saint Louis Courthouse, now fittingly part of the Jefferson National Expansion Memorial, went out of their way to accommodate our requests, and we would like to thank Jerry L. Schober, Superintendent, and Katheen Moenster and Denise Stuhr for their helpful assistance with the courthouse photographs.

The success of this volume also owes a great deal to the four individuals who agreed to pool their considerable expertise as official consultants to the project. The authors are grateful to Jonathan Batkin, Director of the Wheelwright Museum, Santa Fe; Wayne Fields, Associate Professor of English, Washington University; David H. Miller, Dean of the School of Humanities and Social Sciences and Professor of History, Cameron University; and William H. Truettner, Curator of Painting and Sculpture at the National Museum of American Art, Smithsonian Institution.

We are also indebted to a number of individuals and institutions who have allowed us to reproduce materials from their collections or have lent their own expertise to this project: John C. Abbott, Elijah P. Lovejoy Library, Southern Illinois University at Edwardsville; Laurey Allis of Christie, Manson and Woods, Inc.; Rolf Andree, Curator, Kunstmuseum Düsseldorf; James K. Ballinger, Phoenix Art Museum; Lillian Brenwasser of Kennedy Galleries; Anna J. Caffey of the Stark Museum; Nancy Grant Corrigan, Tustin, California; Bill Cuffe, Yale University Art Gallery; Elizabeth Cunningham, the Anschutz Collection; Lorenzo De Masi and the Capitoline Museum, Rome; Lawrence Dinnean and Irene Moran of the Bancroft Library, University of California, Berkeley; Hilarie Faberman, Carole McNamara, and Terry Kerby, University of Michigan Museum of Art; Paula Richardson Fleming, National Anthropological Archives, Smithsonian Institution; Wayne

Furman and Rebecca Waddell of the New York Public Library; Stephen Good, Rosenstock Arts, Denver; Dr. and Mrs. John Grant, Mrs. Samuel Grant, and Mr. Samuel Grant, Jr., Wimar's descendants in Saint Louis; Charles E. Hilburn, Gulf States Paper Corporation; David C. Hunt and Peggy Henderson, Joslyn Art Museum; Beatrice Hurwitz of Simon and Schuster, Inc.; Lawrence Huss of the Dover Free Public Library; Barbara Isaac of the Peabody Museum, Harvard University; Reinhart K. Jost, Department of Germanic Language and Literature, Washington University; Martin Kodner, Saint Louis; Bob Kolbrener, photographer, Saint Louis; Helmut and Inge Krumbach, Düsseldorfer Institut für amerikanische Völkerkunde; Irene Martin, the Thyssen-Bornemisza Collection; David W. Mesker, Saint Louis; Mrs. Maxwell Moran; Lory Morrow, Montana Historical Society; Fred A. Myers, Director, and Anne Morand, Kayelene O'Neal, Margot Schiewing, and Joan Carpenter Troccoli at the Thomas Gilcrease Institute for American History and Art; Jane O'Meara, Inventory of American Painting, National Museum of American Art; the staff of the Department of Paintings at the Louvre; Gerald Peters and the staff of the Gerald Peters Gallery, Santa Fe; B. Byron Price, National Cowboy Hall of Fame; ElRoy Quenroe, Quenroe Associates, Baltimore; Joel L. Samuels, Reu Memorial Library, Wartburg Theological Seminary; Martha A. Sandweiss, Mead Art Gallery, Amherst College; Todd Strand, State Historical Society of North Dakota; Esther Thyssen; George M. White, Architect of the Capitol; Lyle S. Woodcock, Saint Louis; Rudolf Wunderlich, Mongerson-Wunderlich Galleries, Inc., Chicago; and Mark Zaplin, Zaplin-Lampert Gallery, Santa Fe.

This project involved the concerted efforts of the staffs of the Amon Carter Museum and the Gallery of Art at Washington University, and a few individuals should be singled out for special mention. Jan Keene Muhlert, Director of the Amon Carter Museum, and Gerald Bolas, formerly Director of the Gallery of Art at Washington University in Saint Louis, now Director of the Portland, Oregon Art Museum, have lent their unfailing support. At the Gallery of Art, Sharon Bangert, Administrative Assistant, applied her literary skills to manuscript preparation. John D. Magurany, Registrar, conscientiously assisted in coordinating the transportation and installation of the exhibition. At the Amon Carter Museum, Doreen Bolger, Curator of Painting and Sculpture, gave each manuscript a close reading and offered many helpful suggestions. Milan Hughston, Librarian, used his great skills and knowledge of the field to obtain many hard-to-find research items and provided much assistance to all the authors, while Ben Huseman, Curatorial Assistant, performed a number of research tasks. Melissa Thompson, the Museum's Registrar, worked closely with the lenders and efficiently processed a bewildering amount of paperwork related to the exhibition. Nancy Stevens, the editor of this volume, deserves special praise. She coordinated critical suggestions from many readers of the manuscript and greatly assisted the authors with the necessary changes and revisions. In addition, she supervised the production of the volume with the aid of her capable assistant, Karen Reynolds. Finally, the authors would like to extend their appreciation to the book's designer, Jim Ledbetter, for his fine eye for detail and welcome enthusiasm for the project.

1

2

PLATE 2
Indians Pursued by American Dragoons. Oil on canvas, 1853.
Gulf States Paper Corporation, Tuscaloosa, Alabama.

3

PLATE 3
Flatboatmen on the Mississippi. Oil on canvas, 1854.
Amon Carter Museum, Fort Worth.

4

PLATE 4
The Captive Charger. Oil on canvas, 1854.
The Saint Louis Art Museum; gift of Miss Lillie B. Randell.

The Abduction of Boone's Daughter by the Indians. Oil on canvas, 1855.
Amon Carter Museum, Fort Worth.

6

Plate 7
Funeral Raft of a Dead Chieftain. Oil on canvas, 1856.
Gulf States Paper Corporation, Tuscaloosa.

8

PLATE 9
Indians Stealing Horses. Oil on canvas, 1858.
Joslyn Art Museum, Omaha.

10

PLATE 10
Buffaloes Crossing the Yellowstone. Oil on canvas, 1859.
Washington University Gallery of Art, Saint Louis.

Plate 11
Buffalo Crossing the Platte. Oil on canvas, 1859.
The Thomas Gilcrease Institute of American History and Art, Tulsa.

12

Plate 12
Indians Approaching Fort Union. Oil on canvas, c. 1859.
Washington University Gallery of Art, Saint Louis.

PLATE 13
Indians Crossing the Upper Missouri River. Oil on canvas, c. 1859.
Amon Carter Museum, Fort Worth.

14

PLATE 14
The Buffalo Dance. Oil on canvas, 1860.
The Saint Louis Art Museum; gift of Mrs. John T. Davis.

Plate 15
Indian Encampment on the Big Bend of the Missouri River. Oil on canvas, 1860.
The Thomas Gilcrease Institute of American History and Art, Tulsa.

Plate 16
Buffalo Hunt. Oil on canvas, 1860.
Washington University Gallery of Art, Saint Louis.

17

PLATE 17
Portrait of an Indian (Bear Rib).
Oil on canvas mounted on cardboard, c. 1860.
Mr. and Mrs. Gerald P. Peters, Santa Fe.

18

PLATE 18
Buffalo Hunt. Oil on canvas, 1861.
Missouri Historical Society, Saint Louis.

PLATE 20
De Soto Discovering the Mississippi and *Edward Bates*.
Watercolor and oil on wet plaster, 1862.
Saint Louis Courthouse rotunda.
Photograph by Bob Kolbrener, 1990.

Plate 21
The Landing of Laclede and *Thomas Hart Benton*.
Watercolor and oil on wet plaster, 1862.
Saint Louis Courthouse rotunda.
Photograph by Bob Kolbrener, 1990.

PLATE 22
The Year of the Blow and *Martha Washington*.
Watercolor and oil on wet plaster, 1862.
Saint Louis Courthouse rotunda.
Photograph by Bob Kolbrener, 1990.

23

PLATE 23
Westward the Star of Empire (Cochetope Pass) and *George Washington.*
Watercolor and oil on wet plaster, 1862.
Saint Louis Courthouse rotunda.
Photograph by Bob Kolbrener, 1990.

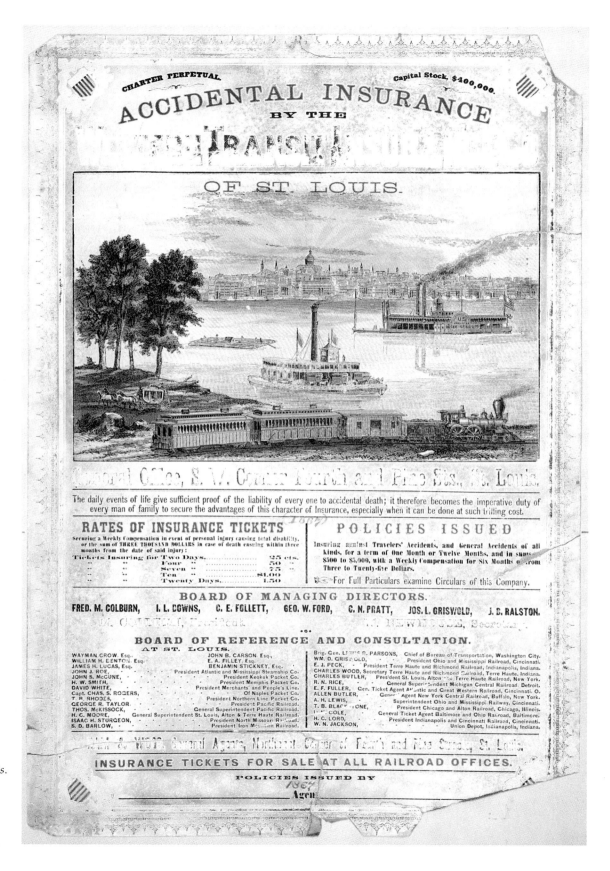

24

Introduction

The decade preceding the Civil War was a period of rapid change in American history, as the nation began consolidating its vast territories west of the Mississippi River. One of the most important of these regions was the land drained by the Missouri River and its tributaries, an area that had already figured prominently as the principal location of the American fur trade for more than half a century. Significantly, it also served as inspiration for numerous artists and writers who traveled the river from the 1830s through the 1850s in search of adventure and knowledge. Their impressions of the people and landscape of the upper Missouri left a valuable record, a complex amalgam of fiction and fact that continues to influence the way most people view the American West.

One of these travelers was Carl Wimar (1828–1862), a German-born artist from Saint Louis, whose shifting vision of the American West coincided with the profound changes in the region just prior to the Civil War. The paintings of his brief but productive career illustrate key themes that occupied nearly every American writer and artist of the period, when national attitudes toward the trans-Mississippi West were often contradictory. Wimar's works effectively bridged the conflicting realms of reality and myth, influencing a later generation of artists who sought to embody a similar spirit of the American West in their own works.

When Wimar returned to Germany for four years of artistic training from 1852 to 1856, he was the only painter in Düsseldorf to concentrate on imaginative themes of the American West—a subject that held special appeal for a European audience. At the time, most of what he knew about the American frontier came from earlier artists and romantic literature. Recognizing the need for firsthand observation, he subsequently made two trips up the Missouri River on fur company steamboats. In 1858 he journeyed as far as Fort Union, then along the Yellowstone

River to a point near the mouth of the Powder River. The following year he was a passenger on the first steamboat to navigate the Missouri as far as Fort Benton. At the time, the upper Missouri region was still open frontier, but federally sponsored exploration was well under way and settlement of the Dakota and Montana territories was about to begin. Wimar was one of only a few artists to take a camera upriver to record the Indians in their native setting, and his photographs and sketches were among the last to be made before the Plains tribes were moved to reservations.

Up to the 1850s, the American frontier was seen as an arena of primitive grandeur, largely untouched by the corrupting influence of white civilization. Wimar's artistic predecessors, among them Karl Bodmer and George Catlin, sought to record an accurate picture of the landforms and Indian tribes on the upper Missouri, but in keeping with the prevailing beliefs of their time, they were not above imposing a romantic schema on such a view. Similarly the works Wimar produced in Düsseldorf were imaginative renderings of popular ideas and gave objectivity only secondary importance. The exotic subjects of these paintings and their evocative settings were drawn from European conventions of the romantic and picturesque and from the imaginative western fiction of James Fenimore Cooper and others. Wimar's predominant theme during this period was the confrontation between the frontier and civilization, and his paintings established precedents for certain subjects, such as attacks on wagon trains and the abduction of white settlers, that would be explored by generations of later artists. Such work effectively illustrates historian Richard Slotkin's concept of "regeneration through violence" as "the structuring metaphor of the American experience."[1]

By the time Wimar returned from Düsseldorf to commence his career as a painter, popular perception of the American West was undergoing significant change. It was no longer considered an arena of conflict and violence, but a great stage of limitless opportunity, into which the nation as a whole projected all its political, social, and economic hopes. Such beliefs had begun to take shape as early as 1835 when the missionary Lyman Beecher, in a tract titled *Plea for the West*, avowed that "the West is destined to be the great central power of the nation, and under heaven, must affect powerfully the cause of free institutions and the liberty of the world." He proclaimed the frontier as "a young empire of mind, and power, and wealth, and free institutions, rushing up to a giant manhood, with a rapidity and power never before witnessed below the sun."[2] Saint Louis in the 1850s reflected Beecher's prophecy: the city was in a period of active expansion after a half-century as the mercantile and transportation center for the trans-Mississippi West. The fur trade, in one historian's words, had become "a smoothly running continental monopoly," centered on the activities of the American Fur Company and propelled by the city's location at the juncture of the Missouri and Mississippi Rivers.[3] But as the decade drew to a close, Saint Louis found itself struggling with Chicago to remain the gateway to the rapidly expanding empire of the West. Carl Wimar joined this debate when he created a series of murals for the new dome of the Saint Louis Courthouse. The cycle depicted Saint Louis' historical role in the development of the frontier and emphasized the city's aspirations as the center for the West's future growth. Unfortunately, these hopes were not to be realized. Wimar's mural cycle was completed as the onrushing events of the Civil War overwhelmed the city, and Saint Louis never achieved the status it so avidly sought.

In 1851 Francis Parkman, commenting on Cooper's western writings, observed that "civilization has a destroying as well as a creating power." Parkman, who saw the destruction of the frontier in the "exterminating of the buffalo and the Indian," was among many who sounded an alarm.[4] Wimar traveled up the Missouri River at this cru-

cial moment in its history, as the Plains Indians began to be confined to reservations, the buffalo hunted nearly to extinction, and the vast open spaces parceled into territories, towns, and farms. Yet he viewed the West with preconceived notions of its romantic beauty and grandeur, and these predispositions remained essentially unaltered. By the time he went upriver, the effects of white civilization were everywhere apparent, yet there is little evidence of this in his drawings. He returned from his two trips with many artifacts, photographs, and sketches depicting the Indian tribes as well as the landscape along the 2,500 miles of the river's length. These careful observations are valuable to historians today, but they record a way of life that, even at the time, was already slipping irretrievably away.

In his studio, Wimar began to utilize these materials to create works that mirrored a significant change in his vision of the American West. While his Düsseldorf paintings focused almost entirely on white experience along the American frontier, his overwhelming choice of subject for later paintings became the Indian and the buffalo. More and more, his paintings turned not to a world that was being discovered, but one that was already lost. Like Cooper, Wimar placed his figures in the "garish light" of a setting sun—an effective symbol for what they both perceived as the nostalgic passing of an era.[5] Before consumption claimed his life at the age of thirty-four, the artist had already achieved celebrated status locally as a painter of the "Great West." As the principal Saint Louis newspaper, the *Missouri Republican*, described it:

Our history teems with material for the painter's pencil and the sculptor's chisel. Our pioneers, with their wild and romantic adventures, remain almost unhonored; the red men are fast disappearing, and there is but here and there a master hand to rescue their curious habits and ceremonies from oblivion; while everywhere the hitherto unbroken solitudes of mountains, forests, broad lakes and rapid rivers, is becoming noisy with the hum of advancing civilization. It is this which we wish to preserve and send to posterity.[6]

The "Great West" was in fact a west of mythic hopes. The wealthy Saint Louis businessmen who purchased Wimar's paintings, as well as the critics who effusively praised them, doubtless believed that the disappearance of the Indians, the buffalo, and the open plains were the inevitable casualties of an age of progress of which Saint Louis' leaders were an important part. Ultimately, the representatives of that progress became patrons of the myth itself—a myth of individual freedom, limitless opportunity, and boundless natural resources.

In the end, even though his creative output was tragically brief, Carl Wimar left a lasting legacy. His art, particularly after his student period, contained many ethnographically accurate details, but its overall effect, conditioned by his historical and cultural milieu, was mythic. At his best, he was the equal of any painter of the American frontier, and many of his works still vividly evoke what a contemporary writer termed the "golden age of prairie romance."[7]

Twenty years after Wimar journeyed up the Missouri River, a kindred soul, Walt Whitman, made his own trip west of the Mississippi to discover what he called the "dominion-heart of America." Like Wimar, Whitman was captivated by the West as the "spirit" of the nation. One may see in Carl Wimar's paintings what Whitman described as "that vast Something, stretching out on its own unbounded scale, unconfined, which there is in these prairies, combining the real and ideal, and beautiful as dreams."[8] Wimar, more than any other artist of his time, portrayed the "real and ideal" of the American West as it began to emerge in the popular imagination. Although the

settlement of the upper Plains soon after the Civil War transformed that region forever, Wimar's and Whitman's vision still affects the character of the nation today.

1. Richard Slotkin, *Regeneration through Violence: The Mythology of the American Frontier, 1600–1860* (Middletown, Conn.: Wesleyan University Press, 1973), 5.

2. Lyman Beecher, *A Plea for the West*, quoted in Rush Welter, "The Frontier as Image of American Society: Conservative Attitudes Before the Civil War," *Mississippi Valley Historical Review* 46 (1960): 597.

3. John Francis McDermott, "Years of Turmoil, Years of Growth: St. Louis in the 1850s," *Missouri Historical Society Bulletin* 23 (July 1967): 306.

4. Francis Parkman, "The Works of James Fenimore Cooper," *North American Review* 74 (January 1852): 151.

5. See Donald A. Ringe, "Chiaroscuro as an Artistic Device in Cooper's Fiction," *Proceedings of the Modern Language Association of America* 78 (September 1963): 351.

6. *Missouri Republican*, October 14, 1860, 2.

7. "Prairie Fancies," *Harper's Weekly*, July 10, 1858, 437.

8. Quoted in Walter H. Eitner, *Walt Whitman's Western Jaunt* (Lawrence: The Regents Press of Kansas, 1981), 11, 35.

Figure 1
Carl Wimar. *Self-Portrait*. Oil on canvas, n.d.
National Portrait Gallery, Smithsonian Insti-
tution, Washington, D.C.

America, you have it better

Johann Goethe (1825)[1]

CHAPTER I

The Indian Painter in Düsseldorf

JOSEPH D. KETNER II

Carl Wimar (fig. 1) was a true German American, and his early paintings reflect the cultures both of Germany, where he was born and where he later studied art, and of the American West, where his family settled when he was an adolescent. By the time he went to Düsseldorf to study, like other American artists, with master German painters, he was ready to synthesize his German and American backgrounds into a distinctive, hybrid vision of western America. The only student in Düsseldorf to paint canvases depicting the American West, he drew his subject matter from romantic notions of the frontier—nourished during his early years in Germany—combined with a decade's experience among frontiersmen and native Americans who passed through Saint Louis. In Düsseldorf he not only developed his skills at painting and composition; he also learned to merge this subject matter with the European history painting tradition to create memorable images of the American West, thus laying the groundwork for his mature work.

Wimar's career is remarkable when one considers the modest means and intellectual background of his family. His father, Ludwig Gottfried Wimar, was a nineteen-year-old scrivener when Carl Ferdinand Wimar was born on February 19, 1828, in Siegburg, a small village

Figure 2
Carl Wimar. *Siegburg. 1852*. Pencil on paper,
1852. Missouri Historical Society.

east of Bonn (fig. 2). Ludwig Wimar died within
a few years after Carl's birth, and the boy's
mother, Elizabeth Schmitz, worked as a washer-
woman.[2] According to family lore, their child
demonstrated a special aptitude for the visual
arts at a very early age: he supposedly began
drawing at the age of three and painting in
watercolors and copying prints after works by
the masters by the time he was ten.[3]

By 1835 his mother had remarried, and her
new husband, a merchant named Matthias
Becker, moved the family to Cologne, just up the
Rhine.[4] In 1839, Matthias emigrated alone to the
United States, searching for better economic
opportunities for his young family. He settled in
Saint Louis, at the edge of the frontier, and soon
opened a public house, the Saint Louis Park,
which became a popular meeting place. His busi-

ness established, Matthias called for his family,
who joined him by 1844. The Becker-Wimar
family settled permanently in the Saint Louis
area; in fact, many of their descendants still live
there.[5]

The family's move to the United States was
part of the first major wave of German emigration in the 1830s and 1840s, a reaction to tumul-
tuous sociopolitical and economic problems at
home.[6] During the 1830s, as liberal Germans
pressed for greater individual freedoms and
economic liberties, a tremendous population
explosion strained the already fragile economy.
German working and merchant classes and intellectuals alike were attracted to the social and economic opportunities and political freedom in
America; over 150,000 emigrated to the United
States during this period.

A number of guides published for prospective emigrants discussed the character and customs of the United States and its German settlements. The most popular of these was by Gottfried Duden, who from 1824 to 1827 had lived on the Missouri River outside Saint Louis and had studied the conditions and possibilities for German emigrants. Impressed by the abundance of natural resources and the social and political freedoms that he found in America, Duden urged his fellow Germans to emigrate directly to Missouri, where "poverty . . . is completely unknown" and merchants and skilled tradesmen thrived. Such an idealized account must have sounded very appealing to Matthias Becker, who probably relied on Duden's emphatic advice to "travel directly to Saint Louis on the Mississippi."[7]

Interest in the United States was not confined to would-be emigrants but was spread across a broad cross section of German society in the early nineteenth century. German scientists and naturalists such as Alexander von Humboldt, Paul Wilhelm von Württemberg, Prince Maximilian of Wied-Neuwied, and Balduin Möllhausen explored and studied the North and South American continents for the origins of man and nature.[8] To philosophers and writers of the Romantic Age, America embodied an idealized vision of unspoiled nature and the natural man; Johann Goethe considered America's primitive forests, mountains, and plains to be the ideal representation of God's work, and the German romantic poet Nicolaus Lenau remarked, "My poetry lives and thrives on nature . . . and in America nature is more beautiful and powerful than in Europe."[9] This fascination with the New World also carried over into the popular culture, where western novels and travel literature spread ideas about frontier America to a broad public. Although earlier novels about the American West had appealed to German audiences, those of

James Fenimore Cooper, first translated into German in 1826, seemed to excite their imaginations the most; by midcentury Cooper was among the most popular foreign authors being read in Germany. His work seems to have spawned a whole genre of native German literature, the *wildwestgeschichten* (wild West stories), and also encouraged the growth of the more traditional genre of *reiseliteratur* (travel literature) about the New World.[10]

Among the first and most successful German authors of wild West stories and American travel literature was a German priest who had fled to the United States in 1823 and assumed the pseudonym Charles Sealsfield. Returning to Germany in 1827, Sealsfield published an account of his travels through the United States and followed it two years later with his first work of fiction.[11] Stories like *Tokeah, or the White Rose* (1829) clearly show the influence of Cooper's *The Last of the Mohicans*; Sealsfield's tales divide native Americans into "noble" and "savage" types, some of whom are "treacherous" and others "noble and grand."[12] Sealsfield established the German prototype for wild West literature, which had an immense appeal, especially among youths.

In a society torn by social and political strife, books about the American West provided a release from the grim reality of the present, and they were more popular in Germany than in any other country during the nineteenth century.[13] A number of native authors who succeeded Sealsfield—most notably Friederich Gerstaecker, Balduin Möllhausen, and, later, Karl May—tended to romanticize western America, viewing the vast wilderness as both God's glorious creation and a sublime and menacing force with which to contend. Particularly, their books concentrated

on the confrontation between European civilization and primitive "savages" and evoked mixed
sentiments, sometimes favoring the civilizing
influence of Anglo-European expansion and
sometimes lamenting the loss of the primitive
wilderness and the natural man.[14] Considering
the high literacy rate in Germany and young
Carl's own precocity, it is safe to assume that
Wimar was familiar with some of the popular literature about America while he was a youth in
the lower Rhineland. He certainly knew of such
works later: while an art student in Düsseldorf
he wrote home that he was working from one of
Cooper's novels.[15]

By the time he reached Missouri as an
impressionable fifteen-year-old, Wimar's vision
of the frontier was undoubtedly colored by
romantic German notions of the American West
that he had learned in the fatherland. His earliest
paintings (now lost) derived from prints in this
romantic vein, and their titles, such as *The
Brigand* (c. 1840–43), *The Captive Maid*
(c. 1840–43), and *A Woodland Scene with Deer*
(c. 1845–50), suggest that the young Wimar
already was immersed in the romantic sentiment
that would influence his future work and his conception of the Missouri River frontier. In addition, his father's public house, situated on the
edge of town, was near the encampment for Indians who came to Saint Louis to trade with the
American Fur Company. According to early
accounts, Wimar possessed a great fondness for
the Indians and was befriended by one of their
warriors, who taught the youth much about the
native lifestyle, culture, and customs.[16]

When Wimar arrived in Saint Louis, he was
at the proper age to learn a trade. Because of his
natural predilection for drawing and painting, his
parents apprenticed him to a local house- and
steamboat-painter, A. C. Wilgus, to learn the
painting trade,[17] which encompassed house, sign,
and coach painting, gilding, lettering, and steam-

boat decorating.[18] Wimar was not satisfied with
the training he received from Wilgus and did not
complete his apprenticeship. Instead, he entered
the studio of the French emigré Leon Pomarede,
a local painter and decorator reputed to have had
European academic training. Pomarede had
received the important commission to decorate
the Saint Louis Cathedral a decade earlier and
also had designed numerous theater sets and
painted easel pictures.[19] Wimar felt he could
learn more about the art of painting, instead of
just the craft, from the Frenchman. Although
Pomarede did not usually accept apprentices, he
did permit Wimar to work in the studio on a trial
basis.[20] By 1846 Wimar was living and working
in Pomarede's atelier as his apprentice.

During his apprenticeship Wimar worked on
Pomarede's Mississippi River panorama, *Portrait
of the Father of the Waters*, a vast painted landscape made to be unrolled before a theater audience as a narrator discussed the scenery and
dramatic lighting and musical accompaniment
enhanced the effect.[21] Early in 1848 Pomarede

33

Figure 3
Leon Pomarede. *A Scaffold Burial.* Oil on
canvas, c. 1851. Peabody Museum, Harvard
University.

Figure 4
Portrait of Charles Wimar. Daguerreotype,
early 1850s. Saint Louis Art Museum; gift of
Miss Elise C. Crecelius in memory of her
mother, Charlotte Overstolz Crecelius.

34

collaborated with the English artist Henry Lewis,
but the two soon clashed, voided their partnership, and produced their panoramas indepen-
dently.[22] Pomarede toured the upper Mississippi
in August 1848 and over the next year took several additional sketching trips to develop material
for his vast project; Wimar reportedly accompanied him on one of these sketching tours in the
summer of 1849. The completed panorama,
which required sixteen months of work, six
thousand dollars, and over five thousand feet of
canvas, opened with great fanfare in Saint Louis
on September 19, 1849. Along with Henry
Lewis' panorama, which had opened two weeks
earlier, and a museum of Indian artifacts, it
became a popular attraction for residents and
visitors in the city.

This fertile environment for frontier projects encouraged Wimar's maturing aesthetic sensibilities, and the tremendous task of painting the
panorama made an indelible impression on him
as well. A number of scenes in the panorama
would be influential in his later paintings, especially the views of a prairie fire, Indian encampments, and a war dance; these subjects and the
panoramic format would reappear a decade later
in Wimar's mature Missouri River landscapes.
It is difficult to compare the style of Wimar's
immature portraits and genre subjects to
Pomarede's few extant paintings, which demonstrate a labored paint handling and a stilted drawing technique. But Pomarede's easel paintings of
Indians, buffalo hunts, and other frontier subjects (fig. 3) were seminal in the development of
Wimar's pictorial imagery. According to Wimar's
first biographer, Pomarede also advised his pro-
tégé to adopt frontier subject matter and "follow
it exclusively, as through it he might achieve a
reputation that, in years to come when the Indians would be a 'race clean gone,' would increase
to a peculiar brightness, not only in this country
but on the continent."[23] This would prove to be

wise counsel.

Around 1850 Wimar (fig. 4) was ready to pursue his profession and opened his own business, advertising with a partner in the 1851 Saint Louis City Directory as "Wimar and Boneau, painters 13 n. Third."[24] The success of this venture and the range of their work is not known, but Wimar's extant canvases suggest that he primarily painted portraits and a few genre subjects composed from prints. Preserved from this period are two cut-paper portrait silhouettes and painted portraits of a number of citizens, including four of the Deppe family—Henry, his wife, and two children (figs. 5 and 6). His most ambitious and interesting early painting is of his half-brother, entitled *Emil Becker and His Dog Dash* (fig. 7). The crudely crafted picture demonstrates a naive understanding of modeling, draftsmanship, proportions, and anatomy (especially evident in the remarkable manner in which the dog's tail grows from his hip). However, it is the artist's most complex early portrait, with a decorative landscape background that marks his progress from standard bust-length portraits. There is a primitive charm in the painting's design and in the sensitive portrayal of the sitter and his pet.

Just a year later Wimar began to experiment with more complex landscapes and genre compositions painted after prints, including *Entrance to*

Figure 5   (left)
Carl Wimar. *Henry Deppe*. Oil on canvas, 1850. Missouri Historical Society.

Figure 6   (right)
Carl Wimar. *Fredericka Peters Deppe*. Oil on canvas, c. 1850. Missouri Historical Society.

Figure 8
Carl Wimar. *The Entrance to the Jeddo River*.
Oil on canvas, 1851. Saint Louis Art
Museum.

Figure 7
Carl Wimar. *Portrait of Emil Becker and His
Dog Dash*. Oil on canvas, 1850. Missouri His-
torical Society.

the Jeddo River (fig. 8). The most ambitious and
undoubtedly the finest work of this early period
is *Three Children Attacked by a Wolf* (fig. 9), in
which three children, who have been gathering
kindling in the woods, gesture dramatically to
defend themselves against a snarling wolf. A
lush, wooded landscape enframes the staged
action. Although family oral tradition has it that
Wimar witnessed this scene as a youth and executed the painting under Pomarede's guidance,
the composition is remarkably similar to a 1791
engraving after Thomas Gainsborough's *Two
Shepherd Boys With Dogs Fighting* (fig. 10). The
gestures of the boy raising the machete, the
frightened youngster, and the dominant dog
appear in Wimar's composition—similarities suggesting that Wimar knew the print after Gainsborough. If so, his imaginative powers were
maturing and he was able to integrate visual
resources from European art with his frontier
subjects. The complexity of the composition and
the skill of his paint handling would indicate that

this work, the climax of Wimar's earliest career, was probably painted just prior to his departure for Düsseldorf, not during his apprenticeship.

Although popular events like panoramas could draw crowds, the cultural environment in Saint Louis during the 1840s and early 1850s was not very encouraging for a young painter aspiring to improve his art: there were no formal art schools, exhibition opportunities were limited, and patronage was modest. Yet the city was a center for artists who chose to depict the frontier. George Catlin had arrived there in 1830, traveled the Mississippi and Missouri River regions for six years, and, after touring his Indian Gallery through the United States and Europe, published the journals and images from

his expeditions.[25] In 1833, the scientific expedition of Prince Maximilian of Wied-Neuwied, accompanied by the Swiss illustrator Karl Bodmer, landed at Saint Louis to carry out ethnographic, botanical, and geological research on the Missouri River. Bodmer's drawings and watercolors preserved some of the finest images of the Missouri River frontier prior to its post-Civil War settlement, and engravings after them were published in 1839 with Prince Maximilian's writings about their explorations.[26] These travel accounts quickly became the primary visual sources for later artists of the western frontier, among them Wimar.

In addition to the artists who had passed through Saint Louis during their artistic and sci-

Figure 9   (left)
Carl Wimar. *Three Children Attacked by a Wolf*. Oil on canvas on board, c. 1851. Missouri Historical Society.

Figure 10   (right)
Thomas Gainsborough. *Two Shepherd Boys with Dogs Fighting*. Oil on canvas, R.A. 1783. The Iveagh Bequest, English Heritage, Kenwood.

38

Figure 11
J. C. Wild. *The Valley of the Mississippi Illustrated*. Lithograph, 1840. From the collections of the Mercantile Library Association, Saint Louis.

exhibitions, the American Art Union, and the many prints after his work, and there are close parallels with Bingham's work in some of Wimar's later paintings.

Inspired by Catlin's Indian Gallery, Charles Deas settled in Saint Louis in 1841, then began touring the Indian territory gathering sketches for his studio paintings. He soon exhibited a large number of Indian paintings and became active in the local arts community. According to Henry Tuckerman, Deas was ideally situated in Saint Louis, where he "found all that a painter can desire in the patronage of friends and general sympathy and appreciation."[28] Unlike Bingham, Deas painted dramatic portrayals of the frontiersmen, the plains, and the natives of the Missouri River frontier—dynamic themes that appealed to Wimar as well.

Like many frontier artists of his era, Wimar avidly studied prints and illustrated books for details, compositional sources, and overall conceptions of the West. In addition to the publications of Bodmer's and Catlin's work, there were a number of other resources Wimar may have used. In 1840 local artist J. C. Wild began issuing a series of portfolios entitled *The Valley of the Mississippi Illustrated* (fig. 11), the first important pictorial record of the Saint Louis region.[29] Felix O. C. Darley also began to illustrate western subjects; his *Scenes in Indian Life* (1843) became immensely popular with the general public. In addition, while Wimar was working on the panorama, McKenney and Hall began to re-release their 1836 series, *The History of the Indian Tribes of North America* (1849–54), which contained prints after Charles Bird King, John Mix Stanley, and others. Each of these resources contributed to Wimar's vision of the West and would reappear in his later images of the Missouri River frontier. Wimar continued to collect prints and illustrated books after he moved to Düsseldorf; in 1853 he wrote to his

entific explorations of the West, a core of artists settled in the area, among them George Caleb Bingham and Charles Deas. Bingham, a regionally recognized portrait painter who had gone east to study art in Philadelphia, returned to Saint Louis in 1845 and began creating his important genre paintings of Mississippi River life.[27] Although it is doubtful that the young Wimar was personally acquainted with the older, highly acclaimed artist at this time, he definitely was aware of Bingham's paintings through local

Figure 12
Emanuel Leutze. *Washington Crossing the Delaware*. Oil on canvas, 1851. The Metropolitan Museum of Art; gift of John S. Kennedy, 1897.

brother, "I have acquired many beautiful things, little by little, engravings and books, which may be very useful to you also."[30]

Another significant influence on Wimar's artistic development was the popularity of genre, history, and landscape paintings of western subjects among Americans between the 1830s and the 1850s. During this age of expansionism, Americans closely associated their national identity with the frontier and the pioneering spirit that settled it. Citizens moving into the unsettled West believed in the progress of civilization and their manifest destiny to control and dominate the continent, a vision that artist-explorers and historical painters conveyed through their visual images during the three decades before the Civil War. Although many artists, including Felix O. C. Darley, William T. Ranney, and Arthur F. Tait, worked from eastern studios and had little contact with the realities of the frontier, they nonetheless helped form conceptions of the

West. Ranney would play a particularly prominent role as a source for some of Wimar's later paintings.

Although these western artists, explorers, and publications helped develop Wimar's artistic vocabulary, the catalysts for his decision to study in Europe were Emanuel Leutze and the Düsseldorf Gallery in New York. The Düsseldorf Gallery, which opened in 1849, offered the American audience its first large-scale exhibition of foreign art works, including Leutze's, and caused great excitement among American artists, critics, and patrons. Wimar seems to have felt a special affinity for Leutze, a German immigrant to the United States who had returned to Düsseldorf to study art, then returned to New York in triumph to exhibit his monumental painting, *Washington Crossing the Delaware* (fig. 12) in November 1851.[31] Reviewed and praised in many publications and hailed by critics as the most important American history painting ever created,[32] this painting became the most recognized image in American art at midcentury.

Wimar was captivated by this work and proclaimed that it "surpasses everything I have seen before."[33] In Leutze he discovered not only a noble expression of American history but a personal inspiration. He could appreciate that a German-American artist, having returned to Europe to study, could then make a significant contribution to American art, and he could understand Leutze's patriotic sentiments for both his homeland and his new country. Leutze proclaimed that "I will always . . . to the German fatherland or to the spirit of Germany remain true . . . [and as] a citizen of the United States . . . [I have] a deep interest in whatever tends to promote the patriotic spirit in the hearts of my countrymen."[34] Wimar shared these feelings, declaring, "I am still proud to be a German. But you should not take that as if I betrayed America."[35] Wimar became determined to follow Leutze's artistic path and study in Düsseldorf.

During the 1850s Düsseldorf was the primary destination for American artists studying in Europe. This was partly due to the attraction of Leutze's atelier and partly to the influence of the Düsseldorf Gallery, where the display of German genre, landscape, and history painting attracted large crowds. Contemporary art periodicals, although not impressed with the imagination shown by the Düsseldorf artists, praised the draftsmanship and design of their paintings. A critic for the *American Art Union Bulletin* in 1850 admonished American artists for their "want of careful and accurate drawing" and recommended academic training in Düsseldorf because of its "strict attention to the elementary principles of painting more particularly to drawing."[36]

The few American art academies in existence did not offer the rigorous technical training that most artists required.[37] This state of affairs forced many American artists, who were largely self-taught, to finish their art training with a tour of Europe, to see its cities and landscape and to learn from its museums, artists, and academies. Study in Düsseldorf offered numerous practical advantages for the American artist in Europe, including good access to the academy and the cultural community and a better system of patronage than in other European art centers.[38] Unlike most academies, the one in Düsseldorf provided instruction in a variety of subjects, including history, genre, and landscape painting. The community also had a vital system of independent ateliers that permitted more academic flexibility and a greater degree of creative freedom for individual artists; in practice, most Americans in Düsseldorf did not enroll in the academy but instead preferred the independent ateliers. Perhaps most importantly, Düsseldorf was a very affordable city compared to some of the larger art centers such as London, Paris, Rome, and Berlin.

The promise of a monetary inheritance from a family friend seems to have encouraged Wimar to travel to Europe for further study, although legal complications ultimately prevented the release of funds.[39] Around December 1851, Wimar left Saint Louis for Düsseldorf. He probably departed from New York, where he could have seen Leutze's *Washington Crossing the Delaware* on exhibition. He also had a letter of introduction to the secretary of the American Art Union from William Curtis of Saint Louis, who wrote that "he is now on his way to the 'Father Land' to study his art under the auspices of older masters than our Western Land can furnish" and who asked the secretary to assist Wimar "for the sake of American Art, under whose banner he will ever be enlisted."[40]

Figure 13
Carl Wimar. *Bonn*. Pencil on paper, 1852.
Missouri Historical Society.

Figure 14
Carl Wimar. *Sieben Gebirge 1852*. Pencil on
paper, 1852. Missouri Historical Society.

41

After his trans-Atlantic voyage of approximately thirty days, Wimar visited Bonn and
reestablished family ties, then began touring the
Rhineland. His first sketchbook, bought in Bonn,
includes riverboat views of the city, the "Sieben-
gebirge" (a range of mountains), and other landscapes along the Rhine (figs. 13, 14). The artist
also returned to Siegburg, his birthplace, and
sketched two scenes of the town and its mental
hospital (figs. 2, 15). These are the most refined
and detailed drawings in the book, suggesting
their intense personal associations for the artist.
Wimar's tour took him as far south as Heidelberg, on the Neckar River, where he made
sketches for his first extant painting from the
Düsseldorf period. *Castle of Heidelberg* (fig. 16),
dated May 1852, depicts the sprawling fortress as
one approaches it from the hills that surround
the city. Wimar composed the foreground in a
traditional manner, with intersecting wedges of
land and balancing tree masses that enframe the

Figure 15
Carl Wimar. *Irrenheil Anstalt in Siegburg*.
Pencil on paper, 1852. Missouri Historical
Society.

Figure 16
Carl Wimar. *Castle of Heidelberg*. Oil on
canvas, 1852. Saint Louis Art Museum; gift
of Mrs. M. F. Hahn.

view. The stylized treatment of the landscape and
foliage demonstrates that Wimar did not have
full command of his medium, and the composition is not well conceived. The painting is most
interesting as a point of contrast with his subsequent work, which was transformed under the
influence of Leutze and the Düsseldorf artistic
milieu.

Wimar did not set up residence in Düsseldorf until the fall of 1852, after Leutze had
returned from touring the United States with
Washington Crossing the Delaware.[41] Although
the young artist moved periodically from one
lodging to another during his first two years of
study, he soon settled into the social and artistic
life of Düsseldorf. Since German was his native
tongue, he could live and communicate comfortably in the culture, unlike most of the Americans
who, with the notable exceptions of Whittredge
and Bierstadt, could not speak the language flu-
ently. Furthermore, he had numerous aunts,
uncles, and cousins in the surrounding towns and
villages. They met regularly and shared family
news, which Wimar dutifully reported home in
his letters. The family network and his fluency
in the language also enabled him to expand his
social life beyond the artistic community.
Shortly after his arrival he was chosen to serve
on the board of the Turnverein (Athletic Club)
and was elected to the Carnival Society.[42]

The gregarious Wimar also interacted easily
with the other artists in Düsseldorf. Pomarede's
old partner from Saint Louis, Henry Lewis,
arrived in Düsseldorf during the summer of 1853
as his panorama of the Mississippi made the con-
cluding leg of its tour. According to Wimar, the
panorama was not successful with the German
audience, but the two artists became close
friends. Wimar remarked that Pomarede, his
former master and Lewis' former partner,
"will probably not like it when he hears that I
am friends with Lewis."[43] For his part, Lewis

described Wimar in various letters as "one of the warmest and truest friends I have," "a great favorite here among the artists," and "a real good, sterling fellow."[44] Lewis established a permanent residence in Düsseldorf and found a publisher for his illustrations of the Mississippi that appeared as *Das Illustrierte Mississippithal* (1854–56). He also worked as Leutze's assistant, escorting his large paintings, including *Washington Crossing the Delaware*, on their tours across Europe. Eventually Lewis studied with the master, noting: "I shall paint for a time with Leutze for the purpose of learning to paint figures more perfectly, for by and by, I wish to paint historical landscapes."[45]

Wimar's relationship with Leutze was instrumental to his artistic development and social success during this period. The master history painter was not only the magnet that drew Wimar to Germany but the focus for all American artists in the city; very receptive to his American brethren, Leutze provided them with entrees to social and artistic groups. The American art magazine, *Crayon*, wrote that "to him . . . all Americans are sent, whether students, amateurs, or tourists: he is always glad to see them, and seems to take real pleasure in doing anything in his power to advance their several schemes."[46] During the early 1850s Leutze's circle in Düsseldorf included a number of American artists besides Wimar: Eastman Johnson had arrived in 1849, followed by T. Worthington Whittredge and James M. Hart in 1850. Albert Bierstadt worked there briefly in 1852 and 1854 but frequently ventured out on his own. William S. Haseltine joined them in 1854, William Trost Richards in 1855, and just before Wimar's return to the United States in 1856, George Caleb Bingham arrived in Düsseldorf to spend two years refining his work.

Leutze was prominent in the local art community as one of the most recognized indepen-

43

Figure 17
Artist unknown. *Carl Wimar*. Lithograph, 1854. Künstler-Verein Malkasten Archives, Düsseldorf.

dent artists and a founding member in 1848 of the Malkasten (Paint Box), which quickly became the center of social life among Düsseldorf's artists. Created as a club with lofty artistic purposes, the Malkasten provided a place for artists to discuss aesthetic issues, exhibit their work, and meet socially. There artists could "congregate in the evening to sup, smoke, talk, drink beer, play billiards, and amuse themselves in various ways. . . . Artists of all grades or merit meet here on terms of their most perfect and genial social equality. . . . A true brotherhood seems to reign among them."[47] As codirector of the guild, Leutze was "one of the most influential men in the Malkasten";[48] in a letter to his parents, Wimar described a banquet at which Leutze and Achenbach, another of Düsseldorf's artistic leaders, were given paper and lead pens to draw "whatever came to their minds . . . the things were then auctioned off on the spot and enormous prices were given for them."[49]

Wimar (fig. 17) was warmly accepted into the club and remained a regular, paying member from December 1852 until he left Düsseldorf in 1856.[50] He even was asked to contribute some drawings to be engraved for the *Artists Album* of 1854.[51] In addition, the Malkasten had a theater, "where comical plays and operas, composed and acted by the artists are performed often."[52] On this stage Wimar displayed his dramatic talents and performed comedy routines to the delight of spectators. Not only was he "one of the most comical characters you can imagine," convulsing an audience "with a very good representation of 'Lucy Long in Costume,'" but he "often astonished the natives here by giving a representation . . . of the natives at home, in full costume with war dance etc."[53] The Germans particularly enjoyed the enactments of Indian rituals, as Whittredge confirmed in his autobiography.[54]

In fact, Wimar's long black hair, swarthy complexion, and collection of Indian artifacts convinced many that he was a native American, and they jokingly referred to him as "the Indian painter"[55]—a double entendre on his physical appearance as well as his choice of subject matter. On one occasion Lewis humorously introduced Wimar to a group of Germans as a native American, and the young artist wrote, "I almost died laughing about the idea that many here believe me to be a descendant of Indians, and I had the hardest time with some of them to talk them out of it."[56] Wimar sometimes exploited this misconception by wearing buckskins (see frontispiece) to call attention to himself and his paintings of American frontier subjects.

Wimar began working on native American themes in his paintings soon after he settled in Düsseldorf. Of approximately twenty paintings that he executed during this period, fully three-quarters of them focused on Indians as the primary subject;[57] for their content and composition, he relied upon a variety of visual and literary sources, both European and American. By the end of his first year of study, Wimar had completed his earliest known Indian paintings, *The Discovery of Boone's Encampment in Kentucky by the Indians* and *The Abduction of Daniel Boone's Daughter by the Indians*, and had established the basic themes, style, and iconography for his subsequent paintings in Düsseldorf. The originality of his subjects stirred the imaginations of his German audience and attracted widespread attention. As Wimar related to his family, "Indian and American topics in general seem to be especially well liked here, and there is nobody else here who does them."[58] His Indian subjects, which would earn critical and popular approval in the Kunstvereins (art unions), were exhibited in Düsseldorf, Cologne, Elberfeld, and Hanover.[59]

All of Wimar's major paintings of his Düsseldorf period deal with confrontation and conflict between the Anglo-European settlers and the native American culture. He represents pioneers battling with or being abducted by the Indians, who in turn are fleeing from encroaching civilization. In these early paintings Wimar drew on art, literature, history, and news accounts for his views of the American frontier. His themes were deeply ingrained in the American national identity of the mid-nineteenth century, including the Daniel Boone myth, the captivity narrative tradition (in both literature and the visual arts), religious iconography, and American history painting. His European academic training guided him in rendering dramatic frontier subjects with compositions and figure poses from the traditions of western European sacred imagery and history painting. But rather than portraying historical figures at an important moment in the grand manner, he focused on dramatic scenes with common, everyday pioneers, making them the heroes and heroines of the frontier and justifying their actions through historical precedent and sacred iconography.

Wimar's scenes of conflict between native Americans and pioneers in the trans-Mississippi territories reflected commonly held beliefs among white Americans and Europeans. He portrayed pioneers either as saints, acting upon their manifest destiny to rule the continent, or as martyrs, redeemed in their sacrifice for the righteous cause. His views of native Americans convey the complex and contradictory attitudes of his contemporaries: Indians could be either savage antagonists or noble representatives of a vanishing culture, forced into flight by the settlers. This popular notion of "good" and "bad" Indians was epitomized in tales like James Fenimore Cooper's *The Last of the Mohicans* (1826), in which the noble and virtuous chief Chingachgook and his son Uncas were pitted against the evil warrior Magua. Wimar's images of native Americans also drew on the romantic European

convention of the "noble savage," the uncivilized man whose virtues were drawn directly from nature and were unspoiled by the influences of western society.[60]

Wimar's four versions of *The Abduction of Daniel Boone's Daughter* serve as a barometer of his artistic development in Düsseldorf. The technical, compositional, and iconographic evolution of this series informs all of his other Düsseldorf paintings. In his first major version of this subject (1853, fig. 18), Wimar depicted Jemima Boone being abducted from her canoe while picking flowers on the banks of a Kentucky river—an event originally mentioned in John Filson's *The Discovery, Settlement and Present State of Kentucke* (1784). Published as a promotional piece to encourage the purchase of real estate in Kentucky, Filson's text included an appendix, purportedly a first-person account of Boone's life and adventures in the exploration and settlement of Kentucky, which contained a two-sentence description of the abduction and subsequent rescue of Boone's daughter and the two daughters of his scout, Flanders Callaway. This account, however, was not expansive enough to have served as source material for Wimar's paintings of the subject, nor was the more contemporary publication by Timothy Flint, *Biographical Memoir of Daniel Boone* (1833). Instead, Wimar seems to have drawn inspiration from *The Mountain Muse* (1813), an epic poem by Boone's nephew, Daniel Bryan. Relating the life of Daniel Boone in florid epic verse, Bryan developed a major section of his book around the dramatic abduction of Boone's daughter and the Callaway sisters as the families settled the territory:

> Back to the bank, their little beechen Boats,
> At Beauty's word, the dexterous rowers
>   shot,
> And o'er the fruit-hung flower-empurpled
>   shore,

45

Figure 18
Carl Wimar. *The Abduction of Daniel Boone's Daughter by the Indians.* Oil on canvas, 1853. Washington University Gallery of Art.

46

which appeared in Samuel C. Metcalf's *Indian Warfare in the West* (1821, fig. 19), depicts all three girls being led away in their canoe by an Indian. This print established the stereotype for this subject and seems to have been the source for Karl Bodmer's lithograph of the *Capture of the Daughters of D. Boone and Callaway by the Indians* (1852, fig. 20), which was part of a commission from a French publisher for a series titled *Annals of the United States Illustrated —The Pioneers.* Bodmer, overloaded with illustration commissions and in poor health, hired Jean-François Millet, his friend from Barbizon who then needed the work, to assist with drawing the figures for this series. The publisher, who called upon Bodmer unannounced to inspect his progress, became extremely upset to find Millet working on the plates and immediately canceled the contract. Only four of the planned one hundred plates had been completed at that time; Bodmer printed these himself, pulling only about six impressions of each plate, and they were never distributed.[62] It is possible that Wimar met the famous illustrator of the West and saw this print in Bodmer's Cologne studio, where he lived when he was not in Barbizon;[63] the subject and setting of these two works suggest a similarity. However, Wimar rejected the compositional format established in Metcalf's book and turned instead to European history painting for the composition and figural arrangement of his first *Abduction* painting.

Wimar's chief compositional source probably was a painting by Leutze, *The Vikings First Landing in America* (1845, fig. 21), in which Viking warriors disembark from their vessel bearing a beautiful blonde woman who symbolizes the fertility of the New World. The triangulation of the main figures in Wimar's painting is a simplification of the figural arrangement in Leutze's *Landing*, and some of the gestures are like those in Leutze's painting. Wimar also may

To gather Garlands to inwreathe their brows
The sweetly-blooming Maidens gaily ran;
When from a dark cane thicket growing
    near,
A band of Ruffian Indians fiercely sprang,
And seizing fair Eliza Callaway,
Her charming Sister Frances too, and Boone's
High-soul'd Jemima, bore them through the
    Brake![61]

Although Wimar did not include the Callaway daughters in his painting, he captured the essence of Bryan's "sweetly-blooming Maidens" in the image of the "high-soul'd Jemima" Boone.

Bryan's account is not believed to be accurate, despite his claims to the contrary. Nonetheless, this incident became a popular subject in the literature on Daniel Boone. Although no other artists painted this subject, several prints of it appeared over the years. One of the earliest,

have borrowed the angle of the boat, grounded on a thickly wooded shore, and the view across the water on the right, toward the luminous horizon in the distance. That his first attempt to capture American frontier subjects relied on his mentor's example confirms the influence of Leutze's history painting style even at the beginning of Wimar's studies.

In choosing a subject from Daniel Boone's life, Wimar joined a number of American painters who depicted this consummate pioneer and icon of national identity. One of the first important explorers of the trans-Appalachian West in the late eighteenth century, Boone was an agent of a real estate company when he led a band of pioneers through the Cumberland Gap to begin American settlement of the Kentucky territory in 1773. Later in life he felt the pressure of the growing population there and moved to the Missouri frontier, where he died in 1820.[64]

By the mid-nineteenth century the story of Boone's life had grown to epic proportions, and he had become the symbol of the American pioneering spirit. As the man who brought civilization into the forests, tamed the wilderness, and subdued its pagan, savage people, he was the central myth-hero of antebellum America.[65]

Thomas Cole's *Daniel Boone and His Cabin on the Great Osage Lake* (1826, fig. 22) was perhaps the first important painting of Boone. Cole portrays Boone before his cabin as the sage of the wilderness, a Rousseauian natural philosopher in a dense landscape; he sits on a wooden throne and wears regal purple leggings that identify him as an aristocrat of the forest.[66] Two decades later, William T. Ranney created a much different interpretation of the Boone myth in his painting of *Daniel Boone's First View of the Kentucky Valley* (1849, fig. 23). Here Boone is depicted as an explorer discovering new territories—subject

Figure 19   (left)
Artist unknown. *Capture of Boone's Daughter*. From Samuel C. Metcalf, *Indian Warfare in the West* (Lexington, Ky.: William G. Hunt, 1821). Mercantile Library Association, Saint Louis.

Figure 20   (right)
Karl Bodmer and Jean-François Millet. *The Abduction of the Daughters of Boone and Callaway*. Lithograph, 1852. Special Collection, Olin Library, Washington University; gift of Mrs. Charles Byran, Jr.

48

Figure 21
Emanuel Leutze. *The Vikings First Landing in America.* Oil on canvas, 1845. Kunstmuseum Düsseldorf, loan of Mr. Horst Volmer, Remscheid.

matter reminiscent of another popular subject, Columbus' discovery of the New World. Ranney's composition forcefully conveys, through the pioneers' gestures toward the horizon, the determination underlying westward expansion. Over a decade later Leutze adapted this composition in his paean to manifest destiny, his famous Capitol decoration, *Westward the Course of Empire Takes Its Way* (1861; see fig. 18 in Angela Miller's essay).[67]

Arguably the most significant painting of the Boone myth at midcentury was George Caleb Bingham's *Daniel Boone Escorting Settlers through the Cumberland Gap* (1851–52, fig. 24), which depicts Boone leading his emigrant party into the rugged wilderness of the Kentucky territory. The iconography suggests traditional European religious imagery, particularly of Moses leading the chosen people to the promised land

and of Joseph leading the Virgin Mary and child on their flight into Egypt. Like Moses, Boone leads his people into the frontier by divine right, and like Joseph he protects the righteous by taking his people from the corrupting influence of society into a natural paradise. This adaptation of religious iconography underscores an attitude among some Americans that national expansion had divine approval.

Wimar's 1853 canvases, *The Abduction of Daniel Boone's Daughter by the Indians* and its possible companion piece, *The Discovery of Boone's Encampment in Kentucky by the Indians* (1853, fig. 25), take an unusual approach to the Boone myth. Instead of concentrating on Boone himself as the heroic pathfinder, Wimar dramatizes events related to Boone's family life. *The Discovery of Boone's Encampment* does not depict Boone at all but focuses instead on the

Indians spying on his camp. The Indians peering down from behind the rocky outcrop seem directly inspired by Bingham's *Concealed Enemy* (1845, fig. 26), which Wimar could have known from its inclusion in the American Art Union exhibition of 1845. Wimar's version, now lost, made a distinctive contribution to the iconography of Boone at midcentury, as did his *Abduction of Daniel Boone's Daughter*, which expanded the Boone myths to include other members of the pioneer's clan. This approach of historicizing the lives of less well-known figures who also heroically brought civilization into the wilder-

ness is typical of Wimar's Düsseldorf-period paintings.[68]

Wimar's *Abduction of Daniel Boone's Daughter* is also a significant example of the American literary and pictorial tradition of the captivity narrative, one of the first indigenous genres of American literature.[69] This tradition dates back at least to Mary Rowlandson's *The Sovereignty and Goodness of God . . .* (1682), which became the prototype for the genre. Her account treated the brutal details of her kidnapping as a trial of her religious resolve, much like God's test of Job, and her eventual escape as

49

Figure 22
Thomas Cole. *Daniel Boone and His Cabin on the Great Osage Lake.* Oil on canvas, c. 1825–26. Mead Art Museum, Amherst College.

Figure 23
William Ranney. *Daniel Boone's First View of the Kentucky Valley.* Oil on canvas, 1849. The Thomas Gilcrease Institute of American History and Art, Tulsa.

50

Figure 24
George Caleb Bingham. *Daniel Boone Escorting Settlers Through the Cumberland Gap.* Oil on canvas, 1851–52. Washington University Gallery of Art.

spiritual redemption in the Puritan ideal. Hundreds of captivity narratives were written in the eighteenth and nineteenth centuries, and over time they evolved from Puritan moral treatises into dramatic, sensationalized pulp literature. Typically, captivity narratives concentrated on the conflict between Anglo-European settlers and native cultures—the civilized, Christian moral system against the savage, pagan society. Usually the captive in these stories was a woman, the embodiment of the civilizing, domestic qualities of Anglo-European society, placed at the mercy of the Indian wilderness.[70] Rape by her native captors was often implied in these works, if not explicitly stated.

Although there was a large body of literature about captivity and abduction, dating back to the Greek myth of Persephone's abduction and the Roman tale of the Sabine women, there were relatively few paintings of these subjects. Nicolas Poussin's *The Rape of the Sabine Women* (c. 1635, fig. 27) depicts rows of standing or kneeling women who protest and resist their abduction; their outstretched arms, raised in defensive gestures, also convey their sexual vulnerability. A subsequent variation on this scene, Jacques-Louis David's *The Sabine Women* (1795–99, fig. 28), apparently influenced western American images of women in the wilderness; as Rena N. Coen has convincingly argued, the heroic women in David's neoclassical prototype embody the civilizing virtues and the advance of western civilization.[71]

John Vanderlyn established a tradition for fine art representations of Indian captivities in America with *The Murder of Jane McCrea* (1804, fig. 29), which depicts a young woman facing imminent death at the hands of two Indians, one of whom has raised his tomahawk. Vanderlyn adapted his image from popularized accounts of a revolutionary war event, in which Jane McCrea was murdered and scalped by Indians escorting

her across enemy lines to visit her fiancé, a Tory officer. Vanderlyn executed this, his first history painting, while he was studying in France; the figural poses are borrowed from European art.[72] The muscular native Americans are derived from antique statuary, while Jane McCrea's pose falls firmly in the western tradition of rape and abduction scenes. Kneeling and terrified, she feebly attempts to protect herself by spreading her arms—a gesture that, along with her torn dress and partially exposed breast, suggests her sexual vulnerability.

Two decades after Vanderlyn's early painting, Thomas Cole painted several scenes from Cooper's *The Last of the Mohicans*, including an 1827 canvas with the same title (fig. 30). In it the captive Cora kneels before Tamenund, pleading for salvation; her arms are upraised like Jane McCrea's, but Cora is not sensuously exposed. In fact, Cole made the entire figure group diminu-

tive in relation to the vast, sublime landscape that was his primary concern. Almost twenty years later, John Mix Stanley contributed to the pictorial tradition of captivity narratives with his *Osage Scalp Dance* (1845, fig. 31). Highly regarded for his documentary images of native Americans on the frontier, Stanley drew from sketches and popular accounts to create this dramatic scene for his Indian Gallery at the Smithsonian Institution. In it, the captive mother protects her child as Osage warriors dance threateningly around her. An overzealous warrior, who is about to cleave her with his hatchet, is restrained by the chief, wearing a presidential peace medal, who stands over the woman. Both the savage warrior and the noble chief were familiar types for Stanley's Anglo-European audience, and the pose of the captive mother falls into the tradition established by Vanderlyn.

The most significant exception to Vander-

Figure 25   (left)
Carl Wimar. *The Discovery of Boone's Encampment.* Oil on canvas, 1853. From Perry Rathbone, *Charles Wimar 1828–1862: Painter of the Indian Frontier* (Saint Louis: City Art Museum, 1946), p. 57.

Figure 26   (right)
George Caleb Bingham. *The Concealed Enemy.* Oil on canvas, 1845. Stark Museum of Art, Orange, Texas.

52

Figure 27   (top left)
Nicolas Poussin. *The Rape of the Sabine Women*. Oil on canvas, c. 1635. The Metropolitan Museum of Art, New York; Harris Brisbane Dick Fund, 1946.

Figure 28   (top right)
Jacques-Louis David. *The Sabine Women*. Oil on canvas, 1799. Musée du Louvre, Paris.

Figure 29   (right)
John Vanderlyn. *The Murder of Jane McCrea*. Oil on canvas, 1804. Wadsworth Atheneum, Hartford, Connecticut.

lyn's prototype is *Captured by Indians* (1848, fig. 32) by Wimar's fellow Missourian, George Caleb Bingham. Bingham's painting incorporates religious figure types: the captives are portrayed as the Madonna and child, while the sleeping Indians are reminiscent of the soldiers asleep at Christ's tomb.[73] Bingham presents this captive as the saintly mother of a nation, destined for salvation in both a spiritual and a physical sense. However, Bingham's Madonna type does raise the question of racial mixing and intermarriage. The child sleeping on the mother's lap is evidently an Indian or mixed-blood child, and the subtle placement of the woman half in the light, half in shadow, further implies that she has intermarried with an Indian.[74]

Although Wimar certainly was aware of the iconographic traditions for paintings of captivity and abduction, he seems to have turned to religious iconography of the Christian martyrs and saints, especially Mary Magdalen, for his portrayal of "the high-soul'd Jemima" Boone. Her kneeling pose, with arms upraised in prayer, is similar to that of Mary Magdalen at the base of Christ's cross in Matthias Grünewald's *Crucifixion* on the Isenheim Altarpiece in Colmar (1510–15, fig. 33). The girl, however, is not as disheveled as Grünewald's Mary Magdalen; although Wimar's preparatory study for the painting (fig. 34) shows her hair, dress, and features as somewhat rough and unkempt, in the finished painting her features are idealized, rather like those of Mary Magdalen in Counter-Reformation and Baroque works such as Georges de la Tour's *Saint Mary Magdalen Meditating* (1630–35, fig. 35).[75]

The parallels between Jemima Boone's pose and the iconography of Mary Magdalen suggest several layers of interpretation. On the superficial level, Jemima Boone is pleading for mercy from her captors and, secondarily, praying for rescue or salvation from the Indians. Metaphorically, she may be seeking redemption from the moral compromise she could suffer at the hands of the Indians; her sexual desirability is clear, and though she is innocent so far, she faces the distinct possibility of sexual violation. Perhaps she also seeks redemption for the pagans who have abducted her. Clearly, in these levels of interpretation, the spiritually pure pioneer woman, the embodiment of civilizing and religious virtues in Anglo-European society, is at risk physically and morally in the pagan, uncivilized wilderness.

The sexual implications in Wimar's 1853 *Abduction* are quite explicit. The virginal white fabric of the young woman's blouse has dropped down her arms, revealing the soft flesh and gentle curves of her shoulder and upper breast. The brown drapery falling across her arms is suggestively arranged, while the brilliant red draped in front of her legs predicts the bloody potential of sexual violation. The rapt gaze of the Indian

Figure 30
Thomas Cole. *The Last of the Mohicans.* Oil on canvas, 1827. Wadsworth Atheneum, Hartford, Connecticut; bequest of Alfred Smith.

Figure 31
John Mix Stanley. *Osage Scalp Dance.* Oil on canvas, 1845. National Museum of American Art; gift of the Misses Henry, 1908.

53

Figure 32
George Caleb Bingham. *Captured by the Indians*. Oil on canvas, 1848. Saint Louis Art Museum; bequest of Arthur C. Hoskins.

54

landing the boat, who is totally engrossed in the presence of his captive, also emphasizes her sexual appeal. Such explicitly sexual overtones are typical of paintings in this era; they also are found in a third type of abduction image, in which an Indian on horseback holds an unconscious white captive in his arms (figs. 36, 37). (The latter pose may have been established by a related subject, Charles Deas' *The Prairie Fire* [1847, fig. 38], which depicts white settlers holding an unconscious woman as they flee a fire.) In such representations, the women's dresses invariably have fallen, exposing their soft flesh and usually their breasts.

The overtly sensual representation in Wimar's *Abduction* reveals prevailing notions about native Americans' sexual mores and their treatment of captive women. During this era it

was popularly believed that Indians raped their female captives—a view encouraged by the captivity narratives. This belief was not necessarily true; woodland Indians, such as those who abducted Boone's daughter, usually ransomed their captives, adopted them into the tribe, or sold them as slaves in Canada.[76] However, Anglo-Europeans tended to believe that the natives practiced a sexually promiscuous life —one more indication to the self-righteous Christians that the native culture had an immoral basis. The larger implication of this attitude was that if the uncivilized Indians could spiritually and physically violate civilized Christians, the morally superior pioneers were justified in dominating and even annihilating the natives.

When Wimar finished his first *Abduction*

canvas in December 1853, his admiring colleagues asked him to keep it on exhibition.[77] This
enthusiastic response encouraged him to create a
more ambitious Indian subject, *The Attack on an
Emigrant Train* (1854, fig. 39),[78] which he began
in December 1853. The new painting was his
most ambitious figure composition to date and
introduced a new subject to western art. Wimar
described his large-scale, multi-figure composition as "a family of settlers which I intend to finish under Leutze's guidance."[79] The painting
presents a group of pioneers behind hastily constructed barricades of an encircled wagon train,
valiantly defending their expedition against an
Indian ambush. Two groups of men shoot at the
attackers, while behind the defenders the
wounded are treated and the women and children
seek shelter. The figures are imaginatively

Figure 33   (top left)
Matthias Grünewald. *Crucifixion* from the
Isenheim Altarpiece. Oil on panel, 1510–15.
Musée Unterlinden, Colmar.

Figure 34   (top right)
Carl Wimar. *The Abduction of Daniel Boone's
Daughter by the Indians*. Charcoal and sepia
on paper, 1853. Saint Louis Art Museum.

Figure 35   (left)
Georges de la Tour. *Saint Mary Magdalen
Meditating*. Oil on canvas, 1630–35. Musée
du Louvre, Paris.

56

Figure 36
Artist unknown. *Indians Abducting Woman.*
Oil on canvas, n.d. The Thomas Gilcrease
Institute of American History and Art, Tulsa.

Figure 37 (right)
After F.O.C. Darley. *Indian Captive.* Oil on
canvas, n.d. Bancroft Library, University of
California-Berkeley.

Figure 38
Charles Deas. *Prairie Fire.* Oil on canvas,
1847. Brooklyn Museum, New York; gift of
Mr. and Mrs. Alastair Bradley.

arranged in four groups of three figures each,
which build a pyramid with its apex at the top of
the central pioneer's ramrod. Each group forms a
discrete unit linked to the other groups by inter-
locking diagonals. Compared to the simple four-
figure group in the just-completed *Abduction,*
this complex composition marked a definite
improvement in Wimar's conceptual abilities.

The pioneers in this painting are defending
not only their train but, symbolically, their perceived right to move west and introduce civilization to the frontier. The imperative of manifest
destiny is represented through figure types
drawn from religious iconography. The bearded
man in the center foreground holds a wounded
pioneer in the pose of Michelangelo's *Pietà*
(1499, fig. 40). The dying settler is posed like
Michelangelo's dead Christ, with wavy hair on
his cradled head and his arm fallen limply to his

57

side. Wimar has even drawn an antique drapery around the fallen man's hips—unlikely attire for a frontiersman—in an obvious attempt to depict the pioneer as a Christ-like martyr struggling with the pagan hordes. The woman and children at the right, who flee the battle seeking shelter, are borrowed from traditional renderings of the massacre of the innocents (fig. 41), the biblical tale of brutal slaughter as Herod attempted to murder the newborn Christ child. These types from religious iconography lend the settlers moral and religious righteousness in their conflict with the pagan natives who savagely assault them. The settlers may be martyred, but they are saviors of the wilderness, bringing civilization to the frontier. Like other American artists who drew on historical and religious precedents to provide a visual context for westward expansion, Wimar participated in this process of

Figure 39 (top left)
Carl Wimar. *Attack on an Emigrant Train.* Charcoal and sepia on paper, 1854. Saint Louis Art Museum.

Figure 40 (top right)
Michelangelo. *Pietà.* Marble, 1499. The Vatican, Rome. From Josef Vincent Lombardo, *Michangelo: The Pieta and Other Masterpieces* (New York: Pocket Books, Inc., 1965), fig. 15.

Figure 41 (left)
Guido Reni. *Slaughter of the Innocents.* Oil on canvas, 1614. Pinacoteca Nazionale, Bologna.

expansionist myth-making. His first version of *The Attack on an Emigrant Train* marked the culmination of his use of religious imagery for historical subjects.

This dramatic scene of Indians attacking a pioneer encampment attracted much attention in the artistic circles of Düsseldorf. Prior to exhibiting the painting in July, Wimar wrote to his parents, "I have received compliments on the same from our accomplished artists here, even though I myself am not content with it."[80] The painting apparently caught Leutze's eye and earned Wimar an invitation to work in the studios of Leutze, Joseph Fay, and Oswald Achenbach. Once he settled into a studio in Achenbach's house in September 1854, Wimar began to progress dramatically in his painting. He saw great prospects in his new study arrangement and wrote that "it is only now that I am going to make rapid progress."[81]

One reason for this optimism may have been anticipation that his finances would improve. During his first years in Germany, Wimar had not sold any works locally, preferring to send them back to Saint Louis for the satisfaction of his family, friends, and colleagues. Unfortunately, although he was turning down offers from numerous interested German patrons, his prized pieces did not sell in the American market, and his entire stay in Germany was fraught with financial problems. His letters home frequently pleaded for cash advances or sales of his paintings to sustain his studies: late in 1853 he wrote, "I have asked [Oberstolz] . . . for a monetary advance, and I hope that he is going to do it, if not, I will be in a quandry which I don't know how to bite myself out of."[82] He complained to his parents in August 1854: "I do not understand how all the other Americans are doing it who are selling all kinds of trash which they send to America, whether this is because they are Americans, or whether the people in other states have

better, or less taste."[83] Even after he had gained critical success, he confessed to his parents that "I have gone into debt considerably."[84] He was fortunate that his strong and broad family network in Germany could assist him with his basic sustenance—both moral and monetary—when he was in need.

Early in 1854 Wimar's financial situation grew so critical that he expected to have to return home with the spring thaw. He was not pleased with the prospect of an early departure just when his work was beginning to demonstrate decided improvement. He realized that he would be interrupting an educational opportunity essential to the development of his painting and feared that "it will probably cause me to do an injustice to art." In experiencing the culture of Europe he had acquired lofty aesthetic goals: "I would still not be content [in Saint Louis] since, due to my constant exposure to art and artists during these two years, I have acquired a principle that is completely different from that which I brought along from America. It has become my firm principle that I would rather be a poor artist than a rich amateur."[85]

Resolving to stay in Düsseldorf to complete his art education, Wimar decided to keep some of his paintings to sell to his German patrons. Initially he was forced to trade paintings for some shirts and gilded frames, but in the summer of 1854 his paintings finally began to sell. He sold a small canvas at the Kunstverein in Hanover and two small flatboat paintings from an exhibition in Elberfeld. His depiction of Mississippi River life, *Flatboatmen on the Mississippi* (1854, fig. 42), is a moonlit scene of boatmen playing music and dancing atop their boat; it is obviously inspired by George Caleb Bingham's *The Jolly Flatboatmen* (1845, fig. 43) and possibly by *Wood Boatmen on a River* (1854, fig. 44).[86]

Although Wimar managed to sell enough works in Germany to continue his studies there, he still had little to money to spare. He had to decline an invitation to join Leutze and some of his other students, including Whittredge, Bierstadt, and Haseltine, on a sketching tour to Munich and Italy in the summer of 1854. Instead, Wimar remained in Düsseldorf and settled into his new studio, which faced the same garden square as the studios of the Achenbachs, Lewis, Leutze, and Whittredge. Established in the heart of the Düsseldorf social and artistic community, Wimar also benefited enormously from Leutze's criticism and advice about his paintings. As with his other protégés, Leutze monitored his progress closely, regularly visiting the younger painter's studio to counsel his artistic development. Wimar clarified this relationship with the independent master when he wrote that although Leutze "has no students in his studio, and he is also not taking any[,] . . . without being a student of Leutze's I am as good as under his direction, he sees everything I do, and he always takes a pleasure in teaching me."[87] Wimar apparently studied drawing with Joseph Fay, a fresco painter who had been trained at the Düsseldorf Academy and was primarily recognized for his mural decorations for the City Hall at Elberfeld.[88] The young artist described him as "a second Pomarede to me, good hearted, and I also hope to profit a lot from him."[89]

Wimar's program of study under these two artists approximated the system instituted when Wilhelm von Schadow assumed control over the Academy in 1826. Von Schadow introduced a system of four classes of study to teach the techniques of drawing and painting in a regimented progression. A student learned the rudiments of drawing from prints, antique statuary, and life in the first two classes, then graduated to a third-level painting class. The courses culminated in a master class that provided students with their own studios and the guidance of a specific professor.[90] Like most Americans, Wimar did not

Figure 42
Carl Wimar. *Flatboatmen on the Mississippi.*
Oil on canvas, 1854. Amon Carter Museum.

Figure 43
George Caleb Bingham. *Jolly Flatboatmen*.
Oil on canvas, 1845. Manoogian Collection.

Figure 44
George Caleb Bingham. *Wood Boatmen on a River*. Oil on canvas, 1854. Amon Carter Museum.

enroll in the extensive and time-consuming coursework of the Academy but instead practiced a condensed version of the program in the independent ateliers associated with it. A typical day began immediately after breakfast: he would work on his canvases in his studio all day, without breaking for lunch, then have a light dinner and go to life drawing classes at the Academy from six to nine p.m.[91] He sketched from nature on the tours and trips that he took on the weekends and holidays. He learned to begin each painting with loose sketches inspired by his tours, prints, or readings; he worked these sketches into compositional drawings, then enlarged and refined them into finished drawings that were the source material for the completed canvas.[92] At each stage of creating the artwork he received advice and criticism from Fay and Leutze. This working method is admirably illustrated by his progression to the finished version of *The Captive Charger* (1854, fig. 45).

Wimar began this painting, which he originally called *Indians as Horsethieves*, when he entered his new studio. His teachers and colleagues had taught him the importance of working from nature, so he started the piece by studying Indian artifacts from his collection and sketching a German officer's horse that had been made available to him. His composition and subject were unique, although it was still acceptable for him to use prints and other artworks for details and design ideas. As he wrote to his parents, "I would no longer think of copying from something, and one is absolutely not allowed to do that here."[93] From his life studies and compositional sketch he worked up a finely rendered finished drawing (fig. 46), then transferred its design and details to the final canvas. For most of his major Düsseldorf works he began with drawings on the same scale as the finished canvases; evidence of roulette marks in some of his final drawings indicates that he used them to transfer

Figure 45
Carl Wimar. *The Captive Charger.* Oil on
canvas, 1854. Saint Louis Art Museum; gift
of Miss Lillie B. Randell.

61

Figure 46
Carl Wimar. *Captive Charger.* Charcoal, pencil, and wash on paper, 1854. Private collection. Courtesy Kennedy Galleries, New York.

the design in the manner of cartoons (see figs.
34, 39, and 46–48).

The Captive Charger was the first painting
that Wimar completed directly under Leutze's
guidance, although he previously had been working under the master's watchful gaze. According
to Wimar, "Mr. Leutze expressed his great satisfaction with my current picture to myself and
others, and said that I had made considerable
progress."[94] In its depiction of a group of Indians
spiriting away an American cavalry officer's horse
in the half-light of sunset, the painting suggests
a narrative of events leading up to this scene.
The Indians' furtive glances over their shoulders
and their sack of booty imply that they have
ambushed a scouting party, killed the officer, and
stolen his horse. These actions can be interpreted

symbolically as an attempt to divert the
encroaching Anglo-European culture, represented by the white horse. Although the Indians
have succeeded in this skirmish, the details of the
painting imply that they are a lost society. Their
sidelong glances and nervous expressions indicate
that they are in flight, and the motifs of a setting
sun and a waning moon over the dense prairie
suggest that they are being pressed ever westward by the pioneers' culture.

By February 1855, after three years of
working through a rigid program of independent
study under the criticism of the masters, Wimar
began to feel that his studies in Düsseldorf were
nearing completion. Writing home on his birthday, Wimar remarked to his parents that, "After
I am finished with my present work, I will leave

Figure 47
Carl Wimar. *Indians Pursued by American Dragoons*. Charcoal and sepia on paper touched with white, 1853(?). Saint Louis Art Museum.

Figure 48
Carl Wimar. *Attack on an Emigrant Train*. Charcoal and sepia on paper touched with white, 1856. Saint Louis Art Museum.

Düsseldorf in any case, come what may,"[95] to seek new artistic stimuli elsewhere. Thwarted in his attempt to travel to Italy, he decided: "My most fervent wish now would be to accumulate enough [money] to go to Munich, or Paris, that would be very useful to me now."[96] Shortly after moving into his new studio he began planning a journey to Paris for August 1855 and started taking French lessons. He also intended to return to the United States during the fall of 1855, tour the Missouri River to study the frontier, then return to Düsseldorf to paint from his sketches. When financial considerations forced him to cancel his trip to Paris as well, he decided to stay on in Düsseldorf to complete five more paintings: *Washington and Delaware Indians at a Council Fire* (1855, location unknown), *Prairie Fire* (1855, location unknown), *Indians Pursued by American Dragoons* (1855), another version of *The Abduction of Daniel Boone's Daughter* (1855), and another of *The Attack on an Emigrant Train*

(1856). The latter two were the largest and most ambitious of his works and the culmination of his artistic achievements in Germany.

Wimar completed another version of *The Abduction of Daniel Boone's Daughter* (1855, fig. 49) in the fall of 1855.[97] This version of the abduction, featuring a raft instead of a canoe, has been widely regarded by modern art historians as one of his finest productions.[98] Wimar realized this himself when he wrote, "It is the largest which I have painted so far, and, I believe, also the best, it shows an abduction on a raft."[99] In this reinterpretation, a noble chief stands over the captive maiden and looks sternly forward as the warriors push the raft through the mist across the shallow waters. The scene, which bears no relation to the accounts of the abduction by Filson, Bryan, or Flint, was probably inspired by one of the most significant history paintings of its time, Theodore Géricault's monumental *The Raft of the Medusa* (1819, fig. 50).

Although Wimar's plans to travel to Paris had been thwarted, he still learned important lessons from the French history painters and evidently became exposed to Géricault's raft through a lithograph made in London in 1820. The angle of Wimar's river raft to the picture plane, the diagonal axes of the poles, and several of the poses are identical to elements in Géricault's painting. In comparison with the canoe version of 1853 (fig. 19), the figural arrangements in the new *Abduction* are more complex and controlled, and the composition is more daring. In borrowing from Géricault's composition, which depicts the abandoned survivors of a French military shipwreck, Wimar also could reflect on the American policy that ignored the rights of the natives, drove them from the land, and abandoned them to be vanquished—an interpretation reinforced by the poses and gestures of the Indians. All of the figures on the raft anxiously look back over their path for the pursuing pioneers, except the chief, who stoically stares forward. While the other Indians face the relentless pursuit of civilization, the chief gazes into the mist and the setting sun that symbolically prophesies his culture's fate. Furthermore, the reclining Indian in the lower left is posed like the ancient Roman sculpture of the *Dying Gaul* (fig. 51), which represents the last soldier of a tribe as he perishes on the battlefield. Thomas Crawford later used this pose in his marble *The Dying Indian Chief, Contemplating the Progress of Civilization* (1856, fig. 52) to convey the same theme of the vanishing civilization in an American context.

Wimar's depiction of the Indians in the 1855 version is far removed from his earlier portrayal of them as savage antagonists. Whereas the Indians aggressively lust for their captive in the 1853 painting, Jemima Boone is alone and untouched in the center of the raft in the later canvas. She is fully dressed, without any of the sexual sug-

Figure 49
Carl Wimar. *The Abduction of Daniel Boone's Daughter by the Indians*. Oil on canvas, c. 1855. Amon Carter Museum.

63

Figure 50
Theodore Géricault. *The Raft of the Medusa*. Oil on canvas, 1819. Musée d'Orsay, Paris.

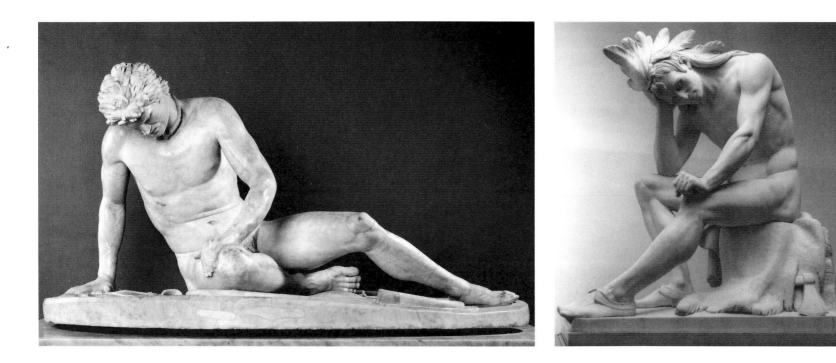

64

Figure 51 (left)
Roman. *Dying Gaul*. Marble. Capitoline Museum, Rome.

Figure 52 (right)
Thomas Crawford. *The Dying Indian Chief, Contemplating the Progress of Civilization*. Marble, 1856. New-York Historical Society, New York City.

gestiveness of the earlier version. The Indians do not seem to threaten her chastity; they do not even appear to notice her presence. The noble chief standing guard over her seems more protective than threatening. It has been suggested that the iconography of this version relates to the ancient myth of Persephone's abduction by Hades, who carried her to the underworld in a bark over the River Styx.[100] The parallel with the ancient myth implies that the Indians in Wimar's painting are taking Jemima Boone into their wilderness world. Furthermore, this work can be read as an escape by the Indians, not only from pursuit by Boone but metaphorically from the white civilization that is rapidly vanquishing their race.

Several of Wimar's later Düsseldorf paintings reflect a similar change in iconography. At the same time he was painting the raft version of *The Abduction*, he used a similar theme of a vanishing culture in *Indians Pursued by American Dragoons* (1855, fig. 53). This theme is most poignantly illustrated by *Funeral Raft of a Dead Chieftain* (1856, fig. 54), which employs the same composition as the raft *Abduction*. In the *Funeral Raft* the deceased chief, crowned with a waning moon, is serenely sent downstream into the misty twilight. Another variation on this theme of the vanishing race is Wimar's *The Lost Trail* (c. 1856, plate 8), in which the Indians search the ground for evidence of a trail, metaphorically suggesting that they have lost their path as a culture. Wimar seems to have borrowed the pose of the primary chief from Charles Deas' famous painting *Long Jakes* (1844, fig. 55), which had appeared in print.

While he was working on *The Abduction*, Wimar was developing his ideas for another version of *The Attack on an Emigrant Train* (1856, fig. 56). This would become his most ambitious and accomplished painting of the Düsseldorf period and a signature image of his brief artistic

career. Begun in February 1855, the painting was not completed until shortly before his departure from Europe in August 1856. In this painting Wimar returned to his themes of conflict, in which the natives are savage warriors repelling civilization's inevitable progress across the frontier. The painter's imagination was sparked by his reading of Gabriel Ferry, a French author of American western stories. Wimar reported in a letter home that he was captivated by a passage in Ferry's *Impressions de Voyages et Aventures dans le Mexique, la Haute Californie et les Régions de l'Or* (Brussels: 1851) that described "a caravan of gold seekers in camp, on the prairie . . . defending themselves against the attack of a band of Indians."[101] Wimar's rendering of the scene was entirely novel in conception and established the prototype for many future images of Indian attacks on wagon trains.[102]

The painting presents a wagon train moving furiously forward at a diagonal out of the picture

Figure 53   (top left)
Carl Wimar. *Indians Being Pursued by American Dragoons*. Oil on canvas, 1853. Gulf States Paper Corporation, Tuscaloosa, Alabama.

Figure 54   (top right)
Carl Wimar. *Funeral Raft of the Dead Chieftain*. Oil on canvas, 1856. Gulf States Paper Corporation.

Figure 55   (left)
Charles Deas. *Long Jakes*. Oil on canvas, 1844. Manoogian Collection.

Figure 56
Carl Wimar. *The Attack on an Emigrant Train.* Oil on canvas, 1856. University of Michigan Museum of Art, Ann Arbor; bequest of Henry C. Lewis.

66

Figure 57
William T. Ranney. *Prairie Fire.* Oil on canvas, 1848. Private collection.

space, while the settlers shoot at the Indians passing on horseback. Two Indians on foot rise from the prairie grass in the foreground to ambush the caravan from the flank. The drama of the narrative is enhanced by the dynamic composition as the orthogonals of the wagon train and Indian horde intersect in the foreground. The artist's conception of the image is thoroughly original; only his own 1854 *Attack* depicted this subject earlier, and the composition remotely relates to just a few pictorial sources. Its closest compositional precedent is William T. Ranney's *Prairie Fire* (1848, fig. 57), a rarity in Ranney's work because it portrays a dramatic frontier subject instead of his usual domestic images of frontier life. Ranney emphasized the drama of dashing horses and the frantic gestures of the pioneers in *Prairie Fire*, and Wimar orchestrated the gold rushers and their horses in a similar manner in his new *Attack*.

Since Wimar's youth in Saint Louis had not allowed for any direct experience of Indian attack, his scene is entirely imaginary in conception. It bears little relation to Indian attacks as they actually occurred on the plains: the wagon appears to be a variation on a European market cart with a canvas top, rather than a western wagon; the grass is inaccurate; and his Indians are wearing whole cloth instead of buckskins.[103] Although Wimar worked from artifacts that his family had sent from Saint Louis and achieved ethnographic accuracy in some of his details,[104] his primary purpose was to create an original and dramatic image of the conflict between the expanding Anglo-European civilization and the frontier's native inhabitants, rather than a literal rendering of one event.

Compared to the 1854 version of *The Attack on an Emigrant Train*, the later composition is tighter and more refined. In the earlier canvas, the focus is on the pyramid of massed figures in the foreground, separate from the Indians in the distance. In the revision Wimar formally integrated the two groups of combatants and rendered the collision course of the two cultures in terms of converging diagonal axes. In the later version he also abandoned the use of figure types derived from sacred art—and their associated moral implications—and concentrated instead on documenting the heroic struggle to settle the frontier.

Wimar had great aspirations for his second *Attack on an Emigrant Train* and planned his departure from Düsseldorf to coincide with its completion. He was even willing to postpone his journey until the canvas was finished to his satisfaction. This apparently caused him to miss his first departure date in the fall of 1855. Early the following spring, with the conclusion of his work in sight, he decided to leave at the end of May. He was confident in his artistic accomplishments and especially pleased by the compliments of his colleagues, writing home that "the best thing is that I see that my work has admirers here."[105] Henry Lewis wrote that Wimar's *Attack* was "a large picture, the finest he has painted. . . . It will add much to his already promising reputation."[106] Wimar had learned much in Düsseldorf and was satisfied with his artistic progress. He also had grown attached to life and art in Germany and realized: "It will not be very easy to leave though since I have very many and also good friends here, who all hope that I am going to return again."[107] In his four years in Germany, he had reunited with a significant portion of the Wimar-Becker clan and had made memorable contributions to the artistic and social life in the community. His legacy to Düsseldorf was the introduction of American frontier subjects, particularly Indians, to the city's genre and history painting traditions.

When Wimar departed for New York in August 1856 he carried the consummate paintings of his four years in Düsseldorf: his 1855

67

version of *The Abduction of Daniel Boone's Daughter* and the just-completed *Attack on an Emigrant Train* (fig. 56), as well as a small copy of his raft *Abduction* (1855, fig. 49) to exhibit in New York upon his arrival.[108] His *Attack* soon became the more influential image; acquired by Missouri Governor Gamble from an exhibition in Boston,[109] the painting was lithographed by Leopold Grozelier in 1860 and released as *On the Prairie* (fig. 58). Distributed nationwide, this print influenced artists for generations and established a central image in the western myth: the Indian attack on emigrant wagon trains.

Shortly after the print was issued, Felix O. C. Darley copied Grozelier's print for his *Emigrants Attacked by Indians* (1860, fig. 59). Although Darley had never traveled in the West, he was perhaps the most successful western illustrator of the era, regularly copying from other western artists such as Catlin and Wimar. In 1860 Prince Napoleon commissioned him to paint four western subjects, one of which was his

Figure 58
Leopold Grozelier, after Carl Wimar. *On the Prairie*. Lithograph, hand colored, 1860. Saint Louis Art Museum.

Figure 59
F.O.C. Darley. *Emigrants Attacked by Indians*. Engraving, 1860. Print Division, Miriam and Ira D. Wallach Division of Art, Prints, and Photographs, New York Public Library; Astor, Lenox and Tilden Foundations.

Figure 60
Thomas Hill after Carl Wimar. *Attack on an Emigrant Train*. Oil on canvas, c. 1861. Private collection. Courtesy Garzoli Gallery, San Rafael, California.

Emigrants Attacked; the paintings themselves are no longer extant but survive in engravings.[110] At the same time, Thomas Hill produced a large-scale painting from the Grozelier print (fig. 60)—possibly Hill's first important painting after he moved to San Francisco from Philadelphia in 1861. The painted copy replicates the print with the exception of the huge billowing clouds that dominate the sky. Hill's painting was one of his earliest western subjects and seems to have been the inspiration for his mature work.

Grozelier's print also inspired Emanuel Leutze to produce *Indians Attacking a Wagon Train* (1863, fig. 61), a variation on Wimar's painting. Leutze portrayed the pioneers feverishly attempting to form a defensive circle with their wagons as the dust rising on the horizon warns of an impending Indian assault. Interestingly, Leutze also created a painting entitled *Indian and Captive* (c. 1862, fig. 62), based on Wimar's canoe *Abduction*. Apparently the older painter gained greater respect for Wimar's images of the frontier after his own tour of the West in 1861, and he turned to his former pupil for precedents to interpret these important themes in Western art.

The influence of Wimar's 1856 version of the *The Attack on an Emigrant Train* was so pervasive that all subsequent western artists had to consider this painting when treating the subject. In the late nineteenth and early twentieth centuries, Frederic Remington and Charles M. Russell interpreted wagon train attacks, and although their works are not directly derived from Wimar, they are informed by this seminal painting. Even contemporary western artists dealing with this subject are influenced by Wimar's precedent. So are modern Hollywood moviemakers: John Ford relied on western paintings, including Wimar's *Attack on an Emigrant Train*, for many of his film stagings.[111]

The paintings that Wimar brought home from Düsseldorf summarized his artistic development and the complex iconography of his works during this period. His canvases explored new figure types, compositional formulas, subject matter, and iconography in western art, while echoing contemporary beliefs concerning the Indian, the pioneer, and the frontier. Influenced by the early western artists, including Bodmer, Bingham, Deas, and Ranney, and by European history painting as exemplified by Leutze, the young artist imaginatively transposed these sources into dramatic, historicized genre paintings that gave heroic stature to pioneers and to western expansion.

Wimar realized that his epic narratives of the West were, thus far, imaginary compositions drawn largely from art and literature. At the end of his studies in Düsseldorf, he felt the need to explore the plains and its inhabitants. Taking the academic method that he had learned in Düsseldorf to the Missouri River frontier, he planned to remain long enough "to collect the necessary

Figure 61
Emanuel Leutze. *Indians Attacking a Wagon Train*. Oil on canvas, 1863. Dover Public Library, Dover, New Jersey.

Figure 62
Emanuel Leutze. *Indians and Captive*. Oil on
canvas, n.d. The Thomas Gilcrease Institute of
American History and Art, Tulsa.

70

studies" and then return to Europe in order to
benefit from its artistic traditions.[112] He was
never to leave the United States again. Once he
returned to America and experienced the Missouri River frontier, he progressed beyond his
fascination with themes of abduction and attack
and began recording for posterity the life, land,
and customs of the plains and its inhabitants,
who seemed to be "fast passing away from the
face of the earth." As the *Crayon* admonished,
"Soon the last red man will have faded forever
from his native land and those who come after us
will trust to our scanty records for their knowledge of his habits and appearance."[113]

Notes

1. Johann Wolfgang von Goethe, "Den Vereinigten Staaten," *Werke* (reprint; Hamburg: 1956), 333.

2. Alfred Englaender, "Der Sohn einer Wäscherin," *Henkel Zeitschrift* [Düsseldorf] (Maerz 1954), 74. See also Perry Rathbone, *Charles Wimar 1828–1862: Painter of the Indian Frontier* (Saint Louis: City Art Museum, 1946), 8.

3. Wimar's first biographer, William Tod Helmuth, noted this in *Arts in Saint Louis* (Saint Louis: 1864).

4. The city directories of Cologne, cited by Helmut and Inge Krumbach of the Düsseldorfer Institut für amerikanische Völkerkunde, note that the Becker family lived there from 1835 until 1843, in the Loehrgasse 24, which was renamed the Agrippastrasse in 1875.

5. For details on the artist's life, consult the primary biographical resources: Helmuth, *Arts in Saint Louis*; Wimar A. Becker and William Romaine Hodges, "Carl Wimar," *Student Life* [Washington University] 14 (January 1890): 68–70, (February 1890): 85–87, (March 1890): 103–5; William Romaine Hodges, *Carl Wimar* (Galveston, Texas: Charles Reymershoffer, 1908); and Rathbone, *Charles Wimar 1828–1862.*

6. Linda Joy Sperling, "Northern European Links to Nineteenth Century American Landscape Painting: The Study of American Artists in Düsseldorf," Ph.D. diss. (University of California, Santa Barbara, 1985), 72.

7. Duden's most influential book, *Bericht uber eine Reise nach den westliches Staaten Nordamericka* (Elberfeld: 1829) is available in translation as *Report on a Journey to the Western States of North America*, ed. James W. Goodrich (Columbia & London: The State Historical Society of Missouri and the University of Missouri Press, 1980); quoted passages are from this translation, 102, 182. For an analysis of Duden's effect on German settlers, see William Bek, "The Followers of Duden," *Missouri Historical Review* 14 (April-July 1920): 436–58.

8. Dee L. Ashliman, "The American West in Nineteenth-Century German Literature," Ph.D. diss. (Rutgers, 1969), 47–48, 55–56, 66.

9. "Editor's Introduction" to Duden, *Report*, xx. Goethe evoked the spirit of the New York in his 1825 poem, *Den Vereinigten Staaten* [The United States].

10. Ashliman, "American West in German Literature," 27, 41. Many of my references to German literature on America during this era are indebted to this important study of the subject.

11. Ibid., 19, 28–30.

12. Ibid., 150–51.

13. George Brooks, "The American Frontier in German Fiction," in John F. McDermott, ed., *The Frontier Re-examined* (Urbana, Ill.: University of Illinois Press, 1967), 156.

14. Ashliman, "The American West in German Literature," 97, 114.

15. Carl Wimar to his parents, 20 June 1854, Missouri Historical Society, Saint Louis. All quotations from Wimar's correspondence are from this collection, unless otherwise noted.

16. This information is contained in Helmuth, *Arts in Saint Louis*, 38; Becker and Hodges, "Carl Wimar," 14: 68; Hodges, *Carl Wimar*, 11; and Rathbone, *Charles Wimar 1828–1862*, 9.

17. Hodges, *Carl Wimar*, 12.

18. Nina Fletcher Little, *American Decorative Wall Painting 1700–1850* (New York: E.P. Dutton & Co., 1972), xix.

19. John F. McDermott, "Portrait of the Father of the Waters, Leon Pomarede's Panorama of the Mississippi," *Bulletin de l'Institut Francais de Washington*, n.s. no. 2 (December 1952): 48. See also McDermott's article, "Leon Pomarede, 'Our Parisian Knight of the Easel'," *Bulletin of the City Art Museum of Saint Louis* 34 (Winter 1949): 8–18.

20. Becker and Hodges, "Carl Wimar," 69.

21. Panoramas of the Mississippi River, bordering on the vast, unknown frontier, were particularly popular; at least five were created during this period. For more information on panoramas, see Perry Rathbone, *Mississippi Panorama* (Saint Louis: City Art Museum, 1950); John F. McDermott, *The Lost Panoramas of the Mississippi* (Chicago: University of Chicago Press, 1958); and Angela Miller, "The Imperial Republic: Narratives of National Expansionism in American Art, 1820–1860," Ph.D. diss. (Yale University, 1985).

22. McDermott, "Portrait of the Father of Waters," 49.

23. Helmuth, *Arts in Saint Louis*, 39.

24. Rathbone, *Charles Wimar 1828–1862*, 12.

25. The principal resources on Catlin are his *Letters and Notes on the Manners, Customs, and Condition of the North American Indians* (London: 1841) and *North American Indian Portfolio* (London: 1844), and William H. Truettner's *The Natural Man Observed: A Study of Catlin's Indian Gallery* (Washington, D.C.: Smithsonian Institution Press, 1979).

26. Prince Maximilian of Wied-Neuwied, *Reise in das Innere Nord Amerika in den Jahren 1832 bis 1834* (Coblenz: 1839); George Catlin, *Letters and Notes on the Indians*. The most thorough studies on Bodmer are published by the Joslyn Art Museum, which holds the bulk of his work. See particularly *Karl Bodmer's America* (Omaha, Neb.: Joslyn Art Museum, 1984).

27. For further biographical information on Bingham, refer to the principal resources on the artist: John F. McDermott, *George Caleb Bingham, River Portraitist* (Norman, Okla.: University of Oklahoma Press, 1959); Maurice E. Bloch, *George Caleb Bingham* (Berkeley: University of California Press, 1967); and Michael Shapiro et al., *George Caleb Bingham* (New York: Harry N. Abrams, Inc., 1990).

28. Quoted in Carol Clark, "Charles Deas," *American Frontier Life: Early Western Painting and Prints* (New York: Abbeville Press, 1987), 60. Refer to this seminal essay on the artist for other biographical details.

29. John F. McDermott, "J. C. Wild, Western Painter and Lithographer," *Ohio State Archaeological and Historical Quarterly* 60 (April 1951): 111–25. See also John W. Reps, *Saint Louis Illustrated: Nineteenth-Century Engravings and Lithographs of a Mississippi River Metropolis* (Columbia, Mo.: University of Missouri Press, 1989). Wild's series of lithographs ran nine issues before the publication folded in May 1842.

30. Carl Wimar to his brother August, 2 November 1853.

31. William H. Gerdts, "On Elevated Heights: American Historical Painting and Its Critics," in William H. Gerdts and Mark Thistlethwaite, *Grand Illusions: History Painting in America* (Fort Worth, Tex.: Amon Carter Museum, 1988), 87.

32. Barbara S. Groseclose, *Emanuel Leutze, 1816–1868: Freedom is the Only King* (Washington, D.C.: Smithsonian Institution Press, 1975), 40.

33. Carl Wimar to his parents, 23 March 1853.

34. Quoted in Sperling, "Northern European Links," 365.

35. Carl Wimar to his parents, 27 August 1854.

36. JWE, April 1850, quoted in Sperling, "Northern European Links." The body of critical literature on American artists in Düsseldorf is modest. The primary works on this subject are Donelson Hoopes, *The Düsseldorf Academy and the Americans* (Atlanta: The High Museum of Art, 1972); Kunstmuseum Düsseldorf, *The Hudson and the Rhine: Die amerikanische Malerkolonie in Düsseldorf im 19. Jahrhundert* (Düsseldorf: Kunstmuseum, 1976); Danforth Museum, *American Artists in Düsseldorf: 1840–1865* (Framingham, Mass.: Danforth Museum, 1982); Sperling, "Northern European Links."

37. Sperling, "Northern European Links," 151. Also see Lois Marie Fink and Joshua C. Taylor, *Academy: The Academic Tradition in American Art* (Washington, D.C.: Smithsonian Institution Press, 1975), 27–29, for a history of the American art academies.

38. Sperling, "Northern European Links," 108–22. In addition to active patrons, the German cities also had a system of art unions (*Kunstverein*) similar to those in America.

39. According to family legend, at some point in the 1840s the Becker family accepted an impoverished Polish immigrant into their home and helped provide for him until he could establish himself. During that time young Carl befriended the houseguest and discussed his artistic ambitions with the immigrant. The Polish man eventually accumulated some wealth and always remembered the assistance from the Becker clan. At his death he bequeathed some of his assets to Carl to help the aspiring artist to study in Europe. This tale is reported in each of the early biographical resources on the artist: Helmuth, *Arts in Saint Louis*, 39; Becker and Hodges, "Carl Wimar," 69; Hodges, *Carl Wimar*, 14; Rathbone, *Charles Wimar 1828–1862*, 12. When Wimar realized that the bequest would not be forthcoming, he wrote to his parents from Düsseldorf: "It does not look good with my inheritance"; undated letter, Missouri Historical Society.

40. William P. Curtis to Andrew Warner, 3 December 1851, New-York Historical Society.

41. Groseclose, *Emanuel Leutze, 1816–1868*, 40.

42. Carl Wimar to his parents, 12 January 1854.

43. Ibid., 2 November 1853 and 6 December 1853.

44. Henry Lewis to his brother George, from Düsseldorf, 1 June 1856, 21 April 1857, and 12 December 1857, Henry Lewis Papers, William L. Clements Library, University of Michigan, Ann Arbor.

45. This new information is derived from a series of letters by Wimar and Lewis regarding the latter's relationship with Leutze. See Wimar correspondence of 23 March 1854, 27 August 1854, Missouri Historical Society; and Lewis correspondence of 1856? and 28 May 1858, Lewis Papers, University of Michigan.

46. *Crayon* 5 (March 1857): 82, 89, quoted in Sperling, "Northern European Links," 108.

47. Sanford R. Gifford to his father, undated (probably June 1856), p. 44, Minnesota Historical Society, Saint Paul.

48. Ibid., 45.

49. Carl Wimar to his parents, 19 September 1854.

50. "Mitgliederliste des Künstlervereins Malkasten," December 1852-September 1856, Malkasten Archives, Stadt Archiv, Düsseldorf. This citation was provided courtesy of Helmut Krumbach and the Düsseldorfer Institut für amerikanische Völkerkunde.

51. Carl Wimar to his parents, 23 October 1854.

52. Sanford R. Gifford to his father, undated (probably June 1856), 44.

53. Henry Lewis to his brother George, 21 April 1857. One playbill lists Wimar as an actor in *Pannemann's Traum*.

54. See John I. H. Baur, ed., "The Autobiography of Worthington Whittredge," *Brooklyn Museum Journal* 1 (1942): 31. Whittredge related that on a sketching trip with a group of German and American artists and some local girls, the Germans asked Whittredge how Indians scalped their victims. The artist, who, unbeknownst to the group, wore a toupee, demonstrated by hanging from a tree and scalping himself before the party. The dramatic gesture caused several of the women to faint, much to the delight of the other members of the party.

55. Carl Wimar to his parents, 6 December 1853.

56. Ibid.

57. The exceptions were the Heidelberg landscape, a portrait of Leutze (now lost), and another typical frontier subject, Mississippi River flatboats.

58. Carl Wimar to his parents, 6 December 1853.

59. Wimar exhibited an attack painting, *Auswanderer, von Indianern angegriffen* [*Emigrants Attacked by Indians*], no. 567, in 1855, and two captivity paintings entitled *Eine Deutsche von Indianern gefangen* [*A German Captured by Indians*], nos. 438 and 566, in 1857 at Hanover. See *Verzeichniss der Drei und Zwanzigsten Kunst-Ausstellung in Hannover* (Hanover: Druck von August Grimpe, 1855); and *Verzeichniss der Fuenf und Zwanzigsten Kunst-Ausstellung in Hannover* (Hanover: Druck von August Grimpe, 1857; citations courtesy the Düsseldorfer Institut für amerikanische Völkerkunde). In his series of Düsseldorf letters in the Missouri Historical Society, Wimar tells of his exhibitions in the other German cities. At the Düsseldorf Kunstverein of 1854, *The Attack on an Emigrant Train* attracted particular attention with its "lure of the exotic." See "Wochentlicher Kunstbericht. Bildende Kunst. Die Kunstvereins-Ausstellung," *Düsseldorfer Journal und Kreis-Blatt* 16 (5 August 1854): 1. The following year, Wimar was identified as one of the more talented figure painters at the Kunstverein exhibition. See E. Schulte, "Die permanente Kunstausstellung," *Correspondenz-Blatt des Kunstvereins fur die Rheinlande und Westphalen zu Düsseldorf* 10 (March 1855): 12.

60. One of the first important studies of this theme in romantic art, literature, and philosophy is Hoxie Neale Fairchild's *The Noble Savage: A Study in Romantic Naturalism* (New York: Russell and Russell, 1961).

61. Daniel Bryan, *The Mountain Muse* (Harrisonburg, Va.: Davidson and Bourne, 1813), lines 547–56 (pp. 160–61). Filson's book was published in 1784 by James Adams of Wilmington, Delaware; a reprint edition was published in Louisville, Kentucky, by John P. Morton and Company in 1930. Flint's account was published in 1833 by E. H. Fleet of Cincinnati.

62. Benjamin Poff Draper, "American Indians—Barbizon Style," *Antiques* 44 (September 1943): 108–10. For additional information on this rare print series see De Cost Smith, "Jean François Millet's Drawings of American Indians," *Century Illustrated Monthly Magazine* 80 (May-October 1910): 78–84; "From Fontainebleau to the Dark and Bloody Ground," *Month at Goodspeed's Book Shop* (Boston) 16 (March-April 1945): 150–54; and the Joslyn Art Museum, *Karl Bodmer's America*, 370.

63. Joslyn Art Museum, *Karl Bodmer's America*, 365.

64. John Filson, *Kentucke* (1930), 49–58.

65. For a particularly insightful discussion of the Boone myth in the visual arts, see Dawn Glanz, *How the West Was Drawn: American Art and the Settling of the Frontier*, in Linda Seidel, editor, *Studies in the Fine Arts: Iconography* (Ann Arbor, Mich.: University Microfilms, 1978, 1982), 2. See also Richard Slotkin, *Regeneration through Violence: The Mythology of the American Frontier, 1600–1860* (Middletown, Conn.: Wesleyan University Press, 1973), 21.

66. The interpretation of these symbols was graciously supplied in conversation with Professor J. Gray Sweeney, Arizona State University, Tempe. Dawn Glanz in *How the West Was Drawn*, 11, associates Boone in this painting with Saint Jerome, the hermetic saint who gained wisdom and salvation through his experience in the wilderness. The religious metaphor gives a sacred interpretation to Boone's role in western expansion. Hoxie N. Fairchild also makes this association in *The Noble Savage*, 142–43.

67. For more on images of discovery, particularly those of Columbus, and on *Westward the Course of Empire Makes Its Way*, see Angela Miller's essay.

68. Mark Thistlethwaite introduced, explained, and compared the ideas of grand manner history painting, genrefied history painting, and historicized genre painting. See "The Most Important Themes," in Gerdts and Thistlethwaite, *Grand Illusions*, 39–45.

69. The critical literature interpreting the significance of the captivity narrative is almost as extensive as the genre itself. Wilcomb E. Washburn edited a monumental compendium of the entire known captivity literature of 311 titles in 111 volumes (New York: Garland Publishers, Inc., 1975). Some of the critical studies used in developing this section on Wimar's captivity scenes include Phillips D. Carleton, "The Indian Captivity," *American Literature* 15 (May 1943): 169–80; Roy Harvey Pearce, "The Significance of the Captivity Narrative," *American Literature* 19 (March 1947): 1–20; Richard Slotkin, *Regeneration Through Violence*; David T. Haberly, "Women and Indians: *The Last of the Mohicans* and the Captivity Tradition," *American Quarterly* 28 (Fall 1976): 431–43; and Pauline Turner Strong, "Captive Images," *Natural History*, no. 12 (December 1985), 50–57.

70. See Slotkin, *Regeneration Through Violence*, which develops a complex interpretation of the creation and development of an American myth-identity through the captivity narrative and the theme of violence.

71. Rena N. Coen, "David's Sabine Women in the Wild West," *Great Plains Quarterly* (Spring 1982): 67–76. Giovanni da Bologna's sculpture *The Rape of the Sabine Women* (1583, Loggia dei Lanzi, Florence) was one of the earliest visual treatments and established the figural type for the western tradition of this subject. See Arlene Popper Levin, "Giambologna's Conception of the *Rape of the Sabine Women*," M.A. thesis (Washington University, 1971).

72. For a thorough discussion of the history surrounding this revolutionary war event and the painting, see Samuel Y. Edgerton, Jr., "The Murder of Jane McCrea: The Tragedy of an American *Tableau d'Histoire*," *Art Bulletin* 49, no. 4 (1967): 481–92.

73. Vivian Green Fryd discusses this interpretation of Bingham's iconography in her article, "Two Sculptures for the Capitol: Horatio Greenough's Rescue and Luigi Persico's Discovery of America," *American Art Journal* 19, no. 2 (1987): 30–31.

74. Angela Miller of Washington University has suggested this interpretation of the painting.

75. For a discussion of the development of the Magdalen iconography, see Marjorie M. Malvern, *Venus in Sackcloth: The Magdalen's Origins and Metamorphoses* (Carbondale, Ill.: Southern Illinois University Press, 1975), 2, 9, 162, 256; and Alan Phipps Darr and Rona Roismann, "Francesco da Sangallo: A Rediscovered Early Donatellesque 'Magdalen' and Two Wills from 1574 and 1576," *Burlington Magazine* 129 (December 1987): 784–90.

76. Carleton, "The Indian Captivity," 173.

77. Carl Wimar to his parents, 6 December 1853.

78. The completed canvas is in a private collection and was unavailable for publication. The illustration for this painting is Wimar's working drawing, from the collection of the Saint Louis Art Museum.

79. Carl Wimar to his parents, 12 January 1854. Wimar also wrote about this painting in several other letters home. On 23 March 1854 he noted that he was working on the piece and would need three to four more months to complete it. By 13 July 1854 he had already shipped the painting back to the United States. However, a version of this subject entitled *Auswanderer, von Indianern angegriffen* was exhibited in Hanover beginning on 25 February 1855 (see n. 59); it is difficult to determine whether this was a copy of or a preparatory study for the finished painting.

80. Carl Wimar to his parents, 13 July 1854.

81. Ibid., 19 September 1854.

82. Ibid., 6 December 1853.

83. Ibid., 27 August 1854.

84. Ibid., 19 September 1854.

85. Ibid., 12 January 1854.

86. Wimar would have known *The Jolly Flatboatmen* from engravings distributed by the American Art Union, and he also seems to have known *Wood Boatmen on a River*, the moonlit night scene which Bingham was working on in the same year.

87. Carl Wimar to his parents, 20 June 1854 or 1855, Missouri Historical Society.

88. R. Wiegmann, *Die Konigliche Kunst-Akademie zu Düsseldorf: Ihre Geschichte, Einrichtung und Wirksamkeit* (Düsseldorf: 1856).

89. Wimar to his parents, 19 September 1854.

90. Sperling, "Northern European Links," has an excellent discussion of the Düsseldorf academic method; see chapter 3, "The Düsseldorf Academy and the American Landscape."

91. See Wimar's letters to his parents, particularly 2 November 1853 and undated letter probably written in late 1854 or early 1855.

92. Three sketchbooks survive from this period, two in the Missouri Historical Society and one the Saint Louis Art Museum, as well as five finished compositional drawings, four in the Saint Louis Art Museum and one in a private collection.

93. Carl Wimar to his parents, 27 August 1854.

94. Ibid., 20 February 1855.

95. Ibid. It is interesting to note that Wimar believed his birthday was on February 20, while the birth certificate clearly states the 19th. See Geburts Urkunde Nro. 20, Gemeine Siegburg, Kreis Det Sieg, Regierungs-Departments vol Köln (reference supplied by Helmut and Inge Krumbach of the Düsseldorfer Institut für amerikanische Völkerkunde).

96. Carl Wimar to his parents, 23 October 1854. Other letters dated 27 August 1854, 19 September 1854, 20 February 1855, 23 April 1855, 17 July 1855, and 27 March 1856 document his various attempts to travel to Paris and Munich and his plans to return to the United States to study the native populations on the Missouri River.

97. This painting, like the 1854 version of *The Attack on an Emigrant Train*, is in a private collection. Since the authors have been denied permission to reproduce it, the figure reference is to Wimar's smaller copy of the 1855 *Abduction*, now in the collection of the Amon Carter Museum. A fourth version of the *Abduction* is no longer extant. It is not known whether this version was a copy of the canoe composition, the raft version, or an entirely different conception of the subject. All four of these paintings were originally purchased by John A. Brownlee of Saint Louis, as recorded in Helmuth, *Arts in Saint Louis*, 3, and Hodges, *Carl Wimar*, 31.

98. Marcia L. Luft argues in "Charles Wimar's *Abduction of Daniel Boone's Daughter by the Indians* 1853 and 1855: Evolving Myths," *Prospects* 7 (1982): 301–14, that the iconography of the later version demonstrates a more enlightened view toward native Americans and is aesthetically superior to the earlier work. She considers the 1853 painting "a rather unimaginative picture rooted in an overworked tradition," while the 1855 version is "a much more original painting which reflected an enlightened approach to the myths of the American West," 301. Indeed, the later canvas is more accomplished in technique, drawing, and composition and conveys a more favorable attitude toward the native Americans; however, the perception of the Indian as the savage antagonist in the canoe *Abduction* was equally relevant to the white society's complex conception of native Americans. Furthermore, the pictorial sources for both paintings are equally derived from the European tradition of history painting. Although the raft *Abduction* is aesthetically superior, the canoe version is not "unimaginative." In a certain sense the earlier picture is more intellectually engaging and demonstrative of contemporary cultural values on many levels. Both paintings treat the issues of the Boone myth, the captivity narrative, and history painting, yet the first canvas introduces religious figural types that influence the interpretation of the work. It also betrays the contemporary obsession with the idea of sexual violation and the desire to see sexually titillating images. Neither of these insights into the iconography of the American frontier is suggested in the 1855 *Abduction*.

99. Carl Wimar to his brother August, 17 July 1855. For contemporary assessments of the painting, see Wimar's letters to his parents, 7 June 1855 and 17 July 1855.

100. Luft, "Charles Wimar's *Abduction of Daniel Boone's Daughter*," 306–7.

101. Carl Wimar to his parents, 23 April 1855. Gabriel Ferry was the pen name of Eugène Louis Gabriel de Bellemare.

102. As David Miller of Cameron University has pointed out, there are two early graphic renderings of Indian attacks on wagon trains: one by Seth Eastman entitled *Emigrants Attacked by Comanches* (c. 1845, watercolor, James Jerome Hill Reference Library, Saint Paul) and another by Balduin Möllhausen, *Cheyenne Attack* (1851, pencil), which was reproduced in the *Graphic* (London, August 26, 1976). However, both pieces are drawings, and it is doubtful that either became publicly known until after Wimar's paintings were executed.

103. There was a great variety in western wagons; see William E. Lass, *From the Missouri to the Great Salt Lake: An Account of Overland Freighting* (Lincoln, Neb.: Nebraska State Historical Society, 1972), 10–11. But Wimar's wagon more closely resembles the European market wagons that were prevalent in Düsseldorf. For other details, see also John C. Ewers, "Fact and Fiction in the Documentary Art of the American West," in McDermott, ed., *The Frontier Re-examined*, 86.

104. In a letter to his parents on 6 July 1855, Wimar requested that the family send Indian costumes from which he could make studies for both his *Abduction* and *Attack* paintings. In their discussions of these paintings, some scholars have focused on particular tribal accoutrements. For example, Patricia Trenton and Patrick T. Houlihan, in *Native Americans: Five Centuries of Changing Images* (New York: Harry N. Abrams, Inc., 1989), 35–37, identify the rifle-bearing native in the 1853 canoe *Abduction* (fig. 29) as a Shawnee carrying a Leman musket. However, ethnographic accuracy did not become a significant aspect of Wimar's work until after his 1858 and 1859 expeditions up the Missouri River.

105. Carl Wimar to his brother August, 17 July 1855, and his parents, 27 March 1856.

106. Henry Lewis to his brother, George, from Düsseldorf, 1 June 1856.

107. Carl Wimar to his parents, 27 March 1856.

108. Carl Wimar to his brother August, 17 July 1855.

109. Helmuth, *Arts in Saint Louis*, 40.

110. John C. Ewers, "Not Quite Redmen: The Plains Indian Illustrations of Felix O. C. Darley," *American Art Journal* 3 (Fall 1971): 93–95.

111. William Howze, "The Influence of Western Painting and Genre Painting on the Films of John Ford," Ph.D. diss. (University of Texas at Austin, 1986).

112. Carl Wimar to his brother August, 17 July 1855.

113. "Indian in American Art," *Crayon* 3 (January 1856): 28, quoted by Fryd in "Two Sculptures for the Capitol," 33.

Eventually, all things merge into one, and a river runs through it.

The river was cut by the world's great flood and runs over rocks

from the basement of time. On some of the rocks are timeless raindrops.

Under the rocks are the words, and some of the words are theirs.

Norman MacLean,
A River Runs Through It[1]

Figure 1
Saint Louis Levee. Daguerreotype by Thomas
N. Easterly, 1853. Missouri Historical
Society.

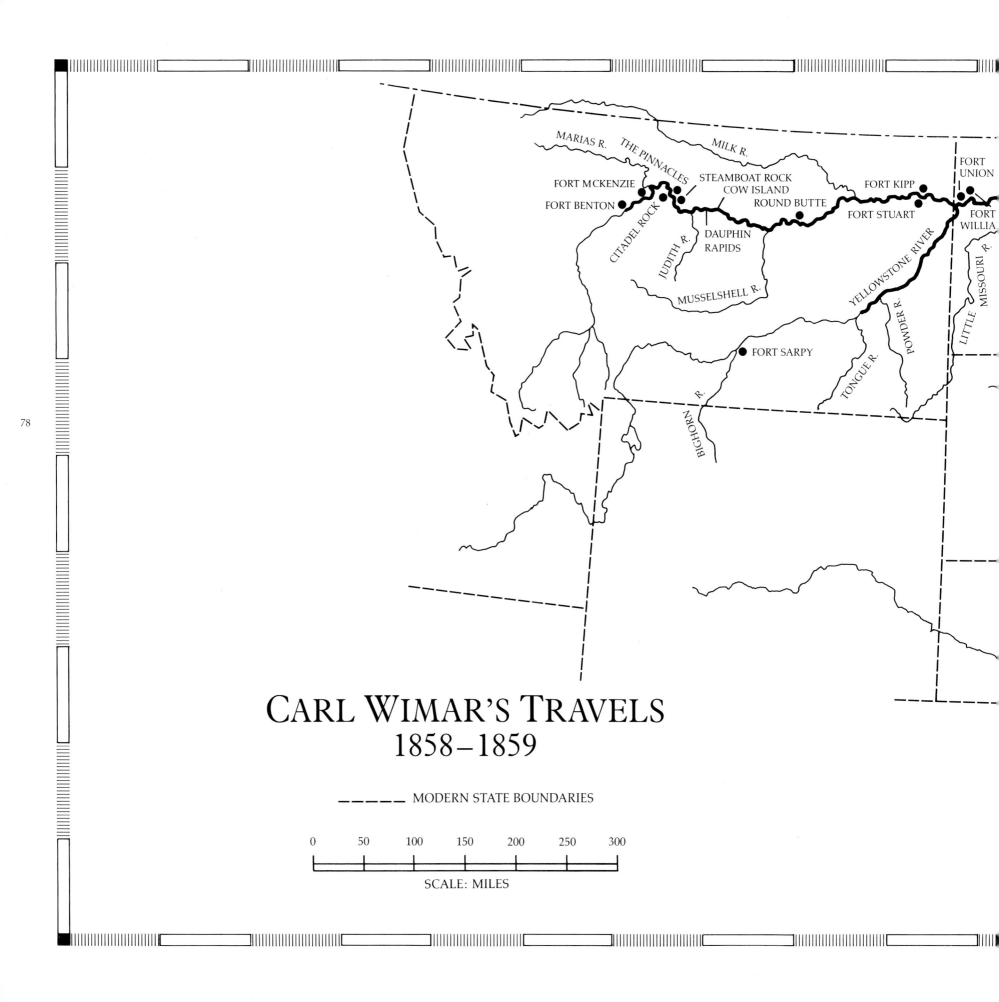

MARIAS R. THE PINNACLES MILK R.

FORT UNION

STEAMBOAT ROCK

FORT McKENZIE COW ISLAND FORT KIPP

FORT BENTON ROUND BUTTE

CITADEL ROCK FORT STUART FORT WILLIA

DAUPHIN RAPIDS

JUDITH R.

YELLOWSTONE RIVER

LITTLE MISSOURI R.

MUSSELSHELL R.

POWDER R.

FORT SARPY

TONGUE R.

BIGHORN R.

CARL WIMAR'S TRAVELS
1858–1859

- - - - - -   MODERN STATE BOUNDARIES

0 50 100 150 200 250 300

SCALE: MILES

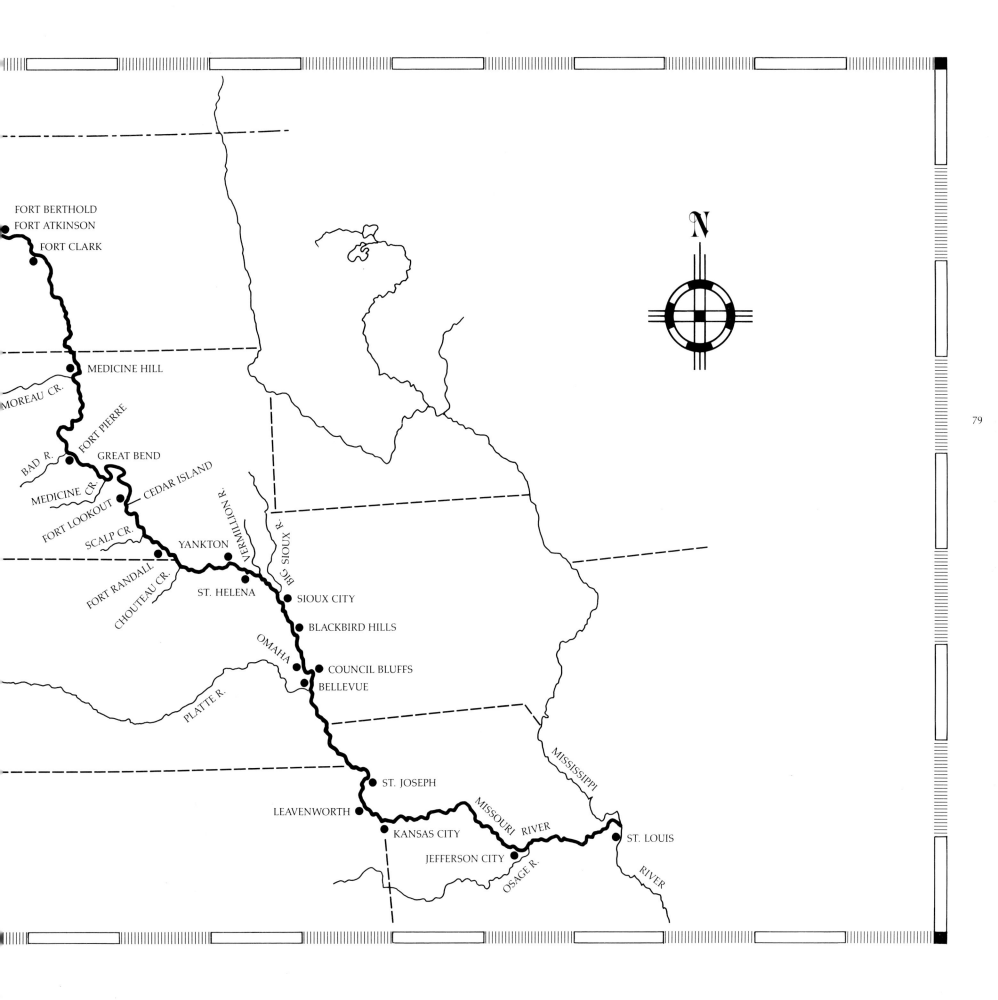

FORT BERTHOLD
FORT ATKINSON
FORT CLARK

MEDICINE HILL

MOREAU CR.

FORT PIERRE

BAD R.

GREAT BEND

MEDICINE CR.

CEDAR ISLAND

FORT LOOKOUT

SCALP CR.

VERMILLION R.

YANKTON

BIG SIOUX R.

FORT RANDALL

CHOUTEAU CR.

ST. HELENA

SIOUX CITY

BLACKBIRD HILLS

OMAHA

COUNCIL BLUFFS

BELLEVUE

PLATTE R.

ST. JOSEPH

LEAVENWORTH

MISSISSIPPI

KANSAS CITY

MISSOURI   RIVER

ST. LOUIS

JEFFERSON CITY

OSAGE R.

RIVER

N

CHAPTER II

An Artist on the Great Missouri

RICK STEWART

For nearly three-quarters of a century, from the time of the Lewis and Clark explorations until the establishment of railroads across the continent, the Missouri River served as the principal highway into the northern portions of the Great Plains and the Rocky Mountains. This great river, coursing over twenty-five hundred miles from its origins in the mountains of southwestern Montana to its juncture with the Mississippi River above Saint Louis, transported large numbers of Anglo-European travelers during the years before the Civil War.[2] One of these was a young Saint Louis painter named Carl Wimar, who journeyed to the upper Missouri River in 1858 and 1859, gathering material for his paintings. In so doing, he became one of the last artists to depict the Indians and the landscape of this region prior to the reservation period, and one of the earliest to photograph the Indian tribes in their native settings. He also was one of the few artists of his time to leave a substantial field record of the geography along the river—an important legacy because modern flood control projects have irrevocably altered much of the original landscape. On his second visit to the frontier, in 1859, Wimar was a passenger on the first steamboat to navigate the Missouri River almost to Fort Benton, nearly 2300 miles upriver. The paintings that he completed following his return reflect his firsthand experience in the untamed West, but they also reveal a conception of that West that had already achieved mythical proportions in the antebellum period. As a result, Carl Wimar's paintings have proven to be among the most significant depictions of American frontier themes.

To a young traveler like Wimar, the Missouri River in the 1850s was not a gateway to the American frontier, but part of the frontier itself, serving the commercial interests of the fur trade with Saint Louis as its mercantile hub (fig. 1). Draining an area well over half a million square miles, the river discharged more than twice the quantity of water as the Mississippi into which it flowed. In its natural state the river was an endlessly twisting chain of snag-infested channels, brush-choked banks, and continuously evolving sandbars that made the Mississippi seem tame by comparison. The annual snowmelt from the mountains and the plains, together with the ice breakup on the river itself, precipitated changes in its course that could happen overnight; yet upriver traffic commenced at the height of the flood season, during May and June, when high water minimized other difficulties for steamboat passage.[3] For the young painter, ascending the river was to be a continual challenge as well as an unforgettable adventure. But despite the threat of danger and the obvious hardships, there were clear artistic benefits for such an excursion. As a writer for the *Cosmopolitan Art Journal* observed in June 1857: "Some of our artists, buried up in their sixth-story studies, would find it to their great profit and good, to 'emigrate' for a season to the Far West to study Nature in her limitless, incomparable magnificence."[4]

By the spring of 1858 Carl Wimar was actively making plans to ascend the Missouri to what he termed "the Indian country." He wrote a letter to his half-brother August Becker, who had relocated to Quincy, Illinois, to open a paint-

ing business of his own, that he was looking into the possibility of joining one of the United States government expeditions as a staff artist. "In that case I could make studies and earn money on the side," he wrote. Certainly the need to earn money was paramount in his plans, for he continued to struggle for a living as an artist, and his family was unable to offer much financial assistance. Although a government commission seems never to have materialized, somehow the artist managed to afford a passage on one of the fur company steamboats that made annual trips upriver to deliver trade goods and Indian annuities to the far-flung frontier posts. By May 17, just three weeks after he had expressed the hope to his brother that he might obtain a government commission, Wimar had determined to travel as a tourist on a steamboat leaving within the week for the upper Missouri. In addition to the sketching supplies that were required for such a trip, he purchased something entirely new: an ambrotype apparatus for making photographs. Ambrotype photography, a successor to the daguerreotype process, was cumbersome and not well suited to use in the field, but Wimar wanted to photograph as well as sketch Indians in their native locale.[5]

Wimar booked passage on the *Twilight*, a steamboat chartered by the trading firm of Frost, Todd and Company. Established in 1856 to compete with Pierre Chouteau, Jr. and his American Fur Company, which dominated the commercial enterprise of the upper Missouri, Frost, Todd and Company had secured a government license to trade with the Indian tribes there. On the morning of May 23, 1858, the *Twilight*, under the command of Captain John Shaw, prepared for its second annual voyage to the Yellowstone River and Fort Union on the upper Missouri. All extraneous fixtures, including the cabin carpets, had been removed to make room for 120 tons of Indian annuities which two agents, Alfred J.

Vaughan and Alexander Redfield, were to deliver under the terms of recent government treaties. The boat also contained seventy-five tons of trade goods and 125 employees of Frost, Todd and Company. One of them, a young Virginian named Henry A. Boller, published an account of his adventures on the upper Missouri in 1867.[6] In addition, two young German Lutherans, Jakob Schmidt and Moritz Braeuninger, who intended to establish a mission with the Crow Indians on the upper reaches of the Yellowstone River, had arranged with Agent Redfield to make the journey with the government's cooperation. The local newspaper also reported that fifteen passengers were making "a pleasure trip," including "Mr. C. Wimar, the talented artist of St. Louis, who will treat our citizens with the finest collection of sketches of Indian life and scenery ever produced in this country."[7]

As Henry Boller described the scene before departure, Captain Shaw stood on the deck calling the roll of the voyageurs, who were "singing, or rather shouting, their Canadian boat-songs with greater energy than music." At eleven o'clock the last plank was drawn aboard, and the *Twilight* slowly swung into the river, its calliope blaring the strains of "Yankee Doodle" and "Oh! Susanna." In a letter to his parents, Boller described the scene as "the passengers hurrahed while the thousands who blackened the levee gave cheer upon cheer" as the steamboat encountered the strong downriver current.[8]

The *Twilight* was a good example of the typical Missouri River steamboat in its golden age. Hiram Chittenden, who wrote a classic history of early steamboating on the Missouri, gives an excellent description of these boats, which Wimar depicted in a number of sketches:

The first-class modern river steamboat was about 220 feet long and 35 feet wide, and would carry 500 tons. It was built with a flat bottom, so that it would draw, say, thirty inches light and fifty loaded. . . . The forcastle was equipped with steam capstans and huge spars, which served a purpose similar to that of the poles on a keelboat pushing the boat over sandbars. . . . The quarters of the crew and steerage passengers were on the boiler deck. On top of the hurricane deck was the texas—a suite of rooms for the officers of the boat. Above the texas stood the pilot-house, high over the river—a very important consideration, for the more directly the pilot could look down the better he could see the channel. The hurricane deck, and particularly the pilot-house, were favorite resorts for the passengers. High above all towered the lofty smokestacks, carrying the sparks well away from the roof of the boat and giving a strong draft to the furnace.[9]

As the *Twilight* steamed through the Missouri countryside, it passed fertile areas that were continuously settled and thick with hardwood forests. Although the river flowed more or less east across Missouri, it still possessed a sinuous current and numerous bends containing treacherous sandbars, islands of snags, and deadly sawyers (trees that had been torn from the banks by the floods, stripped of their limbs by the river ice, and embedded at one end in the river bottom to "saw" up and down with the current, becoming lethal pikes aimed at the hull of an unsuspecting boat). Captain Shaw was experienced enough to remain continually watchful for these perils, which could inflict crippling damage. About four hundred miles upriver from Saint Louis, the *Twilight* reached Kansas City. Though still a small settlement where a few streets had been laid out amidst land covered with timber, the town was rapidly becoming an important terminus for trade goods and passengers bound for

Figure 2
Carl Wimar. *Bellevue*. Pencil on paper,
June 3, 1858. Saint Louis Art Museum.

Figure 3
Carl Wimar. *Iowa Indian Dwelling*. Pencil on
paper, June 3, 1858. Saint Louis Art Museum.

the overland trails.[10]

From Kansas City the river took a more
northerly direction. "The first days of our trip
were pretty boring and I, for my part, was thinking more about you and Saint Louis than the big
tour ahead of us," Wimar wrote to his parents in
one of the few extant letters that he mailed en
route. "[W]e came to Leavenworth, where I used
my ambrotype apparatus for the first time, and
up until now I am very satisfied with my experi-
ments, and I will be able to show you some interesting things in pictures." Beyond the mouth of
the Platte River, the boat arrived at Bellevue,
which for over thirty years had served as an
American Fur Company trading post. More
recently, it had been the location of a Presbyterian mission for the Iowa, Omaha, Oto, Ponca,
and Pawnee tribes. Wimar noted in the letter to
his family that he was producing a number of
sketches in pencil and pastel. He began filling the
first of three small sketchbooks with his impressions of Bellevue, including a view of some log

structures at the outpost (fig. 2). He also noted
that "we passed several Indian tribes, the Iowas,
Poncas, and Omahas without stopping, so I was
only able to make lead pencil sketches of their
huts which are made out of bark, canvas, and
buffalo skins" (fig. 3). But the artist's real subject
was to be the Indians themselves. "[F]rom now
on it will be more interesting every day, because
the boat has to land at each of the upper tribes
and I will have the best opportunity to take
groups."[11]

As the *Twilight* steamed upriver from Bellevue, Wimar made a number of sketches of the
landscape along the way. On June 4, after passing
the mouth of the Vermillion River, the boat was
forced to lay over for a day to repair a broken
rudder. At this point Wimar sketched a group of
figures around an evening campfire and made
two drawings of the riverbanks and undulating
hills, which he identified as in the vicinity of Saint
Helena, in present-day South Dakota.[12] The next
day the steamboat reached the first villages occu-

Figure 4
Carl Wimar. *Captain Constantin Blandowski.*
Oil on canvas, 1861. Saint Louis Art
Museum; gift of Mrs. F. W. Schneider.

84

pied by the Yankton, part of the Sioux Indian
nation. Since many of Wimar's surviving sketches
depict various groups of the Sioux, who were
then achieving dominance over all the other
Plains tribes, it is necessary to briefly describe
their identity and location in the late 1850s to
avoid confusion over terminology employed by
Wimar. The Sioux were divided linguistically
into three groups: Nakota (Santee), Dakota
(Yankton-Yanktonais), and Lakota (Teton). By
Wimar's time the Dakota occupied portions of
the Missouri River frontier south and east of the
Lakota, who continued to pressure other tribes
farther west. The Lakota group comprised seven
major tribes: the Oglala ("scatter one's own");
Brulé ("burnt thighs"); Miniconjou ("planters
by water"); Hunkpapa ("campers at the opening
of the circle"); Sihásapa ("black feet," a different
group than the Algonquian-speaking Blackfeet of

the upper Missouri and northern Rockies); Sans
Arc ("without bows"); and Two Kettles ("two
boilings"). By the time of Wimar's visit, many of
the tribes within the larger divisions tended to
band themselves together whenever it was con-
venient—for purposes of trading, hunting, or
council—even though they saw themselves as
members of separate groups. In 1858 and 1859
the Sioux nation was approaching the height of
its power, and Carl Wimar witnessed the beginnings of their final struggle against rapidly
encroaching white civilization.[13]

As Agent Redfield quickly discovered, relations between the Sioux and the United States
Government were at a low ebb. By a treaty concluded at Fort Laramie in 1851, the Sioux had
surrendered all of their lands lying east of the
Big Sioux River, which today forms the western
boundary of Iowa above Sioux City. On April 19,
1858, a delegation of Sioux in Washington signed
another treaty that surrendered most of their
land lying farther west, between the Big Sioux
and Missouri Rivers, in return for a reservation
of 400,000 acres. In his report filed after his
return, Redfield noted that the area they had
ceded comprised nearly "eleven million acres of
land, much of which is very fine for cultivation
and grazing, and over which our bold and enterprising emigrants are resolved to spread." Unfortunately, as the agent noted, "All the lower
portion of this tribe is well pleased with the
treaty and the sale of their country, but as I proceeded up the river I found much dissatisfaction
on account of it among the upper portion of the
Yanctons [sic] and all the other seven tribes of
the Sioux."[14]

Carl Wimar wrote an account of his journey
upriver, which was published later that year in a
German-language journal. He stated that at the
outset he and his traveling companion, Constantin Blandowski (fig. 4), tried to ally themselves with the American Fur Company, which

appeared "in better odor" among the Indians than the hapless government agents, but in the end they were not successful. Despite the fears he must have had, Wimar obviously resolved to continue his trip and attempt to record the things that he saw. When they reached the Yankton village on June 5, Wimar reported that "the spectacle presented by them was very imposing, and as we neared them they came to the shore and paraded before us, dressed in their most gaudy style." Jakob Schmidt, the young Lutheran missionary, was even more impressed. "I had to admit some fear of these dreaded mighty Sioux," he wrote in his journal. "The Indians were draped in blankets and buffalo skins, those of the chiefs were most highly decorated with many-colored ribbons, strips of cloth, and pearl-like beads." While Schmidt and some others took a stroll through the village, Wimar got busy. "I lost no time in arranging my photographic apparatus, and was enabled in the short space allowed me to take several groups."[15]

Wimar was one of the earliest photographers of the Indians in their native locale and reportedly took a number of photographs of Indians on this trip. However, no ambrotypes have come to light that can be identified with certainty as Wimar's.[16] His pioneering photography of Indians on the Missouri could have been inspired by the activities of other Saint Louis photographers, especially John Fitzgibbon and Thomas M. Easterly. By 1857 Fitzgibbon's photographic gallery at the corner of Fourth and Market streets contained thirteen rooms, some displaying portraits of "the most distinguished celebrities of the age" and others containing "likenesses of chiefs of various tribes of Indians—admitted to be the best collection of Indian portraits in the country." A contemporary noted that Fitzgibbon "has frequently made professional excursions into various parts of the country, and has twice visited the Indian Nations, bringing back with

him each time admirable accessions to his unrivalled collection of Indian portraits." Fitzgibbon's pioneering work must have had an influence on Carl Wimar's decision to ascend the Missouri with a camera of his own. Thomas M. Easterly was hardly less important; he also had traveled extensively and had produced pioneering daguerreotype images of American Indians as early as 1852. Among seventeen daguerreotypes that survive in the Missouri Historical Society, ten portray Sauk and Fox Indians, members of related woodlands tribes, while seven are of Iowas—true Plains Indians. Perhaps Wimar had the opportunity to see Easterly's work or speak with him about the difficulties involved in photographing such subjects. There were many other photographic establishments in Saint Louis as well, so it would not have been difficult for Wimar to secure the supplies or the knowledge for ambrotyping.[17]

Besides taking photographs, Wimar also was able to sketch many of the Indians in the vicinity, including those who attended meetings with the agents. Henry Boller, one of the fur company employees aboard the *Twilight*, recalled that a cabin of the boat was arranged with a semicircle of chairs, and the tribal representatives were formally invited aboard. "The group of Indians comprised the dignitaries of the band, dressed and painted after their own wild fashion," Boller wrote. "A handsome pipe of red stone, filled with chash-hash-ash, or inner bark of the red willow, passed from one to another almost without interruption, and its fragrant odor pervaded the entire apartment."[18] Another passenger, William Napton, clearly recalled Wimar's activities at these councils:

Carl F. Wimar, the gifted St. Louis painter, was making his first trip up the Missouri to get a look at the Indians. He was a tall, slim, lithe man of thirty, a swarthy complexion

85

Figure 5
Carl Wimar. *Indian Portrait Studies*. Charcoal with white, red, yellow, and orange chalk on paper, c. June 7, 1858. Missouri Historical Society.

86

resembling a Spaniard rather than a German, quick, active and indefatigable in the prosecution of his work. When we got to the Indians he was always on the alert for the striking figures among them. On reaching the Indians the agent would invite them to a council, held in the cabin of the boat. On these occasions Wimar would make pencil sketches of the assembled Indians, and he did this work with great rapidity and dexterity.[19]

As the *Twilight* continued upriver toward Fort Randall, it became increasingly obvious that Indian unrest presented a very real threat to the crew and passengers. An account written from the boat recorded: "Arrived at Fort Randall and stayed till the next day, received an escort from Company C, Second Infantry, of forty-one men, under command of Major Wessels, to the mouth of the Yellowstone. We were warned that the Blackfeet, Mineconcas [Miniconjou], Onkpapas [Hunkpapa], and other bands of Sioux, were making threats against the whites." In the face of possible conflict, the young Lutheran missionaries resolved to become martyrs to their cause. "Our pistols remain at rest and the dagger will not come from its sheath, even if we should be attacked and if there is fire and even if we should receive mortal wounds," Schmidt wrote in his

journal. "How could we kill those to whom we intend to bring spiritual life? I must love them even though I should bleed under their hands." [20]

Fort Randall, which had been established two years earlier, was the highest point on the Missouri where United States troops were quartered. Napton recalled that "the officer's quarters and barracks occupied two sides of a quadrangle of about ten acres, forming a level parade ground of prairie sod, in the center of which stood a flagstaff and a bandstand. In the afternoon a fine regimental band regaled us with delightful music that seemed to be enjoyed even by the Indians loafing around the fort." [21] The one-story double log cabins of the military garrison were upstaged

by the only painted frame house at the fort, owned by the representative of Frost, Todd and Company. "Indians are plenty all around this fort, and delegations arriving and departing daily upon national matters, from different tribes, throughout the great west, many of whom are scattered all round the post upon the surrounding eminences and in the groves," wrote a visitor to the fort a few months later. "There is 'Smutty Bear,' 'Red Leaf,' 'Mad Bull,' 'Strike the Ree,' and many other Indian encampments around here, interesting and curious to the stranger." [22]

One of Wimar's sketches that has survived in fragmentary condition depicts the heads of five Indians, three of which appear to be portrait

Figure 6   (left)
Three Yankton Dakota: Struck By the Ree, Charles Picotte, and Smutty Bear. Photograph by Julian Vannerson and Samuel Cohner, McClees Studio, Washington, D.C., 1858. National Anthropological Archives, Smithsonian Institution.

Figure 7   (right)
Struck By the Ree. Photograph by Julian Vannerson and Samuel Cohner, McClees Studio, Washington, D.C., 1858. National Anthropological Archives, Smithsonian Institution.

studies (fig. 5). The figure in the center bears a striking resemblance to Smutty Bear, when compared to a photograph of the chief taken sometime between December 31, 1857, and April 26, 1858, by the McClees studio in Washington, D.C., when the Yankton chief was part of a delegation that visited there (fig. 6). The same photograph also shows the head chief of the Yanktons, Struck By the Ree, who appears to be the figure to the lower right in Wimar's drawing. Another photograph of this chief, taken by the McClees studio in the same period that the group photo was taken, shows Struck By the Ree in an almost identical pose as that shown in Wimar's sketch (fig. 7). In June 1858 the village of Struck By the Ree was located approximately forty miles below Fort Randall, on the river opposite Calumet Bluffs near the mouth of the Niobrara River. In a letter to his parents on June 5, Henry Boller mentioned visiting the chief's camp in that vicinity. "While sitting on a box watching the goods, a dense crowd of Indians around me, the long tresses of some falling over my shoulders and contrasting with mine very strongly," he wrote, "I drew on a smooth lid, an Indian on horseback chasing a buffalo, & some other animals, to the intense astonishment of the gaping crowd of men, women, and children." Despite his purported "mild manner and musical voice," Struck By the Ree was enraged at the encroachments of white settlers on Yankton lands before the government treaty had taken effect. He demanded of Agent Redfield that they be evicted, or the Indians themselves would forcibly remove them. "I found some squatters even in the village of the Man that was Struck by the Ree and they had built a block house with port holes to fire through and had declared that they would not remove," Redfield wrote to his superiors from the Yankton village. Not for the first time, the agent pleaded for additional military troops in the region so the terms of the government treaties could be strictly enforced.[23]

On June 10, nearly one hundred miles above Fort Randall, the *Twilight* stopped at a large village of the upper Yankton tribes. Nearby was the site of what Missionary Schmidt described as "the old, bleak Fort Lookout," a post that had been established in 1856 and abandoned by the army the following year in favor of Fort Randall. Agent Redfield called a council and found the Indians in "ill temper." Furious at the purported sale of their lands, the Indian representatives warned that the upper Sioux tribes would not allow Redfield and his party safe passage beyond Fort Pierre.[24] According to Henry Boller, who was also present, a chief named Medicine Cow, who had met Redfield at the same site the previous year, did most of the threatening. One of Wimar's rough sketches that survives in a fragmented sketchbook depicts an Indian warrior identified by inscription as Medicine Cow. The drawing also contains many notations as to the details and color of the chief's costume.[25]

Not surprisingly, Wimar had little success photographing any of the disgruntled Indians here or farther up the river. "Although the whole of the tribe, dressed in their best habiliments, were encamped upon the shore, I was only enabled to secure the portrait of one chief, for so soon as the camera was planted in a position to secure any appropriate group, the whole of them fled into the surrounding country," Wimar wrote later that year. "Of this chief, however, I obtained quite an excellent likeness."[26] Apart from the photography, the artist did manage to fill his small pocket sketchbook with a number of interesting drawings of subjects on the two-hundred mile stretch of the river that lay between the lower Yankton villages and the upper ones near Fort Lookout. This sketchbook and one other, preserved in the Saint Louis Art Museum, contain sixty-seven pages of drawings whose sequence seems to follow his course upriver. A page in the first sketchbook displays careful likenesses of three well-known Sioux chiefs, all identified with inscriptions (fig. 8). The uppermost head is Bear Rib, the leader of the Hunkpapa, whom Wimar was to depict several times in the course of the next two years. Bear Rib, who was described at the time as "quite an orator and not remarkably bashful," was an important figure in this period. Conciliatory toward the whites, he was eventually murdered for his beliefs in 1862 by members of his own tribe.[27] Below Bear Rib are portraits of two noted chiefs, Iron Horn and One Horn of the Miniconjou, a branch of the Lakota. Both chiefs were also well-known in the period; Iron Horn sat for a photographer in 1859, and Wimar's drawing of One Horn resembles the famous Miniconjou headman of the same name that the artist George Catlin had painted on his trip up the Missouri nearly twenty-five years earlier.[28]

The next page in the sketchbook depicts two more chiefs, Two Bears of the Yanktonais and Iron Nation of the Brulé, two tribes of the upper Sioux that in this period were normally located in the vicinity of Fort Lookout. In his account of the trip Wimar stated that the *Twilight* received representatives of the Hunkpapa and Brulé at some point between Fort Randall and the upriver site. Two pages of drawings indicate Wimar's keen interest in the particular way that Yanktonais men braided their hair and adorned it with feathers.[29] After a few pages of landscape studies, including a feature labeled "Natural Fort," the artist made a series of drawings of Indians inscribed as having been done at Fort Randall. He depicted a number of Indian figures, most identified as Yanktons, including some bundled in decorated blankets or capotes.[30]

After the stormy council at Fort Lookout, the *Twilight* steamed into one of the most notable natural features of the Missouri, the Great Bend (or Big Bend, as it was sometimes

called). Here Wimar made a double-page drawing in his sketchbook that showed the broad river curving around the wooded banks and low-lying hills beyond. The river flowed into a horseshoe pattern over a distance of approximately twenty-two miles, leaving a narrow neck of land a little more than a mile and a half across. Steamboats often discharged groups of passengers to walk across the neck while the boat made its way around the bend, which normally took a day's time. The foot travelers were sometimes able to hunt birds and other small game that could be found in the woods and thickets on the route to the opposite channel. There is no evidence that Wimar or anyone else on the *Twilight* was

Figure 8
Carl Wimar. *Bear Rib, One Horn, Iron Horn.* Pencil on paper, c. June 7, 1858. Saint Louis Art Museum.

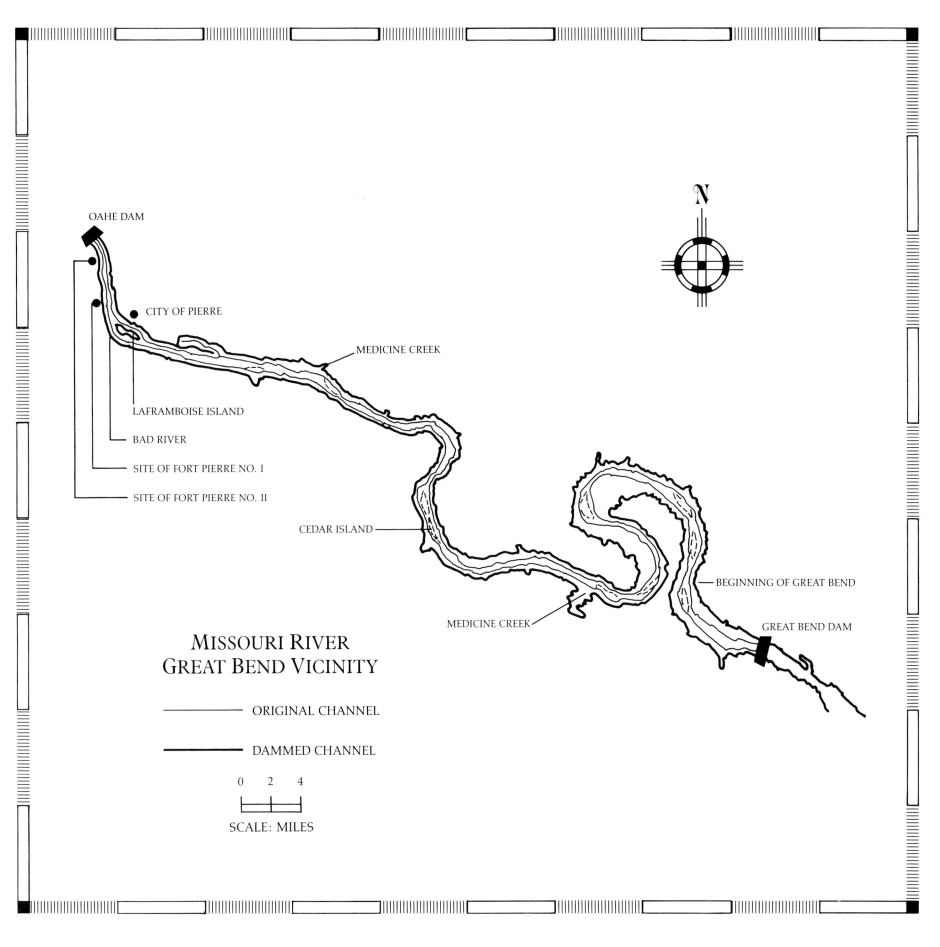

OAHE DAM

CITY OF PIERRE

MEDICINE CREEK

LAFRAMBOISE ISLAND

BAD RIVER

SITE OF FORT PIERRE NO. I

SITE OF FORT PIERRE NO. II

CEDAR ISLAND

MEDICINE CREEK

BEGINNING OF GREAT BEND

GREAT BEND DAM

MISSOURI RIVER
GREAT BEND VICINITY

——————— ORIGINAL CHANNEL

━━━━━━━ DAMMED CHANNEL

0   2   4

SCALE: MILES

allowed to cross the Great Bend on foot during this trip, probably due to the volatile nature of the Indian situation. The artist was to chronicle this feature of the river in greater detail the following year.[31]

Shortly after traversing the Great Bend, the steamboat reached Fort Pierre on June 12, 1858. This famed fur company post had been erected in 1831–32 and named for Pierre Chouteau, Jr., one of the principals of the American Fur Company. Purchased by the U.S. Government in 1855, it was now in its final decline. The river landing there had changed and was no longer adequate, and the buildings were too dilapidated to be salvaged. As a result, Fort Pierre had been abandoned early in 1857 in favor of the new site at Fort Randall two hundred miles downriver. Frost, Todd and Company, who had engaged the *Twilight*, were subsequently appointed custodians of the old fort, but most of its buildings had been either removed or badly vandalized by the time Carl Wimar first visited there.[32] In his report on the trip Wimar noted that the *Twilight* was unable to land at Fort Pierre itself "on account of the low stage of the water," but ascended a mile farther upstream followed by several hundred Sioux in procession along the riverbank. "The chiefs formed themselves in a circle on the shore opposite the boat, their women and children being arranged behind them," Wimar wrote. After some deliberation, a delegation was invited to come aboard. William Napton recalled that the river bottom in the vicinity "was dotted with their lodges as far as we could see from the hurricane deck of the boat." Agent Redfield then entered into what he described as "a long and tedious and disagreeable talk with their chiefs and head men." The Sioux vehemently protested the sale of their lands, and Redfield became alarmed at their "most disturbed and irritated state of mind." In a letter to his superior written aboard the steamboat two days

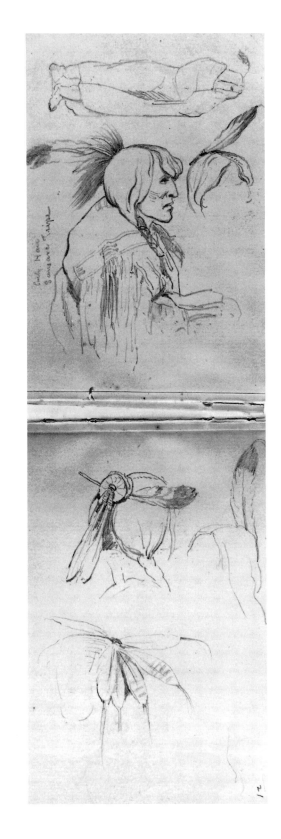

Figure 9
Carl Wimar. *Curly Hair, Sans Arc Tribe, Fort Pierre/ Studies of Feather Adornment*. Pencil on paper, June 12, 1858. Saint Louis Art Museum.

Figure 10
Carl Wimar. *Unidentified Indian, Fort Pierre.*
Pencil on paper, June 12, 1858. Saint Louis
Art Museum.

92

later, Redfield noted that "I think I could not have accomplished my business with them at all but for the presence of the troops with us." Despite the tension, Wimar recorded: "I obtained as many portraits as possible, unseen to them, and also was enabled to catch several groups; of these latter, however, the figures are rather too small on account of the distance at which I was obliged to stand while taking them."[33]

A small sketch, probably done at this council, depicts a warrior in profile identified as "Curly Hair, Sans Arc Tripe [sic]" (fig. 9). Another drawing depicts an Indian with a distinctive headdress wearing a medal around his neck with the inscription "Van Buren 1837" (fig. 10). This individual resembles another that Wimar encountered, as described in the following account by William Napton:

On one occasion above Fort Pierre while the

boat was tied up swinging around against a bluff bank about the same height with the guards of the boat, a great big Indian came creeping up through the willows, squatting down on the bank within a few yards of the boat. He was most ornately and elaborately dressed, completely covered from head to foot with garments of dressed skins, profusely ornamented with garniture of beads, fringe, etc., and, as we afterwards ascertained, was a famous "medicine man." On his head an immense bonnet ornamented with feathers, beads, etc., with a leather strap forming a sort of tail to the bonnet, strung with circular plates of silver, reaching down behind almost to the ground when standing erect. Wimar began preparations for taking his ambrotype, thinking he might get it unobserved, but as soon as he began looking through the camera at him the Indian jumped up, evincing immediately his opposition to the process, at once drawing an arrow from his quiver, and by his hostile demonstrations and talk made Wimar understand that he would not submit. Then Wimar undertook to show him that he meant no harm whatever, exhibiting some pictures he had taken of other Indians, but he seemed unable to understand him and soon disappeared from view through the willow bushes lining the river bank.[34]

The same drawing also displays a small rendering of a dog travois. Henry Boller recalled that the Sioux employed the travois with horses to carry away the annuity goods after the council, and added that there were smaller ones made "for the benefit of the dogs, who are thus unwillingly compelled to make themselves useful."[35]

Two other sketches that were likely done at the Fort Pierre council show a burial scaffold, a tipi, and the rear of a Yanktonais head with the

hair braided in a queue (fig. 11). An entry in Jakob Schmidt's journal, dated June 12 at Fort Pierre, preserves a description of a scaffold nearly identical to the one depicted in Wimar's drawing:

> Four posts, eight feet tall, were stuck in the ground in an elongated quadrangle. On top some horizontal bars were fastened to them on which lay a small chest, as large as it might hold the corpse of a child of four to five years, wrapped in red cloth. Next to it stood a small box, which probably contained clothing and food for the dead, which he might need on the way to the other world. Across the scaffold lay a stick on whose end a string and some feathers (perhaps the headgear) hung and a scalp.[36]

The artist was clearly interested in recording as many aspects of Indian life as possible. This extended to acquiring a number of Indian objects through barter, which he planned to take back to his studio in Saint Louis. "I had supplied myself with many little notions for this purpose," Wimar wrote, "[and] I was enabled to procure a variety of curiosities, costumes, arms, and accoutrements."[37]

Leaving Fort Pierre, the *Twilight* steamed upriver while Wimar made sketches of the passing landscape, including one identified as the mouth of the Moreau River, and a notable feature about thirty miles above that the artist termed "Medicine Hill," near the site of an Indian village.[38] On June 16 he made a rough two-page sketch which shows a large group of mounted Indians arrayed across a broad prairie landscape, some firing their rifles, others dismounted and arranged in an open circle. The *Twilight* had halted on the west bank of the river to meet a large delegation of Yanktonais led by their famous chief, Big Head. According to Wimar's account,

> We had scarcely reached the shore when some three hundred savages galloped towards us in a furious manner, until they

Figure 11
Carl Wimar. *Burial Scaffold and Tipi, Fort Pierre*. Pencil on paper, June 12, 1858. Saint Louis Art Museum.

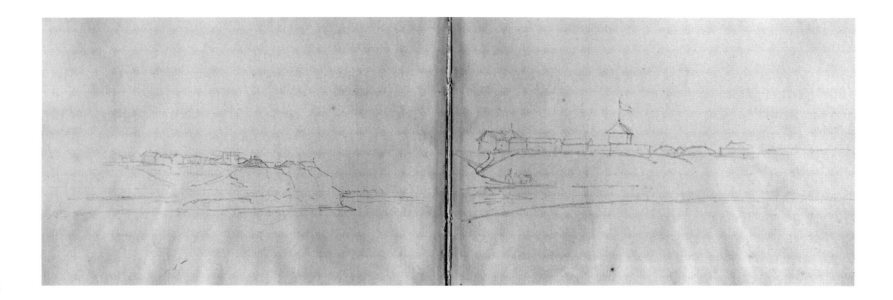

94

were within about one hundred paces of our
party when they suddenly came to a halt
and fired their flintlocks over our heads.
You may imagine our fright when we heard
the whistling balls passing over us, but we
were informed that such proceedings were
intended as a sign of friendship. Some of
their pieces had been aimed so low that their
bullets took effect on the wheel-house of
our steamer. The Indians then descended
from their highly comparisoned horses and
there was a great council formed on the
prairie.[39]

Nine years later Henry Boller remembered the
scene vividly. "A long, dark line of warriors, riding abreast, emerged from the intervening roll of
prairie and with full pomp and panoply advanced
to meet us, headed by the famous chieftain, Big
Head, in person," he wrote. "All were dressed in
shirts of deerskin profusely decorated with scalp-
locks, stained horsehair, and devices worked in
porcupine quills and beads. War eagle feathers
were fastened in their hair and pennons of scarlet

cloth fluttered from the lances." Dismounting,
the Indians seated themselves in a line, holding
their horses behind them. Big Head and his sub-
ordinates advanced to Agent Redfield and his
interpreter, Zephyr Recontre, and shook hands
with solemn ceremony. "It will be recollected
that this chief and his followers have for some
years past been rather conspicuous for their
unfriendly and refractory disposition," Redfield
later noted in his report. Big Head castigated the
terms of the recent treaty, refusing to abide by
the supposed sale of tribal lands. In the midst
of all this, "Wimar the artist endeavored to buy
some arrows of a brave," Boller recalled, "when
the latter, fitting one to his bow replied that he
would 'sooner put one through him.'"[40]

Leaving the environs of Big Head's village,
the *Twilight* pushed on upriver, entering present-day North Dakota. On the eastern side of the
Missouri extensive prairies, rich in grass, opened
to view. On the other side, vertical bluffs averag-
ing two hundred feet in height rose beyond the
cottonwood and willow thickets on the river bottoms. Here Wimar began a new sketchbook with

a view of the landscape on the west side of the river, inscribed as being fifteen miles below Fort Clark. Two more double-page studies depict the broad expanse of the river set against a background of high plateaus. On June 19 the steamboat came in sight of Fort Clark, and Wimar made two sketches of the post as they approached it (fig. 12). The fort, named in honor of William Clark and established in 1831 by the American Fur Company, was situated high on the west bank of the Missouri about eight miles below the mouth of the Big Knife River. Barely visible in Wimar's small drawings of the fort and its environs are the earthen lodges of the Arikara tribe, who had established a semipermanent village near the fur company post. The Arikaras, or Rees as they were sometimes called, were the most northerly extension of the Caddoan stock, which ranged south into Texas. After the smallpox epidemic of 1837 they had become allied with the Mandan and Hidatsa tribes and were bitter enemies of the Sioux. Wimar wrote that the *Twilight* had anchored offshore the previous night at a distance downriver from the fort, in order to avoid "the notorious thieving propensities" of these Indians. "This precaution, however, was not of much avail, as we had been observed by some of their spies, and a short time after midnight the Indians surrounded our craft with their boats made of buffalo hides, and it was actually necessary to have the most vigilant sentinels [as] our guards to prevent us from being robbed," he noted. "This tribe is known to be very desperate, and we found them so."[41]

The Arikaras had moved into the abandoned villages of the Mandan, after the latter had been decimated by smallpox. At the time of Wimar's visit they were raising corn, beans, squash, and pumpkins, which they traded to the Sioux for buffalo hides. In this period the Arikara and other weaker tribes were being continually pushed northward by the advancing Sioux, who

also harassed them in their semipermanent locations. As a demonstration of this, the Sioux regularly burned the prairies in the vicinity of Fort Clark to keep the roving buffalo herds away from the Arikara villages, so the latter would not be able to obtain their own hides. Tribes such as the Arikara were thus entirely at the mercy of the roaming Sioux and were becoming steadily weaker. When Agent Redfield stepped ashore to meet the Arikara on June 19, he found them frustrated and volatile:

> They are at war with a portion of the Sioux, and killing and being killed; stealing and being stolen from; but as they are few and their enemies numerous, they, of course, get the worst of it. . . . They seemed to wish to get rid of the treaty, as if that was the cause of their suffering, and would not receive their annuity presents. The chiefs desired to do so, and to keep the treaty; but the young "braves" in open council forbade their acceptance of the presents, and the chiefs acknowledged that they dared not disobey. They seemed to think the annuity not worthy of their acceptance. In fact, some of the young men were wild and crazy with passion.[42]

As Redfield was returning to the boat after this stormy meeting, he was met by a group of the young braves. Suddenly one of them placed the muzzle of his rifle between Redfield's feet and fired it, causing powder burns on the agent's clothes. Undeterred, Redfield induced twelve of the Arikara chiefs and warriors to come aboard the *Twilight* for additional discussion. After an initial parley the chiefs asked to see the soldiers that were accompanying the boat, who were apparently being kept out of sight. "Our escort was so large that they prudently desisted from making any demonstration," a witness noted in

Figure 13
Carl Wimar. *The White Parflesh, a Chief, and Other Members of the Arikara Tribe, Fort Clark.* Pencil on paper, June 19, 1858. Saint Louis Art Museum.

an account written for the *Missouri Republican.* After a council that lasted over five hours, the Arikaras reluctantly agreed to the agent's wishes and received the annuities.[43]

Surprisingly enough, Wimar was able to record some of his impressions amidst this atmosphere of anger and tension. "The appearance of the military had produced such excitement that I could only procure two daguerreotypes [ambrotypes], from which I painted, without their knowledge, two portraits of their chiefs," he reported. Wimar produced four pages of sketches in his small book that represent the Arikaras and the vicinity of Fort Clark (figs. 13–14). The first three pages contain many studies of the heads of various warriors, with special attention paid to hair style and modes of dress. One of these drawings, however, is identified with the inscription, "The White Parflesh: A Chief of the Arrickarees[sic]." This chief, the principal spokesman at the council, was well known in the period as a senior figure who was more apt to be conciliatory toward the whites.[44] The fourth page

in Wimar's sketchbook depicts an Indian leaning against the bundles of annuity goods that were set ashore, along with two small studies of earth lodges located in the vicinity. Wimar was to depict this type of dwelling a number of times during his trips upriver, and a photograph taken a number of years later shows an abandoned lodge on the west bank of the Missouri River which resembles those in the artist's sketches (fig. 15).[45] Wimar recorded that he walked into the village accompanied by two friends, only to find themselves surrounded by clamoring squaws. "Fortunately I had but trifles about my person, for, as the crowd became more dense, I felt their hands in all my pockets," he wrote. The artist was greatly relieved when a group of men from the boat arrived to rescue them from their predicament.[46]

By the late afternoon the *Twilight* was once again on its way upriver. After a brief stop at a small Mandan village a few miles above Fort Clark, the boat continued upstream past increasingly picturesque bluffs made of soft sedimen-

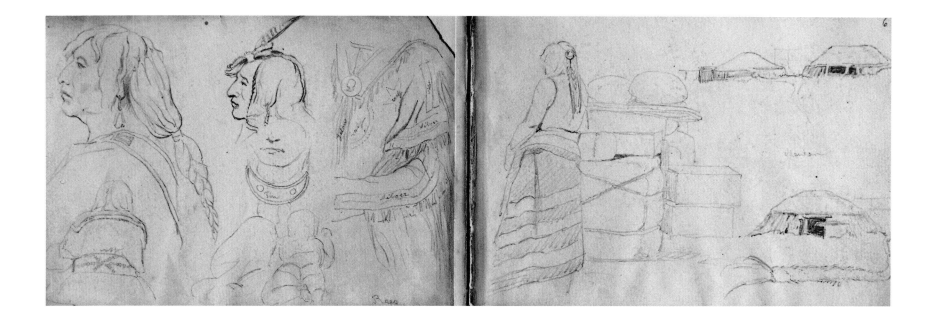

tary rock bearing strata that varied in color from black to white to red. Such formations, susceptible to erosion and bearing very little vegetation, were often referred to as "mauvaises terres" or badlands, a name that was used by many travelers in the mid-nineteenth century to denote almost any type of barren, broken country on the High Plains.[47] On June 20, less than a day after leaving Fort Clark, the steamboat came in sight of Forts Berthold and Atkinson, and Wimar made a small sketch of both (fig. 16). In 1845 the remnants of the Mandan tribe, decimated by disease, had combined with the Hidatsa, or Gros Ventre, and moved to a site called Like-a-Fishhook village, named after a peculiar bend in the Missouri approximately fifty miles north of Fort Clark. The same year Fort Berthold was established there by Bartholomew Berthold of the American Fur Company, as a trading center for the village. In 1858, when Carl Wimar visited the area, a new opposition post, named Fort Atkinson, was being erected about two hundred yards to the north by Frost,

Todd and Company. Henry Boller, who was an employee of the latter, described the post, which was to be his home for the next several years, as "sufficiently spacious for all the requirements of the trade." Wimar's drawing depicts the fort as Boller described it, situated "on the lower end of the high bluff bank, about two hundred feet from the river and nearly the same distance from the Indian village. . . . Three sides of the fort were enclosed with a substantial stockade of hewn timbers, sixteen feet in height."[48]

Wimar also made sketches of one of the earth lodges and the scaffolds that were used to dry buffalo meat and stretch the hides, which were the prime trade item in the period. When the *Twilight* arrived, many of the Indians were away on a buffalo hunt, but there was plenty of evidence that the fortunes of the two tribes had not been good. "These poor, feeble, subdued people I found, as usual, quiet and friendly, and thankful to receive their small presents," Agent Redfield reported. "They are fast wasting away, and unless soon assisted and protected by the

Figure 14
Carl Wimar. *Studies of Arikara Indians and Mandan Earth Lodges, Vicinity of Fort Clark.* Pencil on paper, June 19, 1858. Saint Louis Art Museum.

government the hostilities of the Sioux will utterly annihilate them, and the Arrikarees[sic] also."[49] Although Wimar must have been aware of this, his drawings indicate a detached interest in the Indians' mode of dress. He executed a small sketch of three female figures with children, wrapped in blankets, along with two studies that showed the method of braiding the hair at the back of the head, one of which is labeled "Grovan [sic]." Once again, Wimar attempted to photograph the Indians, with nearly disastrous results:

> I was cautioned by one of our trappers not to endeavor to take a photograph of any of this tribe on account of their superstitious ideas, but the groups were so very picturesque that I could not refrain, and essayed

therefore a trial. Unfortunately, I was unable to hide myself from their keen vigilance, for one of the chiefs watched my proceedings and uttered a few words to his people which had the effect of dispersing them immediately, nor would they again reassemble until the photographic apparatus had been put aside. Our Captain, who understood the Indian language, endeavored to explain to them the nature of my proceedings, after which I made a second attempt, but so soon as I had planted the camera they became so incensed that they aimed their arrows at my person, which you may imagine caused me to immediately desist from further effort. I was informed afterwards that it was the belief of these Indians, that had I secured their portraits

Figure 15
Mandan Earth Lodge, Lewis and Clark Trail, West Bank of Missouri. Photograph by Laton Huffman, n.d. Montana Historical Society.

they would have perished with the small pox. In order to obtain any pictures I was obliged to stand behind a curtain in which a small opening was made through which the focus of the camera was allowed to protrude.[50]

Beyond the juncture of the Little Missouri River, in the Black Hills, the surrounding landscape began to take on a more dramatic effect. "Ranges of towering clay bluffs of the most fantastic shapes, often resembling gigantic ruins, meet the eye," Henry Boller wrote. "All colors are here depicted, from the darkest blue to a bright vermilion [sic], and when the rays of the sun light up their walls and towers the effect is picturesque in the extreme, reminding one of castles of the Old World." Near a place on the river named Cardinal's Point, the *Twilight* was intercepted by a hunting party of Assiniboines, who wished to be taken aboard and carried upriver a short distance to Fort William, where their fellow tribesmen were waiting for their annuities. "Everyone had a piece of buffalo meat hanging on his back or on his side," Schmidt wrote. "They sat down on trunks and chairs, took off their weapons and meat; shared some meat with the white people. I also tried a piece. It was only recently cooked and very soft and tender like the best beef." By one o'clock in the afternoon the boat arrived at Fort William, near the mouth of the Yellowstone River, where a large encampment of Assiniboines awaited its arrival.[51]

The *Twilight* fired three cannon shots as a salute and was answered by two from the fort. After a brief meeting with the Indians, all parties agreed to dismantle Fort William, which had been established in 1833 and named after the trader William T. Sublette, and move it eighty miles farther upriver, into the heart of the Assiniboine hunting grounds. In recent years Sioux

99

Figure 16
Carl Wimar. *Fort Atkinson/ Fort Berthold/ Gros Ventre Lodge.* Pencil on paper, June 20, 1858. Saint Louis Art Museum.

war parties had overrun the original site, running off horses in broad daylight under the guns of the fort and occasionally laying siege to its beleaguered inhabitants. In a short time all of the materiel belonging to the old fort was loaded onto the steamboat, leaving the bundles of robes and peltries to be picked up on the return trip. Wimar seems to have executed a single page in his sketchbook here; it details Assiniboine objects including a decorated musket, a beaded moccasin, and a headband (fig. 17). There are also drawings of the prickly pear and yucca plants which abounded in the region.[52]

Sketches on the following pages depict the cutbanks and steep bluffs that the *Twilight* encountered near the vicinity of Fort William on June 23, as well as the mouth of the Yellowstone River, as it emptied its great flow into the Missouri (fig. 18). Described by many travelers from Lewis and Clark onward, this geographic feature

Figure 17
Carl Wimar. *Studies of Gros Ventre and Assiniboine, Vicinity of Fort William*. Pencil on paper, c. June 22, 1858. Saint Louis Art Museum.

was famous throughout the entire country. The Yellowstone River mouth was over four hundred yards wide, with a volume of water more than equal to that of the Missouri. The junction of the two rivers occurred in an area bounded by wooded thickets; beyond, broad undulating prairies extended many miles and contained an abundance of game.[53] A few miles upstream from this confluence, the Missouri continued to flow in an east-west direction, passing slightly higher ground that was safe from periodic flooding. This was the site of Fort Union, the most famous outpost on the Missouri River frontier, which had been erected in 1829–34 by the American Fur Company. Fort Union is mentioned in many of the descriptive accounts from the period, and it was to serve as one of the most important subjects of Carl Wimar's later career.[54]

The *Twilight* arrived at Fort Union and immediately began unloading the annuities for the Assiniboines, as well as two years' worth of goods promised to the Crows, to be carried up the Yellowstone to a prearranged location near

Figure 18
Carl Wimar. *Confluence of the Yellowstone and Missouri Rivers*. Pencil on paper, June 23, 1858. Saint Louis Art Museum.

100

the mouth of the Powder River. The cargo that remained aboard the boat was destined for the Assiniboine trade at a new fort to be built by Frost, Todd and Company farther upriver. Accordingly, within a few hours the *Twilight* swung away from the banks at Fort Union, leaving Agent Redfield and his crew to talk to the Assiniboine and Crow representatives. Carl Wimar stayed aboard the boat as it steamed upriver to the new site. The next day, at eight o'clock in the evening, the boat arrived at its destination but was forced by a violent hailstorm to anchor on the opposite bank. By early dawn the freight was being unloaded and covered with tarpaulins to protect it from the weather until the new structures could be erected. A drawing in Wimar's sketchbook depicts a level bottomland with wooded areas and tall bluffs in the background; the inscription places the view forty miles above the mouth of the Yellowstone, near the mouth of Big Muddy Creek. This may be the site of Fort Stuart, as the new post was called. "Very beautiful in its primeval solitude was the spot whose tranquility was soon to be rudely broken by the echoing axe of the woodsman, the rifle of the mountaineer, and the varied bustle of the trading-post," Henry Boller recalled. "Timber was abundant and close at hand, the Missouri's waters rolled at our feet, and the grassy prairies were liberally stocked with game. With all these natural advantages, and the greatly diminished danger of incursions from the Sioux, the new post seemed established under the most favorable auspices." By noon the work of discharging the cargo was completed, and farewells were exchanged with those who were to remain at the new location. With a final salute from its cannon and a round of music on the calliope, the *Twilight* rounded a bend and was headed downstream at three times the rate it had taken to ascend. By sunset the boat had reached the banks below Fort Union, and Wimar disembarked with

his companions to rejoin Redfield's party and journey up the Yellowstone. With little delay the steamboat pulled away from shore on its return trip to Saint Louis, which it reached without incident on July 10.[55]

Wimar spent the next eleven days at Fort Union, preparing for the Yellowstone expedition. There is no evidence that he attempted to photograph the Indians here, as the artist John Mix Stanley had done five years earlier. Perhaps his numerous difficulties on previous occasions had finally dissuaded him from the attempt, or he might simply have run out of supplies; more likely, he may have sent the cumbersome photographic apparatus with the *Twilight* on its return voyage. Whatever his reasons for not taking photographs, his sketching did not suffer in similar fashion. Fifteen pages of drawings document his fascination with the Assiniboine Indians and their life near the fort. Curiously, no drawings of Fort Union itself—save a faint rendering in the background of one of the depictions of an Indian subject—seem to have survived from this trip, although the artist was to sketch the area more carefully the following year. At the time of Wimar's visit, the Assiniboine territory ranged north of the Missouri into present-day Saskatchewan, and roughly between the White Earth River on the east and the Milk River on the west. The population of the tribe had decreased markedly, the result of disease and war with the Sioux.[56] In Wimar's faint double-page rendering of the Assiniboine encampment at Fort Union, at least twenty-four lodges are visible. Several tipis, including some with decorations, appear in greater detail in at least two other sketches, along with studies showing racks used for skinning and processing hides or displaying medicine bundles (figs. 19–24). In the corner of one of these pages Wimar represented Broken Arm, chief of the Canoe Band, whom Henry Boller described in his reminiscences as a man of great dignity. How-

Figure 19
Carl Wimar. *Studies of Assiniboine Women, Fort Union*. Pencil on paper, June 23–July 5, 1858. Saint Louis Art Museum.

Figure 21
Carl Wimar. *Studies of Assiniboine and Fire-arms, Fort Union*. Pencil on paper, June 23–July 5, 1858. Saint Louis Art Museum.

Figure 20
Carl Wimar. *Studies of Assinboine Dress/ Tipis and other Structures/ Portrait of Broken Arm, Assiniboine Chief, Fort Union*. Pencil on paper, June 23–July 5, 1858. Saint Louis Art Museum.

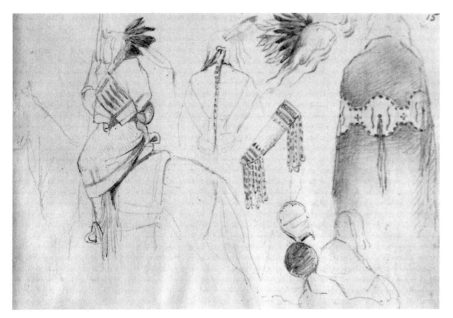

103

Figure 22
Carl Wimar. *Studies of Assiniboine, Fort Union.* Pencil on paper, June 23–July 5, 1858. Saint Louis Art Museum.

Figure 24
Carl Wimar. *Studies of Assiniboine Dress, Horse Trappings, and Dog Travois, Fort Union.* Pencil on paper, June 23–July 5, 1858. Saint Louis Art Museum.

Figure 23
Carl Wimar. *Studies of Assiniboine and Dogs, Fort Union.* Pencil on paper, June 23–July 5, 1858. Saint Louis Art Museum.

Figure 25
Carl Wimar. *Indian Shelter Near Fort Union.*
Pencil on paper, June 23–July 5, 1858. Saint
Louis Art Museum.

104

Figure 26
Carl Wimar. *Abandoned Shelter.* Charcoal
and white chalk on buff paper, c. 1858. Private
collection.

ever, the Lutheran Schmidt was far less praise-worthy of the Assiniboine in general, saying that they had been ruined "in body and soul" by the influence of alcohol. "Not withstanding all their decorations, all beauty has been taken from them and all wild splendor," he wrote. Yet Wimar, who seemed to have befriended the young missionaries during the long trip, recorded the Indians with customary detachment. His sketches are careful visual notes regarding the Assiniboines' mode of dress, including the beadwork, feather, or painted decoration of blankets, capotes, foot-gear, and weapons. It is obvious that Wimar wished to accumulate a storehouse of visual information concerning the Indians that he encountered on the upper Missouri; he was interested in picturesque detail, not the political realities of the rapidly changing frontier. His sketchbook pages also include a number of studies of dogs, some with travois, that attracted the notice of other visitors to the Assiniboine camps in the period. Another sketch represents an Indian shelter made of driftwood and snags (fig. 25); sometimes referred to as hunting lodges or war lodges, these structures were common all along the Yellowstone and Missouri Rivers. A separate, undated drawing from this period depicts a more elaborate example (fig. 26).[57]

On July 1, a minor incident at the fort nearly wrecked the plans of the young Lutheran missionaries. A young Indian woman had died at the site of the new Fort Stuart, and her body had been brought to Fort Union for burial. A funeral procession was organized, led by Alexander Culbertson (fig. 27) of the American Fur Company, Agent Redfield, and Agent Alfred J. Vaughan, all of whom dressed in black for the occasion. Redfield approached Schmidt on Culbertson's behalf and requested that the missionary perform a service over the woman's grave. To Redfield's astonishment, Schmidt refused to do so, because the woman had not been baptized. According to

Schmidt's account, Redfield became very upset and warned: "If you want to be that way, you will not get very far in this country." Despite the Agent's remonstrations, the idealistic young zealots stood their ground. "Everybody was angry with us, especially Mr. Culbertson, who becomes a madman when infuriated," Schmidt wrote. The following day, the two missionaries received a visit from Wimar, who had been sent to inform them that under special instructions from Culbertson, they were not to be conveyed up the Yellowstone to assume their hoped-for mission to the Crows. To Wimar's surprise, the two Lutherans told him they had already decided to make their way westward on their own, since it was apparent that they were unable to overcome the hostility that had been built up over the previous day's incident. "You cannot go alone," Wimar reportedly told them, urging them to reconsider. Agent Vaughan offered to take them to Fort Benton to work with the Blackfeet, a possibility that seemed acceptable if they were unable to reach the Crows. When Redfield once again tried to persuade them to preside over the burials of whites and Indians associated with the fur company, Schmidt again refused. "The painter [Wimar] with whom we have associated was surprised that the Lutherans 'were so fanatic, and that he had never experienced anything like it,'" Schmidt wrote, adding that Wimar "is Roman Catholic; he is a good person; he belongs to the 'great church.'" As it turned out, the impasse was breached when Schmidt allowed that it would be all right for them to give a "devotional speech" at a grave site. Much relieved, Redfield conferred with Culbertson, who declared that the whole matter had been an unfortunate misunderstanding. "Next Monday or Tuesday we will leave on small boats and go up the Yellowstone River toward Fort Sarpy," a gleeful Schmidt noted in his journal.[58]

On July 4, 1858, the eighty-second anniversary of the nation's independence was celebrated at Fort Union. Officers of the day were elected, and the assembled throng, among them some of the most famous names in the fur trade, listened to Agent Redfield speak about "the bravery, greatness, wealth, and influence of the Americans upon the entire world and about the importance of the American government by the people," Schmidt reported. Redfield also gave a brief declaration to the delegation of Assiniboine chiefs and warriors who were present. Alexander Culbertson declined the opportunity to speak, but Robert Meldrum, who had come upriver on the *Twilight*, was not so bashful. A Kentuckian who had intermarried with the Crows, Meldrum was an experienced and much-respected figure on the upper Missouri (fig. 28). Schmidt recorded in his journal:

Figure 27
Alexander Culbertson. Photograph, c. 1865. Montana Historical Society.

105

Figure 28
*Robert Meldrum—Agent to the Crows and
Employee of the American Fur Company.*
Photograph by Cheney's Art Gallery, Oregon
City, Oregon, n.d. Montana Historical
Society.

106

Meldrum was supposed to be the next speaker. He excused himself by saying that he had grown up with the Indians and their ways, and that he was not capable of giving a speech to such an educated and intelligent people. However, if he were permitted to say a few words concerning a different matter, he wanted to remind them that if the Americans were so rich, so powerful as he had just heard, then they should help his people, the poor Indians (pointing at them) who fade away from day to day. Beautiful words! These were the most beautiful and shaming words at the same time. The applause was not very strong.[59]

Soon after that, the congregation was formed into line and marched to "a substantial dinner of buffalo, elk, and antelope" with flags flying and a salute from the fort's cannon. "The occasion furnished an excellent scene for Mr. W[imar], the

talented young artist from your city," stated an anonymous writer to the *Missouri Republican*, "who, by the way, has labored hard, and with success, to preserve on canvas the scenes, customs and habits of a people that are passing away."[60]

On July 6 two mackinaw boats loaded with fur company goods and government annuities left Fort Union for the mouth of the Yellowstone. One of the boats was under the command of Meldrum, the other Redfield. Travelers on Redfield's boat included Wimar, Blandowski, Culbertson, the two Lutherans, an interpreter named Sevier and his son, two hunters from Fort Union, and several others. "The next day, at an early hour, we commenced our slow, laborious and difficult ascent of this large and rapid stream, at this time unusually full," Redfield later wrote in his official report. The mackinaws had to be cordelled upriver, drawn along by groups of men who toiled along the shore. The banks of the river were very rough, overgrown with thickets of cottonwood, ash, willow, and box elder. Steep ravines and marshy flats intersected at various points to hinder progress. "You may easily imagine the labor that we were compelled to undergo when I inform you that it was often necessary for us all to exert ourselves together to move the boats," Wimar later wrote. To make matters worse, the weather was not cooperative. "The men were some days in the water, or deep mud and mire, more than half the time, and the weather was rainy, and, for the season, unusually cool," Redfield reported, adding that they were able to make no more than ten miles per day. Even Schmidt and Braeuninger were pressed into service to help the boats upriver. "It is hard work to penetrate the bushes, without having to pull the heavy boat on top of it," Schmidt wrote. "Faces and hands get sore." Somehow amidst all the toil Wimar found time to record some impressions in his sketchbook, including a hastily

Figure 29
Carl Wimar. *Cordelling a Mackinaw/ Bluffs
Along the Yellowstone.* Pencil on paper,
July 6–26, 1858. Saint Louis Art Museum.

107

drawn sketch of a group of men pulling one of the boats along a high, overgrown riverbank (fig. 29). The drawing on the opposite page shows the steep bluffs that rose above the river, while succeeding sketches depict the broad bottomland the channel sometimes followed. "Its banks are more beautiful than the Missouri," Schmidt observed.[61]

As the party proceeded up the Yellowstone, they employed their hunting skills to bring in game for food. On July 12 five buffalo were seen crossing the river a short distance upstream from the boats. Wimar and a few other passengers went after them, and the artist succeeded in shooting one before it got to the river bank. "We killed, often, many of these animals and generally selected for food the female, leaving the others to the wolves, who followed our track in great numbers and prevented many times our sleep by their prolonged and monotonous howlings," Wimar recalled. "During the night we had a

regular watch to alarm us in case of danger from the Indians, and lighted large fires around our camp to scare away the bears and wolves which were ever on our scent."[62] Wimar was able to make detailed sketches of some of the buffalo which were killed on the voyage upriver (figs. 30–31). According to Wimar's account, the party consumed approximately sixty-four buffalo during the length of the trip. "Each of the party cut from the carcass that portion of the meat which best suited his palate and prepared it for his own use," Wimar wrote. "We cooked without seasoning and nothing could have been more palatable than this food." Another drawing in Wimar's small sketchbook depicted a fallen elk, which also served as sustenance for the travelers.

For Wimar, the Yellowstone expedition was the exhilarating experience of a lifetime. He proudly recorded: "I had the good fortune on one occasion to kill a large bear, of which I brought home a huge paw as a trophy and

Figure 30
Carl Wimar. *Studies of Dead Buffalo, Yellowstone River*. Pencil on paper, July 6–26, 1858. Saint Louis Art Museum.

Figure 31
Carl Wimar. *Studies of Dead Buffalo, Yellowstone River*. Pencil on paper, July 6–26, 1858. Saint Louis Art Museum.

memento." This may be stretching the truth a bit, for Schmidt implied in his journal that another hunter did the killing. Nevertheless, the artist did depict a dead bear in one of the few fully dated drawings from the 1858 trip, which places it on the third day of the journey up the Yellowstone (fig. 32). On July 22, while hunting buffalo with Sevier, Wimar's rifle accidentally discharged, wounding the interpreter in the arm. "On board there were mutterings about the carelessness in handling firearms," Schmidt reported. "The painter became a little ill from dismay. The interpreter said that his wounds were 'nothing' and only carried his arm in a sling. Everything is okay."[63]

Days passed as the two boats continued to struggle upriver. Sometimes the Yellowstone current was too strong for the cordellers, and every person was ordered overboard to assist in the effort. On other occasions, the entire crew of both boats was combined to haul a single boat to

Figure 32
Carl Wimar. *Study of a Dead Bear, Yellowstone River.* Pencil on paper, July 10, 1858.
Zaplin-Lampert Gallery.

a safe position. "One can easily imagine how the clothing suffers with such water, dirt, and bush work," Schmidt wrote. "Then we have to stand on the boat like washerwomen in order to clean our things, or else let them dry on our bodies." Now the landscape along the river began to change, as the channel became narrower and the banks higher. "It is a beautiful view but also dangerous when the cordellers on the top of the barren and steep mountains pull the boat, or when there is only one or two feet of passable path for walking," Schmidt noted. For the first time, horses and mules could pull the boats and relieve the tired and disgruntled cordellers, whose food supply was growing short.[64]

Thunderstorms and cold weather continued to plague the journey. A heavy thunderstorm accompanied by high winds forced the party to abandon the safety of the boats and seek shelter on the shore, "covered with blankets like Indians." On July 26, almost three weeks after they had started, the two mackinaws halted somewhere below the mouth of the Powder River. "It was here determined that our large boat could carry all the goods the remainder of the distance to Fort Sarpy, as horses could here be used to some advantage, the river banks being better," Agent Redfield later wrote, "and as I had become very ill from fever, induced by exposure and a severe cold, I most reluctantly consented to return to Fort Union." The larger mackinaw, with Meldrum, the two missionaries, and eighteen others, pushed on to Fort Sarpy near the mouth of the Bighorn River. The smaller boat—containing the ailing Redfield, the wounded Sevier, Culbertson, Wimar, Blandowski, and two others—turned about and headed back downriver to Fort Union. Before he left the area, Wimar made many studies of the river landscape in the vicinity, including islands of cottonwood and willow beneath the high, striated bluffs that rose above the banks on the north side (fig. 33).[65]

It is apparent that Wimar and his friends had brought with them a preconceived, glorified notion of the Indian from earlier artists and writers like George Catlin, James Fenimore Cooper, or Prince Maximilian and his artist, Karl Bodmer. The following passage from Schmidt's journal, dated the day after Wimar headed downstream, reveals some of Wimar's apparent expectations on his Missouri River trip:

> More Indians came to our noon camp. There must have been about twenty or thirty. All were on horseback, the men as well as the women. I regretted yesterday, and even more today that the painter Wimar had not seen these most attractive people. These would have been the finest for his brush of the entire journey. The passengers on the steamer *Twilight*, who traveled up and back

down the Missouri on this boat, longed to see beautiful, wild figures and believed the further upstream, the better. They never again saw such Indians as the Yanktons [who had been on] the James River not far upstream from Sioux City. By contrast, the most recent which they saw—that is the Assiniboins who have been degraded by drinking orgies—must have destroyed their beautiful fantastic image. They wanted to see "beautiful daughters of the wilderness." Instead, they saw nothing but dirty squaws. They turned their backs on the Far West grumbling and peevish about the books which portray the Indians so magnificently, and hurried south.[66]

Schmidt was not the only observer who noted such expectations; Henry Boller, in a letter to his father written aboard the *Twilight* on June 23, commented that many of those traveling for pleasure were already "completely disgusted with Indian life and Indian scenery":

Figure 33
Carl Wimar. *Landscape Along the Yellowstone River.* Pencil on paper, July 6–26, 1858. Saint Louis Art Museum.

Figure 38
Carl Wimar. *Study of a Steamboat—Rear View*. Pencil on paper, 1859. Missouri Historical Society.

Figure 37
Carl Wimar. *Study of a Steamboat—Front View*. Pencil on paper, 1859. Missouri Historical Society.

deliver the Indian annuities as far as Fort Benton, and they prepared to take goods there by steamboat for the first time. They engaged the *Spread Eagle*, which had made the trip for the company the previous year under its skilled captain, John LaBarge, to carry the bulk of the passengers and freight. However, in order to navigate the more treacherous waters above Fort Union, the *Chippewa*, a smaller, lighter-draft stern-wheeler commanded by Captain M.H. Crapster, was to accompany the *Spread Eagle*. The smaller boat, fully outfitted, pulled away from the Saint Louis landing on May 25 and headed upriver. Two drawings in a small sketchbook of Wimar's may depict the departure of this record-setting vessel (figs. 37–38). Four days later, to the salute of

booming cannon, Captain LaBarge swung the heavily freighted *Spread Eagle* into the Mississippi River current. In addition to Wimar, the boat carried a number of passengers who have since left their mark on history, including Charles Chouteau (fig. 39) and Alexander Culbertson heading the American Fur Company delegation. In addition, they had invited the scientist Ferdinand Hayden to accompany them and gather observations, principally on the geologic formations along the river's length. Chouteau was a founding member of the Academy of Science of Saint Louis, which had been organized two years earlier, and the fur company boats had previously carried Hayden and other scientists on specimen-collecting forays for the Smithsonian

116

Figure 39
Charles P. Chouteau. Engraving by A. H.
Ritchie after photograph, n.d. Montana
Historical Society.

Institution under the Academy's sponsorship.
For this trip, Hayden was to serve as the naturalist for a government surveying party, under
the command of Captain W. F. Raynolds of the
Topographical Engineers, that would explore the
Yellowstone River drainage for proposed wagon
routes. The secretary of the Smithsonian, Spen-
cer F. Baird, also sent a young taxidermist
named John Pearsall to accompany the expedition
upriver, "to make a collection of curiosities in
general, commencing at the mouth of the Missouri, and extending to the Pacific coast." Besides
these men, Chouteau was joined by a fellow
academy member, Dr. Elias J. Marsh, who served
as the boat's physician in exchange for free passage and kept a detailed journal of his trip. In his
list of passengers whose "pleasant company" he
was prepared to enjoy was "Mr. Wimar, a young
German artist of St. Louis. He is very fond of

Indian scenes and takes these opportunities for
observing and taking sketches," Marsh wrote. "I
saw some of his pictures in St. Louis, and they
seemed to me very well done."[76]

That same afternoon the *Spread Eagle*
reached the mouth of the Missouri and for the
next few days proceeded west toward Kansas
City, stopping frequently to load firewood and
additional freight. Above Kansas City at Fort
Leavenworth the boat took on additional passengers, including Jim Bridger, the famed scout,
who had been engaged as the guide for Captain
Raynolds' party. Bridger, Culbertson, and some
of the other mountaineers regaled the passengers
with stories, some undoubtedly embellished,
concerning their collective experiences on the
upper Missouri frontier. At Saint Joseph Captain Raynolds himself joined the boat, as did
Indian Agents Alfred J. Vaughan and Bernard S.
Schoonover. The latter had replaced Alexander
Redfield, who had been assigned to the Yankton
Agency, recently established to serve the Sioux
on their new reservation on the lower Missouri.[77] On June 6 the steamboat passed the
mouth of the Platte River, then stopped at
Omaha City, where Dr. Marsh and the other
passengers saw members of the Pawnee tribe.
Ninety miles above this point the boat passed the
Blackbird Hills, an area well known to travelers
along the Missouri throughout the nineteenth
century. Carl Wimar made a small sketch of
these hills, sparsely covered with timber, the
highest rising approximately three hundred feet
above the river.[78]

On Saturday, June 11, the boat passed the
mouth of the Vermillion River, which cut
through low-lying white bluffs streaked with
reddish stains. Wimar made a drawing of the
river mouth, showing Indian lodges barely visible on the crest of a distant ridge (fig. 40). From
this point onward the artist adopted the technique of horizontally bisecting a piece of paper

Figure 40
Carl Wimar. *Mouth of the Vermillion River.*
Charcoal with white on paper, June 11, 1859.
Mongerson-Wunderlich Galleries, Inc.

117

roughly ten by fifteen inches, upon which he rapidly sketched certain stretches of the river landscape. The drawings seem not to have been bound into a sketchbook, although the many sheets that survive could have been cut out and trimmed at a later date.

Wimar's choice of subjects during his second trip was to be heavily weighted in favor of topographical views all the way to Fort Benton. In this drawing, executed in charcoal with occasional touches of white highlighting, the two channels of the Vermillion River mouth are seen coursing around a sandbar overgrown with brush and timber. In an inscription at the bottom Wimar identified the site, indicating the directional flow of the Missouri River current. The upper drawing depicts the ashy, barren bluffs that followed the river above and below the

mouth. Barely discernible are two figures, possibly Indians, sitting on the riverbank in the lower left foreground. It is possible that the presence of Hayden and other scientists aboard the *Spread Eagle* influenced the artist to follow their interest in the topography of the upper Missouri. The bisected nature of Wimar's drawings, with their obvious interest in topographic detail, also raises speculation that he might have hoped to sell his works to the government or to officials of the fur companies.[79]

Once the steamboat had moved beyond the limits of the last organized settlements and their ready-cut woodpiles, the crew found themselves cutting their own wood for the first time on the journey. "There are generally found enough dead trees for all our wants, but they have to be cut down and in lengths from ten to fifteen feet

Figure 41
Carl Wimar. *Landscape Above Fort Randall/ Mouth of Scalp Creek*. Charcoal and chalk on brown paper, June 14, 1859. Saint Louis Art Museum.

Figure 42
Carl Wimar. *Two Studies of Cedar Island*. Charcoal with white on brown paper, c. June 15, 1859. Saint Louis Art Museum.

and brought on the boat, where they are afterward sawed and split to the proper size," Marsh recorded. Such an activity consumed at least two or three hours daily, doubtless affording time for Wimar to execute some of his sketches. By noon of June 12 the *Spread Eagle* reached the principal Yankton Sioux village, and about thirty warriors and their chief, the venerable Smutty Bear, were invited aboard. The Indians were disappointed to learn that Agent Redfield and the annuities intended for them were not with the boat but still downriver. A few miles farther upriver, a white trader came aboard to sell a number of Indian pipes made of catlinite, a material from the red pipestone quarries in southern Minnesota.[80] The *Spread Eagle* traveled throughout the night, and the following morning, fifteen miles below Fort Randall, Wimar made a double sketch of the sharp-peaked hills on either side of the river. Stopping at Fort Randall, the passengers disembarked to look at the fort and trade with the Indians for additional articles, including

Figure 43
Carl Wimar. *View of La Framboise Island/ Mouth of the Bad River*. Charcoal with white on buff paper, June 18, 1859. Amon Carter Museum.

beaded moccasins and bows and arrows. The boat remained until the following day, when a detachment of thirty soldiers came aboard to accompany Captain Raynolds' party into the Yellowstone country. Again on the river, Wimar drew the landforms above Fort Randall, including a more careful study of the mouth of Scalp Creek (fig. 41) and two studies of a feature identified as Cedar Island (fig. 42)—a name travelers gave to at least four different islands in this area of the river. Such islands were generally covered with growths of red cedar, whose uniform trunks were used by the Indians for lodge poles. Unfortunately, the aromatic wood was also desirable fuel for steamboats, and it was not long before the islands were denuded.[81]

At midday on June 16 the *Spread Eagle* reached the beginning of the Great Bend of the Missouri. This time a number of passengers

went ashore to walk across the neck—a group of irregular hills sparsely covered with timber— and meet the boat the following day on the other side. Although Dr. Marsh does not mention Wimar as one of his fellow adventurers, it is apparent that the artist made the trek and was among those who climbed the hills above the group's campsite to obtain a view of the whole bend of the river. At about ten o'clock the following morning the steamboat picked up its hungry passengers and continued on its way.[82]

Early on June 18 Wimar made a double-page view of the river channel south of La Framboise Island and the mouth of the Bad River (fig. 43), near the site of old Fort Pierre. Shortly afterwards the *Spread Eagle* reached "new" Fort Pierre, built by Frost, Todd and Company a mile or two farther upriver. A group of Sioux chiefs awaited their arrival, and soon a number of

Indian representatives, "decked in full court dress, with feathers and paint in profusion," arrived to meet with Captain Raynolds and Agents Vaughan and Schoonover. Raynolds and his party planned to leave the Missouri at this point, wishing to pass through the Black Hills to reach the Yellowstone and Powder River drainage. All of the chiefs spoke in turn, vigorously objecting to the trespass of their lands. Raynolds withheld delivery of the annuity goods and threatened force until the chiefs realized that their position was hopeless and reluctantly agreed.[83] The principal spokesman for the Sioux delegation at Fort Pierre was Bear Rib, whom Wimar had sketched during his trip to the region the previous year. In the artist's small pocket

120

Figure 44
Carl Wimar. *Bear Rib*. Oil on canvas, 1859.
Private collection.

Figure 45
Carl Wimar. *Bear Rib*. Oil on canvas, 1859.
Missouri Historical Society.

Figure 46
Carl Wimar. *Indian Group and Portrait Studies*. Pencil on paper, 1859. Missouri Historical Society.

sketchbook, containing two pages of population figures for the Indian tribes of the upper Missouri, Bear Rib's name appears at the top of the first page, followed by four columns which list nine Sioux bands and their number of lodges, warriors, and total number of inhabitants. A small oil sketch that also survives shows Bear Rib's head in profile (fig. 44). Another copy of the same sketch, unsigned, is in the Missouri Historical Society (fig. 45); in this copy, Wimar appears to have softened the features of the famous chief. The same head appears in the lower right corner of a drawing depicting a group of Indians gathered in conversation, with the outline of Fort Pierre in the background (fig. 46). Wimar also completed at least one more elaborately finished oil portrait (fig. 47) which seems to reflect the white man's view of this Hunkpapa chief as "a man of great courage and of implacable resolution, faithful to his word, and one to be counted upon in any circumstance."[84]

As he had done a year earlier, Wimar made

Figure 47
Carl Wimar. *Portrait of Bear Rib*. Oil on canvas, c. 1859. Mr. and Mrs. Gerald Peters, Santa Fe.

122

Figure 48 (right)
Carl Wimar. *Indian Burial, Fort Pierre.* Charcoal on paper, c. June 19, 1859. The Dietrich American Foundation, Philadelphia.

Figure 49 (bottom)
Carl Wimar. *Medicine Creek/ Chalk Bluffs— Little Soldier's Village.* Charcoal with white chalk on paper, June 22, 1859. Missouri Historical Society.

some other sketches in the vicinity of the Indian burial ground upriver from the site of old Fort Pierre. One of the drawings shows a wrapped corpse atop a scaffold placed amid the forked limbs of a dead cottonwood tree (fig. 48). "Yesterday afternoon I walked to the old fort and also the Indian burying ground," Dr. Marsh wrote in his journal on June 19. "They bury their dead in trees or artificial scaffolding about eight feet high. There were three or four of the scaffolds with two or three bodies on each, some in boxes, some merely wrapped in cloths." If he did not actually accompany Marsh, it seems reasonable to assume that Wimar made a similar foray. A rough sketch that follows the pages of population figures in the artist's small sketchbook depicts a crude, weatherbeaten tipi under some trees, with the words "Indian gr[ave]" pencilled at the bottom. Again Marsh provides a clue as to the possible subject: "We saw also a wigwam, deserted and torn to pieces by the rain and weather. A year ago a party of Rees came down to steal horses; one was shot and his body was said to have been cut to pieces; a wigwam was erected over his remains, and now are to be seen his skull pierced with bullets, and some other bones, besides his tomahawk, leggins, spoon and other personal property." Returning to the fort, Marsh and his fellow passengers bartered for further Indian articles and exchanged farewells with Captain Raynolds and his surveying party. By eight o'clock in the evening, the *Spread Eagle* was once again on its way upriver.[85]

The badlands country along the river north of Fort Pierre seemed uninviting to the steamboat passengers. Hunters put ashore to proceed upriver tried unsuccessfully to procure game while the boat's crew cut wood. On the afternoon of June 22 Captain LaBarge halted at the site of a permanent agricultural village headed by Little Soldier, a Yanktonais chief. Wimar made a sketch of the country surrounding the small village, including the low hills which rose beyond (fig. 49). Marsh and others visited the settlement and found that the dwellings were "wood and mud huts," not tipis; he reported that these earthen lodges were stifling and unsanitary compared to the animal-skin wigwams that the Sioux customarily used. Soon Little Soldier and six others came aboard the boat for a brief council. Coffee and crackers were passed around, and Wimar may have taken this opportunity to make a sketch of the chief and one of his followers (fig. 50). After a small number of provisions were put ashore, the *Spread Eagle* departed.[86]

Soon the steamboat stopped at Big Head's village, which Wimar had visited the previous year. An unidentified drawing depicting an encampment of tipis near the riverbank and a range of low hills in the background may well be a rendering of this site (fig. 51). The meeting with Big Head, who was in a recalcitrant mood, did not go well from the start. He was openly hostile to Agent Vaughan, with whom he had quarreled in the past, and told Agent Schoonover that he would not accept the government annuities. A witness at the scene reported that Big Head was "bound to do some wickedness—[he

Figure 50 (left)
Carl Wimar. *Portrait of Little Soldier, Yanctonais Chief, and an Unidentified Follower.* Pencil on paper, June 22, 1859. Private collection.

Figure 51 (bottom)
Carl Wimar. *Study of Cottonwood Trees [Big Head's Village(?)].* Charcoal with white chalk on brown paper, c. June 24, 1859. Saint Louis Art Museum.

Figure 52
Carl Wimar. *Na-Sou-La-Tanka* [*Big Head*].
Charcoal with white chalk on buff paper,
c. June 24, 1859. Saint Louis Art Museum.

124

Figure 53
Carl Wimar. *Fort Clark*. Pencil on paper,
June 25, 1859. Private collection.

says] that his heart is bad, he has got to die soon, and he wants to have a great name." Despite this show of anger, Schoonover was able to persuade the chief to accept a small number of provisions. At some point Wimar made a careful sketch of this volatile Yanktonais chief, whom the artist identified with an inscription of his Indian name, Na-Soo-La-Tanka (fig. 52). After waiting a short time for the slower *Chippewa* to catch up, the *Spread Eagle* proceeded on its way.[87]

Early in the morning on June 25 the steamboats reached the vicinity of Fort Clark. Wimar again sketched the hills and plateaus visible beyond the broad arc of the river below the fort and made a much more detailed rendering of the fort itself (fig. 53). "The fort is well situated on a high hill overhanging the river, but owing to the fact of the river channel having changed, it cannot be very closely approached by the steamer," Marsh wrote in his journal. Some of the passengers disembarked to visit the Arikara and Mandan lodges near the post, and Wimar made a number of significant sketches during the few hours of his visit. Two unusually detailed drawings depict the interior and exterior of one of the earth lodges (figs. 54–55), which, a contemporary description noted, averaged forty feet in circumference, supported by a crude framework of poles covered with at least eighteen inches of dirt. Wimar's exterior view shows a lodge with four primary poles and includes a notable feature that Audubon had described during his visit sixteen years earlier: "All these lodges have a sort of portico that leads to the door, and on the tops of most of them I observed buffalo skulls." The other drawing represents the interior of a larger dwelling which Audubon referred to as a "Medicine Lodge." This was supported by eight poles, as evidenced by the carefully drawn plan in the lower left corner. Wimar identified this as an Arikara structure, and he represented at least fifteen Indians huddled in blankets around a central

Figure 54   (left)
Carl Wimar. *Interior of an Arikara Medicine
Lodge, Fort Clark*. Charcoal with white chalk
on paper, June 25, 1859. Missouri Historical
Society.

Figure 55   (right)
Carl Wimar. *Mandan or Arikara Lodge, Fort
Clark*. Charcoal with white chalk on paper,
June 25, 1859. Missouri Historical Society.

fire dug into the floor. A long chain, suspended
from the center of the roof, supported a cooking
pot over the fire, a detail Audubon also mentioned. Dr. Marsh recorded that he visited a
number of these lodges and smoked with the
inhabitants in the hopes of trading with them,
but was not very successful.[88]

Perhaps the most striking drawing that
Wimar executed at Fort Clark was one depicting
two Arikara grave mounds surmounted by three
decorated buffalo skulls and surrounded by a
circle of many others (fig. 56). The burying
ground, a few hundred yards beyond the village,
was visited by many travelers in the period.
The artist made another very faint drawing that
shows three Indian women mourning beneath a
burial scaffold, with earth lodges and a bastion
resembling that of Fort Clark in the background.
Such scaffolds existed alongside the earthen

Figure 56
Carl Wimar. *Arikara Graves at Fort Clark*.
Charcoal with white chalk on paper, June 25,
1859. Peabody Museum, Harvard University.

Figure 57
Carl Wimar. *Portrait of a Mandan*. Charcoal with white chalk on paper, c. June 25, 1859. Missouri Historical Society.

Figure 58
Carl Wimar. *Portrait of Ma-Sai-To*. Charcoal with white chalk on paper, c. June 25, 1859. Missouri Historical Society.

Figure 59
Carl Wimar. *Golden Shell*. Black chalk on grey laid paper, 1859. Saint Louis Art Museum.

mounds in the burial ground; contemporary accounts indicated that disease and war with the Sioux were taking a fearful toll on the village population.

This portion of the upriver trip seems to have inspired a number of individual studies of Indians besides those in the sketchbooks. One drawing depicts a seated Mandan warrior, another the head of an Indian identified as Ma-Sai-To (figs. 57–58). A third example, on a similar type of grey-green paper, is a sensitive portrayal of a young Indian woman whose name is given as Golden Shell (fig. 59). She appears to wear a dress decorated with elk teeth, which were in wide use on the northern plains by the time of Wimar's visit.[89]

Shortly after leaving Fort Clark the *Chippewa*, which continued to lag behind the more powerful *Spread Eagle*, was lashed alongside the *Spread Eagle* for the final push to Fort Union. On June 28 the first buffalo were sighted close to the river, and more appeared as the boats proceeded upriver. Soon the boats overtook two hunters who had been put ashore earlier, and there was general elation as two buffalo carcasses were hauled aboard. Dr. Marsh recorded that one of them was butchered "Indian fashion," by stripping the meat off the bones. The other was quartered to obtain "many good roasting pieces," and this occasion may have prompted Wimar to make an oil sketch, approximately eight by twelve inches in size, depicting portions of a butchered buffalo. Another oil sketch, similar in size and material, contains several studies—a buffalo's nose and fore hoof, a stone axe, a clump of prickly pear, a bush bearing the inscription "hill sage," and a fruit-laden branch labeled "bull berry" (fig. 60). All the plants were common along the upper Missouri; the "bull berry," for example (more commonly known as buffalo berry), was a valuable foodstuff for Indians and white men alike. Wimar may also have used the periods when the boats were halted to execute other studies in oil, including an eight-by-twelve-inch example on paper, now badly chipped, depicting the high bluffs along the river in the vicinity of Fort Union (fig. 61).[90]

At nine o'clock in the evening on July 1 the steamboats passed the mouth of the Yellowstone River, and less than an hour later two salutes were fired to signal their arrival at Fort Union. The following day Charles Chouteau formally purchased the *Chippewa* from its owner and captain, M. H. Crapster, in order to have complete control for the inaugural attempt to take a steamboat as far as Fort Benton, over five hundred miles upriver. River traffic to this far-flung point in the heart of the Blackfeet country was becoming increasingly important, for crews under Lieutenant John Mullan had begun a heroic effort to build the first wagon road from Fort Benton over the Rocky Mountains to Fort Walla Walla, near the Columbia and Snake rivers. Captain Reynolds had earlier supervised placing supplies for

Figure 60
Carl Wimar. *Study of Buffalo Head and Hoof, Stone Hammer, Hill Sage, Bull Berry, and Prickly Pear* [Study for the painting: *The Wounded Buffalo*]. Oil on canvas, 1859. Saint Louis Art Museum.

127

Figure 61
Carl Wimar. *Landscape Study, Missouri River Near Fort Union*. Oil on paper, c. 1859. Saint Louis Art Museum.

128

Figure 62
Carl Wimar. *Missouri River Below Fort Stuart/ View of Fort Kipp*. Charcoal with white chalk on paper, July 4, 1859. Mongerson-Wunderlich Galleries, Inc.

Mullan's party aboard the *Spread Eagle* and *Chippewa*, and Chouteau was determined to furnish the supplies for the coming year directly to them. This meant navigating a stretch of the Missouri River that was both spectacular and dangerous, so Chouteau placed Captain LaBarge in command of the *Chippewa*. The *Spread Eagle* was instructed to remain at Fort Union until the *Chippewa* returned, and at eight o'clock on July 3, the latter was under way, with Carl Wimar and Elias Marsh aboard. "I engaged a crew of 95 men composed chiefly of old voyagers, so as to insure my overcoming all the difficulties represented to exist," Chouteau later wrote, "and had two mackinaw boats of 45 tons capacity each, lashed to her sides to serve as lighters in case of need."[91]

Early the next morning, the *Chippewa* "fired 13 guns in honor of the glorious 4th" and landed at Fort Kipp, a newly built American Fur Company post near the mouth of Big Muddy Creek. On Wimar's previous trip, Frost, Todd and Company had erected Fort Stuart in the same area to serve the Assiniboines; now Wimar sketched Fort Kipp, a few log buildings protected by a small square stockade (fig. 62). On the upper part of the same sheet he sketched the high hills and bluffs along the river below the site. The next day the *Chippewa* made slow progress as Captain LaBarge struggled with channels that had shifted considerably. A stern post on one of the mackinaws was badly damaged, halting the boat at Wolf Point for the balance of the day.[92] On July 6 the *Chippewa* passed the mouth

Figure 63
Carl Wimar. *Mouth of the Milk River [Two Views]*. Charcoal with white chalk on paper, July 6, 1859. Missouri Historical Society.

Figure 64
Carl Wimar. *Mouth of the Milk River/ Bluffs Along the Opposite Bank*. Charcoal with white chalk on paper, July 6, 1859. Missouri Historical Society.

Figure 65
Carl Wimar. *July 9th Round Butte* [*Two
Views*]. Charcoal with white chalk on paper,
July 9, 1859. Missouri Historical Society.

While the *Chippewa* steamed westward,
Wimar made a number of sketches as the landscape on either side of the river began changing
dramatically. Eroded bluffs of ancient sedimentary rock layers displayed a wide variety of
colors; grey-green to dark grey shales often
contrasted with sandstone that ranged from
a variegated buff to a striking opalescent white.
On July 8 Chouteau wrote: "We camped this
evening in sight of the 'Round Butte,' half way
distant to Fort Benton. The channel constantly
shifting its position from one shore to the other,
and the dense forest of cottonwood with which
both banks are lined falling into the river, causes
numerous snags and sawyers. These obstructions
proved very annoying, as they obliged us to shift
the position of our barges many times during the
day." Two views of Round Butte, a dome-shaped
prominence that rose above the surrounding
hills on the south side of the river and was well
known to the voyagers of the period, appear in
one of Wimar's drawings (fig. 65). One view
shows the landmark above a range of low hills
"dotted with scattered groups of dark green
pines," as Prince Maximilian recorded on a visit
twenty-five years earlier.[94]

As the steamboat proceeded beyond Round
Butte, Wimar continued to record the ever-
changing landscape that unfolded before him.
Along some parts of the river the high bluffs
began to reveal a thick layer of whitish sandstone, highly reflective in sunlight. Wimar began
making sketches of this geologic feature, a portion of which is known today as the White Cliffs
area (fig. 66). Some of these drawings represented the landscape above Round Butte precisely
as Maximilian had characterized it: "The mountains continued to increase in height; they were
more and more naked and sterile; their color was
whitish-grey, grey-brown, often spotted with
white, the upper part disposed in horizontal
strata, or in narrow stripes; and some isolated

of the Milk River, the largest of the Missouri's
northern tributaries, and Wimar made several
sketches of the area (figs. 63–64). The artist
sketched the broad valley of the river, over a mile
wide at its confluence with the Missouri and
dotted with cottonwood groves and undergrowth.
At the same time, he made careful renderings of
the "succession of conical and table-hills, composed of different-colored clays in horizontal
strata jutting into the valley," as John Mix Stanley had described them five years earlier. Soon
after, the *Chippewa* passed the farthest point that
any steamboat had ever reached. The river then
began a winding course, passing from one side of
the valley to the other, becoming so shallow that
the boat was forced to spend the next day and a
half shifting cargo into the mackinaws and sparring over the many sand bars. Dr. Marsh noted
that Agent Vaughan and a party of ten men
detached themselves and headed overland to Fort
Benton, which was only half the distance by land
as it was by water. Chouteau, however, was
determined to press on.[93]

summits rose in the most grotesque forms." The Missouri River channel began to narrow somewhat, and the *Chippewa* was able to make better time. Dr. Marsh recorded in his journal that game was plentiful, and several buffalo were killed and butchered. Despite this, the tourists on board were not satisfied. "Our meat has always been abundant, but since leaving the *Spread Eagle* vegetables and pies have been scarce and our ice for the past few days has entirely failed, at which many of our passengers seriously complain," Marsh noted. On July 10 Wimar began keeping a record in his pocket sketchbook of the wildlife that he encountered; the entry for that day listed buffalo bulls, cows, and calves, grizzly bears, and what he termed a "wolf serenade." According to Marsh, the wolves took advantage of the carcasses left by the hunters on shore and "kept up an infernal howling late in the night."[95]

On the afternoon of July 10 the *Chippewa* passed the wide mouth of the Musselshell River, its clear water flowing into the Missouri from the south. Wimar made a few rough sketches of the high banks in an area upstream from this point, adding color notations for future reference. Over the next few days the steamboat passed around a number of timbered islands, while the landscape along the banks of the river grew less verdant. "The scarcity of fuel along the shores gave us convincing proofs that we had fully reached the barren or 'Bad Lands' of the Missouri," Chouteau wrote. Now the channel narrowed, and the current became stronger as it coursed through a number of troublesome rapids. On several occasions the *Chippewa* was forced to lighten its load by transferring part of its cargo to the mackinaws. Such efforts, combined with the constant demand for firewood, delayed the steamboat's progress. On July 11 both Wimar and Marsh noted that a band of elk had been sighted crossing the river and two of them killed during the subsequent chase.[96]

As the *Chippewa* continued its voyage, the hills and bluffs along the river continued to grow higher and more rugged in appearance. "We landed just after dinner at the foot of one of the hills to take on wood, which is scarce in this part of the river, so we are obliged to seize every

131

Figure 66
Carl Wimar. *Studies of White Cliffs, Near Judith River/ July 9th Above Round Butte.* Charcoal with white chalk on paper, July 9 and 16, 1859. Missouri Historical Society.

132

Figure 67
Carl Wimar. *Table Rock Formation, Upper Missouri River*. Charcoal with white chalk on buff paper, July 12, 1859. Private collection.

Figure 68
Carl Wimar. *Fortress Butte[?] Near Cow Island, Upper Missouri River*. Charcoal with white chalk on brown paper, July 12, 1859. Saint Louis Art Museum.

opportunity, and we all went ashore," Dr. Marsh wrote in his journal. "The hills are soft grey sandstone, which readily washes into fantastic shapes. On the top of the hill were three or four columns surmounted by a broad and flat piece of stone of different color." A drawing by Wimar dated the same day depicts a formation that closely resembles Marsh's description, while another, probably done near Cow Island, might represent Fortress Butte (figs. 67–68). Other drawings also inscribed "July 12th" indicate that the artist was captivated by the natural scenery in this area. Prince Maximilian had earlier hoped that "the geologist and the painter might devote a considerable time to examine this part of the country, step by step; they would furnish a work of the highest interest." Although there seems to be no direct evidence that Wimar had read Maximilian's account, the fact remains that many of the artist's subjects coincide with the interests of his German predecessor.[97]

On July 13 the *Chippewa*, with the two mackinaws in tow, approached Dauphin's Rapids, which Chouteau declared "by far the most formidable and dangerous encountered on the river, and until cleared of the many boulders which are all loose, will ever be a serious barrier to steam boat navigation." The mackinaws were cast off, and much freight was put ashore to lighten the steamboat's draft. Attempts were then made to warp the boat over by fixing an anchor to the shore and dragging it forward by means of a steam capstan, but the equipment failed. More freight was offloaded as the crew scoured the surrounding river bottoms for driftwood to be burned in the boilers. After two anxious days the *Chippewa*, its supply of wood seriously depleted, passed through the dangerous area. Marsh and some of the other passengers, possibly including Wimar, spent much of the intervening time clambering about the surrounding country hunting or gathering fossil and rock samples. One

Figure 69
Carl Wimar. *Eroded Hills Near Dauphin Rapids*. Charcoal with white chalk on brown paper, July 14, 1859. Saint Louis Art Museum.

particularly striking drawing, dated July 14, depicts stark hills cut by deep ravines and bathed in deep shadow (fig. 69). The artist notated "Dowfain Rappits [sic!]" in his pocket sketchbook, along with the number of buffalo he had sighted in the area. "Today we have been travelling slowly, having advanced in all about thirty miles," Marsh wrote on July 15. "In three or four places, we met with rapids where the current was so strong that we were unable to pass without leaving our mackinaws on shore to be cordelled a short distance, and this afternoon we abandoned [one of] our mackinaw[s] for good and tied it on shore."[98]

Early that afternoon the *Chippewa* reached the mouth of the Judith River, where four years earlier Governor Isaac I. Stevens had called a council to forge a treaty with the Blackfeet. Here Chouteau expressed "the satisfaction of finding the greatest abundance of wood." Somewhere just below the river's mouth Wimar made a small sketch of a crude Indian shelter surrounded by vegetation. As the steamboat moved above the broad Judith bottomland, the character of the surrounding country again changed. In several drawings dated July 15, Wimar represented steep banks and high eroded hills as the *Chippewa* worked its way past another succession of rapids. On July 16, the second mackinaw was jettisoned, and the steamboat entered a spectacular region which Dr. Marsh described as "the finest scenery that we have anywhere observed in all our course." Another passenger who published an account in the *Missouri Republican* described the "new and grander form" that nature now assumed, where sandstone as white as sea sand intermingled with "masses of dark primitive rock" eroded into extraordinary shapes. "Among the figures made of sandstone are various pinnacles and towers, some resembling ruined churches, cities, and castles," he wrote. "Several have names given to them by the voyagers from resemblances their memory suggests." Throughout the following day, as Captain LaBarge

134

Figure 70
After Karl Bodmer. *Remarkable Hills. On the
Upper Missouri.* Aquatint and engraving.
From Maximilian, Prince de Wied-Neuwied,
*Voyage dans l'interieur de l'Amerique du
Nord* (Paris: Arthus Bertrand, 1840), plate 34.
Amon Carter Museum.

Figure 71
Carl Wimar. *Eroded Rock Formations Along the Upper Missouri.* Charcoal with white chalk on brown paper, July 16, 1859. Saint Louis Art Museum.

Figure 72
Carl Wimar. *Steamboat Rock.* Charcoal with white chalk on paper, July 16, 1859. Mongerson-Wunderlich Galleries, Inc.

135

maneuvered the *Chippewa* upriver, Wimar witnessed an unforgettable display of nature as he struggled to execute a flurry of drawings.[99]

It is revealing to compare Wimar's efforts with those of Prince Maximilian and his artist, Karl Bodmer, who had traveled over this stretch of the Missouri River twenty-six years earlier. Maximilian had described the images that Wimar delineated in his drawings:

Here, on both sides of the river, the most strange forms are seen, and you may fancy you see colonnades, small round pillars with large globes or a flat slab at the top, little towers, pulpits, organs with their pipes, old ruins, fortresses, castles, churches, with pointed towers, etc. Etc., almost every mountain bearing on its summit some similar structure . . . a painter who had leisure might fill whole volumes with these landscapes. As proofs of this we may refer to some of these figures, which Mr. Bodmer sketched very accurately [fig. 70]. . . . In several places where the sandstone summit appeared plainly to represent an ancient knight's castle, another remarkable rock was seen to traverse the mountain in narrow perpendicular strata, like regularly built walls. These walls consist of a blackish-brown rock, in the mass of which large olive-green crystals are disseminated. They run in a perfectly straight line from the summits of the mountain to the foot, appearing to form the outworks of the old castle.[100]

Wimar confined his impressions to rapidly executed drawings in charcoal and white chalk, usually two to a sheet. It is well to remember that Maximilian and Bodmer traveled this section of the river in boats that were cordelled, and alterations in course were often made at the request of the artist. Wimar, on the other hand, was aboard a steamboat which surged through the entire stretch of the river in less than a day; there was little time to create works with any degree of finish. The upper half of one of Wimar's drawings, dated July 16, depicts the

Figure 73
Carl Wimar. *Eroded Rock Formations/ The Pinnacles, Upper Missouri River.* Charcoal with white chalk on paper, July 16, 1859. Amon Carter Museum.

Figure 74
Carl Wimar. *Citadel Rock.* Charcoal with white chalk on paper, July 16, 1859. Washington University Gallery of Art.

"dark walls" mentioned in Maximilian's journal. These were actually dikes of metamorphic rock that had forced their way up through vertical fissures in the older sedimentary layers of sandstone. The lower drawing on the sheet is a close-up view of the same scene, showing one of these dark masses set against the white parapets of sandstone near the summit of one of the hills (fig. 71). The contrast between colors in this landscape was dramatic and evocative, ranging from the glistening white sandstone to the rich, dark shades of the igneous rock. The number of Wimar's hurried sketches reveals his desire to record the basic appearance of some of the more outstanding features. One of these drawings represents Steamboat Rock, a sandstone eminence on the north side of the river which, as a passenger aboard the *Chippewa* asserted, required "no imagination to see two smoke pipes, wheelhouses and general outline of the boat" (fig. 72).[101]

Above Steamboat Rock Wimar sketched one striking topographic feature after another, beginning with the Pinnacles, which Bodmer also had

recorded (fig. 73). Six miles farther on, the boat passed a thin, high wall of sandstone with a window-like opening known to river travelers as the Hole in the Wall; the artist made a double-page sketch of it in his pocket sketchbook. Soon the *Chippewa* passed Citadel Rock, a major landmark on this stretch of the Missouri (fig. 74). A passenger aboard the boat described it as "rising up dark and massive to a height of two hundred feet, presenting a perpendicular surface towards the river, and sloping along the sides upward to a point, while away from the river it first falls perpendicularly, then sinks into the other hills." Wimar made an additional study of this formation with color notations in a page in his pocket sketchbook. There is also a full-page study of cottonwoods and undergrowth along a river bank, bearing the inscription "Citadel July 1859" (fig. 75). A few miles upriver, opposite Kipp's Rapids, Wimar made a full-page rendering of an outcrop that may be Eagle Rock (fig. 76). In an area known as the Stone Walls, where the bluffs rose steeply on either side of the river, Wimar

Figure 75
Carl Wimar. *Cottonwoods on the Missouri.*
Charcoal with white chalk on grey paper,
July 16, 1859. Missouri Historical Society.

Figure 76
Carl Wimar. *White Castles on the Missouri.*
Charcoal with white chalk on paper, July 16,
1859. Missouri Historical Society.

Figure 77
Carl Wimar. *Eye of the Needle; LaBarge Rock
in the Distance.* Charcoal with white chalk on
brown paper, July 16, 1859. Saint Louis Art
Museum.

138

Figure 78
Carl Wimar. *Bluffs Opposite Fort McKenzie.*
Pencil on paper, July 17, 1859. Missouri
Historical Society.

Figure 80
Carl Wimar. *Bluffs in the Vicinity of Fort
Benton.* Charcoal with white on paper,
July 17, 1859. Missouri Historical Society.

Figure 79
John Mix Stanley. *View of Fort Benton.*
Watercolor on paper, 1853. Yale University
Art Gallery.

made a drawing of a peculiar pointed arch of
sandstone high atop the cliffs, today known as
the Eye of the Needle (fig. 77). Just beyond, a
thick, isolated column of dark rock rose above
the river; Wimar made a drawing of it as well,
unaware that it would soon bear the name LaBarge
Rock, in honor of the intrepid captain of the
record-setting *Chippewa*.[102]

Above the area of the Stone Walls the surrounding countryside, in Dr. Marsh's words,
"became tame, mostly prairies and sand hills."
During the day, as the river fell and wood
became increasingly scarce, Chouteau ordered
the last mackinaw to be loaded with goods and
cordelled the final distance to Fort Benton, now
less than fifty miles upstream. On the evening
of July 16 the *Chippewa* halted for the night
at Spanish Island, described as a favorite winter
camping ground for the Indians. Early the following morning the boat reached the mouth of
the Marias River, which cut deeply through a
high, grassy prairie to empty its clear water into
the Missouri. Even though stands of cottonwood,
alder, and wild cherry could be found along the
narrow Marias bottoms, similar growths were

entirely absent along this stretch of the Missouri. "Once we stopped to land and here we procured a few logs," Marsh wrote at this point, "but in starting off, we got on a sand bar and burnt up all the wood we had procured in trying to get off again." At one o'clock in the afternoon on July 17, the *Chippewa* arrived at the site of old Fort McKenzie on the north side of the river at Brulé Bottom, slightly downriver from Fort Benton. "Here our stock of fuel totally gave out . . . without a possibility of replenishing it except by retracing our steps a considerable distance below," Chouteau later wrote in his report. "Observing that the river was falling rapidly, and being but 12 miles distance from Fort Benton, we decided on discharging freight at this point." Thus ended the pioneering effort of Captain LaBarge and the *Chippewa*, twenty-one days and approximately 2270 miles upriver from the city of Saint Louis.[103]

By the time the *Chippewa* halted at the site of Fort McKenzie, which Alexander Culbertson had built in 1832 for the American Fur Company, the fort itself had long since been abandoned and burned. Wimar made a full-page drawing of "a high perpendicular bank of black clay" opposite the fort, which Culbertson had noted some years before (fig. 78). While the freight from the *Chippewa* was being unloaded there for transfer to wagons, Chouteau, LaBarge, and a few others proceeded overland to Fort Benton (fig. 79). There they commandeered a skiff and sounded the final stretch of the river. "I found not less than 3 1/2 feet of water, and all the points and islands well timbered, but too green for steamboat purposes," Chouteau later reported. It seems likely that Wimar accompanied Chouteau and the others to Fort Benton, judging by the few sketches of the region that survive. One of these, bearing an inscription that identifies it as having been done somewhere below Fort Benton on July 17, depicts the "lofty

hills" that Captain Raynolds would report seeing on either side of the river when he visited the area the following year (fig. 80). A small oil sketch by Wimar, now in the Phoenix Art Museum, depicts a river landscape similar to what the artist would have encountered in the vicinity of Fort Benton (fig. 81). Raynolds also noted that the Bear Paw Mountains, rising to the north, did not become visible from the river until three hours downstream; this is a helpful observation, for a half-page drawing by Wimar, depicting a broad river bottom with a high mountain chain rising in the background (fig. 82), bears a faint inscription in the lower left cor-

Figure 81
Carl Wimar. *Landscape—River and Mountains, Upper Missouri River*. Oil on panel, 1858. Phoenix Art Museum; gift of Dr. Ronald M. Lawrence.

139

140

Figure 82
Carl Wimar. *View of the Bear Paw Mountains from the Missouri River [Bear Lake].* Charcoal with white chalk on brown paper, July 18, 1859. Saint Louis Art Museum.

ner that appears to read "Bear Paw." It seems likely that this drawing, dated July 18, was executed at a point below Brulé Bottom, where the river swings in a more easterly direction. The same day the *Chippewa*, with Wimar aboard, had started downstream on the return voyage to Saint Louis, firing its cannon "several times as a salute."[104]

The river level was falling rapidly, and the steamboat encountered greater difficulty on the descent to Fort Union than either Chouteau or Captain LaBarge had expected. "The boat is so light that the currents and winds sometimes sweep her stern down stream, and then as she is a stern wheeler, we often have difficulty in righting her," Marsh recorded in his journal. Late in the afternoon of July 19, after the *Chippewa* had passed the mouth of the Judith River, the danger of being swept against the rocks along the banks became so great that Chouteau ordered thirty feet of the after cabin removed in order to make the boat more navigable. The following day their troubles grew worse. "In descending Dauphin's Rapids, we struck the rocks with great force, breaking many of our bottom timbers, and Burds Rapids came very nearly disabling us entirely,"

Chouteau reported. On the morning of July 21, shortly after passing Round Butte, the steamboat swung around in the current and became stuck fast on a sandbar. "We have been sparring all afternoon and broke both our spars and had to cut others in the woods," Marsh wrote later that evening. Wimar was a witness to all of this and likely accompanied Dr. Marsh and the others on a series of forays to hunt in the surrounding countryside. One full-page drawing, inscribed "July 21th Round Bute [sic]," depicts the high rocky banks that Captain LaBarge so desperately tried to avoid (fig. 83). The *Chippewa* finally managed to break free the following morning, but progress downriver was greatly hindered by low water and numerous sandbars. Time and again the boat halted to take on wood or sound the shallow channel; in the meantime, the passengers amused themselves by hunting and gathering specimens. On the morning of July 26, to the evident relief of all concerned, Captain LaBarge steered the record-setting steamboat toward the riverbank at Fort Union.[105]

Unfortunately, the *Spread Eagle* was nowhere to be seen. Although its orders had been to wait for the *Chippewa*'s return, the larger boat had moved downriver. Within a few hours the *Chippewa* was on its way to catch up, finding the river comfortably high below the mouth of the Yellowstone. On July 27 Captain LaBarge found a cache of wood on shore which the crew of the *Spread Eagle* had cut for them, along with a letter stating the boat had proceeded farther downstream. "This is provoking to us all, as most of our clothes were left on that boat, and we certainly expected to find her at the mouth of the Yellowstone," Marsh complained. "I have only one much worn pair of pants and I must get some antelope skin to patch them. I wore out my shoes some time ago and am now reduced to moccasins, though I have a pair of boots on the *Spread Eagle.*"[106]

The following day the *Chippewa* passed a large camp of Hidatsa, who were on their way back to their village near Fort Berthold after a three-week buffalo hunt. Arriving at the fort, Marsh and two others took advantage of the tribe's absence to steal some skulls from the burying ground, concealing their plunder in their coats until they reached the confines of the boat.

Later that evening, as the *Chippewa* halted at Fort Clark, the passengers and crew learned that a force of Sioux had attacked a party of Arikaras hunting buffalo. While the Arikaras were evacuating their women and children to nearby timber for safety, the Sioux managed to destroy their camp, before being driven off in a pitched battle. "Many of the men were in mourning for relatives slain," Marsh reported. "Their mourning dress is white paint. Two had white painted around their eyes like spectacles, and others had white on different parts of the body." One of Wimar's studies of Indians shows a warrior with Arikara features whose face is painted in a similar manner (fig. 84). As soon as the steamboat was again under way, a number of the passengers discovered that the Indians had pilfered a variety of articles. "So much of our sympathy for their misfortune was changed to a regret that the Sioux had not wiped out the whole nation," Marsh noted with disgust. Evidently the good doctor felt that it was permissible for him to rob the Indian graves, but not for the Indians to help themselves to one of the white man's blankets or

141

Figure 83
Carl Wimar. *July 21st [Near] Round Bute.* Charcoal with white chalk on paper, July 21, 1859. Missouri Historical Society.

Figure 84
Carl Wimar. *Studies of Arikara, Fort Clark*[?].
Charcoal with white chalk on paper, July 28,
1859(?). Missouri Historical Society.

a stray pair of socks.[107]

On July 30, near Little Soldier's village, Marsh recorded that one of the men had killed a rattlesnake and given it to him "to skin for Mr. Wimar, who will put it on an Indian bow after their fashion, or something of the kind." The following morning Marsh wrote in his journal that "Mr. Wimar shot an antelope, and we stopped to get it. It had a beautiful little pair of horns—it is called the Prong-horned Antelope—and I was all morning preparing the head for him." Arriving at Fort Pierre, Chouteau learned that the *Spread Eagle* had left three days earlier. He secured additional provisions and had a brief talk with several Sioux representatives

concerning their war with the Arikara. The following day the *Chippewa* made good time, and early the next morning it caught up with the *Spread Eagle*, which was stuck on a sandbar. "We have all moved on board of her and feel almost at home again," Marsh wrote with an obvious sense of relief. "We found all well and everything in good order, but we have been all day in trying to get off the bar, and at last this evening have succeeded." After struggling past additional sandbars, the two boats reached Fort Randall the evening of August 3; there the passengers had the pleasure of reading some newspapers, including an issue of the *Missouri Republican* only ten days old. The next afternoon the boats paused briefly at the site of the new Yankton Agency directed by Alexander Redfield, who had traveled with Wimar the previous year on the steamer *Twilight*. Redfield and his workers were living in tents and laboring intensely in the oppressive summer heat to establish the agency grounds before the onset of winter. Redfield reported that many of the Yanktons had left to hunt the buffalo and would not return to the agency until the fall. But the buffalo were rapidly dwindling, and the nomadic life of the Plains Indian was entering its final phase.[108]

The *Chippewa* and the *Spread Eagle* only remained at the Yankton Agency for a brief time before continuing on their way downriver, where signs of change were everywhere. Passing the town of Niobrara, the first settlement on the river of the same name, Marsh noted the presence of "a few frame houses, even painted white, while the rest of the prairie is laid off in town lots." Further on, both boats struggled around a succession of sandbars, and relentless hordes of mosquitoes plagued passengers and crew. Their patience was sorely tried in the five days it took to reach Sioux City, the bustling center for the as-yet-undeclared Dakota Territory. In the

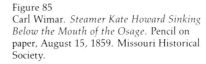

Figure 85
Carl Wimar. *Steamer Kate Howard Sinking Below the Mouth of the Osage*. Pencil on paper, August 15, 1859. Missouri Historical Society.

vicinity of Omaha, the voyagers found the surrounding country in turmoil as Pawnee conflicts with the neighboring Sioux turned into a series of raids on the farms recently established by white settlers on the north side of the Platte River. Now the *Spread Eagle* surged ahead of the smaller *Chippewa*. On August 14 the steamboat hit a snag and barely escaped sinking; fortunately, a rudder broke instead, enabling the *Spread Eagle* to free itself. Downstream the next day, Wimar sketched the wreck of a less-lucky steamer, the *Kate Howard*, which had been irreparably damaged and sunk only a few days earlier (fig. 85).[109]

Finally, at one-thirty in the afternoon on August 16, with cannons firing to note its historic arrival, the *Spread Eagle* reached the Saint Louis levee. (Ironically, the valiant *Chippewa*, which had actually accomplished the record-setting performance, arrived without similar fanfare four days later.) Chouteau lost no time in advertising his historic feat. The day after his arrival the *Missouri Republican* praised the

completion of "one of the most remarkable trips on record in the navigation of the Western rivers." The newspaper described the voyage of the *Chippewa* above the Yellowstone in glowingly optimistic terms, as Chouteau and other entrepreneurs would have wanted it: game was everywhere abundant, the Indians were friendly and quiet, and the actual hazards of the trip had been minimal, they claimed. The notice also singled out Wimar, "a celebrated artist of this city," as one of the more notable passengers on the historic trip, who had "replenished his portfolio with a variety of sketches of Indian life, and the wild scenery of the North West." The reporter went on to say that "Mr. Wimar has been in these regions before, and the public are sufficiently acquainted with the productions of his pencil." A few days later, an anonymous participant on the voyage recounted his impressions of the Missouri River frontier on the front page of the same newspaper. "Already the footprints of civilization may be seen, and the log cabin of the enterprising and speculative farmer dots the

144

Figure 86 (left)
After Carl Wimar. *The Different Forts of P. Chouteau Sr. & Co. Fur Company.* Photograph by J. H. Scholten, c. 1859. Missouri Historical Society.

Figure 87 (right)
Carl Wimar. *Buffalo Head.* Black chalk on grey laid paper, c. 1859. Saint Louis Art Museum.

country far and near . . . the day is not far distant when the iron horse will wend his untiring way through this now wild and picturesque country." The same writer also noted Wimar's presence on the journey, as well as his efforts to record the scenery of "the far western wilds" and "the Indians in their pristine glory." He further observed that "a rich treat" was in store for Wimar's audience once the field sketches were "brought to perfection" in the artist's studio. Wimar, for his part, seemed to revel in the role of a western adventurer; a photograph probably taken soon after his return shows the ruddy-complexioned artist posing confidently in full frontier array (frontispiece).[110]

Wimar celebrated Chouteau's accomplishments in a large-scale drawing which seems to have been intended as a photographic reproduction, because it is inscribed with the artist's name and that of the photographer, John A. Scholten (fig. 86). The artist's renderings of Forts Pierre, Clark, Berthold, Union, Kipp, and Benton are arranged within a decorative framework comprising various Indian artifacts. Four vignettes drawn from the artist's sketches of Indian life—a burial mound, earth lodge, tipi, and burial scaf-

Figure 88   (left)
Carl Wimar. *Buffaloes Crossing the Yellow-stone*. Oil on canvas, 1859. Washington University Gallery of Art.

Figure 89   (bottom)
After the Swim, Herd of Wild Buffaloes, Montana. Photograph by N. A. Forsyth, n.d. Montana Historical Society.

145

fold—appear at the top of the composition. A buffalo head crowns the upper center, above a drawing of Fort Union that includes a steamboat moored on the riverbank; a separate study for this buffalo head survives (fig. 87), although the drawing itself has been lost. A heraldic pair of elk antlers enframes a representation of Fort Benton, which was the newest jewel in the commercial crown of the American Fur Company. Indeed, within a few months of Chouteau's accomplishment, the chief opposition firm of Frost, Todd and Company officially dissolved. Pierre Chouteau and his firm, whose substantial business headquarters in Saint Louis was adorned on the exterior with a huge set of elk antlers in the fashion of those in Wimar's lost drawing, were the undisputed masters of the upper Missouri. Within two years, the discovery of gold in Montana was to propel the Chouteau family fortunes in new directions, beginning another chapter in the history of the upper Missouri River frontier. For Carl Wimar, it was the end of his memorable forays into the wild Indian country; he would never see the West again. Now it was

Figure 90
Carl Wimar. *Buffalo Crossing the Platte*. Oil on canvas, 1859. The Thomas Gilcrease Institute of American History and Art, Tulsa.

time to capitalize on the things he had been fortunate enough to witness before they disappeared forever. A new period of accomplishment in his brief life was at hand.[111]

Soon after his return from the upper Missouri River, Wimar busied himself with a series of paintings based in large part on his frontier experiences. At the end of September 1859, the annual Agricultural and Mechanical Fair opened with great fanfare as "a grand exposition of the wealth and resources of the West." The Fine Art Hall was the center of attraction for the fair's visitors, and Wimar had seven paintings on view there. His were the only artworks singled out for special mention in the fair's annual report. One listed as "Prairie Fire and Buffalo" is known today as *Buffaloes Crossing the Yellowstone*, now in the collection of Washington University in Saint Louis (fig. 88). It is possible that this work was completed prior to the artist's second trip up

the Missouri; it may be one of those works mentioned in a letter to his half-brother, August Becker, on February 3, 1859. Wimar had seen buffaloes crossing a stream during his first trip, and the landscape in the painting resembles the sketches he had made at many points on the Yellowstone. The veracity of the artist's depiction is apparent when it is compared to a similar scene photographed by the Montana photographer N. A. Forsyth a number of years later (fig. 89). However, Wimar had witnessed the prairie fires themselves farther down the Missouri, between Fort Clark and the mouth of the Platte River. The writer for the fair's annual report glowingly described the finished work:

The scene is laid in the wild solitudes of the extensive regions watered by the Yellowstone. The flames are raging on one side of the river, and, to escape their fury, a herd of buffaloes, distracted by fear, in their maddening rush, are swimming the Yellowstone. Some have already gained the opposite side, and are seen scampering and scrambling up one of those high ranges of hills which skirt its banks. All are running up the hill in wild fear and disorder—all but one—and he stands upon the bluff bank of the river—he, the leader and patriarch of the herd; where all is flight and confusion about him, he stands unmoved—the daring leader is waiting for the last of the herd to cross the river. He stands there with his feet growing to the earth, his head slightly stooped and inclined on one side—the position of comfort—and his gaze dauntless, unshrinking, and terrific, is fixed upon those of his frightened followers that are fording the river. In the distance, along the course of the stream, are seen the branching antlers of a stag, which has plunged into the water to escape the fury of the flames, which, from their fervid coloring and natural expression, communicate a scorching atmosphere to the painting that gives force, truth and poetry to the masterly production.[112]

Wimar's artistic aims seemed to have agreed with those of Rudolph Kurz, who wrote that his own frontier paintings endeavored "to be true to nature but chosen from the standpoint of the picturesque and depicted in an aesthetic manner." For Kurz, such works were intended "to satisfy naturalists as well as artists, to broaden the knowledge of the layman and serve at the same time to cultivate his taste."[113] Thus a painter might accurately depict a buffalo herd crossing a particular stretch of the Missouri River or the atmospheric effects of a prairie fire, as long as it was done within the prescribed rules of pictorial construction. This is manifest in another painting Wimar exhibited at the fair, described as "buffaloes at a ford"; the work may be *Buffalo Crossing the Platte*, now at the Gilcrease Museum in Tulsa (fig. 90). Again, this painting

could have been completed before the artist made his second trip upriver, although he had approximately four weeks after his 1859 trip before the fair exhibition opened. The title of this painting implies the area of the confluence of the Platte and the Missouri, but the features of the landscape correspond with many similar areas upriver. In fact, just below the mouth of the Yellowstone, Wimar and his fellow travelers on the *Chippewa* had witnessed "an immense herd of buffalo, more than any we had seen together at one time," according to Dr. Marsh's journal. John James Audubon was one of many travelers who characterized a herd of buffalo as "a beautiful picturesque view," and Karl Bodmer provided more than one visual equivalent of this in the

Figure 91
After Karl Bodmer. *Herd of Bisons on the Upper Missouri*. Aquatint, etching, and roulette. From Maximilian, Prince of Wied, *Travels in the Interior of North America* (London: Ackerman and Company, 1843–44), vol. 2, plate 40. Amon Carter Museum.

148

Figure 92
Carl Wimar. *The Wounded Buffalo*. Oil on canvas, 1859. Washington University Gallery of Art.

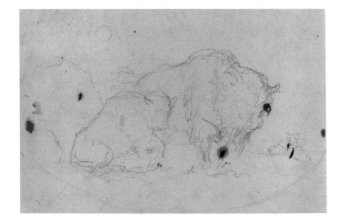

Figure 93
Carl Wimar. *Study of Dying Buffalo Cow*. Pencil on brown paper, 1859. Saint Louis Art Museum.

Figure 94
After Carl Wimar. *Ein Amerik Büffelochse*. Engraving, 1859. Published by Conrad Witter, Saint Louis. Collection of the Glenbow Museum, Calgary, Alberta (70.27.4).

Figure 95
Henry T. Blow. Albumen print by John Scholten, with hand coloring, c. 1870. Missouri Historical Society.

plates which accompanied Maximilian's *Travels*, which Wimar surely knew (fig. 91). Like Bodmer, Wimar employed dramatic atmospheric effects to heighten the sense of the wildness and grandeur of the American frontier. He had seen the spectacular glow of prairie fires against the darkening skies of the open plains, and several of his fellow travelers had extolled the vivid sunsets and other meteorological displays at many points on the two journeys. [114]

Another painting that the author of the fair's annual report considered "expressive of the Promethean fire of inspiration" is known today as *The Wounded Buffalo* (fig. 92). Wimar's depiction elicited a melodramatic description in the report:

It might be appropriately termed the "Infuriated Buffalo," for a buffalo convulsed with

rage and fury is the main subject of the picture, for which everything else is made subservient, and for which everything contributes to heighten the effect and interest. A dam buffalo is lying dead upon the prairie. She has just received her death wound, and from her left side, from the perforation of the bullet, the blood is fast exuding. She has been deserted by all the herd—all except her calf, which stands over her from instinct, and knows not its orphanage; and the male buffalo, maddened with anguish and rage, awaiting with despairing fury the arrival of the hunters, ready for death or revenge. The position of the enraged animal—his nostrils expanded, stretched with his laboring breath, his head lowered for the combat, every muscle dilating with nervous power, and his mouth slightly opened as if the terrific roar was escaping from his lung cells—all were masterly. [115]

The subject of this painting seems to have been derived from the incident on the Yellowstone on July 22, 1858, when Wimar accidentally shot his companion, Sevier, while hunting buffalo. The party had encountered a large group of the animals fording the river; a buffalo cow was wounded, and the two men had gone after it. "They found her on the prairie a good mile from the bank," Jakob Schmidt had written. "Two bulls were with her and since she could go no farther, they would not leave her." A fragmentary study for this work shows that the artist's original conception was a wounded cow protected by a bull, with no calf in sight (fig. 93). Wimar clearly changed his composition to pander to the sensibilities of popular taste; an engraved version appeared in the local newspapers and was marketed as a separate print (fig. 94). "In the distance, on the track of the buffaloes, even the wolves have stopped in their course by the terri-

Figure 96
Carl Wimar. Ambrotype by Andrew J. Fox,
n.d. Missouri Historical Society.

150

fic attitude of the furious leader, and look toward him with hungry, coward, and snarling visages," the annual report's author fulsomely wrote, "while from a mountain cliff which bounds the edge of the prairie, the buzzards are gazing upon the scene, some of them perched upon the rocks, with outstretched necks, looking toward the dead animal, and awaiting impatiently for an opportunity to satisfy their cormorant voracity." Despite the fact that the buffalo cow is clearly not yet dead, the emotional appeal of the painting is evident in the writer's effusive words. According to a contemporary newspaper account, Wimar's works at the fair were "much admired as spirited delineations of his subjects, indicating a freedom of hand and rich coloring that show excelling genius and knowledge of his art."[116]

Although the Fine Art Hall was the center of attraction at the fair, significant changes were under way. "The fact that our home artists will soon have an Artists' Exhibition here has kept from this gallery many pictures, which viewers would have been glad to have seen there," lamented a correspondent for the *Missouri Republican*. The exhibition in question was to be the primary manifestation of a newly formed organization called the Western Academy of Art. This seems to have been the brainchild of Henry T. Blow, a noted patron of the arts in Saint Louis (fig. 95). Besides Blow, nine other individuals co-founded the Western Academy in March 1859, including Wimar, the architect James B. Eads and the painters Ferdinand Boyle and Alban J. Conant. The officers of the academy included Henry Blow as president and Carl Wimar as one of its five "resident professional artists" on the ten-member board of directors. Wimar was also elected librarian, to oversee the formation of a lending library for members of the academy. The efforts of the fledgling academy were warmly received by the Saint Louis press. "Already have a large number of our citizens connected their names with Art by fostering native talent," a writer for the *Missouri Republican* observed, "and these, by cooperating with the Academy, can make St. Louis the center of the Art interests of the Great West."[117] Among those artists possessing "native talent," Carl Wimar was already receiving high praise from contemporary writers for his depictions of western life (fig. 96). "He belongs to our city by adoption, and his name will always be connected with the progress of the Arts in St. Louis," one of them noted.[118]

The inaugural exhibition of the Western Academy of Art opened on the morning of September 28, 1860. The previous day, the Prince of Wales and his retinue, who were visiting the city as part of an American tour, had privately viewed the art on display in the company of Lord Lyons, British Ambassador to the United States, and other dignitaries. "These distinguished visitors expressed great satisfaction with the display of paintings, and particularly with the views of far west scenery by one of our St. Louis artists, Mr. Wimar," noted the *Missouri Republican*. Shortly after the public opening, a catalogue of the exhibition was produced which listed no fewer than 436 individual works of art on view. While many of these represented the efforts of Wimar and other local artists, a larger number were American and European objects from private collections throughout the city. But of all the artists who exhibited at the inaugural exhibition of the Western Academy of Art, none dominated the walls more than Wimar, who displayed no fewer than nineteen paintings.[119]

With the exception of an unidentified portrait and a painting titled *Coming from the Fair*, all of Wimar's works in the exhibition were western subjects, including several large paintings that marked the pinnacle of his brief career. *Buffaloes Crossing the Yellowstone* had been exhibited in the Fine Art Hall at the Agricultural and

Figure 97
Carl Wimar. *Indians Crossing the Upper Missouri River*. Oil on canvas, c. 1859–60. Amon Carter Museum.

151

Figure 98
After Karl Bodmer. *The White Castles on the Upper Missouri*. Aquatint, etching, and roulette. From Maximilian, Prince of Wied, *Travels in the Interior of North America* (London: Ackerman and Company, 1843–44), vol. 2, plate 37. Amon Carter Museum.

Mechanical Fair, which was still in progress when the Western Academy of Art opened its doors. It seems likely that Wimar transferred some of his works from the fair to the Academy exhibition, since exposure at the latter was much more important. Another painting in the exhibition, *On the Missouri, near Judith River*, listed as the property of the artist, is the same as *Indians Crossing the Upper Missouri River*, an undated work now in the collection of the Amon Carter Museum (fig. 97), which clearly was executed after the artist's return from the record-setting journey to Fort Benton. The landscape represents the white cliffs region on the upper Missouri; identical landforms appear in a field sketch made near the mouth of the Judith River on July 16, 1859 (see fig. 66). While there is no mention in any of the travel accounts of Indians making a crossing in this area, the artist could have witnessed this at other points on the river, especially near the forts where the steamboats halted for trade or council. Karl Bodmer illustrated the theme of the crossing in several plates which appeared in Maximilian's *Travels*; one of these, titled *White Castles on the Upper Missouri*, discloses pictorial effects very similar to those in

Figure 99
Carl Wimar. *Indian Encampment on the Big Bend of the Missouri River.* Oil on canvas, 1860. The Thomas Gilcrease Institute of American History and Art, Tulsa.

Figure 100
Carl Wimar. *View of the Missouri River Across the Great Bend.* Charcoal with white chalk on buff paper, June 16, 1859. Missouri Historical Society.

152

Wimar's painting (fig. 98). The vivid coloring of Wimar's scene, with the white bluffs and placid river bathed in the reddish light of the setting sun, becomes a metaphor for the passing of the wilderness.

Other paintings in the exhibition were entirely new to viewers. It is apparent that Wimar had worked at a furious pace in his studio following his return from the upper Missouri. *Big Bend on the Missouri*, also in the artist's possession at the time of the Academy exhibition, is now known as *Indian Encampment on the Big Bend of the Missouri River*, in the collection of the Gilcrease Museum (fig. 99). Once again, Wimar used his first-hand experience on the river to create a panoramic vision of the wild grandeur of the upper Missouri frontier. He had traversed the neck of the Great Bend on June 16 and was among those who ascended the hills above the group's campsite to obtain a view of the entire bend of the river. There he sketched the grand vista that lay before him, in an elaborate double-sheet drawing which served as the basis for the later painting (fig. 100). John James Audubon, who crossed the Great Bend in 1843, pronounced the same view "one of the great panoramas this remarkable portion of our country affords." His words echo Wimar's depiction: "There was a vast extent of country beneath and around us. Westward rose the famous Medicine Hill, and in the opposite direction were the wanderings of the Missouri for many miles, and from the distance we were from it, the river appeared as if a small, very circuitous streamlet."

In the finished painting, Wimar put the middleground, the level plain between the river channels, into deep shadow, as well as portions of the pine-covered ravine to the left. These areas contrast with the reddish-yellow glow of a broad sky illumined by the setting sun on the distant horizon. In the foreground, a group of Plains Indians have tethered their horses for the night

and gather around the light of an evening fire. Beyond the grazing horses a lone sentry, seated at the edge of a hill, gazes out across the landscape. A mounted warrior arrives on the scene, while another, bundled in a striped capote and carrying a long feather-decorated lance, has already dismounted and hurries to join the others around the fire. As a traveler and observer, Wimar had spent the night at this spot on the Great Missouri; as an artist, he substituted a group of Indians and dramatic lighting to create a metaphor for the passing of an era. Like many other artists and writers of the period, Carl Wimar viewed the "Great West" as a paradoxical mixture of realistic experience and mythic expression. "Nature seems to have lavished its gifts on this region," Father Pierre-Jean De Smet observed in 1851, during one of his many trips on the upper Missouri. "But then, what will become of the Indians, . . . who have possessed it from time immemorial? This is indeed a thorny question, awakening gloomy ideas in the observer's mind, if he has followed the encroaching policy of the States in regard to the Indian." De Smet was one of many who realized that the nomadic life of the Plains Indian was nearing its end, and the future of the Missouri River country was soon to be "far unlike the past." *Indian Encampment on the Big Bend of the Missouri River* was not only an evocation of Indian life on the open plains, but a lament for its passing.[120]

Another major painting that Wimar exhibited at the Western Academy of Art was listed as *The Mouth of the Yellowstone*, in the possession of Dr. William Van Zandt, an important patron of the artist's work. This is *Indians Approaching Fort Union*, now in the collection of the Gallery of Art at Washington University (fig. 101). The view is taken from the steep bluffs north of the confluence of the Missouri and Yellowstone Rivers, looking south and west to the badlands that rise along the latter in present-day Richland

Figure 101
Carl Wimar. *Indians Approaching Fort Union.* Oil on canvas, 1860. Washington University Gallery of Art.

154

Figure 102
John Mix Stanley. *Fort Union and Distribution of Goods to the Assiniboine.* Pencil and watercolor on paper, August 1853. Yale University Art Gallery.

Figure 103
After Karl Bodmer. *Fort Union on the Missouri.* Aquatint, etching, roulette, and engraving. From Maximilian, Prince of Wied, *Travels in the Interior of North America* (London: Ackerman and Company, 1843–44), vol. 2, plate 28. Amon Carter Museum.

County, Montana. The broad, dramatic sky is shown at sunset, bathed in dark crimsons, burnt oranges, and pale yellows. The opposition fur company post, Fort William, can be seen on the north side of the Missouri in the middle distance to the left, and the mouth of the Yellowstone a little farther to the right. At the far right, the parapets of Fort Union rise on the near side of the Missouri, along with the tipis of a small Indian encampment. In the foreground, a large group of Indian men, women, and children accompanied by horse and dog travois have halted to survey the broad vista below. Several warriors rear back their horses, firing rifles in the air, while a mounted chief in a feathered bonnet surveys his entourage. Wimar's painting is a romantic paean to the passing of the fur-trading frontier on the upper Missouri.

The painting contrasts with the quieter versions of a similar scene by John Mix Stanley, who visited the fort in 1853 (fig. 102), and by Karl Bodmer (fig. 103). Jakob Schmidt, the young Lutheran missionary who traveled upriver with Wimar in 1858, climbed the same hilltops about half an hour distant from the river to see the same view. "From the top of the highest hill we saw both Fort Union and Fort William, the mountains along the Missouri between the forts, the barren, gray banks along the Missouri, and the Yellowstone River and its banks," he wrote. The mood of Wimar's painting also echoes Prince Maximilian's description of their arrival at Fort Union on June 24, 1833:

> Gentle eminences, with various rounded or flat tops, covered with bright verdure, formed the background; before them, tall poplar groves, and willow thickets on the bank of the river, whose dark blue waters, splendidly illumined by the setting sun, flowed, with many windings, through the prairie. A little further on lay Fort Union,

on a verdant plain, with the handsome American flag, gilded by the last rays of evening, floating in the azure sky, while a herd of horses grazing animated the peaceful scene.[121]

Wimar's painting was obviously intended to suit popular taste and antebellum attitudes toward the Indian. Henry Rowe Schoolcraft, whose multivolume study of the American Indian was assembled between 1851 and 1857, reflected the prevailing view of the "non-pro-gressiveness" of the Indian, who could not adapt to the forces of civilization and was therefore doomed to extinction. Senator Caleb Cushing, the irrepressible champion of Manifest Destiny, asserted in a speech published in 1857 in the *Missouri Republican* that "the tribes of Indians who hunted over the land without occupying it retire before us like the hunted deer and buffalo themselves—deeper and deeper into the inner-most recesses of the continent." A painting like *Indians Approaching Fort Union* was in fact a mosaic of attitudes toward the untamed land and indigenous people of the upper Missouri in the decade prior to the Civil War.

Wimar clearly utilized his field drawings as the solid foundation for his romanticized picto-rial statement, and his claim to accuracy and eye-witness experience were a major selling point. The artist used his powers of observation in a scientific way to strengthen, not undermine, his mythic message. His portrayal of the land and people was highly sympathetic, but also very selective. He adjusted his experiences on the upper Missouri frontier to suit his own romanti-cally held notions about a wilderness that had already passed away by the time he made his own way up the river. Wimar's painting reveals nothing of the great changes that the artist wit-nessed during his two journeys; Fort Union, for example, his symbol of this earlier era, was

156

Figure 104   (left)
Carl Wimar. *The Buffalo Hunt.* Oil on canvas, 1860. Washington University Gallery of Art.

Figure 105   (right)
Carl Wimar. *The Buffalo Hunt.* Oil on canvas, 1861. The Thomas Gilcrease Institute of History and Art, Tulsa.

ordered abandoned within a year after Wimar painted his homage to it. Although many of his field studies remain valuable as historic documents, Wimar's finished paintings depict primitive glory and adventure, closer in spirit to the romantic descriptions by James Fenimore Cooper than to his own time. In this selectivity, Wimar seemed to echo Cooper, who wrote in his preface to *The Prairie* that he might occasionally depart "from strict historical veracity. . . . In the endless confusion of names, customs, opinions and languages which exist among the tribes of the West, the author has paid much more attention to sound and convenience than to literal truth. . . . It was enough for his purpose that the picture should possess the general feature of the original."[122]

One of Wimar's most successful paintings in the exhibition of the Western Academy of Art, and indeed of his entire career, was *The Buffalo Hunt*, which was purchased by Dr. William Van Zandt and eventually bequeathed to the Gallery of Art at Washington University (fig. 104). This painting apparently captivated the Prince of Wales and his entourage, for Lord Lyons com-

missioned a copy of the work, now in the collection of the Gilcrease Museum (fig. 105). The latter is not a precise copy of the original; overall, the lighting has been intensified, and the clarity of elements in the painting has been heightened considerably. Wimar added another Indian pursuer in the far right background and brought the other two into greater focus. In the lower left corner, he signed the work "C. Wimar St. Louis Mo. / 1861," no doubt with a certain degree of pride considering the importance of the commission. As for the first version exhibited at the Western Academy of Art, the actual portrayal of the hunt itself agrees very well with contemporary descriptions of the subject, especially by George Catlin, who witnessed the activity many times and wrote about it in his *Letters and Notes*:

The chief hunting amusement of the Indians in these parts consists in the chase of the buffalo, which is almost invariably done on horseback, with bow and lance. In this exercise, which is highly prized by them, . . . they become exceedingly expert; and are

157

Figure 106
After George Catlin. *Buffalo Chase*. Toned lithograph, hand-colored, 1844. Amon Carter Museum.

able to slay these huge animals with apparent ease. The Indians in these parts are all mounted on small, but serviceable horses, which are caught by them on the prairies, where they are often running wild in numerous bands. . . . In the chase of the buffalo, or other animal, the Indian generally "strips" himself and his horse, by throwing off his shield and quiver, and every part of his dress, which might be an encumbrance to him in running. . . . These horses are so trained, that the Indian has little use for the rein, which hangs on the neck, whilst the animal on the right side [here Catlin refers the reader to his illustration; see fig. 106], giving his rider the chance to throw the arrow to the left; which he does at the instant the horse is pass-

ing—bringing him opposite to the heart, which receives the deadly weapon "to the feather." [123]

Perhaps the most noticeable point of comparison between Catlin's rendition and Wimar's is the relative disparity in size between the buffalo and the mounted Indian. The latter seems more accurate, especially when compared to two other versions of the subject that Wimar probably knew: a plate by Karl Bodmer that accompanied Maximilian's *Travels*, and a print after Peter Rindesbacher that accompanied McKenney and Hall's *History of the Indian Tribes of North America* (figs. 107–108). The similarities among all these works are interesting, but the differences are more revealing. Bodmer's Indian carries a quiver and approaches the animal from the

158

Figure 107 (left)
After Karl Bodmer. *Indians Hunting the Bison.* Aquatint, etching, stipple, and engraving. From Maximilian, Prince of Wied, *Travels in the Interior of North America* (London: Ackerman and Company, 1843–44), vol. 2, plate 31. Amon Carter Museum.

Figure 108 (right)
After Peter Rindesbacher. *Hunting the Buffaloe.* Lithograph, hand-colored, 1837. Amon Carter Museum.

wrong side; in the foreground, a downed buffalo also bears an arrow embedded behind its left foreleg. Rindesbacher, in contrast, has the mounted warrior on the correct side but has depicted horse and rider fully dressed. Catlin shows his Indian drawing his bow well back of the fleeing animal, which contradicts the moment indicated in his description; Wimar, on the other hand, has painted his determined rider about to loose his arrow "at the instant when the horse is passing." The hunter rides on a pad saddle very similar to one that Wimar sketched while visiting Big Head's village in 1858 (fig. 109). The trappings and adornment of the Indians in the finished painting (fig. 110) seem to be from oil studies which he probably made in his studio after his return; his well-stocked studio was described at the time as "a small museum that was sought out by many foreign visitors."[124]

The sense of drama in *The Buffalo Hunt* is greatly heightened by the presence of other rid-

ers, including the central figure with a lance, who have come in from the rear to force the frightened buffaloes into a "surround." All the figures seem to revolve into a carefully orchestrated composition. In the foreground, the mounted Indian has forced his horse between a bull buffalo and a calf; the adult animal, about to receive its death wound, looks with wild eyes toward the equally terrified offspring. While this lends a certain melodramatic quality to Wimar's depiction, several eyewitness observers confirmed the "frightful appearance" of the eyes of such an animal, especially when pursued or wounded. "Of all animals, a buffalo, when close pressed by the hunter, has an aspect the most diabolical," Washington Irving wrote in his narrative of *A Tour on the Prairies.* "His two short black horns, curve out of a huge frontlet of shaggy hair; his eyes glow like coals; his mouth is open, his tongue parched and drawn up into a half crescent; his tail is erect, and tufted and whisking about in the air, he is a perfect picture of mingled rage and terror." Catlin related that the Indian's horse was instinctively afraid of this dangerous and unpredictable animal and "keeps his eye strained upon the furious enemy he is so closely encountering" in order to avoid its horns, "which often are instantly turned, and presented for the fatal reception of its too familiar attendant." Again Wimar indicates a high degree of accuracy by depicting this particular aspect of the chase. Perhaps the best recommendation for the artist's depiction was that of later ethnologists. "Of the many renderings of the buffalo chase I have examined, Charles Wimar's oil painting of 1860 . . . is most satisfying to me as an authentic document," noted John C. Ewers, Ethnologist Emeritus at the Smithsonian Institution, in a ground-breaking study titled "Fact and Fiction in the Documentary Art of the American West." Ewers continued:

> The portrayal of hunting methods shown . . . most nearly conforms to the best eye-witness descriptions of this action I have read in the literature and to the detailed accounts of the buffalo chase recalled for me by aged Blackfoot Indians who had chased buffalo in their young manhood. The action appears to be correct—the mounted bow-man approaching his kill from the buffalo's right, the lancer from its left. Their mounts are small Indian ponies, not big American horses. Their equipment is accurate—including the hair-stuffed pad saddle. My elderly Blackfoot informants told me they preferred to chase buffalo on pad saddles rather than to ride bareback, for the practical reason they could move more freely from side to side and better maintain their balance if their feet were in stirrups.[125]

Wimar's high level of accuracy is also evi-

159

Figure 109
Carl Wimar. *Yanktonais Pad Saddle, Big Head's Band.* Pencil on paper, June 16, 1858. Saint Louis Art Museum.

Figure 110
Carl Wimar. *Indian Clothing and Weapons.* Oil on canvas, c. 1859. Missouri Historical Society.

160

Figure 111
Carl Wimar. *Study for "The Buffalo Hunt"*
Pencil on light brown paper, 1859. Saint Louis
Art Museum.

dent in his depictions of the animals in *The Buf-falo Hunt*. The diminutive, short-nosed Indian pony in Wimar's painting is much more convincing than the long-limbed, thoroughbred-style horses in the works by Bodmer and Catlin. Wimar's buffalo seem more carefully observed, from details such as their slathering mouths to the richly varied colors of their thick coats. William T. Hornaday, who provided a thorough description of the American bison at all stages of its growth in a study published in 1886, noted that a normal bull might stand around five feet at the shoulders and weigh upwards of two thousand pounds. The color and texture of the animal's fur was extremely varied; Audubon termed it somewhere between "a dark umber and a liver-shining brown." In Wimar's painting of *The Buf-falo Hunt*, the difference in coloration of the adult buffalo and the calf was based on the artist's own astute observations. "Unlike the young of nearly all other *Bovidae*, the buffalo calf during the first months of its existence is clad with hair of a totally different color from that which covers him during the remainder of its life," Hornaday wrote. "His pelage is a luxuriant growth of

rather long, wavy hair, of a uniform brownish-yellow or 'sandy' color (cinnamon, or yellow ochre, with a shade of Indian yellow) all over the head, body, and tail, in striking contrast with the darker colors of the older animals." Beyond this, the melodramatic feature of the bull's relationship to the frightened calf is again grounded in reality. According to one reliable observer, a buffalo cow when frightened was apt to "abandon and run away from her calf without the slightest hesitation"; instead, the bulls protected the calves by keeping them on the inside of a traveling herd. Finally, it should be noted that Wimar was scrupulous regarding the depiction of the plants of the shortgrass prairie—all based on studies he had made while foraging along the banks of the upper Missouri. There are recognizable examples of prickly pear and yucca among grasses that tuft and arch like blue grama or buffalo grass, amidst scattered clumps and sprigs of the ubiquitous sagebrush.[126]

Several pencil and charcoal drawings that survive can be seen as preliminary studies for the developed composition of *The Buffalo Hunt*. A very tentative sketch, now in the Saint Louis Art Museum, shows the artist's initial conception of the central Indian coming alongside a barely discernible pair of buffalo, with the Indian and lance lightly pencilled in in the background (fig. 111). In the foreground to the left, Wimar sketched a wounded buffalo dropped to the ground in a manner very similar to Bodmer's version discussed above. Two other drawings on a similar type of paper show the artist exploring the motif of the central mounted Indian and the fleeing buffalo charging to the left, with the hunter behind the animal (figs. 112–113). Here Wimar must have been partially dissatisfied with the pictorial result; in order for the Indian and horse to be visible, they had to be shown dashing slightly ahead of the buffalo. This caused the hunter to be too far forward of his quarry to convey accu-

Figure 112
Carl Wimar. *Buffalo Hunt (Preliminary Sketch).* Pencil on light brown paper, c. 1859–60. Missouri Historical Society.

Figure 113
Carl Wimar. *Buffalo Hunt (Final Sketch).* Pencil and charcoal on light brown paper, c. 1859–60. Missouri Historical Society.

161

rately the highly charged moment of delivering the fatal arrow. In both drawings—and in a small pastel rendering of a *Buffalo Hunt* (fig. 114)— Wimar seems to have struggled initially with the focus of the composition. In the more finished study, he began the central massing of figures that he would effectively achieve in the final painting. The lancer to the right thrusts his weapon in a manner similar to the hunter in F.O.C. Darley's depiction of a buffalo hunt reproduced in *Harper's Weekly* on May 1, 1858 (fig. 115), although in Wimar's oil version of *The Buffalo Hunt* the lance-wielding Indian is significantly different. Many of the trappings that adorn the Indians are closely rendered, and the artist most certainly had seen the red trade-cloth bandoliers and vermillion-painted faces that were noted among the tribes of the upper Missouri in this period. Overall, Wimar's preparatory sketches reveal the artist's desire to refine the composition of the final work from a purely pictorial standpoint without sacrificing the accuracy that he had worked so hard to acquire; he knew that discriminating viewers would judge his painting on both counts.[127]

Figure 114
Carl Wimar. *Buffalo Hunt.* Pastel on canvas, 1860. National Cowboy Hall of Fame and Western Heritage Center, Oklahoma City.

THE BUFFALO HUNT.

162

Figure 115
After F.O.C. Darley. *The Buffalo Hunt*. Illustration from *Harper's Weekly*, May 1, 1858. Amon Carter Museum.

Wimar executed one other significant painting of a buffalo hunt that differs in important ways from the earlier versions. In 1861 Henry T. Blow commissioned two paintings by the artist for his house in Carondelet, now part of south Saint Louis. Wimar only completed one of these before his death: a daring vertical composition, over seven feet in height, titled *The Buffalo Hunt*, now in the Missouri Historical Society (fig. 116). The lack of horizontal space posed a difficult dilemma whose solution is suggested in two of the preparatory sketches for the earlier *Buffalo Hunt*. The buffalo is in front, charging to the left, while the mounted Indian comes alongside behind the animal. This time, however, the horse and rider are slightly elevated above the buffalo so they remain visible to the viewer while maintaining a correct position in terms of the hunt itself. A lighter-colored buffalo calf is shown in the right foreground, emerging from a grassy area and running alongside the bull's left

flank. This aids in keeping the composition centered, as does the placement of an Indian with lance upraised immediately behind and to the rear of the central figure. The lance-bearing warrior is turned away so that his muscled back is all that appears to the viewer, but this effectively anchors the momentum of the central group without drawing too much attention away from it. Wimar has compressed the space in the foreground to convey a great amount of action and detail, while the background is ingeniously orchestrated to bring a strong sense of depth and distance to the scene. The tall vine-laden trees on the right contrast markedly with the open space leading to the badlands formations on the horizon on the left, marked by the dark line of a fleeing buffalo herd. A study for the central figure in Wimar's painting survives, executed in oil on paper (fig. 117). An oil study of a medicine bag made from an otter's skin, probably derived from the artist's Missouri River trips, resembles the

163

example tied to the Indian's waist in the painting (fig. 118). The tribal identity of the Indians has been a matter of some debate ever since the artist's early biographer, Charles Reymershoffer, initiated the discussion in 1907. The most learned opinion identifies the riders as Osage, Pawnee, or other nearby tribes. Wimar visited the Pawnees near Omaha in 1859, and elements such as the shaved head, turban, and bear claw necklace were typical of the tribes bordering on the Missouri River in eastern Nebraska or Kansas. While the positions of the figures themselves can be said to be fairly accurate, the artist has festooned his braves with an array of accessories which seem to be lavishly detailed and highly decorative—possibly to please his patron. The

physical appearance of the Indians is noticeably more idealized, similar to that in the paintings of his Düsseldorf period.[128]

The Buffalo Hunt remains a powerful painting, certainly one of the artist's best. It seems likely that Wimar, as a founding member of an academy dedicated to the advancement of the arts, would have agreed with Rudolph Kurz, his predecessor on the Missouri, who wrote:

No true artist regards as his highest purpose mere reproduction of nature; beauties of nature are daily pleasures from which only the blind are debarred. The artist's task is to improve nature's forms, make perfect her imperfections, strive not only to emulate

Figure 116   (left)
Carl Wimar. *The Buffalo Hunt.* Oil on canvas, 1861. Missouri Historical Society.

Figure 117   (middle)
Carl Wimar. *Study for Indian in [The] Buffalo Hunt.* Oil on paper, 1861. © 1990, Indianapolis Museum of Art; gift of Mr. Jack A. Goodman.

Figure 118   (right)
Carl Wimar. *Medicine Bag.* Oil on canvas laid down on pulpboard, c. 1859. Saint Louis Art Museum.

Figure 119
Carl Wimar. *The Buffalo Dance*. Oil on canvas, 1860. Saint Louis Art Museum.

164

Figure 120
Hidatsa-Mandan Ceremonial Area, Like-A-Fishhook Village. Photograph by Stanley J. Morrow, 1870. State Historical Society of North Dakota.

but to excel her in the creation of beauty. Nature achieves nothing in ideal perfection, but the artist's mind can conceive of ideal beauty and clothe his ideas with correspondingly lovely forms, i.e., idealize them. By that means the human being rises above that which is usual or commonplace. To inspire their fellow beings is the artist's most lofty aim; to that end they should bend their efforts, each according to his ability.[129]

An important painting that Wimar completed in 1860 was not listed in the catalogue of the Western Academy of Art—perhaps because he was still working on *The Buffalo Dance* while the Academy exhibition was under way (fig. 119). Like the artist's earlier paintings, this highly developed composition is an homage to a world that was already gone forever. As far as can be determined, Wimar never witnessed an event like this on either of his journeys to the upper Missouri. The Arikara and Mandan tribes were poor remnants by the time he saw them, and the only songs he heard them sing were laments for their numbers killed by disease or war with the more powerful Sioux.

The Buffalo Dance occurs beneath a moonlit sky painted in dark shades of purple and crimson. The other source of light is a fire in the foreground, which casts a reddish glow amidst the long shadows of the dancing figures. A large group of Indian men, women, and children watch the proceedings on all sides; many are shown atop the roofs of the earth lodges and threshing stages which surround the spectacle. The earth lodge in the center background is recognizable as one that the artist sketched during his visit to Fort Clark on June 25, 1859 (see fig. 55), and a photograph taken eleven years later shows the identical ceremonial area (fig. 120). Many of the Indians in Wimar's painting are wrapped in blue-striped blankets or capotes with bands of decorated bead or quillwork, recalling the figures that appear in the artist's sketches made on the upper Missouri in 1858 (fig. 121). The fur headdress adorned with two feathers on one of the warriors to the far right is derived from a sketch Wimar made at Fort Pierre on June 12 that year (see fig. 10), and the distinctive buffalo horn headdress on the warrior to the left appears in a sketch of Mandan and Arikara objects, including medicine poles, that Wimar made at Fort Clark on his 1859 trip (fig. 122). The tall tripod of poles in the center of Wimar's painting of *The Buffalo Dance*, with bundles of twigs tied to the upper ends, was described by Maximilian in his *Travels* as part of a "medicine establishment" for holy rites. Indeed, Karl Bodmer made a rendering of a Mandan buffalo dance that bears a clear resemblance to Wimar's version (fig. 123). While Bodmer's rendering may have supplied some guidance for the pictorial elements in Wimar's painting, the artist must have read George Catlin's vivid descriptions of the buffalo dance as well (fig. 124). "My ears have been almost continually ringing since I came here, with the din of yelping and the beating of drums," Catlin wrote from a Mandan village on the upper Mis-

165

Figure 121 (left)
Carl Wimar. *Yanktons, Fort Randall.* Pencil on paper, c. June 7, 1858. Saint Louis Art Museum.

Figure 122 (bottom)
Carl Wimar. *Arikara and Mandan Ceremonial Objects.* Pencil on paper, 1859. Missouri Historical Society.

166

Figure 123 (left)
After Karl Bodmer. *Bison-Dance of the Mandan Indians in front of the Medecine [sic] Lodge. In Mih-Tutta-Hankush.* Aquatint, mezzotint, etching, and stipple. From Maximilian, Prince of Wied, *Travels in the Interior of North America* (London: Ackerman and Company, 1843–44), vol. 2, plate 18. Amon Carter Museum.

Figure 124 (right)
After George Catlin. *Buffalo Dance.* Toned lithograph, hand-colored, 1844. Amon Carter Museum.

souri in his *Letters and Notes*, "but I have for several days past been peculiarly engrossed, and my senses almost confounded with the stamping, and grunting, and bellowing of the *buffalo dance*, which closed a few days since at sunrise (thank Heaven), and which I must needs describe to you." Catlin proceeded to narrate the ceremony, which was performed nonstop day and night:

The place where this strange operation is carried on is in the public area in the centre of the village, and in front of the great medicine or mystery lodge. About ten or fifteen Mandans at a time join in the dance, each one with the skin of the buffalo's head (or mask) with the horns on, placed over his head, and in his hand his favorite bow or lance, with which he is used to slay the buffalo. . . . Drums are beating and rattles are shaken, and songs and yells incessantly are shouted, and lookers-on stand ready with masks on their heads, and weapons in hand, to take the place of each one as he becomes fatigued, and jumps out of the ring. . . . The mask is put over the head, and generally has a strip of the skin hanging to it, of the whole length of the animal, with the tail attached to it, which, passing down over the back of the dancer, is dragging on the ground. . . .[130]

Wimar's painting of *The Buffalo Dance* is an exotic travelogue. The artist's first priority was not to chronicle the dance itself, but to evoke its primitive grandeur. In the end, Wimar's excursions on the great Missouri enabled him to achieve legitimacy with his audience for the larger, mythic paintings he created concerning the American West. At the same time, he was conscious of the importance of a timely subject; this is evidenced in his arresting portrait of the

Seminole war chief, Holatamico (Billy Bolek), popularly known as Billy Bowlegs (fig. 125). This chief, the leading figure in the so-called Third Seminole War (1849–58), had led a small band of warriors within a remote area of the Florida Everglades in temporary defiance of government efforts to remove them to a newly created reservation in the Indian Territory. He was the subject of a long feature article in *Harper's Weekly* of June 12, 1858, which included a full-length portrait engraved from a photograph (fig. 126). At the time the photograph was taken, it was noted that he was fifty years old and had two wives, fifty slaves, and great wealth. The central figure in Wimar's painting bears an obvious resemblance to the chief and was likely based on illustrations or photographs, since there seems to be no evidence that the artist ever saw him.

While the features of Billy Bowlegs himself seem related to a specific pictorial source, the other Indians depicted in the work are more problematic. If anything, their features and habiliments are more closely related to the Plains tribes that Wimar knew than to the Seminoles. The crouching figure on the right, for example, possesses a face painted precisely like that of an Indian he had sketched at Fort Union in 1858 (see fig. 20). Likewise, such items as the beaded leggins, otter medicine bag, and striped trade cloth blankets appear to have come from the Plains artifacts in the artist's studio, rather than the Seminoles themselves. But accuracy was not Wimar's aim, for the portrait of *Billy Bowlegs* seems to have had a more compelling reason for its execution: the accelerating events of the Civil War in the western territories. On November 19, 1861, a large force of "Loyal Indians" under the general leadership of the aged Creek chief Opothle Yahola defeated an invading Confederate force at the battle of Round Mountain, south of the Cimarron River. The Seminoles were allies with the Creeks in this important engagement,

Figure 125
Carl Wimar. *Chief Billy Bowlegs (Holatamico)*. Oil on canvas, 1861. Saint Louis Art Museum.

BILLY BOWLEGS, CHIEF OF THE SEMINOLES.—[FROM A PHOTOGRAPH BY CLARK, OF NEW ORLEANS.]

Figure 126
Billy Bowlegs, Chief of the Seminoles. Engraving from a photograph by Clark, New Orleans. From *Harper's Weekly*, June 12, 1858, p. 376.

and Billy Bowlegs was one of their principal leaders. Although the Indians' triumph was to be short-lived, such an action must have had great symbolic value to Union sympathizers in the West in the early months of the war. It is not too far-fetched to imagine that Wimar, himself a supporter of the Union cause, realized the extreme irony of a people who had been so fully exploited by the government now vigorously defending it.[131]

The initial events of the Civil War were a culmination of a long period of sectional conflict that had affected every aspect of life in Saint Louis. "As this agitation increased and intensified, there was a serious widening of the breach between the two classes of the community," wrote a nineteenth-century historian, "and a coalition, political but not social, was formed between the Germans and what may be termed the New England element in St. Louis . . . includ[ing] many of the thriftiest, most enterprising, and most useful citizens of the place, the men who put up the work-shops and built the railroads, who fostered industry and developed trade in every direction. . . . " It is a grave coincidence that during the highly successful exhibition of the Western Academy of Art, Abraham

Lincoln defeated the local favorite, Stephen A. Douglas, in the presidential election. Six months after thirteen thousand Saint Louis schoolchildren enjoyed the fruits of art and culture sponsored by the first institution of its kind in the West, the "dreadful idea" of internecine warfare became a grim reality. Missouri was to suffer the fate of other border states in the conflict; no family was spared the bitter divisions that ensued. One of the early casualties of the war was the Western Academy itself. "The military authorities took possession of the building, and what the organization had collected was quickly scattered abroad," a Saint Louis historian wrote in 1883. "The casts from the antique works now in the reading-room of the Public School Library are all that remain of its possessions." Despite these developments, there were other opportunities for Carl Wimar to apply his productive and memorable trips on the Great Missouri, and he would take full advantage of them in the single year that remained of his brief life. Although he was suffering from the effects of consumption, the artist was at the peak of his career. His depictions the Missouri River frontier had found an appreciative audience, and his stature as an artist seemed to be assured.[132]

NOTES

1. Norman MacLean, *A River Runs Through It and Other Stories* (Chicago: University of Chicago Press, 1976), 104.

2. There is no comprehensive history of the Missouri River to equal Paul Horgan's majestic study of the Rio Grande, *Great River* (New York: Rinehart, 1954). Stanley Vestal's *The Missouri* (New York: Farrar and Rinehart, 1945) is a superficial account originally written for the Rivers of America series.

3. A humorous account of the vexing character of the ever-changing river for the nineteenth-century travelers can be found in George Fitch, "The Missouri River: Its Habits and Eccentricities Described by a Personal Friend," *American Magazine* 63 (April 1907): 639. See also Robert C. Gildart, *Montana's Missouri River* (Helena: *Montana* Magazine, 1986), 11.

4. "A Western Landscape," *Cosmopolitan Art Journal* 1 (June 1857): 114.

5. Carl Wimar to August Becker, April 24, 1858, The Thomas Gilcrease Institute for American History and Art, 3826.2836. Boller wrote to his parents on May 29: "Mr. Paul Weimar [sic] a painter who gained distinction at Düsseldorf is on the boat and intends to remain a year in the Far West painting Indian scenery and incidents. He has an ambrotype apparatus on board." Ray H. Mattison, ed., "Henry A. Boller, Upper Missouri River Fur Trader," *North Dakota History* 33 (Spring 1966): 134. The ambrotype process (as it was called in America) was essentially daguerreotypy on glass. Ambrotypes looked like daguerreotypes, but the positive image secured on a glass plate looked like a negative until the plate was coated with black on the reverse. Like daguerreotypes, ambrotypes were one-of-a-kind images, and rather fragile. The process was short-lived due to the rise of collodion paper photography just before the Civil War. See William Welling, *Photography in America: The Formative Years 1839–1900* (New York: Thomas Y. Crowell Co., 1978), 110–11.

6. Henry A. Boller, *Among the Indians: Eight Years in the Far West, 1858–1866*, ed. Milo M. Quaife (Chicago: R.R. Donnelly and Sons Company, 1959). See also Henry A. Boller, "Journal of a Trip to, and Residence In, the Indian Country," ed. Ray H. Mattison, *North Dakota History* 33 (Summer 1966): 260–315. Boller wrote a great many letters home to his parents which are presented in Mattison, "Henry A. Boller, Fur Trader," 106–219. In 1857 Frost, Todd and Company chartered its first steamboat, the newly built *Twilight*, to carry nearly four hundred tons of freight upriver. Daniel Frost, a former army officer, also had used political connections to secure the government contract to deliver the Indian annuities for that year. For an account of Frost, Todd and Company, see John E. Sunder, *The Fur Trade on the Upper Missouri, 1840–1865* (Norman: University of Oklahoma Press, 1965), 183–84.

7. *Missouri Republican*, July 11, 1858, 2.

8. Boller, *Among the Indians*, 15; Mattison, "Henry A. Boller, Fur Trader," 127. For an overall history of the fur trade, see Hiram M. Chittenden's pioneering two-volume study, *The American Fur Trade of the Far West*, originally published in 1902 (Stanford, Cal.: Academic Reprints, 1954), and the more recent two-volume effort by Paul Chrisler Phillips, *The Fur Trade* (Norman: University of Oklahoma Press, 1961).

9. Hiram M. Chittenden, *Early Steamboat Navigation on the Missouri River*, 2 vols. (New York: Francis P. Harper, 1903), 1: 114–15. Wimar made three rough sketches of a craft similar to Chittenden's description in a sketchbook dated the following year, now in the Missouri Historical Society. See sketchbook 1918.52.2, pages 11, 15, and 67. The *Twilight*, however, was equipped with side wheels, which were less effective on the Missouri River.

10. Information on the original location of historic sites along the Missouri River can be found in the Missouri River Commission, *Map of the Missouri River from Its Mouth to Three Forks, Montana, in Eighty-Four Sheets* (Washington: Missouri River Commission, 1892–95), hereafter cited as *Missouri River Maps*. Kansas City and its environs appear on sheet 14. A good geographical description of the Missouri River between Saint Louis and Kansas City in the middle 1850s may be found in Lt. A. J. Donelson, "Navigability of the Missouri," in *Reports of Explorations and Surveys, to Ascertain the Most Practicable and Economical Route for a Railroad from the Mississippi River to the Pacific Ocean* (Washington: Beverley Tucker, Printer, 1855), 1: 231–33 (hereafter cited as *Pacific Railroad Reports*). Kansas City as it appeared in 1858 is described in William Barclay Napton, "Lewis and Clark's Route Retraveled. The Upper Missouri in 1858," in *Over the Santa Fe Trail, 1857* (Kansas City: Franklin Hudson Publishing Company, 1905), 5.

11. Carl Wimar to his parents, June 1, 1858, Thomas Gilcrease Institute for American History and Art, 3826.2834. Wimar's sketchbooks from the 1858 trip are preserved in the Saint Louis Art Museum. For the location of Bellevue, see *Missouri River Maps*, sheet 23. Historical notes on the site can be found in Norman A. Graebner, "Nebraska's Missouri River Frontier, 1854–1860," *Nebraska History* 42 (December 1961): 215–16. A view of the city with a brief note of its appearance at the time of Wimar's visit can be found in *Frank Leslie's Illustrated Newspaper*, June 5, 1858, 13–14. Bellevue had been a stopping point for four artists who preceded Wimar up the Missouri River. In 1833 Karl Bodmer accompanied his employer, Prince Maximilian of Wied, who described the "green-wooded chain of hills" surrounding the Bellevue Agency, which was "agreeably situated" on the riverbank above some cruder huts. See Prince Maximilian, "Travels in the Interior of North America," in Reuben G. Thwaites, ed., *Early Western Travels, 1748–1846* (Glendale, Cal.: The Arthur H. Clark Co., 1966), 22: 265–67. John James Audubon, who arrived at Bellevue ten years later, agreed that the surrounding hills were luxuriant, for they teemed with various kinds of birds. See Maria R. Audubon and Elliott Coues, *Audu-*

169

bon and His Journals (New York: Charles Scribner's Sons, 1897), 1: 478. In 1851 Rudolph Friedrich Kurz stayed at the Bellevue post for several days and made a number of sketches of the Indians. See J. N. B. Hewitt, ed., *Journal of Rudolph Friedrich Kurz* (Lincoln: University of Nebraska Press, 1970), 64–66. George Catlin also described the Bellevue trading post in his book, *Letters and Notes on the Manners, Customs, and Conditions of the North American Indians* (London: Published by the Author, 1841), 2: 11–12.

12. See sketchbook 61:41, pages 7 verso, 8 verso, 9 recto, and 9 verso, Saint Louis Art Museum. The broken rudder incident is mentioned in the *Missouri Republican*, July 11, 1858, 2. See also Napton, "Lewis and Clark's Route Retraveled," 82–83. The Saint Helena area appears in *Missouri River Maps*, sheet 30. Further commentary about the area near the mouth of the Vermillion River can be found in Johann Jakob Schmidt's daily journal, translated by Gerhard M. Schmutterer in *Tomahawk and Cross: Lutheran Missionaries Among the Northern Plains Tribes, 1858–1866* (Sioux Falls, S.D.: The Center for Western Studies, Augustana College, 1989), 117.

13. Gary E. Moulton, ed., *The Journals of the Lewis and Clark Expedition* (Lincoln: University of Nebraska Press, 1987), 3: 35, 109. See also Royal B. Hassrick, *The Sioux: Life and Customs of a Warrior Society* (Norman: University of Oklahoma Press, 1964), 3–7.

14. A.H. Redfield to A.M. Robinson, September 1 and October 12, 1858, in "Report of the Commissioner of Indian Affairs," 35th Cong., 2d sess., *Senate Executive Document No. 1*, 436. Redfield noted that by the terms of the treaty, the Indians were assured "undisturbed occupancy" for at least one year. "I found, however, that several squatters were already on their lands eagerly endeavoring to seize some of the most desireable points. One company of intruders had actually located in the midst of their village and erected a sort of fortress for their protection." Ibid. Redfield assured the displeased chief that he would ask the military authorities upriver at Fort Randall to have the interlopers evicted. Whether this was accomplished is not known. This incident was also reported in the *Missouri Republican*, July 11, 1858, 2.

15. Perry Rathbone, *Charles Wimar, 1828–1862* (Saint Louis: City Art Museum, 1946), 19. Quotations from Schmidt's journal are taken from Oswald F. Wagner, "Lutheran Zealots Among the Crows," *Montana: The Magazine of Western History* 21 (January 1972): 2–19. Schmidt's journal of his trip ran from May 28 to November 19, 1858. Substantial excerpts were printed in biweekly installments, from February 1 to December 5, 1859, in *Missionblatt*, a Lutheran evangelical periodical published in Nuremberg, Germany. Schmidt, who had immigrated to America in 1856, was an enthusiastic convert to missionary work among the Indians for the Iowa Synod. In a letter to friends in Germany he had declared, "Ever since 1853, when I decided to become a missionary to the Indians, I have been reading all the material about them that I could lay my hands on." Wagner, "Lutheran Zealots," 4. See also Schmutterer's translation of Schmidt's journal for June 5 in *Tomahawk and Cross*, 117–19.

16. The best overview of early efforts to photograph the American Indian is Paula Richardson Fleming and Judith Luskey, *The North American Indians in Early Photographs* (New York: Harper and Row, 1986). The authors briefly note Wimar's activity on 194–95. See also Welling, *Photography in America*, 110–12. The only photographer to precede Wimar on the Missouri seems to have been John Mix Stanley, an artist who accompanied Governor Isaac Stevens' party for the Pacific Railroad Survey in 1853–54. Stevens recorded that Stanley took daguerreotypes of the Indians at Forts Union and Benton. At the latter, he observed that the Indians "were delighted and astonished to see their likenesses produced by the direct action of the sun. They worship the sun, and they considered that Mr. Stanley was inspired by their divinity, and he thus became in their eyes a great medicine man." Stevens, "Narrative of 1853," *Pacific Railroad Reports* 12, part 1, 103–4. Unfortunately, none of these important images appear to have survived. The same fate has befallen the photographic efforts of Solomon Nunes Carvalho, who accompanied John C. Frémont's expedition from Missouri to Utah in 1853. Carvalho described his efforts in a narrative titled *Incidents of Travel and Adventure in the Far West . . .* (New York: Derby and Jackson; Cincinnati: H. W. Derby and Co., 1857), 20–22, 64, 67–68. See also Robert Taft, *Photography and the American Scene* (New York: Dover Publications, 1964), 263, 409, and Walt Wheelock, "Frémont's Lost Plates," *Westerner's Brand Book* (San Diego, 1971), 2: 48–53.

17. Fitzgibbon's activities are described in Jacob N. Taylor, *Sketchbook of Saint Louis . . .* (Saint Louis: G. Knapp and Company, Printers, 1858), 311–14. Some of Fitzgibbon's photographs are preserved in the Missouri Historical Society. A superb daguerreotype, hand-colored, of the Kansas Chief Kno-Shr has been dated to 1853 and is in the Gilman Paper Collection. It was noted that Fitzgibbon was taking daguerreotype views of the Agricultural and Mechanical Fair in 1857, with the idea of having them sent east, where they might be engraved for illustrations in *Leslie's Magazine*. The fair that year also included an exhibition of ambrotypes and daguerreotypes by "Mr. Brown," as well as many ambrotype portraits of prominent St. Louis citizens by Andrew J. Fox, who did a portrait photograph of Carl Wimar in the same period. See the *Missouri Republican*, September 30, 1857, 2. The same guide that mentioned Fitzgibbon also recommended J. J. Outley's "Daguerrean and Ambrotype Gallery" in two locations in the city, claiming that "there is not a Gallery in the United States where a superior collection of plain or colored Ambrotypes can be found." Taylor, *Sketchbook of Saint Louis*, 290. The important work of Thomas M. Easterly remains to be fully investigated. A good introduction is John C. Ewers, "Thomas M. Easterly's Pioneer Daguerreotypes of Plains Indians," *Missouri Historical Society Bulletin* 24 (July 1968): 329–39. Easterly's work is the subject of a long-awaited study, forthcoming, by Dolores A. Kilgo. See her recent article, "Preserving the Legends of the American Frontier: Daguerreotype Portraits by Thomas M. Easterly," *History of Photography* 13 (April-June 1989): 129–32. A very useful overview of early photography in Saint Louis is Charles Van Ravenswaay, "Pioneer Photographers of St. Louis," *Missouri Historical Society Bulletin* 10 (October 1953): 48–71.

18. Boller, *Among the Indians*, 18.

19. Napton, *On the Santa Fe Trail*, 79–80. He added an interesting note: "I saw him paint a portrait of Captain Atkinson, a son of General Atkinson, as we were ascending the river, in the cabin of the boat, which I thought denoted marked artistic skill as well as being a faithful likeness of the man." Ibid., 81. This portrait has not been located.

20. *Missouri Republican*, July 11, 1858, 2; Wagner, "Lutheran Zealots," 5. See also Schmutterer, *Tomahawk and Cross*, 120–21. For Wimar's words on the situation, see Rathbone, *Charles Wimar*, 19–20. For a view of Fort Randall and an account of its appearance in Wimar's time, see *Frank Leslie's Illustrated Newspaper*, July 3, 1858, 68. Wimar made a sketch of the Chouteau Creek mouth, approximately twenty-five miles below Fort Randall, which contains color notations on the hills and bluffs along the river (Wimar sketchbook 62 : 41, Saint Louis Art Museum, 10 recto).

21. Napton, *Over the Santa Fe Trail*, 84. Fort Randall, established by General William S. Harney, was destined to have the longest existence of any garrison on the upper Missouri above Omaha. See the *Missouri River Maps*, sheet 33; Ray H. Mattison, "The Military Frontier on the Upper Missouri," *Nebraska History* 37 (September 1956): 159–82; and Linda W. Slaughter, "Fort Randall," *Collections of the State Historical Society of North Dakota* 1 (1906): 423–29.

22. *Missouri Republican*, September 18, 1858, 2. The same visitor, who dated his report September 6, noted that the army troops had not been paid since the previous December but had been active nonetheless: "The Tepees show off, and the papooses are many, bearing striking likenesses to the officers and men of the army, who are proud of the issue of their loins. One-half of the little ones hovering around the squaws are off-spring of white men."

23. Redfield's letter to Charles E. Mix, Acting Commissioner of Indian Affairs, is dated June 5, 1858, and is reproduced in the National Archives Microfilm Publications, microfilm 234, roll 885, frames 218–19 (hereafter cited as NAMP, M234, R885, F218–19). Boller's letter is in Mattison, "Henry A. Boller, Fur Trader," 137. See also the *Missouri Republican*, June 29, 1858, 2. A more detailed description of these two chiefs can be found in the same newspaper for July 28, 1856, 2. The photograph shows the two chiefs seated on either side of Charles Picotte, who was a nephew of Struck By the Ree. The three men were members of the delegation to Washington, and the photograph was taken sometime between December 31, 1857, and April 26, 1858. It is now in the Smithsonian Institution National Anthropological Archives, and is reproduced in Fleming and Luskey, *North American Indians in Early Photographs*, 31. An additional photograph of Struck By the Ree, taken ten years later, appears on page 33 in the same publication. An interesting letter by Picotte, dated August 3, 1858, describes the site of his uncle's camp as on the river opposite Calumet Bluffs and provides a map of that portion of the Missouri. See NAMP, MC234, R885, F180–83. Another photograph of Smutty Bear appeared as a lithographed reproduction in Ferdinand Vandiveer Hayden, . . . *Contributions to the Ethnography and Philology of the Indian Tribes of the Missouri Valley* . . . (Philadelphia: C. Sherman and Sons, Printers, 1862), 460. Hayden wrote that "the figures on the plates accompanying this are copied from photographs taken in the Indian country, under the direction of Mr. J. D. Hutton, Topographical Assistant to Captain William F. Raynolds, T.E., and published by permission of the latter." Ibid., 457. Hayden accompanied Raynolds on an exploratory survey of the Yellowstone River in 1859. They traveled up the Missouri on the same steamboat as Carl Wimar that year.

24. Schmutterer, *Tomahawk and Cross*, 122; Redfield, 1858 Report, 437. For a corroborative account of the stormy council, see the *Missouri Republican*, July 11, 1858, 2. The American Fur Company boat had a similar encounter a week later; see the same newspaper for June 29, 1858, 2. Fort Lookout was located on the southern boundary of the lower Brulé Indian Reservation, but the site is now flooded by the waters of the reservoir behind Fort Randall dam. See Mattison, "Military Frontier on the Upper Missouri," 165, and Merrill J. Mattes, "Report on Historic Sites in the Fort Randall Reservoir Area, Missouri River, South Dakota," *South Dakota Historical Collections* 24 (1949): 543. Augustus Meyers, one of the young soldiers who built the fort, recalled the appearance of the site: "The river channel was on that side and the banks high enough not to be overflowed. The wooded bottom-land extended two hundred yards back from the river, then ascended fifty feet above the water in an easy grade to a plateau. . . . About a mile west of the river the land became rugged and hilly. There were plenty of woods in sight along the river banks as far as we could see." Augustus Meyers, "Dakota in the Fifties," *South Dakota Historical Collections* 10 (1920): 175–76, 185. Fort Lookout was apparently built on or near the site of an earlier trading post of the same name, which had served as the principal trading center on the Missouri before the establishment of Fort Union in 1828. See Merrill J. Mattes, "*Under* the Wide Missouri," *North Dakota History* 21 (1954): 152. When Prince Maximilian visited the older fort in 1833, it was the uppermost of the Missouri River Indian agencies. He described the physical appearance of the fort itself as well as the topography, and noted the presence of Yankton and Yanktonais dwellings nearby. See Maximilian, "Travels," in Thwaites, *Early Western Travels* 22: 303–4.

25. Wimar sketchbook 64 : 41, Saint Louis Art Museum, 5 verso. This sketchbook is larger than the first three pocket-sized sketchbooks and contains lined paper. Many of the pages were torn out at a subsequent date. The identifiable sites that remain come in a sequence from Fort Pierre downriver past the Omaha Indian settlements. It is likely (though not irrefutable) that Wimar filled this sketchbook on his return trip in September 1858. Medicine Cow is mentioned in Boller, *Among the Indians*, 21, and in Will G. Robinson, "Digest of Reports of the Commissioner of Indian Affairs—1853–1869," *South Dakota Historical Collections* 27 (1954): 210.

26. Rathbone, *Charles Wimar*, 20.

27. See the account of Bear Rib furnished by a traveler on the American Fur Company steamboat *Spread Eagle*, published in the *Missouri Republican*, June 29, 1858, 2. For a detailed account of the chief's demise, see the note by Charles DeLand in Frederick T. Wilson, "Old Fort Pierre and Its Neighbors," *South Dakota Historical Collections* 1 (1902): 366–68.

28. Iron Horn is mentioned as a treaty signer in Robinson, "Digest of Reports of the Commissioner of Indian Affairs," 249. The oil sketch is in the Missouri Historical Society (1950.117.2). The photograph of Iron Horn is reproduced as a lithograph in Hayden, *Contributions*, 459. Catlin's description of One Horn appears in his *Letters and Notes* 1: 211. His painting of the chief is illustrated in William H. Truettner, *The Natural Man Observed: A Study of Catlin's Indian Gallery* (Washington: Smithsonian Institution Press, 1979), fig. 81. See also Hassrick, *The Sioux*, 167. The Miniconjous precipitated the infamous Grattan massacre in 1854, which in turn caused General William S. Harney to lead his troops west to fight the rather dishonorable battle of Blue Water, then to establish Forts Lookout and Randall. See Robinson, "Digest of Reports of the Commissioner of Indian Affairs," 175, and William H. Goetzmann, *Army Exploration in the American West, 1803–1863* (Lincoln: University of Nebraska Press, 1979, reprinted from the earlier edition by Yale University Press, 1959), 409–10.

29. See Wimar sketchbook 61:41, Saint Louis Art Museum, 10 verso–12 verso, and Rathbone, *Charles Wimar*, 20. Two Bears and Iron Nation are mentioned in Redfield's report for the previous year. See Robinson, "Digest of Reports of the Commissioner of Indian Affairs," 211. A photograph of Iron Nation, taken in 1867 by Alexander Gardner, is reproduced in Fleming and Luskey, *North American Indians in Early Photographs*, 34. Early accounts sometimes referred to the Yanktonais as the Yanktons of the North, and there is some confusion over the names in this period. For a brief account of the tribe and their movements, see Hassrick, *The Sioux*, 29–30.

30. See Wimar sketchbook 61:41, Saint Louis Art Museum, 13 recto–18 recto. The "natural fort" in Wimar's drawing closely resembles a site named Tower Reach in the government maps made between 1878 and 1892. This feature is approximately eight miles below Fort Randall. Capotes were common among the Northern Plains tribes. These long hooded coats were often decorated with trade items, including bright cloth and beading. See Ronald P. Koch, *Dress Clothing of the Plains Indians* (Norman: University of Oklahoma Press, 1977), 82.

31. *Missouri River Maps*, sheet 38; Audubon and Coues, *Audubon and His Journals* 1: 514–15. The trip was also mentioned by Audubon's traveling companion Edward Harris; see John F. McDermott, ed., *Up the Missouri with Audubon: The Journal of Edward Harris* (Norman: University of Oklahoma Press, 1951), 96. Wimar's drawing, inscribed "G Bend," is in Wimar sketchbook 61: 41, Saint Louis Art Museum, 18 verso-19 recto. Prince Maximilian and Karl Bodmer made a similar jaunt; see Maximilian, "Travels," in Thwaites, *Early Western Travels* 22: 312–14. The distances of the bend doubtless changed with regularity, given the unpredictability of the river channel. One account published in the *Missouri Republican* on June 29, 1858, claimed the river distance as fifty miles, but this was exaggerated. Lieutenant Donelson, who surveyed the area for the Pacific Railroad Survey, noted that the river course flowed east, then northwest, then east, then southwest; the river distance was given as twenty-five miles, with only two and one-half miles across the neck. See Donelson, "Navigability of the Missouri," *Pacific Railroad Reports* 1: 240–41. Today the Great Bend has been adversely affected by Big Bend Dam, which was completed in 1967. Most of the historic sites, original riverbanks, islands and sandbars, and countless Indian sites for a ninety-mile stretch of the river to present-day Pierre, now lie underwater. Ray H. Mattison, who completed a survey of the bend before its banks were altered and inundated, described the distance as 22.0 miles around the loop and 1.6 miles across the neck. The distances reported by the river travelers of the nineteenth century vary widely; it seems likely that the bend would have closed itself somewhat by Mattison's time. See Ray H. Mattison, "Report on the Historic Sites in the Big Bend Reservoir Area, Missouri River, South Dakota," *South Dakota Historical Collections* 31 (1962): 243–86. Mattison gives an excellent map of the sites affected between pages 246 and 247; his brief account of the history of the Bend itself appears on page 252. See also Mattes, "Historic Sites in the Fort Randall Reservoir Area," 564–65.

32. For the best brief overview of Fort Pierre, see Ray H. Mattison, "Report on Historical Aspects of the Oahe Reservoir Area, Missouri River, South and North Dakota," *South Dakota Historical Collections* 27 (1954): 24–28. The account of General Harney's foray into Sioux territory in 1856 and the abandonment of the fort are detailed in Mattison, "Nebraska's Military Frontier," 164–65, and much more thoroughly in Wilson, "Old Fort Pierre and Its Neighbors," 285–91. Wilson also details the initial establishment of the fort, together with a description of the site by George Catlin, who visited there in May or June 1832 (270–75). Prince Maximilian's lengthy comment on the fort and its environs in 1833 can be found in his "Travels," in Thwaites, *Early Western Travels* 22: 315–29. Audubon mentions his stop in Audubon and Coues, *Audubon and His Journals* 1: 526–27. Rudolph Kurz described the fort in 1851 and made sketches there; see his *Journal*, 71, 175. Augustus Meyers, who arrived at Fort Pierre with the army troops in 1855, described the old stockade as being situated on high bottomland, with a commanding view of the river in either direction. "To the north, on the bank of the river, less than a half mile away, there was an Indian settlement of about twenty-five lodges," Meyers recalled. "It was there that the Indians who came to trade usually camped." Meyers, "Dakota in the Fifties," 132–33. The geographical area is shown in *Missouri River Maps*, sheet 40.

33. Rathbone, *Charles Wimar*, 20; Napton, *Over the Santa Fe Trail*, 85; Redfield, 1858 Report, 437; A. H. Redfield to Charles E. Mix, June 14, 1858, NAMP, M234, R885, F223–25. Both Wimar and the writer of the account in the *Missouri Republican* (July 11, 1858, 2) state that the council was held on the boat; Napton maintains that the assemblage was too large and the meeting was held on a flat plain on the shore.

34. Napton, *Over the Santa Fe Trail*, 80–81.

35. Boller, *Among the Indians*, 23–24. "The dogs, whose flesh is eaten by the Sioux, are equally valuable to the Indians. In shape they differ very little from the wolf, and are equally large and strong." Maximilian, "Travels," in Thwaites, *Early Western Travels* 22: 310.

36. Schmutterer, *Tomahawk and Cross*, 124. Thaddeus Culbertson, a visitor to Fort Pierre in 1850, stated that nearby were scaffolds of similar type, surmounted by trunks and boxes wrapped in blankets that contained the bones and belongings of the dead. See Thaddeus Culbertson, *Journal of an Expedition to the Mauvaises Terres and the Upper Missouri in 1850*, Smithsonian Institution, Bureau of American Ethnology, Bulletin No. 147 (Washington: U.S. Government Printing Office, 1952), 77. A few years later Augustus Meyers described them as having been made of forked sticks and poles that were set on high ground, adding that the burial sites were frequently plundered by white visitors. See Meyers, "Dakota in the Fifties," 144–45.

37. Rathbone, *Charles Wimar*, 20.

38. The drawings are in Wimar sketchbook 61:41, Saint Louis Art Museum, 22 verso–27 recto. The Moreau River, which entered the Missouri about 1300 miles above Saint Louis, was named for a French trader who was murdered by his Cheyenne wife. See *Missouri River Maps*, sheet 44. The origin of the name is described in Maximilian, "Travels," in Thwaites, *Early Western Travels* 22: 335. Thaddeus Culbertson described the river as "a small stream, although larger than most others here. The banks of the Missouri for some miles below are gently ascending hills with round tops, and they are covered with short grass, enough to give them a very pleasing appearance." See Culbertson, *Expedition to the Mauvaises Terres*, 89. Audubon termed it a "handsome stream"; see Audubon and Coues, *Audubon and His Journals* 1: 531. A description of the general area can also be found in the *Missouri Republican*, June 29, 1858, 2. Unfortunately, the site is now under the water of a modern reservoir. See Mattison, "Historical Aspects of the Oahe Reservoir Area," 78.

39. Rathbone, *Charles Wimar*, 21. The drawings are in Wimar sketchbook 61:41, Saint Louis Art Museum, 27 verso–29 recto.

40. Mattison, "Henry A. Boller, Fur Trader," 142; Boller, *Among the Indians*, 24–25; Redfield, 1858 Report, 437–38. Jacob Schmidt also left a vivid description of the scene: "How should I describe it? They came riding toward us as a front, these wild lords of the wild prairie on their courageous, mischievous horses, and holding quietly the shortened and filed gun in their hand. Untouched hangs the quiver with its arrows and bow on their backs. All shots were only for welcoming, a joyous greeting. And behold! In front of that array of wildly beautiful riders walked proudly and dignified in their stately regalia two Indian chieftains, only a few steps before their neighing horses. What a view!" Schmutterer, *Tomahawk and Cross*, 128. The peacefulness of Big Head's band is echoed by the author of the steamboat memorandum in the *Missouri Republican*, July 11, 1858, 2. William Napton recalled that "Big Head made a great speech, in which he gave some excuse for not attending the general council at Fort Pierre, claiming to be altogether peaceful and friendly, and anxious to accept the annuities from the great father at Washington. Big Head was a heavy built ugly Indian unlike most of his tribe, who were generally tall, well-proportioned, fine-looking fellows." *Over the Santa Fe Trail*, 88. Big Head made plenty of trouble for the Indian Agency in 1856, the year of General Harney's expedition. See

the *Missouri Republican*, August 9, 1856, 2, for a description of one meeting (where Two Bears, also drawn by Wimar, was present), and a full account in Chester L. Guthrie and Leo L. Gerald, "Upper Missouri Agency: An Account of the Indian Administration on the Frontier," *Pacific Historical Review* 10 (March 1941): 53–54.

41. Rathbone, *Charles Wimar*, 21–22; *Missouri River Maps*, sheet 51. For the sketches, see Wimar sketchbook 60:41, Saint Louis Art Museum, 1 recto–4 recto. Fort Clark had originally been built as a station for the Mandan, but by 1845 that tribe had moved upriver after being decimated by a smallpox epidemic. At that point the Arikara occupied the old Mandan village. By 1860 the Arikara also moved upriver, and the post was abandoned and dismantled. It is now a North Dakota State Historic Site. In the 1950s, slight mounds and hollows marking the outline of the old stockade were still visible, as were circular depressions of the old earth lodges. See Ray H. Mattison, "Report on Historic Sites in the Garrison Reservoir Area, Missouri River," *North Dakota History* 22 (1955): 17–18. Fort Clark was described by many travelers prior to Charles Wimar. See Prince Maximilian, "Travels," in Thwaites, *Early Western Travels* 22: 344–55, 23: 232–37; Audubon and Coues, *Audubon and His Journals* 2: 10–15; Culbertson, *Expedition to the Mauvaises Terres*, 95–99; and Kurz, *Journal*, 72–73. A traveler in 1862 described the abandoned site; see "Diary of James Harkness, of the Firm Labarge, Harkness and Company," *Contributions of the Historical Society of Montana* 2 (1896): 346. For a good overview of the Arikara, see Edwin Thompson Denig, *Five Indian Tribes of the Upper Missouri*, ed. John C. Ewers (Norman: University of Oklahoma Press, 1961), 41–62.

42. Redfield, 1858 Report, 438. See also Redfield to Charles E. Mix, June 21, 1858, NAMP, M234, R885, F226–27. Alfred J. Vaughan, Indian Agent for 1856, reported that the Arikara gathered 4000 bushels of corn. The previous year, due to a frost on the 15th of August, they only produced one-third that amount. In 1857, A. H. Redfield found a large encampment of Sioux near the Arikara village, there for trading purposes. He noted that "the Sioux were very independent and asserted that all they wanted was to have access to traders and wanted neither annuities or soldiers." See Robinson, "Digest of Indian Commissioner Reports," 203, 212. Lieutenant Rufus Saxton described the Sioux practice of burning the prairies in *Pacific Railroad Reports* 1: 265.

43. *Missouri Republican*, July 11, 1858, 2. In a letter written to his superiors on February 3, 1858, Redfield had urged that U.S. Army troops be stationed at Forts Pierre, Berthold, and Clark to protect the sedentary tribes from the warlike Sioux. See NAMP, M234, R885, F187. The incidents are also recorded in a letter from Henry Boller to his parents dated Saturday, June 19. See Mattison, "Henry A. Boller, Fur Trader," 143–44.

44. Rathbone, *Charles Wimar*, 22. The drawings are in Wimar sketchbook 60:41, Saint Louis Art Museum, 4 verso–6 recto. A good contemporary description of The White Parflesh can be found in Boller, *Among the Indians*, 30, 351. One unfinished painting attributed to Wimar and now in the Gilcrease Museum is an oval portrait identified as a Mandan

173

man (0126.1595). It appears to have been copied from a photograph; the intensity of the subject's expression seems related to the qualities of the latter.

45. Ferdinand Hayden, who visited Fort Clark several times in the 1850s, described the appearance of these structures as being "built up by planting four posts in the ground in the form of a square, the posts being forked at the top to receive transverse beams. To the beams other timbers are attached, the lower extremities of which describe a circle, or nearly so, the interstices being filled with small twigs, the whole thickly overlaid with willows, rushes, and grass, and plastered over with mud, laid on very thick. A hole is left in the top for the smoke to pass out, and another in the side for the door." Hayden, *Contributions*, 352. See also Culbertson, *Expedition to the Mauvaises Terres*, 97. Prince Maximilian gave a rather thorough description of the Mandan lodge when that tribe was at the peak of its development; see Maximilian, "Travels," in Thwaites, *Early Western Travels* 23: 269–73.

46. Rathbone, *Charles Wimar*, 22. For the unsanitary conditions that year, see Boller, *Among the Indians*, 28–29. Fifteen years earlier John James Audubon had been appalled by the filth and disease he saw around him at Fort Clark, and he described it in lurid detail. See Audubon and Coues, *Audubon and His Journals* 2: 10–16.

47. For good contemporary descriptions of the Mauvaises Terres, see Audubon and Coues, *Audubon and His Journals* 2: 148–52, and Culbertson, *Expedition to the Mauvaises Terres*, 139–45.

48. Boller, *Among the Indians*, 75, 78; *Missouri River Maps*, sheet 53. Boller sketched a plan of Fort Atkinson and gave a detailed description of its layout in his journal; see Mattison, "Henry A. Boller, Fur Trader," 156–58. The site of Fort Berthold, Fort Atkinson, and Like-a-Fishhook village is now under the water of the Garrison Dam reservoir, a casualty of progress. Fort Atkinson was named after Edward G. Atkinson, a local representative of Frost, Todd and Company. The whole area underwent many changes after Wimar's visits in the late 1850s. In 1862 the Arikara moved up to the vicinity of Like-a-Fishhook village, and Fort Clark was subsequently abandoned. The three tribes—Arikara, Hidatsa, and Mandan—became the Affiliated Tribes, which exist to the present day. The same year that the Arikara arrived, the American Fur Company gained possession of Fort Atkinson, abandoned the older Fort Berthold, and gave that name to the newer fort. This second Fort Berthold was almost entirely destroyed by fire in 1874, at the beginning of the final Sioux uprising. For a good overview of these tangled affairs, see Mattison, "Historic Sites in the Garrison Reservoir Area," 8, 33–38. Alexander Culbertson visited Fort Berthold in 1851 and noted that the Indians practiced agriculture there as they did at Fort Clark. See his comments on the tribes in *Expedition to the Mauvaises Terres*, 99–101. Rudolph Kurz spent some time at Fort Berthold in 1851; see the *Journal*, 73–77. Lieutenant Donelson described the area surrounding Fort Berthold in 1853; see the *Pacific Railroad Reports* 1: 243. For other accounts of this area, including a history of the absorption of Indian culture to the present day, see Mattes, "*Under* the Wide Missouri," 162–63. More helpful information can be found in Wilson, "Old Fort Pierre and Its Neighbors,"

359–61. For a thorough report on archaeological excavations made in the area, see G. Hubert Smith, *Like-A-Fishhook Village and Fort Berthold, Garrison Reservoir, North Dakota* (Washington, D.C.: National Park Service, United States Department of the Interior, 1972).

49. Redfield, 1858 Report, 438–39. See also the *Missouri Republican*, July 11, 1858, 2. Redfield's letters to his superiors reveal an increasing sense of frustration with the unchecked power of the fur companies. "The rivalry between the Fur Companies is very *sharp* and *bitter* and has I *know* a very unfavorable effect upon the Indians. The influence and example and conduct of the half breeds and other employees of these companies is also most pernicious—Liquor is being introduced into the country by half breeds from Red River and *secretly* I think by *other* parties. To detect or arrest these abusers the Agent has but little opportunity or power and I wish the *trade* was stopped *entirely* and *every half breed and white man expelled* from the country except the Indian Agents." Redfield to Charles E. Mix, June 21, 1858, NAMP, M234, R885, F226–28. A visitor to the area in 1856 did not observe the same level of desperation; see the *Missouri Republican*, June 29, 1858, 2. The Gros Ventres of the Missouri (Hidatsa) were distinguished in this period from the Gros Ventres of the Prairie (Atsinas), an Algonquian-speaking tribe who lived farther west. See the excellent explanation of this in Moulton, *Journals of the Lewis and Clark Expedition* 3: 206–7. For a recent overview of this tribe, see Loretta Fowler, *Shared Symbols, Contested Meanings: Gros Ventre Culture and History, 1778–1984* (Ithaca and London: Cornell University Press, 1987). Earth lodges of the type depicted in Wimar's drawing are reproduced in O.G. Libby, "Typical Villages of the Mandans, Arikara, and Hidatsa in the Missouri Valley, North Dakota," *Collections of the State Historical Society of North Dakota* 2 (1908): f.p. 498. A more complete study may be found in Gilbert L. Wilson, *The Hidatsa Earthlodge* (New York: The American Museum of Natural History, Anthropological Papers 33, 5, 1934).

50. Rathbone, *Charles Wimar*, 22–23. Rudolph Kurz, the young Swiss artist who had preceded Wimar to the area seven years earlier, found similar problems when he too was inspired to sketch the "picturesque" Indians. He had been surprised to find that they regarded painting and drawing as "bad medicine," writing in his journal that "they look with dread upon an artist as the forerunner of pestilence and death." Under the circumstances, Wimar was fortunate to have avoided an ugly incident. See Kurz, *Journal*, 76.

51. Boller, *Among the Indians*, 35–38; Schmutterer, *Tomahawk and Cross*, 133; *Missouri River Maps*, sheets 54, 60. The *Twilight* passed the mouth of the Little Missouri River on June 21. Wimar made a quick sketch of the area with the inscription, "Little Missouri Blak[sic] Hills"; see Wimar sketchbook 60:41, Saint Louis Art Museum, 9 recto. Meriwether Lewis was the first white explorer to describe this area, writing in his journal on April 12, 1805, that the Little Missouri flowed through broken country to a point southwest of the Black Hills, adding that "the colour of the water, the bed of the river, and its appearance in every respect" resembled the greater Missouri. See Moulton, *Journals of the Lewis and Clark Expedition* 4: 26. Today, the mouth of the Little Missouri is inundated by the reservoir of Garrison Dam. See Mattison,

"Historic Sites of the Garrison Reservoir Area," 43. For other descriptions of this area, see Maximilian, "Travels," in Thwaites, *Early Western Travels* 22: 367; Audubon and Coues, *Audubon and His Journals* 2: 20–21; and the *Missouri Republican*, June 29, 1858, 2. A report in the *Missouri Republican* (July 11, 1858, 2) noted that the boat arrived at Fort William thirty-one days and two hours out of Saint Louis, "which, considering the state of the river, was an extraordinary[ly] quick trip." Gary Moulton notes: "The Assiniboines called themselves *Nak'ota* and spoke a dialect of the Sioux language. Although closely related, the two groups maintained distinct identities from their first mention by whites in 1640. By the time of Lewis and Clark the Assiniboines, like the Sioux, were nomadic buffalo hunters, ranging north of the Missouri on both sides of the present United States-Canadian border, in northeastern Montana, northwest North Dakota, and northern Saskatchewan. Their linguistic relationship with the Sioux did not preclude hostilities between the two." *Journals of the Lewis and Clark Expedition* 3: 230.

52. These events are summarized in Boller, *Among the Indians*, 39–40; Schmutterer, *Tomahawk and Cross*, 134; and in the *Missouri Republican*, July 11, 1858, 2. See also the *Missouri River Maps*, sheet 60. For Wimar's drawings, see sketchbook 60: 41, Saint Louis Art Museum, 9 verso–12 recto. Fort William was the first opposition post on the upper Missouri. Later a military post, Fort Buford, was erected nearby, and the area is now the Fort Buford Historic Site, maintained by the State of North Dakota. For a thorough description of Fort William at its beginning, see Charles Larpenteur, *Forty Years a Fur Trader*, ed. Elliott Coues (Minneapolis: Ross and Haines, Inc., 1962), 51–53. For an overview of its history, see Wilson, "Old Fort Pierre and Its Neighbors," 354–55, and Mattison, "Historic Sites in the Garrison Reservoir Area," 63–65.

53. For descriptions of the confluence of the Yellowstone and Missouri Rivers, see Moulton, *Journals of the Lewis and Clark Expedition* 4: 66–71; Maximilian, "Travels," in Thwaites, *Early Western Travels* 22: 373; Audubon and Coues, *Audubon and His Journals* 2: 28; Lieutenant Donelson in the *Pacific Railroad Reports* 1: 243–44; Boller, *Among the Indians*, 40; and the *Missouri Republican*, August 9, 1856, 2, and June 29, 1858, 2.

54. For a detailed description of Fort Union, see Edwin Thompson Denig, "Description of Fort Union," in Audubon and Coues, *Audubon and His Journals* 2: 187. Denig wrote his description of the fort at Audubon's request on July 30, 1843, and it still remains the most important eyewitness source. Another valuable account of the fort at the beginning of its illustrious history can be found in Maximilian, "Travels," in Thwaites, *Early Western Travels* 22: 376–93. Among the more notable visitors in the middle 1850s was a group of "St. Louis ladies" who arrived on the steamboat *Spread Eagle*, claiming to be "the first white women who had ever ascended the Missouri River to this point." See the account in the *Missouri Republican*, August 9, 1856, 2. Fort Union declined rapidly as a trading post after Wimar visited there in the late 1850s. It was briefly occupied by military troops in 1864–65, then abandoned two years later in favor of the new military post, Fort Buford, at the site of old Fort William a few miles downriver. At that point, most of the salvageable buildings at Fort Union were pulled down and used at the new fort.

Today a replica maintained by the National Park Service stands where old Fort Union once stood, and the Missouri River flows by at a greater distance from the old channel. Charles Larpenteur, who entered Fort Union as a clerk with the fur company and afterwards took charge of the whole operation, has chronicled its history, including its rise and fall, in *Forty Years a Fur Trader*. See also Mattison, "Historic Sites in the Garrison Reservoir Area," 65–69, and Erwin N. Thompson, *Fort Union Trading Post: Fur Trade Empire on the Upper Missouri* (Medora, N.D.: Theodore Roosevelt Nature and History Association, 1986).

55. Boller, *Among the Indians*, 40–45. Wimar's drawing is in Wimar sketchbook 60: 41, Saint Louis Art Museum, 14 recto. John Mix Stanley also sketched this area in 1853; see Stevens, *Pacific Railroad Reports* 12, Part 1, 89. Fort Stuart was named in honor of Colonel A. D. Steuart, "late paymaster of the United States Army"; see the *Missouri Republican*, July 11, 1858, 2. The precise location of Fort Stuart seems uncertain, although most of the commentators list it as being somewhere near the mouth of the Poplar River, which would be about eighty miles upriver from Fort Union, a distance verified by Wimar and Boller. Eight miles below Poplar River was a site named Elk-Horn Prairie, "an elevated plain extending five miles along the river, and gradually rising towards the high hills eight or ten miles distant," as it was described in the *Missouri Republican* on June 29, 1858, 2. However, Charles Larpenteur's account differs from Boller in terms of location. Larpenteur states that in 1859 he was put in charge of Fort Stuart, which was in run-down condition and had been relinquished by Frost, Todd and Company. He gave the location as thirty-five channel miles from Fort Union. Larpenteur later vacated this site for a new one upriver near the mouth of Poplar River. Since Boller and Larpenteur were partners at the time the fort was relocated, it seems possible that the former, writing his account many years later, confused the old site with the new one. However, this does not explain why Wimar claimed a distance of eighty miles in his account; it will be recalled that Wimar's drawing, cited above, shows a site forty miles above the Yellowstone, near the mouth of Big Muddy Creek. If this were indeed the site of the new fort, then it agrees with Larpenteur's account. See Larpenteur, *Forty Years a Fur Trader*, 306–9, 318–21, and editor Thwaites' note in Boller, *Among the Indians*, 42–43. In 1858 the *Twilight* was preceded up this stretch of the river by the *Spread Eagle*, which navigated as far as it could until halted by shallow water at a point fifty miles below the mouth of the Milk River, where it deposited goods for the American Fur Company to be freighted overland to Fort Benton. The account of this voyage is given in the *Missouri Republican*, June 29, 1858, 2. The *Twilight* met its end in September 1865, when it sank one-half mile above Napoleon, Missouri. See Charles N. Kessler to Charles Reymershoffer, June 20, 1919 (Reymershoffer Papers, Missouri Historical Society).

56. For a history of the Assiniboine, see Denig, *Five Indian Tribes*, 63–98, and Hayden, *Contributions*, 379–89.

57. Schmutterer, *Tomahawk and Cross*, 139. See Wimar sketchbook 60: 41, Saint Louis Art Museum, 13 recto–20 verso. Boller's account of his visit to Broken Arm's camp in September 1858 includes mention of the dogs that customarily accompanied the Assiniboine, as well as the

activity of the women dressing buffalo hides and meat, which were subsequently exchanged with the whites for trade goods. See *Among the Indians*, 125–44. John Mix Stanley, who visited a Piegan camp a few years earlier, noted that the travoised dogs could travel "twenty miles a day, dragging forty pounds." See his comments in the *Pacific Railroad Reports* 1: 448. Maximilian gives a good description of the appearance and dress of the Assiniboine in his "Travels," in Thwaites, *Early Western Travels* 22: 388–93. When Isaac Stevens and John Mix Stanley visited the Assiniboine at Fort Union in 1853, they also mentioned the large number of dogs. See the *Pacific Railroad Reports* 12: 73. Hayden remarked on the dogs as beasts of burden and described Assiniboine camp life in his *Contributions*, 386–89. For an excellent description of the dog travois of the Gros Ventres, see Gilbert L. Wilson, "The Horse and the Dog in Hidatsa Culture," *Anthropological Papers of the American Museum of Natural History* 15, Part II (New York: American Museum Press, 1924), 281–85. Audubon's note on the tree burial is in Audubon and Coues, *Audubon and His Journals* 2: 38. Descriptions of the rude hunting lodges appear in many sources, beginning with Lewis and Clark; see Moulton, *Journals of the Lewis and Clark Expedition* 4: 108–9. Maximilian wrote of them as protective bulwarks for war parties; see his "Travels," in Thwaites, *Early Western Travels* 23: 42–43.

58. Schmutterer, *Tomahawk and Cross*, 142–45. For information on Alexander Culbertson, see Jack Holterman, *King of the High Missouri: The Saga of the Culbertsons* (Helena and Billings, Mont.: Falcon Press Publishing Company, 1987).

59. Schmutterer, *Tomahawk and Cross*, 148. Meldrum, the son of a Presbyterian circuit rider, had intermarried with the Crows. Known to them as "Round Iron," he was an expert on their language and customs. See Sunder, *The Fur Trade on the Upper Missouri*, 126.

60. *Missouri Republican*, October 29, 1858, 2.

61. Rathbone, *Charles Wimar*, 23; Redfield, 1858 Report, 440; Schmutterer, *Tomahawk and Cross*, 151. Wimar's sketches of the whole Yellowstone trip are contained in Wimar sketchbook 60: 41, Saint Louis Art Museum, 21 recto–38 verso. A copy of the "Articles of Agreement" between Redfield and Alexander Culbertson for transport of the goods up the Yellowstone, dated June 26, 1858, is reproduced in NAMP, M234, R885, F239–40. From the Missouri, the Yellowstone travels through an elevated plain in valleys that vary from hundreds of yards to over a mile in width. These are bordered by steep bluffs of rock and clay, which appear in Wimar's sketches. In 1858, there was much timber, even dwarf pine and fir on the bluffs. Grass was plentiful, as was game. Normally the Yellowstone's waters began to rise in April, peaking in June. It seems that the runoff was later than usual in 1858, adding to the difficulties that Redfield and his party encountered. Today the land alongside the river has been much changed by agriculture, but happily, the river itself remains the last major free-flowing waterway in the nation. Contemporary descriptions of the Yellowstone and its environs were given by Ferdinand Hayden, who accompanied an exploratory expedition of the Yellowstone under Captain W. F. Raynolds in 1859; see his *Geological Report of the Exploration of the Yellowstone and Missouri Rivers* (Washington: Government Printing Office, 1869), 6–7, 58–59. Captain Raynolds gave his own summation in his report titled "Exploration of the Yellowstone," 40th Cong., 1st sess., *Senate Executive Document No. 77* (1867), 8–9. Hiram Chittenden described the mackinaw boat as a flat-bottomed boat, sometimes as long as fifty feet with a twelve-foot beam, with a large rudder. The cargo was placed in the center of the craft and wrapped securely. Wimar's drawings of the mackinaw agree with these features. These boats were likely manufactured at the chantier (French for boatyard) of Fort Union, which was located twenty-five miles upriver. See Chittenden, *Early Steamboat Navigation on the Missouri River*, 94–95.

62. Schmutterer, *Tomahawk and Cross*, 152–53; Rathbone, "Charles Wimar," 23–24.

63. For the three pages of buffalo drawings, see Wimar sketchbook 60: 41, Saint Louis Art Museum, 22 recto, 31 verso–32 recto. Two elk studies are on 26 verso, 27 recto. The drawing of the dead bear measures 5 x 7 1/4 inches and is in a private collection; it may have been part of a sketchbook. Wimar's comments are cited in Rathbone, *Charles Wimar*, 23–24. Schmidt's account of Wimar's hunting accident is in "Jahrt des Missionars Schmidt auf dem Yellow-Stone River," *Missionblatt*, No. 11 (June 1, 1859), 1. The author is indebted to Dr. David Miller of Cameron University for the translation, and to Joel L. Samuels, Director of the ReuMemorial Library at the Wartburg Theological Seminary in Dubuque, Iowa, for his assistance with the pertinent issues of the *Missionblatt* which contain excerpts of Schmidt's journal. Alexander Redfield reported that "we found game very abundant along the river, especially buffalo, elk, deer, antelope, etc. Over fifty buffalo and many other animals, including two grizzly bears, were killed by our party on the trip." 1858 Report, 441. In 1851, Rudolph Kurz had been able to make studies of the buffalo in the Yellowstone country in similar fashion. After one of the animals was felled, Kurz made "exact drawings as I could, showing different views of the fallen bison." Kurz, *Journal*, 140. It is interesting to trace the decreasing range of the buffalo herds in the 1850s; it is apparent that their vast numbers were dwindling long before the buffalo hunters began to take their destructive toll. John James Audubon and his traveling companion, Edward Harris, witnessed "very great numbers" below Fort Pierre; see Harris' comments in *Up the Missouri With Audubon*, 85. On the other hand, Ferdinand Hayden, who accompanied Lieutenant G. K. Warren's exploratory expedition through the Dakota country twelve years later, flatly stated that "many of them are fast passing away, and in a few years those upon which the Indian is now dependent will become extinct." Hayden, "Exploration," 78–79.

64. Schmutterer, *Tomahawk and Cross*, 153–55.

65. Redfield, 1858 Report, 441; "Jahrt des Missionars Schmidt," 43–44.

66. "Jahrt des Missionars Schmidt," 43–44. The author is once again indebted to David H. Miller of Cameron University for the translation of this passage.

67. Mattison, "Henry A. Boller, Fur Trader," 146.

68. Schmutterer, *Tomahawk and Cross*, 158–59; Redfield, 1858 Report, 476–77; Rathbone, *Charles Wimar*, 24; Wagner, "Lutheran Zealots," 7; Raynolds, "Exploration of the Yellowstone," 146. Wimar and his fellow travelers were certainly not the first to have their ideal images soiled by reality. John James Audubon continually complained about the "false" impressions he had received from Catlin's account of the Indians on the upper Missouri. See Audubon and Coues, *Audubon and His Journals* 1: 27. Eight years later, Rudolf Kurz also condemned Catlin's "Yankee humbug," although he admitted that "with the exception of several instances where the author talks big, the book contains a great deal that is true." See Kurz, *Journal*, 130. For the drawings, see Wimar sketchbook 60 : 41, Saint Louis Art Museum, 28 recto–38 verso. A description of Fort Sarpy was recorded by Captain W. F. Raynolds during his sojourn to the Yellowstone region in 1859: "We found the trading-house situated in the timber on what during high water would be an island, a channel, now dry, passing to the south of it. The 'fort' is an enclosure about 100 feet square, of upright cottonwood logs 15 feet high, the outer wall also forming the exterior of a row of log cabins which are occupied as dwelling houses, store houses, shops and stables. The roofs of these structures are nearly flat, and formed of timber covered to the depth of about a foot with dirt. . . . No flanking arrangements whatever exist, and the 'fort' is thus a decidedly primitive affair." Raynolds, "Exploration of the Yellowstone," 50. Further comments on Fort Sarpy may be found in Lieutenant James H. Bradley, "Affairs at Fort Benton, from 1831 to 1869," *Contributions of the Historical Society of Montana* 3 (1900): 261, and Wilson, "Old Fort Pierre and Its Neighbors," 363. In 1859 Ferdinand Hayden estimated the Crow Nation to number 450 lodges. "The country usually inhabited by the Crows, is in and near the Rocky Mountains, along the sources of the Powder, Wind, and Big Horn rivers, on the south side of the Yellowstone, as far as Laramie Fork on the River Platte. They are also found on the west and north side of that river, as far as the source of the Mussel-shell, and as low down as the mouth of the Yellowstone. That portion of their country lying east of the mountains, is perhaps the best game country in the world. From the base of the mountains to the mouth of the Yellowstone, buffalo are always to be found in immense herds." *Contributions*, 392.

69. Rathbone, *Charles Wimar*, 24; Redfield to A. M. Robinson, September 30, 1858, NAMP, M234, R885, F230.

70. *Missouri Republican*, October 24, 1858, 2.

71. "Domestic Art Gossip," *Crayon* 5 (December 1858): 353–54.

72. The Indian artifacts in the Missouri Historical Society bear the following accession numbers: the buckskin quiver, bow, and arrows, 1918.29.1; the pipe bag, 66.2245; and the beaded bandolier 66.1989. Another object, a fire bag (66.1975), seems later in the century, and it is doubtful that Wimar collected it. The author would like to thank Magdalyn Sebastian, Registrar at the Missouri Historical Society, for her valuable assistance with information and photographs. Jonathan Batkin, Director of the Wheelwright Museum in Sante Fe, generously assisted in the identification of the objects. A typescript of the probate inventory of the artist's estate, which bears the reference number 6292, is in the John Francis McDermott papers in the library of Southern Illinois University at Edwardsville. Additional items in the inventory included four oil paintings in various sizes, an "assortment of sketches in crayons," twenty-seven small "pictures in frames," an assortment of "small sketches," eighty-one "pieces in an unfinished condition," and a group of forty-seven "small lithographs and engravings (all damaged)." Wimar's location was listed as 123 North 18th Street in 1859; see the *St. Louis Directory—1859* (Saint Louis: R.V. Kennedy and Co., 1859), 514. In 1860, his address was given as 291/293 Carr Street; see the *St. Louis Directory* (Saint Louis: R.V. Kennedy and Co., 1860), 551.

73. For an overview of the objects exhibited in the Art Hall of the Agricultural and Mechanical Fair, see the *Missouri Republican*, September 7, 1858, 2. Brownlee had exhibited two paintings by the artist at the fair the previous year, one of which was identified as an abduction of Daniel Boone's daughter by Indians. See the *Missouri Republican*, September 30, 1857, 2. The experiences of Schmidt and Braeuninger make fascinating reading. Unfortunately, their hopes for a permanent mission never materialized; the following year Schmidt was felled by illness, and Braeuninger disappeared on the Powder River, presumably killed by the Sioux. However, later Lutheran missionary efforts were successful. See Wagner, "Lutheran Zealots," 11–19.

74. Charles Wimar to August Becker, February 3, 1859, and March 14, 1859, Gilcrease Institute of American History and Art, 3826.2840, 3826.2835.

75. *Missouri Republican*, May 8, 1859, 2; May 20, 1859, 2. For the development of Omaha and Nebraska City in this period, see Graebner, "Nebraska's Missouri River Frontier," 223–26.

76. See the *Missouri Republican*, August 22, 1859, 2, and "Journal of Dr. Elias J. Marsh," *South Dakota Historical Review* 1 (January 1936): 82. See also the *Missouri Republican*, July 26, 1859, 2, and Sunder, *Fur Trade on the Upper Missouri*, 175–76, 202–3. The Academy of Science of Saint Louis was organized March 10, 1856, and incorporated January 17, 1857. The Academy was initially housed in rooms at the Saint Louis Medical College. Within a few years the Academy boasted a substantial collection of books and specimens; some of the latter were collected by Charles Chouteau and others on the upper Missouri. Unfortunately, the library and museum of the Academy were almost totally destroyed by fire in May 1869. For a brief history of the institution, see J. Thomas Scharf, *History of Saint Louis City and County. . .* (Philadelphia: Louis H. Everts and Co., 1883), 1: 899–900, and a more recent study by John R. Hensley, "Transacting Science on the Border of Civilization: The Academy of Science of St. Louis, 1856–1881," *Gateway Heritage* 7 (Winter 1986–87): 18–25. The roster of Captain Raynolds' party included a number of specialists, including some other artists. Besides Hayden and Piersall, there was J. D. Hutton, topographer and photographer; J. H. Snowden, topographer; H. C. Fillebrown, meteorologist and assistant astronomer; Anton Schonborn, artist; and Dr. M. C. Hines, surgeon and assistant naturalist. See Raynolds, "Exploration of the Yellowstone," 18. A brief autobiographical account of Raynolds' life, dated October 20, 1858, is reproduced in NAMP, M234, R506, F228–34.

77. "Journal of Dr. Elias J. Marsh," 83–85. Jim Bridger (1804–1881) is widely regarded as one of the most accomplished scouts of the period. For a study of his life, see J. Cecil Alter, *Jim Bridger* (Norman: University of Oklahoma Press, 1962). Zephyr (or Xavier) Recontre (dates unknown) was a prominent interpreter in the Dakotas in this period, frequently employed by the government. He was Agent Redfield's interpreter for the 1858 trip. According to a note by the unnamed editor of Dr. Marsh's journal, Recontre always began his translations with the phrase, "He says, says he, that he says."

78. The principal hilltop of the Blackbird Hills was known as the burial place of the Omaha chief, Washinga-Sahba, who "was buried, sitting upright on a live mule. . . . When dying, he gave orders that they should bury him on that hill, with his face turned toward the country of the white man." Maximilian, "Travels," in Thwaites, *Early Western Travels* 22: 277; "Journal of Dr. Elias J. Marsh," 86–87; *Missouri River Maps*, sheet 26. Wimar's charcoal drawing of this site, in fragmentary condition, is in the Saint Louis Art Museum (60:47). George Catlin left a lengthy account of Blackbird in his *Letters and Notes* 2: 5–7. Blackbird's grave was noted by Lewis and Clark and Audubon as well; their accounts are printed in Audubon and Coues, *Audubon and His Journals* 1: 485–86. An account written aboard the *Spread Eagle* during the 1858 trip states: "Between this [Omaha] and Sioux City we pass a beautiful series of bluffs, known as Blackbird Hills, on the highest and most prominent peak of which, Blackbird, a noted, bold, tyrannical and very exacting Indian Chief, was buried on horseback, his horse still living. The mound or grave can still be seen at a long distance." *Missouri Republican*, June 29, 1858, 2. On the same voyage, Henry Boller observed in a letter to his parents: "Passed the grave of the celebrated chief Blackbird. The picture of Catlin's is like it, the scenery more wild and beautiful every mile." Mattison, "Henry A. Boller, Fur Trader," 129. The geographical appearance of the area from the mouth of the Platte River to the Blackbird Hills is described by Lieutenant Donelson in the *Pacific Railroad Reports* 1: 235–38. It is interesting to note that within forty years after Wimar's trip, the Missouri River in this area had shifted course as much as several miles from the channels that had existed prior to the Civil War. A map illustrating these changes in the area around the Blackbird Hills is reproduced in Chittenden, *Early Steamboat Navigation on the Missouri* 1: f.p. 79. Today, according to one historian, the site of Blackbird's grave is "covered with dense timber and brush, and neither the Missouri River nor the valley can be seen from the crest. The place is unmarked on modern maps, it is unnoted on highway signs, and even persons living within a mile know nothing of its history or the origin of its name." Roy E. Appleman, "Lewis and Clark: The Route 160 Years After," *Pacific Northwest Quarterly* 57 (January 1966): 8–9.

79. "Journal of Dr. Elias J. Marsh," 88. Apparently the mouth of the Vermillion River has shifted to the south since Wimar's time. The formations in this area include Niobrara chalk stained with iron oxides, which sometimes weathers to a bluish-gray, as well as Pierre shale, "the youngest Cretaceous unit in the region . . . a dark gray to black marine shale which makes up the bedrock on the valley walls of the Missouri River." Moulton, *Journals of the Lewis and Clark Expedition* 2: 503, 507; 3: 39, 48. Other descriptions of this area are given by Lieutenant

Donelson in the *Pacific Railroad Reports* 1: 239, and by Ferdinand Hayden in Lieutenant G. K. Warren, *Explorations in the Dacota Country, in the Year 1855* (Washington: A. O. P. Nicholson, Senate Printer, 1856), 10.

80. Smutty Bear, whom Wimar had sketched and possibly photographed the previous year, made a favorable impression on Dr. Marsh. "The chief was rather aged, but was fine-looking and evidently superior both physically and mentally to all his warriors. He had a deep-toned voice and spoke freely with a good deal of gesticulation. One of the gentlemen afterward took his photograph, with which he was much pleased, and requested to have one taken for himself." See "Journal of Dr. Elias J. Marsh," 89–90.

81. See the *Missouri River Maps*, sheet 34. Today this entire stretch of the river, from the upper Cedar Islands down beyond the mouth of Scalp Creek, is inundated by the waters of Fort Randall Dam. The Wimar drawings for this phase of the trip are *Natural Fort 15 Miles Below Fort Randel [sic]*, Missouri Historical Society (1950.116.2.17); *Two Studies* (which includes the inscription, "Above Fort Randle[sic])," Saint Louis Art Museum (78:47); *Western Landscape and Study of the Mouth of Scalp Creek*, Saint Louis Art Museum (73:47); and *Two Studies of Cedar Island*, Saint Louis Art Museum (66:47). For the stopover at Fort Randall, see the "Journal of Dr. Elias J. Marsh," 90, and Raynolds, "Exploration of the Yellowstone," 19. The Scalp Creek area is described by Hayden in Warren, *Exploration of the Dacota Country*, 70, as well as in Mattes, "Historic Sites in the Fort Randall Reservoir Area," 492–93. The cedar islands were described in some detail by Maximilian; see his "Travels," in Thwaites, *Early Western Travels* 22: 292–97. Lieutenant Donelson provides another description of one of them, adding that it also contained ripe wild strawberries in abundance. See the *Pacific Railroad Reports* 1: 240. Hayden related that the islands "have an area of several hundred acres, and are covered with a dense growth, so crowded that the largest trees are not more than two feet in diameter. A large quantity of fine timber might be selected from these islands with an advantage to the remainder. They are also the resort of myriads of birds and larger animals, which gather to these places to rear their young undisturbed." Hayden in Warren, *Exploration of the Dacota Country*, 70. William B. Napton, who had gone upriver with Wimar in 1858, stated that the trees grew so straight and knot-free that they were used for a variety of things at the trading posts; see *Over the Santa Fe Trail*, 89. For accounts of the inundation of this stretch of the river and the best explication of the various cedar islands, see Mattes, "Historic Sites in the Fort Randall Reservoir Area," 491–92, 502–3, 528.

82. "Journal of Dr. Elias J. Marsh," 90–93; Audubon and Coues, *Audubon and His Journals* 1: 513–18. Audubon was accompanied by his assistant, Isaac Sprague, who produced at least two watercolors of their trip across the neck of the Great Bend, one of which is a view from a vantage point nearly identical to that of Wimar. These are reproduced in McDermott, ed., *Up the Missouri with Audubon*, f.p. 96. George Catlin wrote: "Scarcely anything in nature can be found, I am sure, more exceedingly picturesque than the view from this place." *Letters and Notes* 1: 74. Maximilian also ascended the steep hills at this point to gain a similar view. See his "Travels," in Thwaites, *Early Western Travels* 22:

312–13. Today most of the area along the original channel lies under the waters backed up by Big Bend Dam. See Mattison, "Historic Sites in the Big Bend Reservoir Area," 252. See also Mattes, "Historic Sites in the Fort Randall Reservoir Area," 564–66.

83. One of the eyewitnesses to this stormy encounter was not optimistic, noting that the chiefs "were not willing to be held responsible for the acts of their young men, or of any stray war parties, which might commit depredations upon the exploring party. My impression is, that the Indians have already commenced a series of annoyances which will end in open war with them." *Missouri Republican*, July 26, 1859, 2; "Journal of Dr. Elias J. Marsh," 93–94; Raynolds, "Exploration of the Yellowstone," 19–21. According to the newspaper account, one of the "annoyances" caused by the Indians was that "the prairie for some three hundred miles above Fort Pierre was on fire, or had lately been burned off as we came down. The old traders are of the opinion that this has been the act of the Indians, and that they have burned every particle of vegetation from Fort Pierre to the Black Hills." Captain Raynolds' account of the council included an eloquent passage attributed to Bear Rib: "When I get land it is all in one piece, and we were born and still live on it. . . . If the white people want my land, and I should give it to them, where should I stay? . . . . My brother, look at me; you do not find me poor, but when this ground is gone then I will be poor indeed. . . . If you were to ask me for a piece of this land I would not give it."

84. Philippe Régis Denis de Keredern de Trobriand, *Army Life in Dakota* (Chicago: The Lakeside Press, R.R. Donnelly and Sons Company, 1941), 118. De Trobriand's is the best account of Bear Rib's devotion to the white cause and his eventual murder in 1862 by members of his own tribe; see 118–23. Wimar's pages with population figures are from the 1859 sketchbook in the Missouri Historical Society (1918.52.2.32–33).

85. "Journal of Dr. Elias J. Marsh," 95. The sketch of the burial wigwam is from the 1859 sketchbook at the Missouri Historical Society (1918.52.2.31). While at Fort Pierre, the *Spread Eagle* and *Chippewa* were overtaken by the steamer *Florence,* in the service of the opposition fur company. Aboard that steamer was Henry Boller, who had journeyed upriver on the *Twilight* the previous year. The *Florence* forged ahead to reach the mouth of the Yellowstone in twenty-three days, a record time. See the *Missouri Republican*, July 17, 1859, 2.

86. "Journal of Dr. Elias J. Marsh," 96; *Missouri River Maps*, sheet 48. The exact location of Medicine Creek is uncertain. Mattison, in his "Report on Historic Sites in the Big Bend Reservoir Area," 258, 268, lists two separate streams by that name about thirty miles apart below Fort Pierre. The lower one seems more likely since the name was in use in Wimar's time. Today both areas are inundated. It is entirely possible that Wimar made the drawing of Medicine Creek well before finishing the sheet with the sketch of Little Soldier's village.

87. "Journal of Dr. Elias J. Marsh," 97–99; *Missouri Republican*, July 26, 1859, 2. Another drawing, in the collection of the Saint Louis Art Museum (80 : 47), depicts a small group of tipis seen beyond a cottonwood grove that may be a closer view of Big Head's encampment. Although the countryside is similar, it is impossible to identify it with

certainty. The drawing of Big Head in the Saint Louis Art Museum was previously listed as an unidentified subject; the author is indebted to Jonathan Batkin for identifying the inscription as Big Head's Indian name.

88. "Journal of Dr. Elias J. Marsh," 99; *Missouri Republican*, June 29, 1858, 2; Audubon and Coues, *Audubon and His Journals* 2: 13. The Saint Louis Art Museum's drawing (52 : 47) of the hills and flat-topped bluffs bears the inscription "below Fort Clark" in the lower left corner; it occupies the upper half of a sheet, with the lower half blank. The lodges are also described by Maximilian in his "Travels," in Thwaites, *Early Western Travels* 23: 269–72, and by Culbertson in his *Expedition to the Mauvaises Terres*, 97. In 1862 Lewis Henry Morgan visited the site of the Arikara village at Fort Clark, which had been abandoned; see his remarks in Leslie A. White, ed., *Lewis Henry Morgan: The Indian Journals, 1859–1862* (Ann Arbor: University of Michigan Press, 1959), 161.

89. See the descriptions in the *Missouri Republican*, August 9, 1856, 2; June 29, 1858, 2. The Mandan are glowingly described by Lieutenant Rufus Saxton in the *Pacific Railroad Reports* 1: 265–66. A drawing showing a Mandan wrapped in a blanket, dated June 25, 1859, is in a private collection in Saint Louis. The ethnologist Lewis Henry Morgan described one of these graves during his visit in 1862: "The best or most conspicuous grave was that of an Arikaree[sic] chief who was killed by the Sioux a few years ago. A large mound was raised over the grave about four feet high and oblong about six or eight feet. There was another grave close beside it and mound over it. On the top of the chief's grave were two buffalo skulls, side by side, their horns wound with red bands, and the forehead of one spotted with vermillion. The soil or sod was cleared for a space of five feet around the mound and lined with a circle of buffalo skulls of which I counted seventeen. They made about two-thirds of a circle and were on the side of the chief's mound and to show that they were placed there for him, and not for the adjoining mound." Morgan, *Indian Journals*, 162. The faint rendering titled *Indian Burial* is in the Saint Louis Art Museum (87 : 47). Henry Boller, during his visit in 1858, wrote: "The dead, dressed in their best garments, are laid on scaffolds in the open air, and after they decay and fall to pieces the skulls are arranged in circles, the bones collected and buried, and the mounds surmounted with a buffalo skull." Boller, *Among the Indians*, 29. Lieutenant Maynadier, second-in-command to Captain Raynolds on the exploratory expedition to the Yellowstone, stopped at Fort Clark on the return trip and spoke with an Arikara chief who told him that his people were few and would not last much longer, "because the Sioux were always prowling about to kill them, and even in the cornfields at the village women had been shot and scalped." See "Exploration of the Yellowstone," 151. For information on elk teeth as a form of decoration, see Robert H. Lowie, *Indians of the Plains* (Garden City, N.Y.: The Natural History Press, 1954), 50–51.

90. "Journal of Dr. Elias J. Marsh," 101–3. The oil study of butchered buffalo is in the Saint Louis Art Museum, 55 : 47. A small pocket sketchbook, now in the Missouri Historical Society (1918.52.2.64), contains several pages of drawings of common plants. One of these, bearing the inscription "Prairie Pflanzen," includes studies of the ubiquitous joe pye

weed, Culver's root with its pink blossoms, the nutritious service berry, and red willow or dogwood (which the artist labeled with the Indian name "kinnikinnick," from the fact that its inner bark was an ingredient in Indian tobacco). The buffalo berry rivaled the chokecherry as the favorite fruit that grew in abundance along the upper Missouri. Both have an acidic taste; the plant was described by Catlin in his *Letters and Notes* 1: 72–73. According to Edwin Thompson Denig, who wrote in the early 1850s, buffalo berries were dried and made into soup or used as an ingredient in pemmican; *Five Indian Tribes of the Upper Missouri*, 12 and n. 10. Other interesting examples of Wimar's landscape studies in the Saint Louis Art Museum include an oil on paper study of eroded bluffs (56 : 47), a broadly painted depiction of isolated groups of trees on a prairie with high hills in the background (57 : 47), and a study in oil on canvas of a line of trees along a riverbank, beneath a sky streaked with dark clouds (65 : 41). The latter clearly shows evidence of having been tacked at the corners onto a board. There is also a fine small study of the artist's own hands, that seems to have been done on the 1859 trip (54 : 47).

91. "Journal of Dr. Elias J. Marsh," 103–5; *Missouri Republican*, July 26, 1859, 2; "Early Navigation on the Upper Missouri River. Report of Charles P. Chouteau to the Secretary of War of a Steamboat Expedition from St. Louis to Fort Benton, 1859," *Collections of the Historical Society of Montana* 7 (1910): 253. Information on the Mullan Road can be found in David Lavender, *Land of Giants: The Drive to the Pacific Northwest, 1750–1950* (New York: Doubleday and Company, 1958), 332–33. For Mullan's full report, see "Report and Map of Capt. John Mullan, United States Army, of His Operations While Engaged in the Construction of a Military Road from Fort Walla Walla, on the Columbia River, to Fort Benton, on the Missouri River," 37th Cong., 3d sess., *Senate Executive Document 43* (1863).

92. "Journal of Dr. Elias J. Marsh," 105; Chouteau, "Early Navigation of the Upper Missouri River," 254; Raynolds, "Exploration of the Yellowstone," 114; *Missouri River Maps*, sheet 62. One of the other double-image sheets bears the inscription "Above Fort Stuart July 4th 1849 [sic]" and is in a private collection in Saint Louis, while the second one, bearing the inscriptions "July 4th 1859" on the upper sketch and "Above Fort Stuart" on the lower, is in the possession of Mongerson-Wunderlich Galleries, Inc. For a description of the Missouri from the Yellowstone to the Milk River, see Stevens, *Pacific Railroad Surveys* 1: 163. Captain Raynolds called the Big Muddy "a very insignificant stream, containing but little water"; Raynolds, "Exploration of the Yellowstone," 114.

93. For the quoted sources on the Milk River and its vicinity, see Stevens, *Pacific Railroad Reports* 1: 93, 165, and 12, part 1: 90; Moulton, *Journals of the Lewis and Clark Expedition* 4: 124; and Stanley, *Pacific Railroad Reports* 1: 447. See also *Missouri River Maps*, sheet 65. The progress of the *Chippewa* is noted in Chouteau, "Early Navigation of the Upper Missouri River," 254, and "Journal of Dr. Elias J. Marsh," 105. The Milk River was noted to be fairly small, though similar to the Missouri in terms of its features. Further descriptions can be found in Maximilian, "Travels," in Thwaites, *Early Western Travels* 23: 46; Cul-

bertson, *Expedition to the Mauvaises Terres*, 114; and more thorough descriptions by Lieutenant C. Grover in the *Pacific Railroad Reports* 1: 496, and Raynolds, "Exploration of the Yellowstone," 112. Today the area lies at the eastern end of the vast Fort Peck Reservoir.

94. "Journal of Dr. Elias J. Marsh," 106–7; Chouteau, "Early Navigation on the Upper Missouri River," 254; *Missouri Republican*, August 23, 1859, 2; Maximilian, "Travels," in Thwaites, *Early Western Travels* 23: 54–55; *Missouri River Maps*, sheet 67. Wimar's drawing of Bouche's grave is in the possession of Mongerson-Wunderlich Galleries, Inc. Another drawing depicting a horse and figure in the upper portion and a river landscape bearing the date "July 8th" below is in the Saint Louis Art Museum (70 : 47). The single drawing representing the dark looming masses and inscribed "July 8th near round Bute[sic]" is in the Missouri Historical Society (1950.116.2.23). Lieutenant C. Grover described Round Butte as "a conical-shaped mountain, about a mile and a half from the river, which is so peculiar on account of its position and regularity of form, that it has become a landmark, and is called half-way between Fort Benton and the Yellowstone, though its distance is somewhat greater from the former than the latter place"; *Pacific Railroad Reports* 1: 495. Captain Raynolds also mentioned it in his "Exploration of the Yellowstone," 112. Brief information on the geology of the upper Missouri may be obtained in Gildart, *Montana's Upper Missouri River*, 6–11; the best source for a more specialized view is David Alt and Donald W. Hyndman, *Roadside Geology of Montana* (Missoula: Mountain Press Publishing Co., 1986). Unfortunately, today it is impossible to see this area as Wimar did, since all the low ground is inundated by the waters of Fort Peck Reservoir. The area along the Missouri from Fort Peck Dam to a point approximately 125 airline miles upriver now lies within the boundaries of the Charles M. Russell National Wildlife Refuge, which occupies nearly one million acres. Information or maps of this stretch of the river may be obtained by contacting the office of the Refuge Manager, Charles M. Russell National Wildlife Refuge, Box 110, Lewistown, Montana 59457.

95. Maximilian, "Travels," in Thwaites, *Early Western Travels* 23: 53–54; "Journal of Dr. Elias J. Marsh," 107. Wimar's sketchbook notations, running from July 10 through 17, can be found in the pocket volume in the Missouri Historical Society (1918.52.2.40). There are a number of drawings dated July 9th depicting the landscape along the Missouri River above Round Butte. Two sheets are in the Missouri Historical Society (1950.116.2.10,15); these show the stratified bluffs above a chain of low hills. Another is in the Saint Louis Art Museum (69 : 47), which depicts some of the bluffs with summits heavily eroded into grotesque shapes. A fainter rendering in charcoal or coarse graphite illustrates some odd-shaped formations and is in the possession of Mongerson-Wunderlich Galleries, Inc. Finally, two sketches on one sheet, now in a private collection in Saint Louis, depict additional hills and bluffs heightened with white chalk.

96. Moulton, *Journals of the Lewis and Clark Expedition* 4: 171; "Journal of Dr. Elias J. Marsh," 108; Chouteau, "Early Navigation of the Upper Missouri River," 254–55; *Missouri River Maps*, sheet 69. Two sketches of the area upriver from the Musselshell are in the 1859 pocket

sketchbook in the Missouri Historical Society (1919.52.2.3–4). Further descriptions of the region can be found in Maximilian, "Travels," in Thwaites, *Early Western Travels* 23: 58–59; the report by Lieutenant Grover in the *Pacific Railroad Reports* 1: 247, 493–94; Raynolds, "Exploration of the Yellowstone, 112–13; and Hayden, *Geological Report of the Exploration of the Yellowstone and Missouri Rivers*, 8, 93–94.

97. "Journal of Dr. Elias J. Marsh," 108–9; Maximilian, "Travels," in Thwaites, *Early Western Travels*, 64–65; *Missouri River Maps*, sheet 71. A study of the pillar-like rock formations is also in the Saint Louis Art Museum (79:47). Another example dated July 12 depicts two views; the upper shows a stretch of river flanked by steep hills, while the lower illustrates an eroded bluff with a summit of flat capstones (Saint Louis Art Museum, 81:47). In addition, Wimar's pocket sketchbook has a rough sketch, dated July 12, of a rock in the shape of a castle turret (Missouri Historical Society, 1918.52.2.19). Again Maximilian's words come to mind: "I have already described these mountains when speaking of the white castles, but here they begin to be more continuous, with rough tops, isolated pillars, bearing flat slabs, or balls, resembling mountain-castles, fortresses, and the like, and they are more steep and naked at every step." Ibid. Another drawing in the sketchbook, dated July 11 seems to depict the vicinity of Cow Island or a similar locale, where cottonwood groves abounded and the hills had not yet closed in on the banks (Missouri Historical Society, 1918.52.2.43). Lieutenant Grover described this vicinity very well in the *Pacific Railroad Reports* 1: 493, as did Captain Raynolds six years later in "Exploration of the Yellowstone," 111. Cow Island is also mentioned in Chouteau, "Early Navigation on the Upper Missouri River," 255. Today Cow Island lies just inside the boundaries of the wild and scenic stretch of the Missouri River, as do the Badlands formations described above.

98. "Journal of Dr. Elias J. Marsh," 110–11; Chouteau, "Early Navigation on the Upper Missouri River," 255; *Missouri Republican*, August 23, 1859, 3; *Missouri River Maps*, sheet 72. Wimar's brief note on the notorious "Dowfain Rappits" is in the Missouri Historical Society (1918.52.2.40). Dauphin Rapids was known to Maximilian, who mentioned it was named "after one of our *engagés*, who had fallen into the river at this place." However, in a note at the bottom of the same page R.G. Thwaites asserts: "According to [Alexander] Culbertson's reminiscences, they were named for Antoine Dauphin, who was here detected in a liaison with a Blackfoot woman. He was one of the first victims of smallpox in 1837." Maximilian, "Travels," in Thwaites, *Early Western Travels* 23: 67. In September 1853 Lieutenant Grover observed the rapids when the river was at its lowest point: "Here a gravel bar extends across the whole river, and a small gravel island near the middle divides the stream into two branches, of nearly the same depth, and causes a bend in the channel of both; in addition to this, boulders of a ton weight are frequently found in and near the channel. The depth of water in the channel was twenty inches; its rate did not exceed four and one half miles per hour. The current is stronger here than at any other point on the river." *Pacific Railroad Reports* 1: 248; see also 492. Isaac Stevens, Grover's commander, observed that the river's current through the rapids was three feet deeper in June, during flood season; see ibid., 12, part 1: 235. James Willard Schultz, who was one of the first people to "float"

the Missouri as a sightseer, described Dauphin Rapids as he encountered them in 1903: "Years before the Government engineers had run a long wing dam out from the south shore at this point, throwing all the water into one deep channel. But the ice had battered it season after season, wearing it away, and as I looked now I could only see a line of white foam where it had once stood. The roar of the water was sullen and menacing." James Willard Schultz, *Floating on the Missouri*, ed. Eugene Lee Silliman (Norman: University of Oklahoma Press, 1979), 38.

99. Chouteau, "Early Navigation of the Upper Missouri River," 255; Moulton, *Journals of the Lewis and Clark Expedition* 4: 215–16, 220; "Journal of Dr. Elias J. Marsh," 111; *Missouri Republican*, August 23, 1859, 3; *Missouri River Maps*, sheet 73. The drawing of the Indian shelter, with an inscription that reads "below Mouth of Judith July 15th," appears in the pocket sketchbook in the Missouri Historical Society (1918.52.2.48). Another page in the same sketchbook depicts the eroded sides of steep bluffs, with color notations added by the artist. An inscription in the lower right corner identifies it as having been done above the mouth of the Judith River on July 15th (1918.52.2.22). A very fine drawing done with charcoal and white highlighting, now in the possession of Mongerson-Wunderlich Galleries, Inc., represents a high rock formation identified by an inscription that reads "July 15th above Mouth of Judith." Similar formations are depicted in a drawing executed with identical materials, now in the Saint Louis Art Museum, which has been misidentified in the title as having been done along the Yellowstone (64:47). Descriptions of the Judith River vicinity are given by Lieutenant Grover in the *Pacific Railroad Surveys* 1: 491–92; Captain Raynolds in "Exploration of the Yellowstone," 110–11; and its geologic character in Hayden, *Geological Report of the Exploration of the Yellowstone and Missouri Rivers*, 93. Schultz noted in *Floating on the Missouri*, 35, that "the Blackfeet call it O-to-kwi-tuk-tai—Yellow River, on account of the quantities of yellow 'paint' or ochre which is found near its source. The large flat here at its mouth and the Sage Creek flat opposite, were favorite camping places with them, good trails leading out to the plains north and south, and the wide flats affording ample room to graze their herds in sight of their lodges." For an account of the treaty council between Governor Stevens and the Indians, see Lieutenant James H. Bradley, "Affairs at Fort Benton, from 1831 to 1869," *Montana Historical Society Contributions* 3 (1900): 274–75.

100. Maximilian, "Travels," in Thwaites, *Early Western Travels* 23: 78–79. These formations appear in *Missouri River Maps*, sheet 74. Pierre-Jean De Smet, a Jesuit missionary who traveled through this area in September 1846, described the formations as "exhibiting the most fantastic shapes and fissures and offering to the astonished imagination a vast variety of comparisons: think of urns of all figures and forms; of round and square tables of all dimensions; of pillared pulpits, fantastically carved; thousands of rocky excrescences, in the forms of big and little mushrooms; then come altars with their candelabra, forts, castles, and miniature cities." Hiram M. Chittenden and A. T. Richardson, eds., *Life, Letters, and Travels of Father Pierre-Jean De Smet, S.J., 1801–1873* . . . (New York: F.P. Harper, [1904]), 2:601–2.

101. *Missouri Republican*, August 23, 1859, 3. For other comments on Steamboat Rock and the notable features in this area, see the "Journal of Dr. Elias J. Marsh," 111–12; Raynolds, "Exploration of the Yellowstone," 111; and *Missouri River Maps*, sheet 73. Lewis and Clark's comments concerning this region also reflect a sense of awe; see Moulton, *Journals of the Lewis and Clark Expedition* 4: 225–32. Other studies of the metamorphic dikes, dated July 15 and 16, are in the Saint Louis Art Museum (76:47). Another single drawing in the Missouri Historical Society was mistakenly identified as having been made in the vicinity of Round Butte; dated July 16, it shows a view of the steep formations, layered with white sandstone, on either side of the river not far from Steamboat Rock (1950.116.2.20). Karl Bodmer's representation of this feature is reproduced in *Karl Bodmer's America*, 223. In a footnote to Lewis and Clark's comments on this region, Moulton wrote: "During the glacial period, ice forced the Missouri River to cut a new channel from near Virgelle to Fort Peck Dam, Montana. The channel here has been cut more than three hundred feet deep through late Cretaceous formations of the Claggett Shale, Eagle Sandstone, and Marias River Shale. The most conspicuous of these is the nearly white sandstone of the Virgelle Member of the Eagle Sandstone. Red-brown iron concretions up to eight feet in diameter occur at the top of the Virgelle Member in many places. The concretions are very resistant to erosion and protect the softer, underlying sandstone. Sandstone not protected by concretions erodes away leaving columns and pillars of white sandstone. Various degrees of protection by overlying materials has produced a variety of geometric figures." Moulton, *Journals of the Lewis and Clark Expedition* 4: 233, n. 1. Today this entire stretch of the river comprises part of the 138-mile-long Upper Missouri Wild and Scenic River, under the supervision of the Bureau of Land Management, United States Department of the Interior. A number of brochures and excellent maps of the sites mentioned in this essay may be obtained from the Lewistown District office of the Bureau of Land Management, Airport Road, Lewistown, Montana 59457.

102. *Missouri Republican*, August 23, 1859, 3; "Journal of Dr. Elias J. Marsh," 112; Raynolds, "Exploration of the Yellowstone," 111; *Missouri River Maps*, sheet 74. The sketch of The Hole in the Wall is in the 1859 sketchbook, Missouri Historical Society (1918.52.2.6). For Bodmer's versions of these two subjects, see *Karl Bodmer's America*, 228, 230. James Willard Schultz wrote: "The Hole in the Wall! Never a traveler on the Upper Missouri but remembers that wonderfully thin, high wall of sandstone. From the top of a high ridge it juts straight out over the valley and then drops straight down, hundreds of feet, to the level of the plain. Some fifty feet back from its fall, and perhaps twenty from its crest, some blocks of the stone have dropped out, leaving an oblong, jagged hole. When we came in sight of it, for a moment the sun shone through it, illuminating a bit of hill and river with an intense light, and leaving all the rest of the valley in dark shadows"; *Floating on the Missouri*, 21–22. Citadel Rock was mentioned by many travelers in the period; Maximilian claimed the name had been given to it by traders. See his remarks in his "Travels," in Thwaites, *Early Western Travels* 23: 80; Bodmer's watercolor is reproduced in *Karl Bodmer's America*, 234. During the Pacific Railroad Surveys, Lieutenant Grover stopped at the base of Citadel Rock, which he stated was forty feet square, adding that

"there are many cavities in its faces large enough to hold a good-sized apple, which are sometimes lined with crystals of carbonate of lime." See the *Pacific Railroad Reports* 1: 490, and Stevens' comments on the same locale in 12, part 1: 98, 220. The lower sketch accompanying the Eye of the Needle may represent Fortress Butte. Marsh described "the chapel" as a tower of rock with an "arched Gothic doorway" on top; "Journal of Dr. Elias J. Marsh," 112. Captain Raynolds seems to have noted it as having the shape of "a perfect horseshoe"; "Exploration of the Yellowstone," 111. The drawing that appears to be an isolated rendering of LaBarge Rock is in the possession of Mongerson-Wunderlich Galleries, Inc. For Bodmer's renderings, see *Karl Bodmer's America*, 235–37.

103. Chouteau, "Early Navigation of the Upper Missouri River," 255–56; "Journal of Dr. Elias J. Marsh," 112; *Missouri River Maps*, sheet 75. The Marias River is a good-sized stream that drains a large area to the Rocky Mountains. Its principal tributaries are the Cutbank, Two Medicine, Badger, Birch, and Dupuyer Creeks. Lewis and Clark thought the Marias to be the main stream of the Missouri and followed it for a distance until they realized their mistake; see Moulton, *Journals of the Lewis and Clark Expedition* 4: 246–49. The Marias River country, including its confluence with the Missouri, was extensively described in the *Pacific Railroad Reports*; see Isaac Stevens' comments in 1: 93, 98, 165, and 229. Lieutenant Grover also described the area of the junction of both rivers in 12, Part 1, 489. Captain Raynolds arrived at this site a year later and noted that the Missouri below the mouth of the Marias changed from a "limpid blue color" to one of "ashy whiteness." See "Exploration of the Yellowstone," 110.

104. Information on the *Chippewa*'s final leg of the journey is contained in the "Journal of Dr. Elias J. Marsh," 112–13, and Chouteau, "Early Navigation on the Upper Missouri River," 255–56. Culbertson's very interesting report on old Fort McKenzie can be found in Audubon and Coues, *Audubon and His Journals* 2: 188–95. Maximilian and Bodmer had numerous adventures at this historic fort; see Maximilian, "Travels," in Thwaites, *Early Western Travels* 23: 87–95. Bodmer's studies of the area are reproduced in *Karl Bodmer's America*, 269–72. A number of accounts of Fort Benton and its region were penned for the *Pacific Railroad Reports*. Isaac Stevens wrote: "The ascent from the wide grassy plain in which the fort is located to the high table-land is somewhat abrupt, the only passage on a level with the plain being close to the river on the south, and very narrow. Fort Benton is smaller than Fort Union. Its front is made of wood, and the other sides adobe or unburned brick" (vol. 12, part 1: 101). Stanley's view is reproduced as Plate XXIV in the same volume; additional comments by Stevens and Lieutenant Grover can also be found in vol. 1: 97–98, and 488, respectively. Agent Alfred Vaughan chronicled the interesting efforts to establish a farming community for the volatile Blackfeet in letters to his superiors. See his letters to A. M. Robinson dated September 10 and December 27, 1858, in NAMP, M234, R30, F221–28 and F239–40, respectively. Alexander Culbertson wrote another view of this activity; see his letter to Charles E. Mix, dated March 4, 1858, in NAMP, M234, R30, F176–78. Captain Raynolds' observations are in his report of the "Exploration of the Yellowstone," 109–10. Another intriguing sketch dated July 18 in the artist's pocket sketchbook (Missouri Historical Society, 1918.52.2.63)

depicts high bluffs along the river and bears an inscription that seems to begin with the words "Labarche [sic] Landing." The location of this site is unknown, but the formation on the left of the drawing bears a resemblance to LaBarge Rock.

105. *Missouri Republican*, August 23, 1859, 3; "Journal of Dr. Elias J. Marsh," 112–15; Chouteau, "Early Steamboat Navigation on the Upper Missouri," 256.

106. "Journal of Dr. Elias J. Marsh," 115.

107. Ibid., 115–18.

108. Ibid., 118–19. Redfield reported his activities in two letters to his supervisor, Colonel A. M. Robinson, dated July 17 and August 8, 1859. These are reproduced in NAMP-M234, R959, F127–29 and F137–39. On July 17 Redfield wrote: "The point selected for the Agency is one of the most beautiful on the Missouri river and about 15 miles below U.S. Fort Randall. I brought with me canvas and tents, under which I am now sheltering my people and the goods. I found the greater part of the Yanctons forty miles below here at the old and principal village of the tribe. I gave them some provisions and took the two principal chiefs on the boat and brought them up here, requiring the tribe to remove up here to receive their annuities under the treaty." In doing this, Redfield forced the tribe to abandon their semipermanent village and cornfields, undermining what little stability the Yanktons had achieved in the first place.

109. "Journal of Dr. Elias J. Marsh," 121–22. On July 22, 1859, the editor for the Sioux City *Eagle* had noted: "This new territory is now open for settlement, although the time allowed the Indians in which to remove has not yet expired. There is a large amount of beautiful farming land in Dacotah [sic], and we doubt not much of it will be taken up next year by hardy pioneers, as from all quarters we hear of parties forming for the new territory." This appeared in the *Missouri Republican*, August 4, 1859, 2. Reports on the Pawnee unrest can be found in the *Missouri Republican*, June 30, 1859, 2, and July 18, 1859, 2. For a note on the sinking of the *Kate Howard*, see the *Missouri Republican*, August 15, 1859, 2. The *Chippewa*, for all its accomplishment, suffered a sad fate on the upper Missouri the following year, as revealed by the following notice: "*Chippewa*, bound for Benton, burnt in disaster bend. The owners, the American Fur Company, were smuggling alcohol through to Benton, for Indian trade, and one of the deck-hands, in the act of stealing a drink, took a candle and gimlet and proceeded into the hull of the boat, and in drawing the alcohol it ignited, and the boat caught fire. She was loaded with Indian annuity goods, and also goods for the American Fur Company. There were about 25 kegs of powder on board. When the fire reached the powder, the boat blew up. Packages of merchandise were found three miles from the disaster." Quoted in "Steamboat Arrivals at Fort Benton, Montana, and Vicinity," *Contributions to the Historical Society of Montana* 1 (1876): 317.

110. For the report of the *Spread Eagle*'s return, see the *Missouri Republican*, August 17, 1859, 2. The anonymous account appeared in the same newspaper on August 22, 1859, 1. Another report published the next day (p. 3) by an anonymous writer seems to be in the style of Dr. Marsh's narrative.

111. For a scholarly overview of the events of the period, including the dissolution of the partnership of Frost, Todd and Company, see Sunder, *Fur Trade on the Upper Missouri*, 208–9. Scholten, who must have known Wimar, is an interesting figure. Born in Prussia, he had immigrated with his parents to Hermann, Missouri; in 1855 he began a two-year apprenticeship in photography with Andrew J. Fox. The *Saint Louis Directory* for 1859 lists him as a "daguerrian" at 297 South 5th (419), while the 1860 edition places his "ambrotype and photographic gallery" at the corner of 5th and Convent (288). Apparently Scholten was the first to introduce the carte-de-visite to Saint Louis. His studio was completely destroyed by fire in 1878, with an irreparable loss of over 30,000 photographs. Information on his life is taken from an unidentified clipping in a scrapbook assembled in the 1880s, now in the Alphabetical Files at the Missouri Historical Society; see also Van Ravenswaay, "Pioneer Photographers in St. Louis," 69.

112. M. Hopewell, M.D., *Report of the Fourth Annual Fair of the St. Louis Agricultural and Mechanical Association of September 1859* (Saint Louis: George Knapp and Company, 1859), 126–27. The report listed the following works by Wimar lent by Dr. van Zandt: "Buffalo (No. 112 in the catalogue)," "Prairie Fire and Buffalo (No. 113)," and "View of Fort Snelling, and Indians returning from the hunt (No. 114)." In addition, John A. Brownlee lent "Discovery of Boone's Encampment in Kentucky, by the Indians (No. 128)," "The Capture of Boone's Daughter by the Indians (No. 129)," "Seminole Indians returning from a Foray, having captured a Dragoon's horse (No. 130)," and "Jolly Flat-boatmen by moonlight (No. 131)." A newspaper account praising these paintings as "very spirited and faithful" can be found in the *Missouri Republican*, September 27, 1859, 2.

113. Kurz, *Journal*, 3–4.

114. *Missouri Republican*, September 27, 1859, 2, and September 25, 1860, 2; Audubon and Coues, *Audubon and His Journals* 2: 26; "Journal of Dr. Elias J. Marsh," 115–18. William Napton recalled of the 1858 trip: "The long twilight of this high latitude enabled the boat to run in clear weather almost if not quite as late as ten o'clock, and little time was lost by darkness, and we were also favored with several magnificent displays of the Aurora Borealis, exceedingly brilliant, lighting the entire northern half of the sky for hours at a time." Napton, *Along the Santa Fe Trail*, 91. There is no evidence that Wimar photographed any buffaloes on his 1858 trip, but Solomon Carvalho seems to have done so while accompanying the Frémont Expedition five years earlier. Encountering large herds between Walnut Creek and the Arkansas River, he wrote: "I essayed, at different times, to daguerreotype them while in motion, but was not successful, although I made several pictures of distant herds." Carvalho, *Travels and Adventures in the Far West*, 64.

115. Hopewell, *Report of the Fourth Annual Fair*, 127.

116. *Missouri Republican*, September 30, 1859, 2; Hopewell, *Report of the Fourth Annual Fair*, 127. Charles N. Kessler, writing from Montana to Charles Reymershoffer on June 20, 1919, observed that the turkey buzzards in Wimar's painting were not common as far north as the Yellowstone River; Reymershoffer papers, Missouri Historical Society.

117. The Act of Incorporation as well as the constitution of the Western Academy of Art is reproduced in the *Catalogue of the First Annual Exhibition of the Western Academy of Art* (Saint Louis: The Missouri Democrat Book and Job Office, 1860), a copy of which is in the Missouri Historical Society. A contemporary profile and portrait of Henry T. Blow can be found in Richard Edwards and M. Hopewell, *Edward's Great West and Her Commercial Metropolis, Embracing a General View of the West and a Complete History of St. Louis. . . .* (Saint Louis: Published at the Office of "Edwards's Monthly," a Journal of Progress, 1860), 226–27. The comments on the upcoming "Artists' Exhibition" are in the *Missouri Republican*, September 29, 1859, 2; the observation about the Academy's importance can be found in the same newspaper for October 14, 1860, 2. The exhibition of the Academy was timed to take advantage of the large number of visitors in Saint Louis for the annual fair. See M. Hopewell, M.D., *Report of the Annual Fair of the St. Louis Agricultural and Mechanical Association, of September 1860* (Saint Louis: George Knapp and Company, 1861), 94–95.

118. *Missouri Republican*, October 14, 1860, 2.

119. *Missouri Republican*, September 28, 1860, 1; *First Exhibition of the Western Academy of Art*, 5–18. There were many portraits by recognized artists such as Chester Harding, George Peter Alexander Healy, Thomas Sully, and William Wilgus, as well as Western Art Academy members Alban G. Conant and Manuel L. De Franca. Genre subjects were represented by the work of William H. Beard, John George Brown, John Gadsby Chapman, Eastman Johnson, and Thomas S. Noble, along with paintings by founding academy member Ferdinand Boyle. Many landscapes adorned the walls, including a number of examples by Albert Fitch Bellows, Thomas Birch, Thomas Doughty, Sanford Gifford, Regis Gignoux, John Frederick Kensett, Henry Lewis, Joseph Rusling Meeker, and William Sonntag. Meeker, a skilled practitioner who had studied at the National Academy of Design in New York City, had recently relocated his studio to Saint Louis. Apart from these artists, there were several others whose work reflected the subject matter of the West. George Caleb Bingham exhibited paintings titled *Flatboatmen in Port, County Election, Election Returns*, and *Lighting a Steamer over a Bar*. Charles Deas was represented with a single example titled *Canadian Voyageurs*, while Seth Eastman had three paintings titled *Indian Spearing Fish, Landscape and Indians*, and *Chasing Buffalo*. Henry Isaacs, a Saint Louis artist who traveled up the Missouri with Wimar on the 1859 trip, had a single oil on display, *Scene on the Upper Missouri*, lent by Charles P. Chouteau. Besides the work by Isaacs, Chouteau lent two works each by Wimar and Kensett. Henry T. Blow lent paintings by Boyle, De Franca, Lewis, Meeker, Sully, and Wilgus. The most generous patron, however, was another Academy founder named James E. Yeatman. He lent forty-two works to the exhibition, including examples by Bingham, Chapman, Deas, De Franca, and Eastman. Information on Isaacs is difficult to obtain. The *St. Louis Directory* for 1859 lists a Henry Isaacs as a bookkeeper for Pierre Chouteau Jr. and Company (261); the following year the same Isaacs is listed, along with Henry G. Isaacs, an architect (247). The latter was to achieve a prominent career in Saint Louis; perhaps, as a young man, he journeyed upriver for the adventure. Unfortunately, there is nothing in the literature on Isaacs to corroborate such speculation.

120. Audubon and Coues, *Audubon and His Journals* 1: 513–18. Chittenden and Richardson, *Life, Letters, and Travels of Father Pierre-Jean De Smet* 2: 645–46.

121. Schmidt's account can be found in Schmutterer, *Tomahawk and Cross*, 145–46. For Stevens' interesting description of the area north and south of Fort Union, see the *Pacific Railroad Reports* 1: 92. Maximilian's comments are in his "Travels," in Thwaites, *Early Western Travels* 22: 373. It is important to note that two artists followed in Wimar's footsteps up the Missouri River in 1860 and 1861. The earlier of the two was William Jacob Hays, who was to build a successful career as a painter of the buffalo and who journeyed as far as Fort Stuart, where he remained for a brief period before starting back to Saint Louis. A fine drawing of Fort Union, dated June 16, 1860, is in the Amon Carter Museum. The best overview of Hays' trip can be found in Robert Taft, "The Pictorial Record of the Old West: II: William Jacob Hays," *Kansas Historical Quarterly* 14 (May 1946), 145–65. The other artist, William de la Montagne Cary, traveled on the *Spread Eagle* and *Chippewa*, as Wimar had done. Many of the artist's sketches and paintings are preserved in the Gilcrease Museum, and some subjects are identical to those depicted by Wimar. Cary's early journeys need further study, but the reader may find helpful information in Mildred D. Ladner, *William de la Montagne Cary: Artist on the Missouri River* (Norman: University of Oklahoma Press, 1984).

122. An excellent analysis of Schoolcraft's antebellum attitudes toward the American Indian (and by extension the wild frontier) can be found in Robert E. Bieder, *Science Encounters the Indian, 1820–1880* (Norman: University of Oklahoma Press, 1986), 146–93. Caleb Cushing's remarks were published in the *Missouri Republican*, May 1, 1857, 1. The order for Fort Union to be abandoned was communicated in the same newspaper on May 30, 1860, 2. Cooper's words are quoted from his preface to *The Prairie* (first published in 1827) in Blake Nevius, ed., *Cooper: The Leatherstocking Tales, Volume I* (New York: The Library of America, 1985), 881. One recent historian has written: "An important American historian in his own right, Cooper differentiated with the utmost care between the order of truth necessary for the historian and that required for imaginative works. Like the painters, he sought to achieve a balance between the generalized fidelity to American experience which would convey an exact sense of its nature and quality and yet embody a religious, patriotic, and ethical idealism which transcended the immediate aspects of that experience." James F. Beard, "Cooper and His Artistic Contemporaries," *New York History* 35 (1954): 125.

184

123. Catlin, *Letters and Notes* 1: 251–52; Catlin's illustration of the hunt (Plate 107 in the original volume) is reproduced in this essay from the larger hand-colored version taken from Catlin's *Indian Portfolio* (Amon Carter Museum, 1972.46.5). The story of Lord Lyons' commission is related in Rathbone, *Charles Wimar*, 27.

124. See the description of Wimar's studio in the *Duesseldorfer Anzeiger*, December 29, 1862.

125. John C. Ewers, "Fact and Fiction in the Documentary Art of the American West," in John Francis McDermott, ed., *The Frontier Reexamined* (Urbana: University of Illinois Press, 1967), 84. Catlin's additional comments are in *Letters and Notes* 1: 252. Irving's description is in his narrative *A Tour on the Prairies*, first published in 1835 but issued by the author in a new edition in 1859 (Norman: University of Oklahoma Press, 1956), 173. John James Audubon had a nearly identical reaction: "I think that I never saw an eye so ferocious in expression as that of the wounded buffalo; rolling wildly in its socket, inflamed as the eye was, it had the most frightful appearance that can be imagined; and in fact, the picture presented by the buffalo as a whole is quite beyond my powers of description." Audubon and Coues, *Audubon and His Journals* 2: 62–63. For another positive opinion on the ethnographic accuracy of Wimar's version, see Herman Ten Kate, "On Paintings of North American Indians and their Ethnographical Value," *Anthropos* 6 (1911): 531. Ewers' use of the term "Blackfoot" over "Blackfeet" is explained in the following letter he wrote to Mrs. Dana O. Jensen at the Missouri Historical Society on July 4, 1967: "As for Blackfoot vs Blackfeet it is a bit confusing. Anthropologists invariably use Blackfoot—singular or plural. Most others use Blackfoot (singular) and Blackfeet plural. Both refer to the same tribes, and I refuse to be too much concerned over which forms are used—because they don't really mislead anyone." Ewers went on to say that the native term for the tribe is "Sikskika," which properly translated means "Blackfoot." However, the legal name of the tribe given under the Indian Reorganization Act of 1932 is "Blackfeet;" for that reason, the tribe itself opted for the latter.

126. William T. Hornaday, *The Extermination of the American Bison, with a Sketch of its Discovery and Life History* (Washington, D.C.: U.S. National Museum, 1887), 397–406. For information on the plants of the Upper Plains, see Theodore Van Bruggen, *Wildflowers, Grasses and Other Plants of the Northern Plains and Black Hills* (Interior, S.D.: Badlands Natural History Association, 1983). For a view of the shortgrass prairie, see Ruth Carol Cushman and Stephen R. Jones, *The Shortgrass Prairie* (Boulder, Colo.: Pruett Publishing Co., 1988).

127. Darley, though influential, had never been to the trans-Mississippi West when this illustration was executed. See John C. Ewers, "Not Quite Redmen: The Plains Indian Illustrations of Felix O. C. Darley," *American Art Journal* 3 (Fall 1971): 88–98. It is worth adding that the theme of the buffalo hunt was one of the elements of a musical composition which premiered in Saint Louis in September 1858, titled "Hiawatha" and described as a musical "tone-painting." Some of the other movements included "Shores of the Missouri" and "Indian Serenade"; see the *Missouri Republican*, June 23, 1858, 2.

128. Henry T. Blow's commission is mentioned in Rathbone, "Charles Wimar," 27–28. George Catlin described such bags in detail; see his *Letters and Notes* 1: 36–39. The Reymershoffer papers at the Missouri Historical Society (group 74–0072) preserve a number of letters from various individuals regarding the painting. W. F. (Buffalo Bill) Cody claimed that the Indians in *The Buffalo Hunt* were Blackfeet, but he was clearly mistaken (Cody to Charles Reymershoffer, March 15, 1907). W. H. Holmes, writing from the Smithsonian Institution, was more helpful: "According to our Mr. Mooney, who is well acquainted with all the tribes of the middle west, the Indians represented are Osage, Kaw, Oto, or Missouri, all of which are closely cognate tribes of Siouian stock, who formerly occupied southeast Kansas and adjacent portions of the Indian Territory" (Holmes to Reymershoffer, January 19, 1907). In a later letter, Holmes expanded his comments by saying that in 1860 the Kaw and Oto Indians occupied southeast Kansas and southeast Nebraska, respectively: "My guess would be that this encounter occurred on or near the lower Kansas River, between a Kaw and Oto Indian"; Holmes to Reymershoffer, July 2, 1907). Major Gordon W. (Pawnee Bill) Lillie was even more certain of the location, claiming that the hills in the distance were the Wichita Mountains, "just west of Fort Sill," looking from the east (Lillie to Reymershoffer, October 12, 1907).

129. Kurz, *Journal*, 189. Kurz's views were echoed by Blow and other members of the board of the Western Academy of Art: "The rich merchant will become the friend and patron of the arts, and will surround himself with tasteful elegance, instead of a display of mere gingerbread tinsels, so to speak, and his house will become a palace of the beautiful and a center of social and refined intercourse. The mechanic, by accustoming himself to contemplate a symmetry of form will acquire a taste which shall aid him in his vocation. And young people, by coming in contact with good pictures, will find the soul within them yearning for the true, the beautiful, and the good. New sources of enjoyment, infinite and varied, will be opened to them, while regions of refined pleasure, heretofore closed or unexplored, will be laid bare to their delighted senses, and the more they enjoy the more they will be prepared for higher gratification." *Missouri Republican*, October 7, 1860, 3.

130. Catlin, *Letters and Notes* 1: 126–28; Maximilian, "Travels," in Thwaites, *Early Western Travels* 23: 340. For additional views of Like-A-Fishhook Village and information on the threshing stages which are depicted in Wimar's painting and Morrow's photograph, see Gilbert L. Wilson, "Agriculture of the Hidatsa Indians: An Indian Interpretation," *Bulletin of the University of Minnesota, Studies in the Social Sciences*, No. 9 (November 1917): 49–57, 98–99. See also Smith, *Like-A-Fishhook Village and Fort Berthold*, 28–29. Morrow documented the entire area, and his photographs are an invaluable record of the site as Wimar must have known it. See Wesley R. Hurt and William E. Lass, *Frontier Photographer: Stanley J. Morrow's Dakota Years* (Lincoln: University of Nebraska Press and the University of South Dakota, 1956), 72–73. A very crude pencil sketch of one of the central figures, together with three studies of legs and footgear, is in the Saint Louis Art Museum (83:47, recto). Captain William F. Raynolds visited the Mandan village at Fort Berthold in 1859 and described the forked poles and scaffolds visible in

the Wimar and Bodmer renditions as being frameworks for drying vegetables and game. See Raynolds, "Exploration of the Yellowstone," 149.
Herman Ten Kate gives high marks to Wimar for his depiction of this
event; see his remarks in his article "On Paintings of the North American Indian and their Ethnographical Value," 532.

131. "American Painters: Their Errors as Regards Nationality," *Cosmopolitan Art Journal* 1 (June 1857): 116; *Harper's Weekly*, June 12, 1858,
116. For a brief overview of the fortunes of Billy Bowlegs (whose name
is commonly written as Holatter Micco or Holata Mico) and the events
in the Indian Territory during the Civil War, see Edwin C. McReynolds,
The Seminoles (Norman: University of Oklahoma Press, 1957), 264–312.
The painting of *Chief Billy Bowlegs (Holatamico)* is in the Saint Louis
Art Museum (9:1938).

132. Rathbone, *Charles Wimar*, 28. See also J. Thomas Scharf, *History
of Saint Louis City and County, from the Earliest Periods to the Present
Day* (Philadelphia: Louis H. Everts and Company, 1883), 2: 1591, 1621.
The Missouri Historical Society contains many fine manuscript collections whose letters reveal the political, social, and cultural conflicts of the
period leading up to and including the Civil War. Alexander Badger,
writing on May 5, 1861 from Fort Vancouver, Washington Territory to
his sister Alice Clayton, expressed alarm for the fortunes of Saint Louis
and the "dreadful idea" of civil war. Badger Collection, Missouri Historical Society. The phenomenal success of the Western Academy exhibition is chronicled in several issues of the *Missouri Republican*, as well
as references in letters from Henry T. Blow's wife, Minerva, to their
daughter. "Your dear father never looked better in his life, and is in fine
spirits," she wrote on November 11; "he is busy this week with seeing
the free schools at the Academy. Yesterday 1500 attended and he made
them quite a speech. Today the normal school is expected, and before
the week is over 13,000 children will have enjoyed the beautiful collection—father enjoyed their pleasure very much and says he has never
engaged in anything which gratified him more." Minerva Blow to Susie
E. Blow, November 11, 1860. Blow family papers, Missouri Historical
Society. Further information on the attendance and success of the exhibition may be found in the *Missouri Republican*, October 4, 1860, 3;
October 7, 1860, 3; October 23, 1860, 3; and November 17, 1860, 3.

[W]e have been informed that the "star of empire," arrested in its giant march westward, has come to a dead pause; and now, fixed in mid-heaven, sheds down its glorious beams from the precise zenith of St. Louis. The Mississippi Valley is one mighty, unbounded, prolific domain of present and future power, glory, and refinement, and St. Louis is its centre.[1]

Professor O. M. Mitchell (1857)

St. Louis, . . . the centre of the vast empire . . . must, I truly believe, ere long make her seat here, or hereabouts, grasping an ocean in each hand, with her feet upon the great gulf of the South, and holding on to the north pole with all her teeth.[2]

William J. Flagg (1857)

Figure 1
Rotunda, Old Courthouse, Saint Louis.
Photograph by Bob Kolbrener, 1990.

A Muralist of Civic Ambitions

ANGELA L. MILLER

Early in 1862 Carl Wimar began work on a series of mural decorations—four lunettes, four allegorical figures, and four bust-length portraits—for the rotunda of the Saint Louis Courthouse (fig. 1). Wimar had barely completed the commission late that year when, according to the legendary account, the artist laid aside his brushes and died of the tuberculosis that had sapped his strength since at least the previous year.[3] The mural commission that brought Wimar's career to a close also symbolically closed an era in the city's history, as the grand vision of empire-building that it projected began to fade. Many of the city's hopes for the future had turned upon securing the route of the transcontinental railroad that would link the Mississippi Valley to the West Coast.[4] The city had vied energetically for that honor, but in July 1862, shortly before Wimar completed his courthouse cycle, the war-plagued federal government announced that Chicago, not Saint Louis, would be the point of origin for the Pacific Railroad.[5]

Just as the Eads Bridge would symbolize Saint Louis' economic and cultural aspirations after the war, the courthouse was the prewar symbol of the city's youthful ambition to become the new seat of American empire. Wimar's murals expressed that civic spirit in its broadest his-

torical dimensions. Combining history, allegory, and portraiture, the courthouse cycle depicted the epochal events, ideals, and personalities that had shaped the history of the Mississippi Valley and that would mold its future, as envisioned by Saint Louis' leading pro-Union citizens in the early years of the Civil War. Projecting a mythic future out of a mythic past, Wimar and his collaborators selected a series of key episodes to weave a usable historic narrative that served multiple political and cultural functions. This conception matched the efforts of European artists from the seventeenth century to the nineteenth to place history in the service of politics, through artistic allegories that carried a readable message for the present. It also drew upon and contributed to an imagery of regional and national self-definition being developed concurrently by other American artists; its historical allusions have parallels in the paintings, political rhetoric, and historical writings of the mid-

nineteenth century.

The courthouse which stands today (fig. 2) was begun in 1839 and originally was adorned with a small hemispheric dome sheathed in copper. The Renaissance-style dome set upon a colonnaded drum, reminiscent of Saint Peter's, was begun in 1859. This new dome, designed by William Rumbold, employed a patented system of cast and wrought iron inspired by the example of Thomas U. Walter's dome for the United States Capitol (fig. 3), which had been selected in a competition of 1850 and was still under construction.[6] In what may have been a calculated rivalry, Saint Louisans pushed to complete their dome in 1862, several years before the Walter dome was finished.[7]

Well before Wimar furnished an explicit iconography for the courthouse, Saint Louisans had looked to the building as a stalwart reminder of their role in bringing civilization and order to the young Valley of the Mississippi. Cruciform

Figure 2 (left)
Courthouse, Saint Louis. Photograph by R. F. Adams, 1865. Missouri Historical Society.

Figure 3 (right)
Capitol, Washington, D.C. Photograph courtesy of Architect of the Capitol.

Figure 4
Panoramic View of Saint Louis. Photograph by Robert Benecke, 1864. Missouri Historical Society.

in shape, with projecting Greek Revival temple fronts on the east and west and with shorter north and south facades of engaged pilasters, the courthouse stood where the city's founder, Pierre Laclede, supposedly had first surveyed the site for his trading post.[8] Situated one block north of the major thoroughfare of Market Street, the courthouse, following completion of the new dome, dominated Saint Louis' skyline and radiantly symbolized the city's prominence (fig. 4 and plate 24).

With its four arms marking the cardinal directions, the courthouse was also metaphorically situated at major geographic, historic, and cultural junctures. On an East/West axis, Saint Louis was a terminus for existing rail lines to the East and a point of departure for new lines leading to the West. In 1849 delegates had adjourned to the courthouse from around the nation for the National Railroad Convention, chaired by Stephen Douglas, and had heard Missouri Senator Thomas Hart Benton reprise his earlier calls for a national road to the Pacific to consummate the

fabled "passage to India."[9] Benton, who that year had introduced a bill in Congress for a railroad route through Saint Louis, urged: "Let us beseech the National Legislature to build the great road upon the great national line which suits Europe and Asia—San Francisco at one end, Saint Louis in the middle, the national metropolis and great commercial emporium at the other; and which shall be adorned with its crowning honor,—the colossal statue of the great Columbus,—whose design it accomplishes, . . . pointing with outstretched arms to the western horizon, and saying to the flying passengers: 'There is the East, there is India!' "[10] Benton's vision of an imperial West would play a significant role in Wimar's mural cycle.

Running counter to this East/West axis, both geographically and historically, was the North/South axis. Missouri was a border state, and Saint Louis was inevitably drawn into the economic and political struggles between North and South. The courthouse itself had been the site where in 1850 the district court granted

freedom to Dred and Harriet Scott—a decision reversed in 1852 by the Missouri Supreme Court, which met elsewhere in the city. The Dred Scott decision and the ensuing legal battles fought in Saint Louis itself over slavery and the jurisdiction of states did much to widen the rift between local pro- and anti-slavery forces.

Wimar and his civic-minded associates realized that Saint Louis had much to lose both economically and politically from a dismemberment of the Union. Wimar's own pro-Union stance is revealed in a drawing, *Reconciliation* (fig. 5), apparently intended as a study for a panel in a Saint Louis restaurant. *Reconciliation* depicts an allegorical figure of Liberty, with pileus cap held aloft, wearing a starred robe symbolizing the Union and clasping the hands of figures representing North and South. The North, on the left side of the drawing, is surrounded by cupids bearing anchors and ships' masts; smokestacks appear in the distance. The South, on the right side, is accompanied by a sunburst with palm trees and other tokens of the lush semitropical

climate with which the region had become associated. Beneath the group is an eagle bearing a shield. This symbolic group indicates the perceived importance of commerce as a means of bridging political and economic divisions between North and South in the 1850s. This perception carried over into the courthouse decorations as well; Wimar's half-brother and collaborator, August Becker, executed a related mural (no longer extant) on the upper portion of the courthouse dome, above Wimar's murals, showing scenes of "the leading products of the North, corn and wheat," and "the products of the South, the pineapple and the sugar-cane."[11]

But the commercial harmony thus projected could not forestall the events of 1861. The Civil War in Missouri opened on May 10 of that year, when Union forces captured nominally neutral Camp Jackson and catalyzed secessionist feelings at many levels. Elected governor Claiborne Jackson and much of his cabinet defected to the Confederate cause that November, and though the state soon came under the pro-Union governor-

192

ship of Hamilton R. Gamble, guerrilla war in southwestern Missouri continued throughout the spring and summer of 1862.[12] To Unionists, the courthouse was a highly visible symbol of the federal presence and a reassuring testament to the city's loyalty within an embattled state. Saint Louis' leaders must have considered well the meaning of recent events for the city's claims that it was a key post along the axis of empire: to be a viable candidate for the proposed transcontinental railroad, the city would have to demonstrate its loyalty to the North. The decorations for the courthouse became a logical place to convey this burden of civic and political meaning and to show that Saint Louis was destined to play a major role in the settlement of the West.

Wimar's own role in the courthouse commission came about through the efforts of William Taussig, a member of the Saint Louis County

Court (a body largely responsible for county government) and of the special Committee of the Board in charge of the courthouse decorations.[13] In Taussig's words, the Board of County Commissioners "wanted to let the job in open competition and to the lowest bidder, and it was some trouble to induce them to leave the matter to a special committee."[14] The contract, granted January 22, 1862, actually went to August Becker, more than likely for financial reasons; though Wimar's works were central to the courthouse decorations, he received payment from his half-brother.[15]

Taussig, a cultured German emigré, supervised the project and collaborated with Wimar and Judge Wilson Primm, the city's midcentury historian, in formulating the cycle. Judge Primm (1810–1878), who according to one biography was instrumental in transforming Saint Louis from a French colonial outpost into "a thoroughly American city," was an ideal man to help formulate the courthouse cycle. His memory was richly stocked with exemplary passages from the city's history, and he possessed the proper combination of chronicler and prophet to integrate local history within the broader sweep of nation-building.[16] Ultimately, Wimar and Taussig selected the subjects depicted on the south and west sides, while Judge Primm chose the events to be represented on the east and north.[17]

As Commissioner Taussig later recalled: "The themes of the 4 main pictures were most carefully selected and [it was] decided they should symbolize the discovery and development of the far West. . . . It took the artist but a few days to bring those ideas in firm and clear cut lines to paper and I remember well how full of life and forceful drawing the different groups were conceived by Wimar."[18] The planned cycle wove past and future together in a prophetic narrative characteristic of both historical writing and painting in the mid-nineteenth century. The spectator's act of reconstructing meaning out of a series of discrete events paralleled the contemporaneous effort of historians, from George Bancroft to E. L. Magoon, to salvage the historical record from randomness and reveal its larger significance.

The most significant portion of the mural scheme consisted of four lunettes around the circumference of the dome. These lunettes are meant to be seen from the second-floor landing or third-floor balconies rather than from ground level, where their diminutive figures are difficult to read. Their elongated, predominantly horizontal format and curved surfaces must have challenged Wimar's powers of composition, as well as furnishing him a rather small working surface on which to project his grand vision. As happened with the German muralists whose example Wimar emulated, in their realization the lunettes inevitably fell short of his conception. The sheer scope of what he was trying to convey—nothing less than the four phases of empire—defied any effective translation into the material medium of fresco.

Although the historical backdrop of Wimar's cycle was the Civil War, his images concentrated instead on four stages of western conquest and settlement. The lunettes themselves define the origins and historic destiny of Saint Louis as the gateway to the West—an escape route, albeit an illusory one, from the tensions of the present to the hopes of the future. The grand cycle of empire begins on the south lunette of the rotunda with *De Soto Discovering the Mississippi*. Next in the sequence, on the east or riverside lunette, is the *Landing of Laclede* at the site of Saint Louis. On the north lunette Wimar painted a scene from the early history of the French colony of Saint Louis, *The Year of the Blow*. Finally on the west lunette Wimar leaped forward temporally and geographically to paint *Westward the Star of Empire*, a sunset landscape of a pass in the Rocky

Mountains.

In the courthouse rotunda, what appears at first to be a random selection of real and imagined events from the history of the Mississippi Valley is in fact a carefully coordinated symbolic program of linked episodes. De Soto, typologically associated with both Columbus and Pierre Laclede, opens the historic cycle on the south side of the rotunda; the gate of the Rockies completes it on the west side. Episodes from the early European history of discovery and exploration in the New World, here as elsewhere in American art of the antebellum period, were symbolically associated with the westward migrations of the nineteenth century.[19] Numerous other iconographic and historical links tie together the discrete subjects of the four murals, which progress from the Spanish discovery to the French and then American settlement of the Mississippi Valley; from the sixteenth through the eighteenth and nineteenth centuries; from the friendship and peace of the initial Spanish and French conquest, through the frontier warfare generated by British antagonism, to a bright future of American expansion. As the first three lunettes look backward toward origins, the final looks forward toward future prospects. In this context the present is merely implied as an expansive possibility, a moment prepared by history and consummated by a glorious future.

The subject of the south lunette, *De Soto Discovering the Mississippi* (fig. 6), was already well established in American art and culture by the time Wimar tried his hand at it. William Ranney, Peter Rothermel, and Seth Eastman all painted subjects relating to De Soto's discovery of the Mississippi or his burial.[20] The best-known precedent was William Powell's painting of 1853, *Discovery of the Mississippi by De Soto, AD 1541* (fig. 7), commissioned by the federal government to adorn the rotunda of the Capitol in Washington. Wimar repeated a number of themes from

194

Figure 6
Carl Wimar. *De Soto Discovering the Missis-*
sippi. Watercolor and oil on wet plaster, 1862.
Old Courthouse, Saint Louis. The white spots
are areas where the paint has flaked away.

Powell's treatment and other representations of
the New World's early history: assumptions
about a docile and willing Indian population awed
by the superior physical and spiritual authority
of the conquerors; of the providential ascendancy
of European Christianity over native cultures
and of the predestined character of European
conquest and settlement; and finally, of the
importance of enterprise—both spiritual and
secular—in overcoming the adversities of an
uncolonized wilderness.

Critics responding to Powell's painting took
up the theme of mastering obstacles that hindered the West's economic and political integra-
tion into the nation. The editor of the *New York*
Daily Times invoked it to establish the relationship between past and present that made De Soto
an appropriate subject for a national painting:

> The . . . great ideas that belong to our his-
> tory—ideas of Providence, Religion, Human-
> ity, Commerce, Enterprise, Discovery—are
> embodied in these works of the creative pen-

Figure 7
William H. Powell. *Discovery of the Missis-*
sippi by De Soto, AD 1541. Oil on canvas,
1853. United States Capitol Art Collection.

cil. . . . The history of this continent so far
as its northern half is concerned, is inti-
mately identified with our national history,
and hence, if our artists cannot find inspir-
ing themes in the events celebrated in our
own annals, we know of nothing more
appropriate than those interesting occur-
rences that opened the way for our civilization. They have certainly a peculiar relation
to Anglo-Saxon memories—to American
progress—to the taste and feelings of our
national mind and being, . . . The mind of
the country—at least its intelligent mind—
is conversant with those *grand preparatory
events*; it acknowledges their fellowship
with our immediate historic records. All
of them are really links in the same great
chain, and, therefore, our painters do well to
embody them in the efforts of the pencil.[21]

The phrase "grand preparatory events" recalled a
familiar midcentury tendency to explain contemporary events through secular typology. Earlier

Figure 8
Carl Wimar. *Landing of Laclede.* Watercolor
and oil on wet plaster, 1862. Old Courthouse,
Saint Louis.

195

Figure 9
Carl Wimar. *The Landing of Laclede: Study
for Old Courthouse Murals.* Pencil and wash
on light brown paper, horizontal format with
rounded top, c. 1862. Saint Louis Art
Museum.

figures from Europe's imperial past—Columbus, De Soto, La Salle, and Cortez, among others— had prepared the historical stage for the Anglo-Saxon conquest, the final act in the discovery and colonization of the New World by the Old.[22] Their shades were summoned to bear witness to the miraculous changes that the current massive energies of settlement were bringing to the continent:

> Could De Soto and La Salle be awakened from the sleep of death and behold the exhibition of to-day; could they mark the contrast between the woods and wilds and solitudes of this western country then, and the life and bustle and advanced civilization which are now abounding here, how would they ponder this wonderful change with astonishment! Instead of the forest waste inhabited by wild beasts and reverberating with the yell of the savage, they would find splendid cities, gorgeous steamers, the hum of machinery, and a country teeming with the farms and homes of happy freemen extending from the rising to the setting sun.[23]

To nineteenth-century eyes, De Soto was an ideal type of the new order, despite the fact that he had served a regime that most Protestant Americans considered tyrannical and corrupt. They saw him as an emissary of Christianity, whose mission was spiritual as well as political, combining raw military force with the benevolent hand of Christianity. Although relations between Catholics and Protestants in nineteenth-century America were often violent with cultural prejudice, this image of the power of Christianity bringing a native population to heel allowed Catholics and Protestants alike to believe in the necessity and goodness of western colonization. Nineteenth-century images of De Soto also

emphasized his role as proto-entrepreneur, intent on establishing good relations with his trading partners and finding in Christianity the moral and spiritual foundation on which to build a secure economic empire.

In Wimar's treatment of De Soto, the equestrian figure of the Spaniard advancing toward the seated, passive natives dominates the frieze. The arrangement of figures closely recalls Powell's work, in which the primary group of Indians is situated near the banks of the river, facing the Spanish conquerors who enter like a driving wedge from the woods along the Mississippi. Wimar, however, has added some details not included in Powell's treatment, such as the gesture of Indian friendship and generosity in the maiden who bends down before De Soto, offering a platter of fruits that symbolize the natural bounty promised to European conquerors. Such images were entirely imaginary, of course; in reality De Soto's exploration of the Mississippi Valley was characterized by constant warfare with the region's native peoples.[24] Wimar probably invented Indians for his frescoes to emphasize the theme of trade, vital to the cycle and more fully developed in the next lunette.

Wimar established careful links between the De Soto subject and *The Landing of Laclede* (fig. 8), the mural next to it on the east or river side of the courthouse. Pierre Laclede, arriving at the site of Saint Louis in December 1763, opened the subsequent act in the imperial drama: the settlement of the Mississippi Valley.[25] According to the logic of types, he was associated not only with De Soto but with other figures of entrepreneurial and commercial importance to Saint Louis. Wilson Primm, in an address delivered on the anniversary of the city's founding, set Laclede next to Columbus, Cartier, La Salle, and Hennepin as the most recent historical figure in a long line of men possessing "sagacity of mind and an enduring firmness of purpose," who had struggled to control "the resources of a region so vast and unexplored." Like Columbus and De Soto, Laclede had "a combination of the qualities which were required for such an undertaking." He was history's appointed agent, "sent forth as the moving cause of great and wonderful results."[26] Behind Laclede stood De Soto, and behind De Soto, in the minds of Wimar's contemporaries, stood Columbus, the mythic prototype of all subsequent discoverer figures. Wimar's contemporaries, here as elsewhere, were called upon to locate the underlying logic within the complex web of events.

Wimar emphasized the specifically commercial and trade-related nature of Laclede's venture, as he had De Soto's. Again he represented the origins of Saint Louis as a harmonious encounter between Indian and white. Although contemporaneous histories of the city's founding make no allusion to such an event,[27] Wimar may have decided to include Indians to emphasize the benign nature of Laclede's original colonizing venture. The French government in New Orleans had granted Laclede exclusive trading privileges with the Indians of upper Louisiana, and the success of his commercial venture—monopolizing the fur trade in this region of the West—depended upon the good will and peaceful cooperation of the Indian populations along the Missouri and upper Mississippi rivers. Showing native Americans openly embracing the French traders encouraged the notion that Saint Louis' commercial destiny was foreordained and capable of surmounting any and all obstacles—human as well as natural. Thus Laclede and his men, on board the flatboat that brought them up the river, stand in gestures of greeting and friendship as they are pulled ashore toward the waiting party of Indians. A pencil and wash study (fig. 9) for the mural shows the French trader doffing his tricorner hat and extending his arms. Near him is an unfurled banner with the words "St.

Louis"; on shore an Indian chieftain with feathered headdress extends his arm, holding a peace pipe.[28] In the finished mural, Wimar reportedly included a spring of water to welcome the voyagers—perhaps making use of older classical myths that associated founding figures with sacred springs and other manifestations of divine approval.[29]

Although Wimar relied on verbal sources for the particulars of the second lunette, his broader conception of the landing of Laclede owed much to earlier and contemporaneous paintings of first encounters between European conquerors and native peoples.[30] One prototype for such images was Columbus' own first encounter; perhaps the earliest statement of the theme was Theodore DeBry's engraving of Columbus landing in the Indies and being greeted by Indians bearing gifts.[31] A far better-known example of the theme, however, was John Vanderlyn's *Landing of Columbus at the Island of Guanahani, West Indies, October 12, 1492* (1846, fig. 10), painted for the United States Capitol rotunda.

In celebrating Saint Louis' place in the larger drama of nation-building, Wimar paralleled numerous other examples of artistic (and literary) myth-making in the prewar decades. Visual and verbal narratives of origination helped secure for the nation's states and regions an important place in the sequence of colonizing ventures—from John Smith to Roger Williams, from the Pilgrims to Henry Hudson and Bartholomew Gosnold—that expanded the geographic and political boundaries of the continent. Indeed, in the mid-nineteenth century artists created a kind of regional gallery of originating myths, each visually recounting the moment when Europeans first entered a place or region or first established essential relations with the local Indians. Iconographic precedents for Wimar's mural include the New Yorker Robert Walter Weir's

197

198

Figure 10 (left)
John Vanderlyn. *Landing of Columbus at the Island of Guanahani, West Indies, October 12, 1492.* Oil on canvas, 1846. United States Capitol Art Collection.

Figure 11 (right)
Robert Walter Weir. *Landing of Henry Hudson, 1608, at Verplanck Point, near Peekskill, New York.* Oil on canvas, 1835. Private collection. Courtesy of Christie, Manson and Woods International Inc.

Landing of Henry Hudson, 1608, at Verplanck Point, near Peekskill (1835, fig. 11) and Virginia-born John Gadsby Chapman's several treatments of the first encounter theme, including his *First Ship* (whereabouts unknown: exhibited 1837 at the National Academy of Design, engraved in 1842) and his *Good Times in the New World (The Hope of Jamestown)* (1841, fig. 12).[32] John Mix Stanley also painted a *Landing of Captain John Smith at Jamestown* (fig. 13). New Englanders likewise represented their own origins; Charles Hitchcock painted *The Landing of Roger Williams at State Rock* (fig. 14) and two artists from New Bedford—William Allen Wall and Albert Bierstadt—both painted the subject of Bartholomew Gosnold's landing on the site later to become a major whaling port.[33]

Each of these paintings functioned for its respective region as Wimar's painting of Laclede's landing functioned for Saint Louis and its economic hinterlands; each identified a founding figure along with the particular moment, sacred to historic memory, when the European history of

the region began. Such subjects also acted as a form of local apologetics and promotion, as various cities, states, and regions gained a heightened self-consciousness about their role in the life of the nation. Saint Louisans, in an effort to establish a distinctive genealogy that demonstrated their importance to the nation, created their own version of the discovery myth, commemorated first in the scene of De Soto's discovery of the Mississippi. Historical logic, however, required that the baton of empire be passed to the French—the actual settlers of the Mississippi Valley and later the allies of the Americans in their revolution against the British.

Judge Primm chose not only the subject of Laclede's landing but that of the next lunette in the series, *The Year of the Blow* (fig. 15), which shows Indians ambushing a group of French settlers in the woods along the Mississippi. In the distance, along the shores of the river itself, is the stockaded village of Saint Louis. The foreground is strewn with the bodies of those killed in the attack, while men and women settlers

Figure 12
John Gadsby Chapman. *Good Times in the New World (The Hope of Jamestown)*. Oil on panel, 1841. Virginia Museum of Fine Arts, Richmond; Paul Mellon Collection.

199

Figure 13
John Mix Stanley. *Capt. John Smith and Party Landing at Jamestown*. Oil on canvas, n.d. The Thomas Gilcrease Institute of American History and Art, Tulsa.

Figure 14
Charles Hitchcock. *The Landing of Roger Williams at State Rock*. Oil on canvas, 1847. The Thomas Gilcrease Institute of American History and Art, Tulsa.

Figure 15
Carl Wimar. *The Year of the Blow*. Watercolor and oil on wet plaster, 1862. Old Courthouse, Saint Louis.

flee in an effort to alert the town. The episode depicted in the mural occurred in 1780, seventeen years after the young settlement of Saint Louis, like all French lands west of the Mississippi, had been ceded back to Spain. In 1780, some twenty of Saint Louis' French colonists lost their lives during a surprise attack by Indians allied to the British. According to the view prevalent in the mid-nineteenth century, the British had bribed the Spanish governor, Leyba, into betraying his French charges; even though the governor was vindicated following his suicide over the episode, popular accounts continued to cast him as a traitor figure. Judge Primm compared him to Benedict Arnold, who had likewise been "seduced into defection from his duty."[34]

As elsewhere in the cycle, a specific rationale motivated Primm's choice of the third subject. The attack was a fitting instance of the adversities suffered by the young settlement, caught as it was in the machinations of imperial rivals. Such episodes endowed Saint Louis' lowly beginnings with heroic dimensions. In addition, however, an event which took place during the American Revolution furnished a frontier counterpart to the struggles of eastern colonists against their British rulers. In the second quarter of the nineteenth century, as Revolutionary subjects furnished eastern painters with grand historical themes,[35] western cities such as Saint Louis eagerly sought out analogous episodes. The actions and courage of the French settlers anticipated the vaunted bravery and enterprise of American citizens in the historical epoch about to open. A Father O'Hanlon wrote of the French settlers of Saint Louis: "Their defense against this attack and that bold spirit manifested on the occasion were in keeping with the deeds of their brethren, the French, who took part in the American Revolution; while their course of action has

Figure 16
Carl Wimar. *Westward the Star of Empire*.
Watercolor and oil on wet plaster, 1862. Old
Courthouse, Saint Louis.

given them the right to say, that, on the occi-
dental shores of the Mississippi river, they were
the first to battle against English oppression and
English ambition." Historians of the city emphasized those aspects of French colonial culture in
the Mississippi Valley that most matched the
Anglo-Saxon qualities admired by Saint Louis'
midcentury civic promoters. Early in the twentieth century, historian Walter Stevens commented that "there was a good deal of the
instinct of Americanism in St. Louis as early
as 1780."[36]

That the landscape of the Mississippi River
is the setting for three of the four lunettes
underscores the river's importance in the city's
history and in the lives of Saint Louisans. The
river served not only as the avenue of trade but
as the ligature of union, the natural backdrop to
Saint Louis' economic growth and increasing
political strength as the premiere city of the

West. By midcentury a major theme occupying
the city's historians was its predestined role in
the future of the nation, which seemed guar-
anteed by its geographical position below the
juncture of the Missouri and the Mississippi,
the West's major river arteries. Together these
rivers furnished nearly continuous fluid path-
ways to both the Atlantic and the Pacific. To
midcentury western promoters, who believed in
the necessary, indeed providential link between
the natural features of the continent and its
political associations and structures, Saint Louis
seemed "to have been formed by nature, for the
site of a great and populous city, and to have
been intended for the *depot* of the greater part
of the western country." Only "enterprise and
industry," those quintessentially Anglo-Saxon
virtues, were needed to realize its destiny, for
"[t]he immense superiority which its locality
gives it, will always ensure the monopoly of the

commerce, and render it the mart of the mineral, agricultural, and fur countries which lie above it on both sides of the Mississippi River."[37]

The lunette which completed Wimar's cycle was situated, appropriately, on the west side of the courthouse, aligned with the westward movement of empire that was its subject. Alternately called *Westward the Star of Empire* and *Cochetope Pass* (fig. 16), the lunette was the only landscape subject in the cycle, representing a mountain pass at sunset, bordered by rocky bluffs. In this western wilderness the only signs of life are the herd of buffalo that scatter in opposite directions in the foreground of the composition, and the white canvas tops of a wagon train in the distant right background, threading its way through the defile. The lower portion of the sky is roseate with the last rays of the setting sun.[38]

The title *Cochetope Pass* clearly identifies the topical significance of the scene for Saint Louisans, while the allegorical phrase "Star of Empire" signals in a more general way the westward migration of settlers from their jumping-off point at Saint Louis. The phrase was used in a speech made at the Railway Celebration of 1857 (quoted at the beginning of this essay); "the star of empire" as an image invoked the larger process of expansion, which would realize America's historic mission to occupy the continent and Saint Louis' own role in the westward movement. In addition, however, when joined through its other title—*Cochetope Pass*—with the promotion of the Pacific railroad, the phrase carried a more precise relevance.[39] Cochetope Pass was regarded by many in Saint Louis, in the words of an 1862 newspaper article about the courthouse murals, as "the natural gateway of the Central Pacific Railroad."[40] It was also the pass in the Rockies associated with the 38th/39th parallel route that Senator Thomas Hart Benton had tirelessly promoted since the mid-1840s. For Ben-

ton's constituents, Wimar's fourth mural was laden with geopolitical associations, cast in the biblical imagery of the promised land and blessed by the totemic power of the buffalo.

The railroad was at the center of Saint Louis' vision of empire; the ambitions it unleashed were as hard-coined as the materials out of which it was constructed. A writer for the *Missouri Republican* summed up the prevailing local sentiment when he wrote in 1858: "Nothing is better demonstrated than the fact that no city, however great, can long maintain its onward progress without railroads, in competition with those that enjoy such privileges. Chicago is a marked instance of railroad importance. . . . Will St. Louis and Missouri, whose interests in the matter are one, wake up to their true position before their arteries are cut in all directions . . . ?"[41]

The idea of a transcontinental highway had a long history; the nation's increasingly urgent need for secure connections with its new western lands after the Mexican-American War in 1848 and the discovery of gold in 1849 brought it once again to the fore.[42] A new era of federal commitment opened on March 2, 1853, when the United States Congress finally passed the Pacific Railroad Survey Bill, appropriating federal funds for army-directed surveys of four proposed routes across the continent. These four surveys (see map) consisted of the northern or Whitney survey, so-called because of its association with the original route proposed by Asa Whitney, which was headed by I. I. Stevens and passed between the 47th and the 49th parallels; the Central or Buffalo Trail survey (the route endorsed by Benton), which passed between the 38th and 39th parallels through Cochetope Pass and was headed by Lieutenant John W. Gunnison; the 35th parallel survey headed by Lieutenant Amiel Weeks Whipple, originating in Fort Smith, Arkansas and passing along the Canadian River valley to

THE PACIFIC RAILROAD
SURVEYS 1853–5

•••••••••••• WHITNEY/STEVENS ROUTE (47th/49th Parallel)

•••••••••• GUNNISON/FRÉMONT ROUTE (38th/39th Parallel)

— — — — WHIPPLE ROUTE (35th Parallel)

•••••••••• POPE/PARKE ROUTE (32nd Parallel)

++++++++++ TRANSCONTINENTAL RAILROAD AS BUILT

FORT VANCOUVER

FORT SNELLING (ST. PAUL)

CHICAGO

MISSOURI

RIVER

OMAHA

SAN FRANCISCO

COCHETOPE PASS

FORT LEAVENWORTH

ST. LOUIS

SOUTH-WEST BRANCH

ROLLA

SPRINGFIELD

LOS ANGELES

CANADIAN RIVER

MISSISSIPPI RIVER

FORT SMITH

FORT WASHITA

FORT YUMA

N

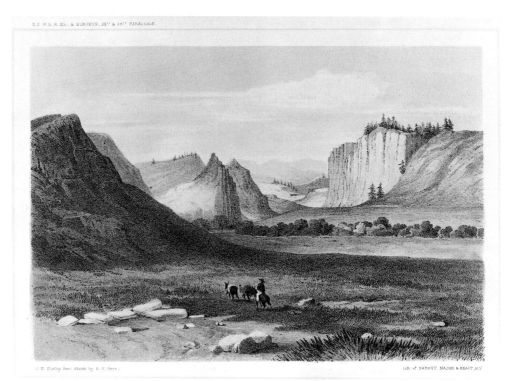

U.S. P. R. R. EX. & SURVEYS, 38TH & 39TH PARALLELS

J. M. Stanley from Sketch by R. H. Kern.   Lith. of SARONY, MAJOR & KNAPP, N.Y.

COO-CHE-TO-PA PASS

View looking up Sahwatch Creek Sept'r 1st

Figure 17
John Mix Stanley after R. H. Kern. *Coo-Che-To-Pa Pass View looking up Sahwatch Creek, September 1st [1853].* Color lithograph, 1855. Amon Carter Museum.

Albuquerque and Los Angeles; and a fourth survey along the 32nd parallel, jointly conducted by Lieutenants J. G. Parke and John Pope.[43] These surveys, however, failed to resolve the question of the best route, and nature itself proved a less-than-reliable court of appeal, proving no one route indisputably superior to the others. Benton's route, however, received a serious setback when Gunnison and a small party of his men were massacred by Paiute Indians, and Gunnison's surviving field notes did little to reassure those favoring the 38th/39th parallel route, which seemed to involve inordinate tunneling and bridging.[44] Refusing to concede defeat, Benton relied on the more encouraging testimony of two other cross-continental treks along the

38th/39th parallel that year—a privately sponsored expedition led by Benton's son-in-law John C. Frémont and an unofficial government-financed expedition led by Lieutenant Edward Fitzgerald Beale.[45]

Frémont had been associated with westward expansion since the early 1840s, when he first acquired his reputation as "the Pathfinder," and in 1848–49, Benton had raised private funds for him to conduct a survey across the Rockies. This earlier expedition, characterized as "one of the greatest disasters in the history of American exploration," had ended in the deaths of one-third of Frémont's team, caught in impassable winter snows in the San Juan Mountains of Colorado after they wandered off the planned route.[46] Frémont's 1853 expedition, though also fraught with difficulties, proved more promising, as did Beale's expedition of the same year.[47] Their reports confirmed what Benton wished to hear; in 1853 the senator wrote that Cochetope Pass was "worthy to open the door from the East to the great western slope of the North American continent."[48] Saint Louis, of course, would be the hinge of this great imperial system of transportation.

Although the report of Beale's expedition was accompanied by four lithographic views, Wimar based his courthouse mural on a view taken by Richard Kern, the artist accompanying the Gunnison survey, who had lost his life in the 1853 massacre. Kern's sketch of the pass was the source for John Mix Stanley's lithograph, published as "*Coo-Che-To-Pa Pass. View looking up Sahwatch Creek, September 1st [1853]*" in the official volume on the 38th/39th parallel survey (fig. 17).[49] The geological forms shown in the Kern-Stanley view—most notably the undulating vertical ridges of the bluff on the right, the pointed form just off of left-center, and the more sloping profile of the ridge nearest the left foreground—match almost precisely the forms shown in Wimar's mural, leaving little doubt about the source for his view.

The herd of buffalo that Wimar included in the foreground had multiple associations. First, Cochetope Pass was a buffalo migration route; its very name was the Paiute word for buffalo, while the Spanish called it the "Puerto del Cibolos" or "Gate of the Buffaloes." As evidence that Cochetope was the most "perfect" and "natural" route over the Rockies, Senator Benton pointed to the buffalo themselves, "those best of engineers, whose instinct never commits a mistake, and which in their migrations for pasture, shelter, and salt, never fail to find the lowest levels in the mountains, the shallowest fords in the rivers, the richest grass, the best salt licks, the most perma-nent water, and always take the shortest and best routes between all these points of attraction." Buffalo migration routes thus presented "a triumph of instinct over science; and we shall claim the benefit of it if any book-taught engineer shall ever have the temerity to dispute the excellence and supremacy of the Coochatope [sic] pass."[50]

Wimar included an emigrant wagon train in his representation, a strange detail given that Cochetope was not commonly used as a route for westward migration.[51] Benton himself, however, in a speech made before Congress in 1855, had quoted Frémont's description of the route as "an open easy wagon way."[52] By arguing that the natural flow of emigration was through this particular pass in the Rockies, Benton and his supporters could claim that iron rails would merely consummate a connection with the Pacific already established by nature. Carefully avoiding the taint of political self-interest, Benton presented his advocacy of the 38th/39th parallel route as an unbiased recognition of the choice dictated by geography itself.[53] But in this case, the evidence of nature and geography remained contested. Although Frémont and Benton struggled heroically to put a good face on the recent expedition, its difficulties, along with the murder of Gunnison as leader of the official survey, gave rival routes a significant edge over the 38th/39th parallel.[54]

Compounding the problems for Benton's route was the existence of a rival faction in Saint Louis itself that favored another route, along the 35th parallel. This route originated in Fort Smith, Arkansas, but would connect with Saint Louis by way of the South-West Branch through Springfield. Its more southerly course offered the advantage of potentially uniting the pro-Southern faction in Missouri.[55] The spokesman for the 35th parallel route, Missouri Congressman John S. Phelps, had powerful support from numerous quarters and, like Benton, vigorously protested his national, nonsectional interests.[56] Beginning in the late 1850s, the Saint Louis–based *Missouri Republican* published a series of scathing denunciations of Benton's "Central" route in favor of the 35th parallel route, which they claimed was the "natural channel of travel."[57] The controversy, the paper declared, "so far as it has been permitted to divide the citizens of St. Louis, must be regretted as both ill-considered and mischievous. . . . Subsequent surveys thoroughly and finally exploded 'Cochetope,' and the rubbish from that explosion being by this time cleared out of the path, we can now see our way better to the true 'Central Route.'"[58] The local debate over which route was superior, continuously fueled by the heat of regional rivalries, would not go away.

Furthermore, advocates of both the 38th/39th and 35th parallel routes attacked the southern interests behind the 32nd parallel route, which had the support of Buchanan's secretary of war, Jefferson Davis.[59] Given the charged sectional dimension of the problem, *any* choice would be bound to antagonize other parties. Yet supporters of the Pacific railroad project had insisted throughout the 1850s that this undertaking could deflect sectional tensions. In 1857, the governor of Maryland, speaking at the opening celebration for the Ohio and Mississippi Railroad's newly completed link to Saint Louis, claimed that "in these times of threatened disruption and disunion, and whilst men are wickedly calculating the value of the confederacy, . . . these ligaments of iron with which you are drawing us into closer neighborhood and most ready intercourse with each other, are so many ties to bind us together . . . as one indissoluble and united people."[60] Edward Miller, chief engineer for the South-West Branch, wrote: "Every iron railroad which passes from one State into another, is a bond of union between them; and along this track will spring up new States, welded

by great iron links to all their quarrelsome elder sisters. . . . There is nothing equal to good bars of American iron, for keeping together things that have a tendency to fly off at a tangent; and as a 'union saver' alone, this railroad will be worth ten times its cost."[61]

In 1858, President Buchanan, citing the increasingly urgent need to defend the nation's western states and territories, called for a renewed commitment to the construction of the Pacific Road.[62] By this time, Benton had redirected his efforts toward a call for private financing by "enlightened capitalists."[63] Western states were prepared to underwrite their own railroads, with an eye to linking up eventually with the trunk line.[64] Following the secession of southern states in 1860, however, the far southern 32nd parallel route was dropped from consideration, and Benton's route received an additional boost from the fact that the 35th parallel route passed through Springfield in the contested southwestern portion of the state, and then through Fort Smith in Arkansas, a Confederate state.[65] Although Benton himself had died in 1858, others took up his cause. On the eve of the passage of the Pacific Railroad bill, the 38th/39th parallel route once again staked an equal claim to consideration with the other routes.[66]

The choice of Cochetope Pass for the subject of the lunette on the west side of the courthouse rotunda may thus have been more than a tribute to a defunct vision. When Wimar began the commission in March 1862, the final decision on the route was still several months away.[67] His inclusion of the pass in his cycle therefore carried a rhetorical function, commemorating Benton's regionally based vision of expansion and making a last-ditch appeal for the inevitable and necessary rightness of the 38th/39th parallel as the route of empire. *Cochetope Pass* further underscored Saint Louis' loyalty to the Union and its belief in the extension of free northern institutions into the West. The emigrant train in the background of Wimar's mural carried freehold farmers, not slaveholders—a demonstration even more appropriate in the context of a federal courthouse. Although the program for the courthouse murals, worked out in the midst of war, pressed Saint Louis' claim to being the source of a better and stronger union, bound together this time by iron ties, its location in a divided state became one factor favoring the choice of Chicago as the Pacific railroad's point of departure. Wimar's and the commissioners' efforts to demonstrate their city's pro-Union stance, and thus to strengthen the legitimacy of their claim to the major rail connection between West and East, in the end proved futile.[68]

In evoking the symbolic importance of the Cochetope Pass, Wimar relied upon an older imagery—the quasi-biblical vision of a new promised land—unrelated to the issue of the railroad per se. The emigrants passing through the darkening valley move in the direction of the setting sun; left in shadow are the buffalo who scatter through the foreground in apparent fright at the encroachments of white settlers.[69] The composition is organized as a sharp contrast between shadowed foreground and light-filled distance, present and future; the human conquest of the West measures the gap.

The providential symbolism associated with the westward movement was more fully developed and exploited by two of Wimar's contemporaries, Emanuel Leutze and Albert Bierstadt. Like Wimar, both artists were of German origin, and both had spent periods of time in Düsseldorf, where they mastered a theatrical manner of representing historical themes in their treatments of westward expansion. There are notable connections between Wimar's *Westward the Star of Empire* and Leutze's fresco in the United States Capitol, *Westward the Course of Empire Takes Its Way* (fig. 18), completed in December 1862.

Although Wimar made no recorded trips to Washington, D.C., during this or any other period, he may have received or read reports of Leutze's mural. The two artists had enjoyed a close association between 1852 and 1856, while both were in Düsseldorf, and even before Wimar returned to the United States, Leutze may have discussed with his American colleagues his conception for a large mural symbolizing the movement westward.[70] In addition, notices and descriptions of the fresco were published prior to its completion, and verbal networks of information kept German-American artists and others who had studied in Düsseldorf abreast of major artistic events in both the United States and Germany. Whatever the reason, the coincidence

Figure 18
Emanuel Leutze. *Westward the Course of Empire Takes Its Way*. Fresco, 1862. United States Capitol Art Collection.

207

Figure 19
Albert Bierstadt. *The Oregon Trail.* Oil on canvas, 1869. Butler Institute of American Art, Youngstown, Ohio.

in the subject matter of the two murals, if not in their conception, appears to be part and parcel of the broader parallels between the United States Capitol and the Saint Louis Courthouse buildings. Given the close architectural similarity between the two, the commissioners of the courthouse may have known of the various decorative schemes then under way to furnish the Capitol with a suitable iconography of American empire.[71] Certainly the echo of Leutze's title in Wimar's mural suggests at least a superficial link, although, as has been noted earlier, the phrase "The Star of Empire" probably had an independent, more local source of inspiration. Commissioner Taussig in his letter of 1886 attributed the words to Benton himself. They are a variant of George Berkeley's resounding "Westward the course of Empire takes its way"; the phrase begins the final stanza in Berkeley's *Verses on*

the Prospect of Planting Arts and Learning in America, written in 1723, and had considerable popular currency throughout the mid-nineteenth century.[72]

More striking than the links between the two works, however, are their differences. Leutze's mural places the human action at the very center of the composition; his conception is preeminently theatrical with its tableau-like, staged arrangement of figures, shown in the finally triumphant but soul-trying moments of the terrible passage across the Continental Divide en route to the promised land. Wimar, far more modest in his pictorial ambitions, only hints at the human agents whose entry opened up an entire new era in the history of the West.

The restrained character of Wimar's treatment is even more apparent when contrasted with Albert Bierstadt's *The Oregon Trail* (1869, fig. 19), in which a series of emigrant wagons moves ponderously westward, into the setting sun that blazes with millennial intensity on the horizon. For Bierstadt, a master of visual rhetoric tuned to the sensibilities of his public, the way west became a holy pilgrimage rife with symbols of sacrifice and spiritual triumph—skulls scattered on the wayside, trees whose bleak branches are feverishly outlined against the sunset sky, and splendid bursts of light promising exaltation and redemption at the end of the journey. There is little room here for doubting the inevitable virtue and benevolence of the process. In the late 1860s, scenes of western expansion and frontier trial had acquired different meanings, alluding to the recently fought war and to the resurrected hope for the future which the West seemed to promise. For both Leutze and Bierstadt, sacrifice simply confirmed the nation's moral and spiritual victory over terrible odds.[73]

Comparing Wimar's mural to the paintings of Leutze and Bierstadt reveals something of Wimar's own divided loyalties as, at the end of his career, he approached a subject whose historical scope had no precedent in his work. Wimar's vision of the West, situated within a complex exchange of cultural gains and losses, was less amenable to symbolic resolutions than Leutze's single-mindedly heroic, eastern-based view or Bierstadt's post-war view. Wimar chose as his major actors not those men and women shown in Leutze's mural at the vanguard of westward expansion, but the buffalo whose death knell was sounded by their appearance.[74] Wimar's apparent ambivalence about the epochal changes that accompanied the opening of the frontier is not surprising. Between 1859, when he returned from the second of two voyages up the Missouri, and 1861, he had completed some of his most visually eloquent paintings on the subject of the buffalo. He painted these animals as a natural symbol of the power and wild beauty of the

West, as well as its doomed fragility; they are shown fording rivers in the mingled blaze of sunset and raging prairie fires (*Buffaloes Crossing the Yellowstone*, plate 10); being hunted by Indians (*The Buffalo Hunt*, plates 16 and 18); or expiring from a bullet wound in the cold, steely dusk of a western day (*The Wounded Buffalo*, see fig. 92 in Rick Stewart's essay).[75] Now in 1862, at the end of his brief career, Wimar returned to the subject of the buffalo to paint Cochetope Pass, "The Gate of the Buffalo," in a work that was intended to celebrate the prospective opening of the West. Given the celebratory program of the courthouse cycle, Wimar's mural of the pass at sunset is notably muted, even somber—as much an elegy for the passing of the buffalo as a trumpet call for the opening of the frontier.[76] Yet associated as his career had been with the primitive West of conflict and romantic savagery, Wimar was prepared, like most of his contemporaries, to cast his lot with the future. If there is regret in *Westward the Star*, it is neutralized by the historical determinism of the cycle as a whole.

Two other phases of Wimar's program for the rotunda round out its symbolic message. The first consists of four allegorical figures of Justice, Liberty, Commerce, and Law, painted on the walls of the interior abutments supporting the dome. Since these figures later suffered greatly at the hands of painters hired to spruce up the fading murals, they are best examined through the three extant drawings that Wimar made preliminary to painting them. At least one of the drawings, squared for transfer, also reveals something of Wimar's working procedure, perhaps learned from his academic training in Düsseldorf or from his first master, Leon Pomarede.

The four figures, approximately nine feet in height, are the allegorical "supports" of social order in the West, testifying in the language of antiquity to the extension of civilized institutions

210

Figure 20
Carl Wimar. *Justice*. Oil on canvas, c. 1862.
Missouri Historical Society.

Figure 21
Carl Wimar. *Law*. Oil on canvas, c. 1862.
Missouri Historical Society.

Figure 22
Carl Wimar. *Liberty*. Oil on canvas, c. 1862.
Missouri Historical Society.

across the continent. Wimar relied here on thoroughly conventional classical symbols: the blindfolded female figure of Justice holds scales in her left hand, sword in her right; Law is a woman writing in a book inscribed with that word, held up by a putto; Liberty holds pileus, fasces, and wreaths, and is accompanied by an eagle with a shield and an American flag (figs. 20 through 22); and Commerce is "the winged Mercury, born of the brain of Jove, tripping fleetly over the globe, bearing the sceptre of power, while beneath him are the symbols of navigation and transportation."[77]

Despite the universal language with which Wimar represented the major principles of social order, there is a more topical import to his four allegorical figures, alluding as they do to the moral and social bulwarks of the American Union.[78] Many northerners felt that the events of 1861 and the secession of southern states had violated the spirit of law and justice, and that the institution of slavery violated liberty. Commerce was the long-heralded if largely northern "glue" of the Union, promising to create bonds between the sections that would transcend differences in their respective social and economic orders. Wimar's choice of figures, therefore, may have been intended as a pointed reference to those very principles that pro-Union northerners considered to be most lacking in the South and most central to the northern vision of the republic.

Beneath the four lunettes themselves are four portraits that complete Wimar's contribution to the courthouse rotunda. George and Martha Washington appear on the west and north sides respectively, Edward Bates on the south side, and Thomas Hart Benton on the east (figs. 23 and 24). The presence of the nation's founding couple, more than a generalized tribute to the republican ideal, once again marked the pro-Union loyalties which the courthouse commission was meant to confirm. These portraits

Figure 23
Carl Wimar. *Thomas Hart Benton*. Watercolor and oil on wet plaster, 1862. Old Courthouse, Saint Louis.

Figure 24
Carl Wimar. *Edward Bates*. Watercolor and oil on wet plaster, 1862. Old Courthouse, Saint Louis.

211

are clearly based on paintings by Missouri artist George Caleb Bingham (1856; Saint Louis Mercantile Library Association), which in turn were based upon Gilbert Stuart's "Athenaeum" portraits of the founding couple.[79] Benton's portrait explicitly linked his Unionist sentiments not only with his advocacy of the Pacific railroad but with his opposition to slavery, most forcibly enunciated in the final years of his life.

Edward Bates' portrait next to Benton's was a further tribute to Missouri's pro-Union statesmen.[80] Bates (1793–1869), like Benton, had long been involved in railroad promotion; in 1851 he broke the earth for the first rail link with the territory west of Saint Louis, and six years later he gave a keynote address at the opening of the Ohio and Mississippi Railroad, which completed the city's first rail link with the East. He shared Benton's vision of a transcontinental railroad opening trade with Asia and also actively promoted ties with the East.[81] Also like Benton, Bates was a tireless campaigner for Saint Louis' national interests, stressing that the valley it dominated belonged to neither North nor South but to the nation, and characterizing the region as "a divinely appointed bulwark of our institutions," providentially situated to bridge the growing political divisions between the sections. Although born in Virginia and himself a slaveholder, Bates was a Whig opposed to the extension of slavery into the territories and to the repeal of the Missouri Compromise. In 1860 he ran against Lincoln for the Republican presidential nomination and later became Lincoln's Attorney-General.[82] Even more tellingly, Bates was the brother-in-law of Hamilton R. Gamble, who had summoned loyalists to resist secession at a Union rally in the rotunda of the courthouse on January 12, 1861, and who became governor of Missouri's provisional Union government after the elected governor defected later that year.[83] Bates' inclusion among Wimar's portraits

in the courthouse rotunda honored not only his promotion of the Pacific railroad but his dedication to preserving the Union.[84]

Wimar's courthouse cycle is one of the earliest instances of fresco decoration in nineteenth-century America. In 1862, when Wimar began the courthouse commission, there were only a handful of American precedents for its use in large-scale public projects. These precedents, found in Washington, were not necessarily known to Wimar, and while they merit mention, we must look farther afield for possible sources. Wimar's years of study in Düsseldorf suggest some answers to the questions of why he turned to fresco at this stage in his career, and what artistic ambitions this medium may have served for him.

The history of publicly sponsored art in the United States began with the Revolution and the ensuing need to decorate public buildings with works of art that both celebrated the new republic and endowed it with a noble pedigree. The decoration of the United States Capitol furnished the leading instance of the role government could play in encouraging history painting commensurate with the new nation's political achievements. Such paintings, however, took the form of large-scale oil works on canvas by the nation's leading artists. John Trumbull set the tone for these publicly commissioned works with his series of Revolutionary War subjects, conceived for the decoration of the rotunda and purchased by Congress between 1819 and 1824. To fill the remaining vacant spots in the rotunda, Congress commissioned additional paintings memorializing key episodes in the spiritual and secular conquest of America.[85]

Later phases of embellishment elsewhere in the Capitol exploited fresco—a medium associ-

Figure 25
Constantino Brumidi. *Calling of Cincinnatus from the Plow.* Fresco, 1855–56. United States Capitol Art Collection.

Figure 26
Constantino Brumidi. *Calling of Putnam from the Plow to the Revolution.* Fresco, 1855–56. United States Capitol Art Collection.

214

Figure 27
Constantino Brumidi. *Thomas Jefferson, Secretary of State*. Fresco, after 1859. United States Capitol Art Collection.

ated in Europe with public decoration. Until the self-conscious Beaux-Arts revival of fresco decoration toward the end of the nineteenth century, public murals in this medium were most often the work of Italian- and German-trained artists. Constantino Brumidi painted the earliest frescoes in the Capitol in 1855–56 in the House of Representatives; on two lunettes on the east and west walls of the Agriculture Committee room he depicted the *Calling of Cincinnatus from the Plow* and a parallel subject from America's Revolutionary history, *Calling of Putnam from the Plow to the Revolution* (figs. 25 and 26).[86] Brumidi's choice of medium was a logical one, given the long and continuous history of fresco painting in his native Italy, and he had the training in fresco technique that American artists lacked. Working on flat rather than curved lunettes, of larger size than Wimar's, Brumidi painted frieze-like compositions; his figures, situated close to the wall plane, appeared large and easily readable, while background details were kept to a minimum and scaled down accordingly. Elsewhere in his Capitol decorations the Italian artist included portrait busts of cabinet members (fig. 27) in conjunction with allegorical or historical scenes—a format similar to Wimar's use of the portrait bust in the courthouse. Brumidi's neo-Rococo ceiling decorations, however, with their Old World associations and pastel frivolousness, brought down the wrath of American artists, who felt that such a decorative language was inappropriate to a republic and who were also angered that government commissions were being given to foreigners.[87]

Wimar may have been exposed to this derivative style of decoration through Leon Pomarede, the man to whom he was apprenticed when he first began painting as a youth in Saint Louis.[88] Like Brumidi, Pomarede had the advantage of European origins and of greater familiarity with both the techniques and possibilities of fresco. The French artist gave Wimar his first lessons in large-scale decoration, and as late as 1855, having mastered a new sophistication of technique, Wimar could still write to his parents, "I still have great respect for Pomarede although he is very strange at times, I owe him a lot, to be sure."[89] An 1858 guidebook to Saint Louis described Pomarede as "by profession a fresco-painter—*peintre en fresque.*"[90] Nonetheless his fresco method was anything but orthodox. In the late 1850s Pomarede painted a large-scale fresco cycle at the Merchants' Exchange, a building begun in 1856 and completed the next year. The authors of the 1858 guidebook did not consider the cycle "true fresco" but credited him with approximating the appearance of fresco in oil, "with some advantages that fresco does not possess. . . . The method adopted by him is called encaustic, and consists essentially in the use of oil colors upon a prepared ground, so as to present a dead absorbent surface, avoiding the *reflections* of light, which render painting in oil unsuitable for such works."[91] The veneration with which fresco was held in the mid-nineteenth century is conveyed by its description as "in every respect . . . [the] grandest walk" of art, "designed for the decoration of great public buildings—princely halls, forums, senate-chambers and churches. . . . It is only in fresco-painting, indeed, that the very grandest achievements of the imagination are possible in the art of painting."[92]

Wimar apparently did not heed warnings that in fresco, petty detail would be lost on domes and ceilings. In other respects, however, Wimar's courthouse murals do recall aspects of Pomarede's work. Wimar may have derived the idea of using oil paints for fresco from Pomarede, with disastrous consequences. He may also have been able to consult both Pomarede himself and his frescoes at the Merchants' Exchange once he received his courthouse commission. Like the courthouse, the exchange, designed by one of the city's most prominent architects, George I. Barnett, was a building of considerable symbolic importance, embodying the proud commercial history and current mercantile stature of the city. The "Hall" or Exchange Room occupied most of the second floor and culminated in a rotunda sixty feet in diameter and fifty-eight feet above the floor.[93] Pomarede was commissioned to paint the pendentives of the dome, choosing allegories of "the four quarters of the globe"—America, Europe, Asia, and Africa. Pomarede's choice of allegory for the four continents was one to which Wimar readily adverted in his rotunda decoration for the four allegorical figures of Justice, Liberty, Commerce, and Law. The decorations in the Hall of the Merchants' Exchange—even taking with a grain of salt the claim that "there is not, perhaps, one of the same size anywhere that is in some respects so striking"—remained an important local precedent as well as an inducement for Wimar to surpass the productions of his teacher.[94]

One other instance of American mural decoration contemporaneous with Wimar's commission was Leutze's *Westward the Course of Empire*, iconographically related, as we have seen, to *Cochetope Pass*. Unlike Wimar's lunettes, Leutze's mural was done in a technique known as stereochromy, or "waterglass painting," in which pigments were mixed with water and painted on the plaster, then coated with a solution of potassium or sodium silicate which, when it dried, left a thin film that sealed the painting.[95] The invention of stereochromy, offered as an improvement upon the fresco medium, occurred within the broader context of the widespread German interest in mural painting. Since these two signal instances of large-scale mural painting, commissioned concurrently, were both executed by German-American artists trained in Düsseldorf and steeped in the artistic

215

culture of the German states at midcentury,[96] we must ultimately look to developments in Germany for the sources of both Leutze's and Wimar's public murals.

Through the late nineteenth century Düsseldorf painters furnished one of the two main currents of official history painting in Germany (the other being Munich), and they influenced both Wimar and Leutze as they took up the challenge of creating a nationalist iconography for the United States. As a student in Düsseldorf between 1852 and 1856, Wimar would have had ample opportunity to observe the continued involvement of German artists with subjects of legendary and historical significance for an emerging regional—and national—identity.

The ideal of a communal art of fresco served religious and national aspirations for which easel painting remained inadequate. The German mural movement originated soon after the turn of the nineteenth century, when German artists in Italy had an opportunity to learn fresco technique following the most rigorous precedents of Renaissance practice and employing scale-sized cartoons. The call for a "rebirth" of German art around public mural decoration as it had flourished from Giotto to Raphael preoccupied artists of the Rhineland for the next three generations, extending to the years of Wimar's Düsseldorf training.[97]

By the mid-nineteenth century, fresco carried a status similar to that of the "international Gothic" style of the fourteenth century, alone considered suitable to the exalted purposes of decorating important civic and state buildings.[98] When Leutze and Wimar were in Düsseldorf, at least one grandly scaled public fresco cycle was under way in Germany—Alfred Rethel's 1847 cycle of the life of Charlemagne for the city of Aachen. Charlemagne's Christian empire served artists of the Rhineland time and again as a fitting subject with which to create an imperial

history and national mythology equal to the political ambitions of the present.[99] A number of other cycles produced under the auspices of the German mural movement also were nationalist in subject matter. Schnorr von Carolsfeld's 1827 Niebelungen cycle, Carl Friedrich Lessing's frescoes at the Schloss Heltorf outside of Düsseldorf, and those of Hermann Plüddemann, all painted between 1826 and 1841, served the call for the political unification of Prussia.[100] During these decades, Düsseldorf-trained history painters received governmental and communal commissions for town halls, schools and universities, theaters, and private residences. Such commissions included a series of fresco decorations for the Elberfeld City Hall, painted between 1841 and 1844 by Heinrich Muecke, Hermann Plüddemann, Lorenz Clasen, and Joseph Fay.[101] It was the last—Fay—who may have furnished Wimar with a more direct link to the revival of fresco; the two occupied adjoining studios, and Wimar wrote home that he studied with the older man, who was "a second Pomarede to me."[102] In 1854, Wimar may have traveled to Elberfeld, where he exhibited two paintings, and thus may have had an opportunity to study the frescoes in the City Hall.[103] Lessing, an artist who exercised a powerful influence on Leutze during his Düsseldorf years, may have been another link; his involvements with fresco probably filtered through Leutze to Wimar during the latter's brief repatriation. The passionate enthusiasm of Rhineland artists for a monumental public art—one that heroized the German past and the ideal of cultural unity—must have left a lasting mark on the artist from Saint Louis.[104]

As a student in Düsseldorf, Wimar could have absorbed not only how the past could be put to political and rhetorical use, but also the specific approach to fresco composition taken by the German history painters. His own preference for frieze-like arrangements of figures parallel to the wall plane was a device that appears repeatedly in the frescoes of the Nazarenes and other German muralists. In both there is little developed sense of recessional space behind the central figures, but rather a flat scenic backdrop.[105] German precedent might also have given Wimar the idea of mixing allegory with historical or literary narrative.[106] German history painting as it developed at the Düsseldorf Academy combined naturalism with the compositional terseness of the first generation of German mural artists. The second generation of history painters, largely dispensing with allegorical elements, furnished a more compelling example for Wimar of how to draw contemporary relevance out of historical themes.[107] Wilhelm Schadow's dictum while director of the Academy—"the strictest possible conception of the subject and the most naturalistic representation of the same"—could apply as well to the ambitions of both Leutze and Wimar as they tackled their respective commissions.

One further connection may be drawn between Wimar's mural cycle in Saint Louis and contemporaneous German developments: at certain key points each was informed by a similar Hegelian vision of history. According to the Hegelian logic at work within the serial paintings of Peter Cornelius in Munich, each successive historical epoch contained the seeds of the next; the physical perfection of ancient Greece inspired a dialectical impulse toward the spiritual perfection of Christianity. A related logic may also be discerned in the choice of subjects for the Saint Louis courthouse murals. Although Wimar may not have had a direct knowledge of Hegel, he may well have internalized certain patterns of thinking; Hegelian ideas also could have been conveyed to him through one or more of the German members of the commission in charge of the Courthouse. Whatever the source, in presenting the history of the Mississippi Valley as four phases of colonization, his murals show a

Hegelian logic: the initial peaceful phases of Spanish conquest and French colonization (thesis) were followed by a phase of rivalry between imperial powers (antithesis), as Indians allied to the British attacked the young French settlement under Spanish rule. The final phase, summed up in Cochetope Pass, culminates in the United States' eventual settlement and control of the continent—the fruition of its superior technological and spiritual authority. The railroad linking East and West, anticipated by the peaceful movement of pioneers guided by a Christian spirit, becomes the logical culmination, or Hegelian synthesis, of the dialectical play of historic agents in the trans-Mississippi West.[108]

Wimar's murals reminded residents of their city's key place in the history and future of the West. Conceived and executed in a politically charged climate, however, the mural cycle embodied both the dream of empire and its contradictions, projecting a nobly unfolding plan in the midst of events that threatened its very foundations and that called into question the providential blessing that enabled it. Wimar's mural cycle offers its fullest content as much by what it fails to show as by what it celebrates. Depicting past and future, it suppresses the conflicted present; Saint Louis, the expansive but contested city of 1862, appears nowhere. Like most narratives, the point of Wimar's cycle was less to describe than to invent and shape, to remake its object—the history of European settlement of the Mississippi Valley—in the image of the civic desires and aspirations of the city's Anglo elite at midcentury.

Running through these grandly conceived historic themes, however, was another, more immediate context: the Civil War and the final months of debate over the choice of route for the

217

Figure 28
August Becker, after Carl Wimar. *Founding of Saint Louis*. Oil on canvas, c. 1862? Missouri Historical Society.

Pacific railroad. Each of these imbued the events from the city's more distant history—the exploration and early settlement of the Mississippi Valley—with a certain uniform hue, drawing them together through a historical logic that was mainly in the telling. In the mid-nineteenth century, the art of narrative carried an enormous rhetorical power, used on numerous occasions to build an empire. For rhetoric inspired conviction, and conviction was required for the endless urban promotion, political and civic lobbying necessary for the city to realize its self-appointed historic destiny. Visual persuasion, reinforced by a hallowed iconography of historic types, would teach the public, secure its loyalties, and propel the city toward the ever-retreating mirage of its imperial destiny.

Like the hopes they represented, the murals suffered at the hands of history. Wimar had executed them with an unstable mixture of oil, gouache, and watercolor on poorly prepared plaster,[109] and as dampness seeped through the shell of the dome, his paint began to flake. There was a heavy-handed restoration in 1880 by an emigré Italian named Miragoli, followed by other restorations; one by Wimar's half-brother August Becker in 1888 was probably the most extensive.[110] In the end, Becker's hand, rather than Wimar's, is most fully represented on the courthouse murals today—an ironic twist of fate, given that Becker had received the original commission. Compared with the murals, Becker's own copy of the courthouse's *Landing of Laclede* (fig. 28) furnishes stylistic evidence of his role in repainting his half-brother's work. Given Becker's habit of deferring to Wimar's superior talents— he made numerous copies after Wimar's paintings—it is unlikely that he significantly altered Wimar's composition. Indeed Becker reputedly put a stop to the work of his predecessor Miragoli, who was in the process of repainting, under the guise of retouching, Wimar's originals.[111]

The cumulative effect of these restorations on the murals has been to obscure, if not obliterate, the presence of Wimar's own hand while preserving his original composition.[112] The courthouse murals cannot therefore be relied upon to give a fair glimpse of Wimar's abilities in the final year of his life. Nonetheless, although their artistic value is compromised, their iconographic and historic importance remains, for they represent the first example west of the Alleghenies of an ambitious civic decorative scheme directed at establishing one city's role in the history of both region and nation.[113]

The civic ambitions recorded in Wimar's murals have been periodically rekindled, invigorated by renewed awareness of the city's urban failures and successes, its dreams of empire and its complex history. Nearly a century after the completion of the courthouse decorations, Eero Saarinen accentuated the symbolic importance of the older building by placing his Gateway arch on an axis with it and reinforcing the directional impulse that was evident in the courthouse's major East/West orientation. In doing so, he reemphasized the grand illusions of an earlier age, embodied in the Saint Louis Courthouse and the murals that are Wimar's legacy to his fellow Saint Louisans.

NOTES

1. Professor O. M. Mitchell, engineer of the Ohio and Mississippi Railroad, quoted in William Prescott Smith, *The Book of the Great Railway Celebrations of 1857* (New York: D. Appleton and Co., 1858), 243.

2. William J. Flagg, a member of the Cincinnati City Council, quoted in Smith, *Great Railway Celebrations*, 245.

3. This account probably made its first appearance in William Tod Helmuth's "Biographical Sketch of Charles Ferdinand Wimar" in *Arts in Saint Louis* (Saint Louis: 1864). The account was repeated in later biographies such as William Romaine Hodges' *Carl Wimar* (Galveston, Tex.: Charles Reymershoffer, 1908), 26; and "Missouri Miniatures: Carl Wimar," *Missouri Historical Review* 37 (January 1943): 208, 212–13.

4. See William H. Goetzmann, *Army Exploration in the American West, 1803–1863* (New Haven: Yale University Press, 1959), 218; and Robert R. Russel, "The Pacific Railway Issue in Politics Prior to the Civil War," in *Antebellum Studies in Slavery, Politics, and the Railroads: Faculty Contributions* (School of Graduate Studies, Western Michigan University), series 5, no. 1 (June 1960): 88–89.

5. The final route was a compromise involving four subsidiary or branch lines running through Omaha, Kansas City, Atchison, and Sioux City, while the main trunk line continued on through Chicago. Saint Louis was relegated to the Kansas City branch line. See Maury Klein, *Union Pacific: Birth of a Railroad, 1862–1893* (Garden City, N.Y.: Doubleday and Co., Inc., 1987), 13 passim.

6. Stella M. Drumm and Charles Van Ravenswaay, "The Old Courthouse," *Glimpses of the Past* 7(1940): 39, states that the patented dome design employed in Saint Louis was the first of its kind in the United States.

7. Lawrence Lowic, *The Architectural Heritage of Saint Louis, 1803–1891: From the Louisiana Purchase to the Wainwright Building* (Saint Louis: Washington University Gallery of Art, 1982), 74–75. J. Thomas Scharf, *History of Saint Louis City and County*, 2 vols. (Philadelphia: Louis H. Everts and Co., 1883), 1: 732–33, describes the interior and the design of the dome.

8. See Walter B. Stevens, *Saint Louis, The Fourth City, 1764–1909*, 3 vols. (Saint Louis, 1909), 1: 20.

9. See especially Benton's congressional speech, 18th Cong., 2d Sess., *Register of Debates in Congress*, Senate, 1: 712–13 (March 1, 1825). Benton's involvement with the idea is discussed in Henry Nash Smith, *Virgin Land: The American West as Symbol and Myth* (Cambridge, Mass., and London: Harvard University Press, 1970), 19–30. In 1818, Benton first proposed a scheme "for the navigation of the Missouri and Columbia rivers," which he defended until 1846, thereafter shifting his energies to the proposal for a Pacific Railway, to be financed by the sale of public lands in California and Oregon. See J. Loughborough, *The Pacific Telegraph and Railway* (Saint Louis: 1849), 20.

10. Quoted in Floyd Calvin Shoemaker, *Missouri and Missourians: Land of Contrasts and People of Development*, 5 vols. (Chicago: Lewis Publishing Company, 1943), 1: 749–50.

11. "Completion of the Saint Louis Courthouse," 3, typescript from *Daily Missouri Democrat*, July 4, 1862, in Saint Louis County Court Records, 1860–1877, RU 106, Box T-JA, Courthouse Archives (now administered by the National Park Service).

12. For an analysis of Missouri politics during the war years, see William E. Parrish, *Turbulent Partnership: Missouri and the Union, 1861–1865* (Columbia: University of Missouri Press, 1963), 23–32, 33–34.

13. On Taussig, see William Hyde and Howard Conard, eds., *Encyclopedia of the History of Saint Louis*, 4 vols. (New York, Louisville, Saint Louis: The Southern History Company, 1899), 4: 2218.

14. Taussig to Mr. Pretorius, "Mural Paintings in the Courthouse by Wimar," September 29, 1886; a translation of this letter, originally published in German in the *Westliche Post*, is in the Courthouse Archives. Taussig also recalled that when he and John F. Fisse were appointed to the commission, they had already decided that Wimar should do the work.

15. "Construction of the Courthouse, 1854–1877: Specifications and Contracts," RU106, Box T-JA-2, Office of the Superintendent, Series 9, Planning Records, Courthouse Archives. Saint Louis County Court records show that between March 20, 1862, and October 23, the commission paid Becker $2,965. One final payment for $30 was made on January 22, 1863. These records seem to contradict Taussig's own assertion that "it was finally decided that the pictures and decorating of cupola should be given to him and Mr. Becker . . . for $1000—. . . where the contract, after much kicking about the wasting of so much money, was finally approved." Taussig to Pretorius; recalling the event a quarter of a century after the fact, Taussig may have been wrong. The mistaken figures were repeated in Hodges' early biography, *Carl Wimar*, 25.

16. On Primm's career see Hyde and Conard, *Encyclopedia of Saint Louis* 3: 1817.

17. This assertion is in Taussig's letter to Pretorius, September 29, 1886, and in "Completion of the St. Louis Courthouse," 5.

18. Taussig to Pretorius, September 29, 1886. He also recalled attending "many conferences . . . in regard to ideas and designs, which took place in Wimar's studio."

19. See William Truettner, "The Art of History: American Exploration and Discovery Scenes, 1840–1860," *American Art Journal* 14, no. 1 (Winter 1982): 4–31; and Vivien Green Fryd, *'The Course of Empire': Art in the United States Capitol, 1815–1860* (New Haven: Yale University Press, forthcoming in 1991).

20. These are, respectively, *Burial of De Soto*, c. 1847, unlocated; *De Soto Discovering the Mississippi River*, c. 1844, Saint Bonaventure University Art Collection, Saint Bonaventure, New York, and a series of watercolors Eastman did for Henry Schoolcraft. Johann M. Culverhouse's *Burial of De Soto*, 1875, Yale University Art Gallery, is a somewhat later representation of De Soto's accomplishments.

Local interest in the explorers of the Mississippi River was demonstrated in a series of articles entitled "Legends of the Mississippi," which appeared in the *Missouri Republican* in 1858. De Soto was the subject of one such sketch on August 22, 1858. Other subjects included La Salle on August 8 and Marquette and Joliet on June 28 and September 19, 1858.

21. Editor of the *New York Daily Times*, "Our National Paintings," December 2, 1853; reprinted in "Opinions of the Press," in *William H. Powell's Historical Picture of the Discovery of the Mississippi by De Soto . . .* (New York: Baker, Godwin, and Co., 1854), 15, emphasis added. This pamphlet is in the collection of the New York Public Library.

22. Truettner, "The Art of History," 9, notes that between 1840 and 1860, the percentage of exploration and discovery scenes grew steadily.

23. William H. Travers, Speaker of the Maryland House of Delegates, quoted in Smith, *Great Railway Celebrations*, 237.

24. On De Soto's "discovery" of the Mississippi River, see Miguel Albornoz, *Hernando De Soto: Knight of the Americas* (New York and Toronto: Franklin Watts, 1986), 321–24.

25. The date for Saint Louis' founding is sometimes given as February 1764, when fourteen-year-old Auguste Chouteau returned to the site of Saint Louis with a working party to build the colony. See James Neal Primm, *Lion of the Valley: Saint Louis, Missouri* (Boulder: Pruitt Publishing Company, 1981), 9.

26. Judge Wilson Primm, "Address on the Founding Day," reprinted in "Article I—St. Louis—Its Early History," *Western Journal* 2, no. 2 (February 1849): 74. Typical of the uses that history served in the mid-nineteenth century, the article aimed "to connect some of the leading facts in [Saint Louis'] early settlement, with those relating to its development as a commercial city," 71.

27. However, one version of the theme, which appears in "Legends of the Missouri . . . Marquette and Joliet," *Missouri Republican*, June 28, 1858, relates an encounter, at the shore of the river, between these two French explorers and the Indians of the region.

28. On back of the drawing, perhaps in Wimar's hand, is the inscription: "First setler! The Landing of La Clede on the western shore of the Mississippi River, where now stands the great city of St. Louis."

29. This spring is not visible in the mural today but is noted in contemporary descriptions; see "Completion of the St. Louis Courthouse," 5.

30. An example of Wimar's reliance upon verifiable particulars was the depiction of Laclede's boat; according to "Completion of the St. Louis Courthouse," 3, this was based on the oral account of a Mr. Laconte, an elderly Frenchman from Carondelet who claimed to have seen the barge used by Laclede and his men and sketched it from memory for Wimar to use in his reconstruction. Laconte also described Laclede. Walter B. Stevens' 1909 account, *Saint Louis, The Fourth City*, 18, described Laclede's crafts as "low hulls" resembling the "rudely constructed barges of the present day. . . . About the center of each boat was a stubby, strong mast, well braced. Tied to the mast was a rope several hundred feet long." This "cordelle" was pulled by cordellers who walked along the river bank dragging the hull after them. As Rick Stewart's essay illustrates, this method was still used on the upper Missouri in the nineteenth century.

31. DeBry's widely circulated engravings were copied by artists such as the anonymous painter of a work at the Thomas Gilcrease Institute of American History and Art in Tulsa, *Columbus' First Landing in the Indies* (n.d.). The painting is based on an engraving in volume 1 of DeBry's *America* (Frankfurt: 1617), 6.

32. Weir's interest in the Hudson theme may have been encouraged by Gulian Verplanck, a prominent New Yorker who bought his painting and who was a commissioner for the decoration of the United States Capitol rotunda. Weir did a second, larger version of the Hudson theme c. 1838. Bierstadt also painted a *Discovery of the Hudson River* in 1875, possibly as a commissioned work.

John Gadsby Chapman painted a *Landing of Columbus*, published in the *New-York Mirror* on January 7, 1837, p. 14. Junius Brutus Stearns painted *First Ship: Indians Sighting Ship on the Horizon in 1853* (private collection), a subject that could refer either to Jamestown or to Plymouth, among several possibilities. Thomas Pritchard Rossiter also painted the theme.

33. The Roger Williams theme was also treated by Isaac Noyes, possibly from Rhode Island, in *The Landing of Roger Williams* (n.d.: Rhode Island Historical Society).

34. Primm, "Address on the Founding Day," 78. A similar account of Leyba's role in the attack appears in Stevens, *Saint Louis: The Fourth City*, 70.

35. See William H. Gerdts and Mark Thistlethwaite, *Grand Illusions: History Painting in America* (Fort Worth, Tex.: Amon Carter Museum, 1988).

36. Stevens, *Saint Louis, The Fourth City*, 70.

37. Judge Wilson Primm, "Early History of Saint Louis," *Missouri Historical Society Collections* 4, no. 2 (1913): 168.

38. A potential threat to this train of settlers is implied in the figures that appear to be silhouetted on the blufftops gazing down at the scene in the pass. However, these shapes are difficult to read and are nowhere mentioned in descriptions of the west lunette. They may conceivably have been added by a restorer.

39. For another example of the association between the phrase "Star of Empire" and the railroad, see Theodore Kaufmann's painting *Westward the Star of Empire* (c. 1867, John W. Barriger III National Railroad Library, Saint Louis Mercantile Library), which shows a train barrelling through the wilderness at night, its floodlight cutting through the darkness in a head-on collision with the spectator. Andrew Melrose's *'Westward the Star of Empire Takes its Way'—Near Council Bluffs, Iowa* (c. 1865, E. W. Judson, New York) is a related work.

40. "Completion of the Saint Louis Courthouse," 5.

41. "Letter from the White Cloud. Steamer White Cloud, Missouri River, July 22d, 1858," by "Commerce," in *Missouri Republican*, July 29, 1858.

42. The official call for a grand national railroad that opened the controversy over routes was first issued by Asa Whitney in January 1845 when he petitioned Congress on behalf of the project. See Henry Nash Smith, *Virgin Land*, 30–34; Klein, *Union Pacific*, 8; Leroy R. Hafen and Ann W. Hafen, eds., *Central Route to the Pacific* (Glendale, Cal.: Arthur H. Clark Co., 1957), 14–24. See also Goetzmann, *Army Exploration in the American West*, 209–12. In addition, Benton himself, in a *Speech of Mr. Benton, of Missouri, on the Pacific Railroad Bill*, House of Representatives, January 16, 1855 (Washington, D.C.: Congressional Globe Office, 1855), 19, pointed to the discovery of gold in 1849 as another urgent reason for a transcontinental railroad, which would save the precious metal, "the life's blood of our daily industry!" from a lengthy and dangerous passage of six thousand miles around the tip of South America or across the Isthmus of Panama. J. Loughborough, *The Pacific Telegraph and Railway*, 25, makes a related plea for a railroad on the grounds of commercial, social, and political ties of "feeling and interest." Benton himself noted in 1853 that the annual migration to the West from the Missouri frontier amounted to "forty or fifty thousand," requiring "responsible action on the part of the government"; "Letter from Col. Benton to the People of Missouri. Central National Highway from the Mississippi River to the Pacific," reproduced in Hafen and Hafen, *Central Route to the Pacific*, 53.

43. These four routes had been winnowed down from the eight which had originally received support from various factions. See Goetzmann, *Army Exploration in the American West*, 75–95, 265. A fifth route, along the 41st and 42nd parallels, was surveyed by E. G. Beckwith, continuing Gunnison's uncompleted survey from Salt Lake City to San Francisco Bay in 1854; this route was finally chosen as the Central Pacific Route in the 1860s. In addition, the assembly of Washington Territory, doubtful about the feasibility of the far northern route, authorized Frederick West Lander to conduct an independent reconnaissance from the South Pass to Puget Sound; ibid., 283. Lander's findings were included in the *Pacific Railroad Reports* 2, part 3: 5–44.

44. Goetzmann, *Army Exploration in the American West*, 286.

45. The best source for the Beale expedition is Gwin Harris Heap's *Central Route to the Pacific, from the Valley of the Mississippi to California: Journal of the Expedition*, originally published in 1854. See the Hafens' introduction, 13–24, to the 1957 edition of Heap's journal, in which they describe the published journal as "Benton's ammunition in his further campaign for the Central route" (21). On Benton's support for the Beale and Frémont expeditions, see Goetzmann, *Army Exploration in the American West*, 284.

46. William H. Goetzmann, *Exploration and Empire*, quoted in David Weber, *Richard Kern: Expeditionary Artist in the Far Southwest, 1842–1853* (Fort Worth: Amon Carter Museum, 1985), 46. See also Thomas Hart Benton, *Thirty Years' View*, 2 vols. (New York: D. Appleton and Co., 1858), 2: 719–21; Leroy R. Hafen and Ann W. Hafen, eds., *Frémont's Fourth Expedition: A Documentary Account of the Disaster of 1848–49 . . .* (Glendale, Cal.: Arthur H. Clark Co., 1960), which reproduces the artist Richard Kern's diary from the expedition; Weber, *Richard Kern*, 17–50.

47. In his 1853 report, Frémont noted several encouraging features of the pass, including its gradual gradient on the east side. Frémont also described the "singular facilities and extraordinary comparative advantages for the construction of the proposed route," which included ample water and wood and "land fit for cultivation" along the waterways leading to the pass. Above all, it was central "to business and population," directly uniting Saint Louis, "the greatest commercial point in the Valley of the Mississippi, with the greatest commercial point on the coast of the Pacific." See "Letter from Colonel Frémont to the Railroad Convention, April 1850," reproduced by Benton in his "Letter . . . to the People of Missouri," in Hafen and Hafen, eds., *Central Route to the Pacific*, 36, 38, 41.

Gwin Harris Heap's journal of the Beale expedition gave a description of the crucial pass in the Rockies that fully justified Benton's enthusiasm. Heap proclaimed the area of the Cochetope Pass and beyond "a wonderful gap, or, more properly speaking, a natural GATE, as its name denotes in the Utah [Ute] language. On each side, mountains rise in abrupt and rocky precipices, the one on the eastern side being the highest . . . the bottom of the Pass was level and at right angles with the Sahwatch valley." Ibid., 137.

48. "Letter from Col. Benton to the People of Missouri," 49. Frémont's expedition of 1853–54 was an effort to vindicate the Cochetope Pass route for winter use. Once again his men suffered terribly, this time in the Wasatch Mountains several hundred miles farther west of Cochetope Pass.

49. There is some variation in the spelling of the name "Cochetope"; such lexicographic variations are characteristic of the period. Stanley's lithograph is in "U.S. Pacific Railroad Explorations and Surveys, 38th and 39th Parallels," vol. 2 of the *Reports of Explorations and Surveys to Ascertain the Most Practicable and Economical Route for a Railroad from the Mississippi River to the Pacific Ocean* (Washington, D.C.: United States Congressional Publication, 1855).

222

50. *Speech of Mr. Benton on the Pacific Railroad Bill*, 14–15.

51. I thank David Miller of Cameron University, Lawton, Oklahoma, for this information.

52. Benton also stated that over forty wagons laden with goods and emigrants had gone through the pass in the summer of 1853, twenty of them with the government-sponsored Gunnison expedition of that year, the remaining without guides. *Speech of Mr. Benton on the Pacific Railroad Bill*, 14–15.

53. In his *Thirty Years' View*, 721, Benton wrote that the 38th/39th parallel was "the route for the Central Pacific Railroad, which the structure of the country invites, and every national consideration demands."

54. David Miller and Mark Stegmaier, in *James F. Milligan: His Journal of Frémont's Fifth Expedition, 1853–1854; His Adventurous Life on Land and Sea* (Glendale, Cal.: Arthur H. Clark Co., 1988), 96, have gone as far as to say that these setbacks "marked the death knell of the Benton-Frémont route."

55. Goetzmann, *Army Exploration in the American West*, 289, 302–3. The so-called "South-West Branch," running diagonally across the state to link up with the 35th parallel route, was only begun in 1858, reaching Rolla in 1860.

56. Phelps was elected to Congress in 1845 and served nine consecutive terms. In 1862 he was appointed military governor of Arkansas by President Lincoln. Though he began his career as a Benton Democrat, he eventually supported Stephen Douglas in 1860 and was a conditional Unionist during the war. See Shoemaker, *Missouri and Missourians*, 1: 633, 641–42. On Phelps' role in promoting the 35th parallel route, see Goetzmann, *Army Exploration in the West*, 248; and H. Craig Miner, *The Saint Louis-San Francisco Transcontinental Railroad: The Thirty-Fifth Parallel Project, 1853–1890* (Lawrence: The University of Kansas Press, 1972), 5, 22.

57. "The 'Central Route,'" *Missouri Republican*, February 7, 1858.

58. "The 'Central Route' to the Pacific," *Missouri Republican*, January 24, 1858. Other statements fueling the controversy included Edward Miller, Civil Engineer, "The Highway of Nations. Great National Pacific Railroad," ibid., May 5, 1858, and "Letter from Col. Bonneville, U.S.A., Albuquerque, N.M., March 14, 1858," ibid., May 15, 1858. As early as 1850, Thomas Allen wrote in *Pacific Railroad Commenced: Address to the Board of Directors of the Pacific Railroad Company . . .* (Saint Louis, 1850: Printed at the Republican Office), 34, that the 35th parallel route was the best qualified as a *national* route serving the needs of both empire and of North and South. This pamphlet is in the Mercantile Library, Saint Louis. See also Goetzmann, *Army Exploration in the West*, 263.

59. Phelps and his supporters repeatedly attacked the 32nd parallel route, which, given the pro-Southern leanings of the President himself, posed a real threat to contending routes. His views were put forth in a number of articles in the *Missouri Republican*: "The Pacific Railroad," February 19, 1858; "The Route of Travel and Transportation Across the Continent," March 4, 1858; "Railroad to the Pacific Ocean," March 11, 1858; "Speech of Hon. Mr. Polk in Senate—April 15th, Pacific Railroad Bill," April 22, 1858, and in *A Letter from Hon. John S. Phelps to Citizens of Arkansas in Relation to a Pacific Railroad* (Saint Louis: 1858), reprinted in the *Missouri Republican* of January 28, 1858. One of Benton's attacks on the southern route is in "Substance of Colonel Benton's Speeches at Kansas, Westport, and Independence, May 6th and 7th," reproduced in Hafen and Hafen, eds., *Central Route to the Pacific*, 61. W.R.E., author of "Pacific Railroad," in the *Missouri Republican*, February 8, 1858, appealed to Congress to "see these advantages and pass the bill ere the sectional storm, already premonished, bursts its fury upon them and swallows up all other considerations." See also Goetzmann, *Army Exploration in the West*, 266.

60. William H. Travers, Speaker of the Maryland House of Delegates, quoted in Prescott Smith, *Great Railway Celebrations*, 237.

61. *The Highway of Nations: The Great National Pacific Railroad* (reprinted from the *Journal of the Franklin Institute*, n.d.), 8. Pamphlet in the collection of the Saint Louis Mercantile Library Association.

62. *Letter from Hon. John S. Phelps to Citizens of Arkansas*, 3, states that the renewed interest in the Pacific Railroad in early 1858 resulted from "urgent military reasons" tending to the selection of the 32nd parallel route by the federal government.

63. William Nisbet Chambers, *Old Bullion Benton: Senator from the New West* (Boston: Little, Brown, and Co., 1956), 410.

64. See Russel, "The Pacific Railway Issue," 89, on local aspirations to connect with the eventual Pacific railway. By late 1856 the Pacific Railroad Company of Missouri had completed 125 miles to Jefferson City and staged an elaborate and ill-timed celebration, which ended in disaster when the Gasconade Bridge, a 760-foot-long temporary structure, collapsed under the combined weight of Saint Louis' leading citizens; some forty-three were killed and injured. See Paul W. Gates, "The Railroad of Missouri, 1850–1870, *Missouri Historical Review* 26 (January 1932): 126–41, and Miner, *Saint Louis–San Francisco Railroad*, 25.

65. Russel, "The Pacific Railway Issue," 96–97, claimed that the influence of the abolitionist Republican Party rendered the choice of a southern route "well-nigh hopeless." See Miner, *Saint Louis–San Francisco Railroad*, 29–41, for the impact of sectionalism and war on the future of the South-West Branch and its ambitions to connect with the final transcontinental route.

66. *Congressional Globe*, 37th Cong., 2d sess., p. 2755. The most accurate list of the routes being considered by Congress and their specific features appeared in a table in the *Congressional Globe*, 37th Cong., 2d sess., p. 1862. Some variation exists in how the secondary sources identify these routes. In any case, the final choice of route—along the 40th/

42nd parallel—followed the route of the Oregon-California Trail, approximating Interstate 80.

67. Even after the congressional decision of 1862, the promise of other transcontinental routes, along with the main Pacific railroad, kept the issue alive. But though other routes were constructed in the late nineteenth century, none followed the 38th/39th parallel.

68. The *Encyclopedia of the History of Saint Louis* 3 : 1847, baldly states that without the intervention of the Civil War, Saint Louis would have secured the transcontinental route.

69. See for instance the interpretation of the work given in the *Saint Louis Republic* ("Paintings Typical . . . To Be Preserved," February 5, 1905): a herd of buffalo "driven westward by the encroachments of the White man and his civilization."

70. Leutze's earliest documented idea for the mural dates from 1857, when he suggested the subject of "The Emigration to the West" to Montgomery Meigs, the man in charge of Capitol decoration, but he may have been mulling over the idea while still in Germany. See Barbara S. Groseclose, *Emanuel Leutze, 1816–1868: Freedom is the Only King* (Washington, D.C.: Smithsonian Institution Press for the National Collection of Fine Arts, 1975), 60–62, 96. Leutze received the commission and submitted his first oil sketch in 1861. For more on Wimar's relationship with Leutze, see Joseph Ketner's essay in this volume.

71. See Fryd, *'The Course of Empire'*.

72. Thomas Cole notably inverted the celebratory meaning of the phrase in his five-part series of paintings *The Course of Empire* (New-York Historical Society, 1833–1836). For further discussion of the phrase see Angela Miller, "The Imperial Republic: Narratives of National Expansion in American Art, 1820–1860," Ph.D. diss. (Yale University, 1985), 90–92.

73. Benton himself employed a similar biblical and typological symbolism when he compared himself to Moses, pointing the way to the promised land; "Speech of Mr. Benton of Missouri," 16. His antagonists, accordingly, were compared to the ten messengers who sent back "evil reports" of the Promised Land, misleading the rebellious children of Israel and detaining them for forty years in the wilderness. So the great lands of the West "also must expect to be evilly reported upon; but truth is powerful and must prevail."

74. By 1853, Gwin Harris Heap noted in his journal of the Beale expedition that the herds of buffalo that had originally furnished both the Utah and Spanish designations of the Pass had been diminished by "the constant warfare carried on against them by Indians and New Mexicans," *Central Route to the Pacific*, 138. The westward migration of Anglo-European settlers only accelerated this process.

75. Also included in this group is *Buffalo Crossing the Yellowstone*, which is compositionally related to *Cochetope Pass*. Wimar also executed a wash and chalk drawing on brown paper of "Buffaloes in the Cochetopa

Pass of the Rocky Mountains," in a private collection; this work is listed as no. 58 in Perry Rathbone, *Charles Wimar 1828–1862: Painter of the Indian Frontier* (Saint Louis: City Art Museum, 1946).

76. Taussig noted this, writing to Pretorius that "[w]hile in the picture by Leutze the wild, adventurous side of the group of immigrants is brought out, it was the pathetic side that appealed to Wimar more, whose immigrant group showing the fatigues of travels toils along in winding line through some canyon farther onwards toward the beautifully setting sun."

77. No drawing exists for the fourth allegorical figure of Commerce. The descriptions of the finished frescoes in "Completion of the Saint Louis Courthouse," 3, differ somewhat from Wimar's preliminary drawings, indicating that he made some changes. These descriptions are probably more reliable since Wimar's original frescoes may have been altered during restoration. In addition to these drawings, there is a sheet of light brown paper in the Saint Louis Art Museum containing recto and verso studies related to Wimar's allegorical figure of Justice; on one side are two figures of Justice, holding sword and scale, and on the reverse is a seated male figure, identified as "Drago" [sic] the lawmaker, leaning on a column with tablet in hand, along with a second study for the same. Other commentators identified the figure of the lawmaker as Solon; see, for instance, "Completion of the Saint Louis Courthouse," 3.

78. According to one account, these "memorable monuments of the genius of the artist" were suggested by the architect, William Rumbold, in consultation with Taussig and Lightner, president of the Board of County Commissioners. The other two figures were selected by the Committee members in charge of the courthouse decorations (ibid.).

79. Bingham had copied these while in Boston in 1856 and subsequently gave them to the Saint Louis Mercantile Library Association, where they reside today. See E. Maurice Bloch, *The Paintings of George Caleb Bingham: A Catalogue Raisonné* (Columbia: University of Missouri Press, 1986), 100, 209. I am indebted to Doreen Bolger for bringing the source of the courthouse portraits to my attention.

80. In addition, Wilson Primm had read law with Bates; Primm, responsible for selecting two of the subjects for the mural cycle, may have played some role in the presence of his mentor's portrait in the courthouse.

81. Stevens quotes him in *Saint Louis, The Fourth City* 1: 481: "When you have constructed the road to the frontier of the Missouri, what power can stop it there? Beyond lie the extended plains of the Missouri and the Arkansas, New Mexico, Utah, California, Oregon, the Pacific and the old Eastern World."

82. On Bates' career, see *Encyclopedia of the History of Saint Louis* 1: 116–18.

83. Parrish, *Turbulent Partnership*, 34 passim. On Bates' service to the provisional government, see 76. Gamble and Wimar were directly con-

nected: Gamble bought Wimar's *Attack on an Emigrant Train*, one of his late and most successful Düsseldorf paintings; see Joseph Ketner's essay.

84. John C. Frémont, Benton's collaborator in the field and co-conspirator in his efforts to prove the viability of the Central (Cochetope Pass) route, did not appear within Wimar's mural scheme. The artist did, however, execute a portrait of him as a northern general, a position he briefly occupied in the Union campaign on the Missouri frontier (1861: private collection). Frémont, on horseback, appeared beside Captain Constantin Blandowski and Colonel Franz Sigel in a triple equestrian portrait painted in grisaille to be engraved. Blandowski, Wimar's friend and companion on his 1858 trip up the Missouri River, died at the capture of Camp Jackson near Saint Louis on May 10, 1861, soon after this portrait was painted.

On Frémont's bungled efforts as Commander of the Department of the West, headquartered at Saint Louis, see Parrish, *Turbulent Partnership*, 48–76. This incident was only the last of a series of failed or badly mismanaged undertakings in Frémont's checkered career.

85. On the history of public patronage before the Civil War, see Lillian B. Miller, *Patrons and Patriotism: The Encouragement of the Fine Arts in the United States, 1790–1860* (Chicago and London: University of Chicago Press, 1966), especially 33–84 on the Capitol commissions; also Fryd, *'The Course of Empire'*.

86. Brumidi's fresco work is reproduced in *Art in the United States Capitol* (Washington, D.C.: Government Printing Office, 1976), 314–17. The room, H-144, is now the House Committee on Appropriations.

87. See Miller, *Patrons and Patriotism*, 79–84.

88. Wimar's half-brother and courthouse collaborator, August Becker, also studied with Pomarede at a later date. In 1834 Pomarede decorated the interior of the new cathedral at Saint Louis; more than likely, however, this decoration did not involve fresco work, since most of the surfaces of the Old Cathedral were wood rather than plaster. See John McDermott, "Portrait of the Father of Waters: Leon Pomarede's Panorama of the Mississippi," *Bulletin de l'Institut Francais de Washington*, n.s. no. 2 (December 1952): 48.

89. Wimar to his parents, April 23, 1855, Missouri Historical Society. Evidently time had mellowed his terse observations, written from Düsseldorf on December 6, 1853, concerning the derivative character of his old teacher: "Everything that Pomarede had painted, I have seen either in engraving or pictures."

90. Jacob N. Taylor and M. Crooks, *Sketch Book of Saint Louis: Containing a Series of Sketches . . .* (Saint Louis: George Knapp and Co., 1858), 59.

91. It is unclear just what the authors here are referring to; encaustic generally was a term reserved for the employment of wax as a medium.

92. Taylor and Crooks, *Sketch Book*, 59.

93. See Lowic, *Architectural Heritage of Saint Louis*, 77–79.

94. Taylor and Crooks, *Sketch Book*, 60.

95. This technique, employed in the decoration of the House of Lords in London, was invented in Munich and offered certain advantages over true fresco, in that the pigment was applied to dry plaster and sections could be painted over more than once, in theory at least. Stereochromy proved too difficult and unstable a medium for most artists and was abandoned by the end of the century. On stereochromy, see F. W. Fairholt, ed., *A Dictionary of Terms in Art* (Virtue, Hall, and Virtue, 1854); Ralph Mayer, *A Dictionary of Art Terms and Techniques* (New York: Crowell, 1969); Ian Chilvers and Harold Osborne, eds., *The Oxford Dictionary of Art* (Oxford: Oxford University Press, 1988). I am indebted to the research of Anne Morand for this information.

96. William Taussig, perhaps aware of this connection as a German himself, mentioned Leutze's "celebrated painting in the Capitol in Washington," in his 1886 letter to Pretorius. It is impossible to know whether Taussig made this connection at the time of Wimar's painting, or after.

97. Led by Peter Cornelius, these artists, later known as the Nazarenes, executed their first important commission in 1815—the Casa Bartholdi fresco cycle illustrating the Old Testament story of Joseph. After 1817 the cartoons for the Casa Bartholdi were put on permanent exhibition at the Stadel Institute in Frankfurt, where artists could study them firsthand and through engravings. See William Vaughan, *German Romantic Painting* (New Haven and London: Yale University Press, 1980), 229. As director first of the Düsseldorf and then of the Munich Academy, Cornelius vigorously promoted instruction in fresco painting. See Richard Muther, *The History of Modern Painting*, 4 vols. (London: J. M. Dent and Company, 1907), 1: 151.

Prince Ludwig of Bavaria proved an important patron of the Nazarenes, giving numerous commissions in Munich to Cornelius and his associates. See Muther, *History of Modern Painting* 1: 143; Rolf Andree et al., *Kunst des 19. Jahrhunderts im Rheinland* (Dusseldorf: Schwann, 1979), 3: 146. Ludwig turned to Cornelius to decorate the Ludwigskirche in Munich, for which the latter modestly chose the Creation and the Last Judgment. Another influential commission, from the town of Frankfurt, went to Alfred Rethel in 1839. Commissions for public murals also went to Moritz Schwind for the Habsburg Hall in the Palace of Munich, his frescoes in the Kunsthall and Hall of Assembly at Karlsruhe, and at the Castle of Hehenschwangau. See Muther, *History of Modern Painting*, 174–75.

98. See Keith Andrews, *The Nazarenes: A Brotherhood of German Painters in Rome* (Oxford: At the Clarendon Press, 1964), 83; also Vaughan, *German Romantic Painting*, 163–90.

99. As Rethel himself stated in his written program, "Among the successors of Charlemagne, not one was able to revive the glory of this great emperor. The Carolingian empire nearly succumbed to the pressures of the times; downtrodden national feeling was seeking to compen-

225

sate itself for its miserable present through loving consideration of its grand past, and the revered figure of the mighty Charlemagne became a national ideal." Rethel might just as well have been writing about his own generation rather than Otto's. On Rethel and the Aachen commission, see *Kunst des 19. Jahrhunderts im Rheinland* 3: 174–80, from which this passage is taken. My thanks to Margot Schiewing of the Gilcrease Institute for her help in translating this text.

100. Intended for Ludwig's Munich residence, the Niebelungen cycle was left uncompleted in 1867. Schnorr had also been commissioned to decorate the state rooms of the imperial palace with scenes from German history that included Charlemagne, Barbarossa, and Rudolf of Habsburg. See Andrews, *The Nazarenes*, 62–64; Muther, *History of Modern Painting* 1: 139. The Schloss Heltdorf frescoes were privately commissioned by Franz Graf von Spee; their subject was the history of the Emperor Friedrich Barbarossa who, since his rediscovery in the mideighteenth century, had been a central figure in the pantheon of Prussian nationalists. The particular choice of themes from Germany's imperial past, however, reflected German intellectuals' concerns with historical precedents for their own vision of a unified Prussian state. See *Kunst des 19. Jahrhunderts im Rheinland* 3: 147, 153.

101. On this commission, see *Kunst des 19. Jahrhunderts im Rheinland* 3: 167.

102. Wimar also wrote that he hoped "to profit a lot from him." Fay is mentioned in several of Wimar's letters home, dated September 19, 1854; October 27, 1854 (in which Wimar described Fay as "[m]y actual Professor . . . who also devotes a lot of effort to me"); June 20, 1855; and an undated letter in which Wimar once again mentions that Fay was devoting "a lot of attention to me." The connection was established in the literature on Wimar; "Missouri Miniatures," 209, states that Joseph Fay and Leutze were Wimar's professors in Dusseldorf.

103. Carl Wimar to parents, July 13, 1854. Again in a letter of September 19, 1854, Wimar mentioned a painting on exhibit in Elberfeld. That he was aware of Fay's contribution to the Elberfeld fresco series is evident in this letter; he incorrectly gives full credit to Fay for "the frescoes in the city hall in Elberfeld."

104. I would like to thank Esther Thyssen, currently completing a dissertation at Yale University on American artists in Düsseldorf, for her informed assistance with this material.

105. On the characteristics of the Düsseldorf history style, evident in the frescoes painted by such men as Lessing, E. J. Bendemann, and others, see *Kunst des 19. Jahrhunderts im Rheinland* 3: 154.

106. An example is Johann Friedrich Overbeck's Casino Massimo frescoes in Rome, which used allegorical figures on the ceiling while giving the walls over to the narrative of Tasso's *Gerusalemne Liberata*; see

Andrews, *The Nazarenes*, 49–50. The combination of allegory and history, however, was common; examples include the Heltdorf decorations as well as the frescoes for the Hall of Bonn University, a commission given in 1818 to Cornelius and his students.

107. Vaughan, *German Romantic Painting*, 221.

108. Saint Louis had direct links with Hegelian modes of thought; the Saint Louis Philosophical Society, dedicated to the study of Hegel, was established in 1866, but these ideas were certainly known there earlier. On the history of Saint Louis German and American intellectuals' fascination with Hegel, see William Goetzmann, *The American Hegelians: An Intellectual Episode in the History of Western America* (New York: Alfred A. Knopf, 1973).

109. Hodges, *Wimar*, 27, reports that Professor H. C. Ives of the Saint Louis Art Museum "made a careful examination and found that in spots water color, oil color and gouache had been . . . blended together," apparently to create "the peculiarly beautiful color tones and hues found in the mountains, valleys and plains of our Western country."

110. Miragoli was contracted by the city to retouch the courthouse murals in 1880, indicating that by that date they were already in poor condition. In 1905, Professor E. H. Wuerpel of the Washington University School of Fine Arts was given the job of filling in the flaking areas of the mural without actually painting over it (U.S. Government Memorandum, National Park Service, October 2, 1975, Courthouse Archives). In 1921, one James Lyons, a house painter with larger ambitions, was set to work by the Director of Public Safety in Saint Louis to "touch up" two of Wimar's frescoes: *The Year of the Blow* and *Westward the Star*. He was also preparing to repaint the portraits of George and Martha Washington, Thomas Hart Benton, and Edward Bates (substituting Lincoln, Grant, and Roosevelt but leaving George Washington) before he was stopped by outraged citizens. See *Post-Dispatch*, February 12, 1922. This article also recounts a discredited story that the murals were repainted "by a couple of sign-painters" in 1865. A WPA restoration was also planned, but evidently never carried out. See *Post-Dispatch*, June 21, 1942, which also recaps the Lyons incident.

111. Saint Louis *Globe Democrat*, November 20, 1889.

112. "The real Wimar art has long ceased to exist," "Missouri Miniatures," 213.

113. The most recent effort of cleaning and restoration, undertaken by the National Park Service that has administered the Courthouse as a national historic site since 1941, was concluded in 1986. The present vivid effect of the rotunda, with its rose and blue-green color scheme, is the product of this last restoration, which did not, however, involve Wimar's murals.

226

Appendix

CHECKLIST OF ART WORKS BY CARL WIMAR

Horse, 1830s
Charcoal and graphite, 7½" × 10¾"
Verso: "Pencil sketch Claimed to by by [sic] Carl Wimar"
Missouri Historical Society, Saint Louis (1933.50.1)

The Brigand, c. 1840–43
Oil on canvas, 32" × 26"
LL: "C. Wimar"
Verso: "No. 3"
Lost; formerly Mr. Barton Wagner, Farmington, Missouri

The Captive Maid, c. 1840–43
Oil on canvas, 32" × 26"
LL: "C. Wimar"
Lost; formerly Mr. Barton Wagner, Farmington, Missouri

Woodland Scene with Deer, c. 1845–50
Oil on canvas, 32" × 26"
LL: "C. Wimar"
Lost; formerly Mr. Barton Wagner, Farmington, Missouri

Estate Portrait, 1849
Watercolor on paper, 13" × 18½"
LR: "CFW 1849"
Gallery Forty-four, New Hartford, Connecticut

Portrait of Emil Becker and His Dog Dash, 1850
Oil on canvas, 30½" × 25"
Missouri Historical Society, Saint Louis (1948.1.1)

Portrait of an Unknown Man, 1850
Oil on canvas, 30" × 25"
LR: "C. Wimar 1850"
Missouri Historical Society, Saint Louis

Ambros. Honer (?), 1850
Paper cutout silhouette, approx. 4" × 3"
LC: "Ambros. Honer . . . (?) . . . Carl Wimar St. Louis 24/11/50"
Missouri Historical Society, Saint Louis

Hermann Kemp, 1850
Paper cutout silhouette, approx. 4" × 3"
LC: "Hermann Kemp? C. Wimar St. Louis 26. Nov. 1850"
Missouri Historical Society, Saint Louis

Portrait of Henry Deppe, 1850
Oil on canvas, 30" × 25"
Missouri Historical Society, Saint Louis (1953.16.1)

Portrait of Fredericka Peters Deppe, c. 1850
Oil on canvas, 30" × 25"
Missouri Historical Society, Saint Louis (1953.16.2)

Portrait of Henry Deppe, Jr., c. 1850
Oil on canvas, 30" × 25"
Missouri Historical Society, Saint Louis (1953.16.4)

Portrait of Sophia Deppe, c. 1850
Oil on canvas, 30" × 25"
Missouri Historical Society, Saint Louis (1953.16.3)

Attributed to Wimar
Edward Eggers, c. 1850
Oil on canvas, 24" × 20"
Missouri Historical Society, Saint Louis

Entrance to the Jeddo River, 1851
Oil on canvas, 29⅛" × 36¹⁵/₁₆"
LL: "C. Wimar 1851"
Saint Louis Art Museum (71:1954)

Three Children Attacked by a Wolf, c. 1851
Oil on canvas on board, 47½" × 41½"
LL: "Carl Wimar"
Missouri Historical Society, Saint Louis (1967.42.1)

Castle of Heidelberg, 1852
Oil on canvas, 21½" × 26"
LL: "C. Wimar May 1852"
Saint Louis Art Museum (15:1984)

Sketchbook, 1852
Pencil, 4⅝" × 7½"
Missouri Historical Society, Saint Louis (1918.52.5)

Sketchbook, c. 1852–56
Pencil on paper, 5" × 3⅜"
"Aufmerksakeit Bernhard"
Saint Louis Art Museum (91 : 1947)

The Abduction of Daniel Boone's Daughter by the Indians, 1853
Oil on canvas, 40" × 50"
LL: "C. Wimar Dusseldorf 1853"
Washington University Gallery of Art, Saint Louis

Discovery of Boone's Encampment in Kentucky by the Indians, 1853
Oil on canvas, 26" × 33"
LR: "Carl Wimar 1853"
Formerly Mr. L. S. Dennig, Saint Louis

The Abduction of Daniel Boone's Daughter by the Indians, 1853
Charcoal and sepia on paper, 36" × 44"
Saint Louis Art Museum (188 : 1955)

Flatboatmen on the Mississippi, 1854
Oil on canvas, 19⅛" × 23⅝"
LR: "1854/C. Wimar, Du"
Amon Carter Museum, Fort Worth (1969.35)

Sketchbook, 1854
Pencil, with ink and watercolor highlights, 6¼" × 10¼"
Missouri Historical Society, Saint Louis (1918.52.4.1)

The Captive Charger, 1854
Oil on canvas, 30" × 41"
LL: "Charles Wimar, Duess. 1854"
Saint Louis Art Museum (181 : 1925)

The Attack on an Emigrant Train, 1854
Oil on canvas, 39⅜" × 49½"
LL: "Charles Wimar, Duss. 1854"
Private collection, Saint Louis

The Attack on an Emigrant Train, 1854
Charcoal and sepia on paper, 36¾" × 49"
Saint Louis Art Museum (79 : 1950)

The Captive Charger, 1854
Charcoal, pencil, and wash on paper, 18" × 24"
LL: "Charles Wimar. 1854"
Private collection, New Jersey

Indian Campfire, c. 1854–56
Oil on canvas, 20⅜" × 24⅞"
Bancroft Library, University of California, Berkeley

Indians Pursued by American Dragoons, 1855
Oil on canvas, 33" × 46"
LR: "Charles Wimar Dusseldorf 1855"
Gulf States Paper Corporation, Tuscaloosa

The Abduction of Daniel Boone's Daughter by the Indians, 1855
Oil on canvas, 44½" × 60½"
LR: "Charles Wimar/Dusseldorf 1855"
Private collection, Saint Louis

Indians Pursued by American Dragoons, 1855
Charcoal and sepia on paper, 30¾" × 42⅞"
Saint Louis Art Museum (256 : 1960)

Massacre of Wyoming Valley, 1855
Watercolor, 18" × 24"
LR: "C.W. 1855"
William Harmsen, Denver, Colorado

The Abduction of Boone's Daughter by the Indians, c. 1855
Oil on canvas, 18⅝" × 25¼"
LR: "Carl Wimar"
Amon Carter Museum, Fort Worth (1965.1)

Massacre at Wyoming Valley, c. 1855
Oil on canvas, 30" × 40"
Private collection, Los Angeles

Funeral Raft of a Dead Chieftain, 1856
Oil on canvas, 11¼" × 16"
LR: "Carl Wimar 1856"
Gulf States Paper Corporation, Tuscaloosa

Sketchbook, 1856
Pencil, 3¾" × 5⁵⁄₁₆"
Missouri Historical Society, Saint Louis

The Attack on an Emigrant Train, 1856
Oil on canvas, 55¼″ × 79″
LR: "Charles Wimar Dusf. 1856"
University of Michigan Museum of Art, Ann Arbor

On the Warpath, 1856
Oil on canvas, 10¼″ × 12½″
LR: "Carl Wimar/1856"
Formerly Mrs. Joseph L. Werner, Saint Louis

Indian Buffalo Hunt, 1856
Oil on board, 11¾″ × 14⅞″
LL: "Carl Wimar.1856"
Private collection, Dallas, Texas

The Attack on an Emigrant Train, 1856
Charcoal and sepia on paper, 32⅞″ × 48¼″
Saint Louis Art Museum (76 : 1950)

The Lost Trail, c. 1856
Oil on canvas, 19½″ × 30½″
Thyssen-Bornemisza Collection, Lugano, Switzerland

The Attack on an Emigrant Train, c. 1856
Oil on canvas, 37″ × 52″
Thomas Gilcrease Institute of American History and Art, Tulsa

Portrait of Adam Lemp, 1857
Oil on canvas, 46″ × 35¾″
LR: "C. Wimar"
Missouri Historical Society, Saint Louis (1971.34.1)

Portrait of Mrs. Adam Lemp (Louise Bauer), 1857
Oil on canvas, 47″ × 35¼″
LR: "Cha. Wimar/1857"
Missouri Historical Society, Saint Louis (1971.34.2)

Portrait of Mrs. Adam Lemp (Justine Claremont), 1858
Oil on canvas, 46″ × 35¾″
LR: "Carl Wimar 1858"
Missouri Historical Society, Saint Louis (1971.34.3)

Indians Stealing Horses, 1858
Oil on canvas, 16½″ × 20″
LL: "C. Wimar 1858"
Joslyn Art Museum, Omaha

Sketchbook I, 1858
Pencil on paper, 5⅞″ × 4⅛″
Saint Louis Art Museum (61 : 1941)

Sketchbook II, 1858
Pencil on paper, 7½″ × 5 /14″
Saint Louis Art Museum (60 : 1941)

Sketchbook III, 1858
Pencil on paper, 6½″ × 4½″
Saint Louis Art Museum (62 : 1941)

Dead Bear, 1858
Pencil, 5″ × 7¼″
LL: "10 July 1858"
Zaplin-Lampert Gallery, Santa Fe

Upper Missouri River Bank, c. 1858
Oil on wood, 6″ × 9½″
Phoenix Art Museum

Landscape, River and Mountains, Upper Missouri River, c. 1858
Oil on wood, 8″ × 13¾″
Phoenix Art Museum

Attributed to CFW
Cecilia Becker Kehrmann, 1858–59
Oil on canvas, 43″ × 35½″
Missouri Historical Society, Saint Louis

Attributed to CFW
Statius Kehrmann, 1858–59
Oil on canvas, 42½″ × 35¼″
Missouri Historical Society, Saint Louis

Bear Rib, 1859
Oil on canvas, 7¼″ × 4½″
LC: "Bear Rib"
Missouri Historical Society, Saint Louis (1950.117.1)

Bear Rib, 1859
Oil on canvasboard, 7½″ × 4½″
LL: "C. Wimar"
LL: "Bear Rib"
David W. Mesker, Saint Louis

229

Iron Horn, 1859
Oil on canvas, 7¼″ × 4½″
LC: "Iron Horn"
Missouri Historical Society, Saint Louis (1950.117.2)

Portrait of Pawnee, 1859
Oil on canvas, 6½″ × 5½″
LL: "C. Wimar 1859"
LC: "Pawnee"
Missouri Historical Society, Saint Louis (1962.200.1)

Portrait of Padoucee, 1859
Oil on canvas, 6½″ × 5½″
LL: "C. Wimar 1859"
LC: "Padoucee"
Missouri Historical Society, Saint Louis (1962.201.1)

Portrait of Rudolf Mackwitz, 1859
Oil on canvas, 24″ × 20″
LR: "C. Wimar 1859"
Missouri Historical Society, Saint Louis (1962.199.1)

The Adam Lemp Brewery, Saint Louis, 1859
Oil on canvas, 35¼″ × 54⅛″
LL: "C. Wimar 1859"
Saint Louis Art Museum (690 : 1949)

Buffaloes Crossing the Yellowstone, 1859
Oil on canvas, 24¼″ × 48¼″
LR: "Charles Wimar 1859"
Washington University Gallery of Art, Saint Louis

The Wounded Buffalo, 1859
Oil on canvas on board, 17⅝″ × 27⅝″
LR: "C. Wimar 1859"
Washington University Gallery of Art, Saint Louis

Buffalo Crossing the Platte, 1859
Oil on canvas, 15¾″ × 30″
LL: "C. Wimar 1859"
Thomas Gilcrease Institute of American History and Art, Tulsa

Mounted Indian Hunter (detail from *The Lost Trail*), 1859
Charcoal on paper, 9¾″ × 8″
LR: "C. Wimar/59"
Missouri Historical Society, Saint Louis (1950.116.2.27)

Ne-Sou-A-Quoit (after Charles Bird King), 1859
Watercolor and charcoal on paper, 15½″ × 10½″
LR: "Ne-Sou-A-Quoit a Fox Chief/the Bear in the Forks of a tree."
Missouri Historical Society, Saint Louis (1950.116.2.34)

Sketchbook, 1859
Pencil on paper, 3¹¹⁄₁₆″ × 6⅛″
Missouri Historical Society, Saint Louis (1918.52.2.1)

View of the Missouri River Across the Great Bend, 1859
Charcoal with white chalk on buff paper
Missouri Historical Society (1950.116.2.11)

Medicine Creek/ Chalk Bluffs—Little Soldier's Village, 1859
Charcoal and white chalk on buff paper, 10½″ × 14⅝″
Upper Scene LL: "Medicine Creek"
Lower Scene LL: "Chalk Bluffs little Soldier Vill[age] 22th June 1859"
Missouri Historical Society, Saint Louis (1950.116.2.14)

Interior of an Arikara Medicine Lodge, Fort Clark, 1859
Charcoal and white chalk on buff paper, 10¾″ × 15¾″
LL: "C. Wimar/59"
Missouri Historical Society, Saint Louis (1950.116.2.26)

Mandan or Arikara Lodge, Fort Clark, 1859
Charcoal and white chalk on paper, 7⅞″ × 10⅛″
Missouri Historical Society, Saint Louis (1950.116.2.28)

Studies of Arikara, Fort Clark [?], 1859
Charcoal and white chalk on paper, 14½″ × 10″
LL: "C. Wimar/59"
Missouri Historical Society, Saint Louis (1950.116.2.30)

Arikara Graves at Fort Clark, 1859
Black and white crayon, 15″ × 9½″
"Arikara Graves at Fort Clark June 25, 1859"
Bushnell Collection, Peabody Museum, Harvard University

Mandan Brave, 1859
Pencil, 14″ × 10¼″
LL: "C. Wimar"
LR: "Mandan June 27th 1859"
Private collection, Saint Louis

Above Fort Stuart, Upper Missouri River, July 4, 1859
Charcoal with white on paper, 10″ × 15¼″
LL: "Above Fort Stuart July 4th"
Mongerson-Wunderlich Galleries, Chicago

Above Fort Stuart July 4th 1849 [?], 1859
Pencil and highlight on buff paper, 9″ × 14″
CL: "Above Fort Stuart July 4th 1849[?]"
Mr. Samuel Grant, Jr., Saint Louis

Mouth of the Milk River/ Bluffs Along the Opposite Bank, 1859
Charcoal and white chalk on buff paper, 10½″ × 15¼″
CR: "Milk River"
LR: "July 6th"
Missouri Historical Society, Saint Louis (1950.116.2.12)

Mouth of Milk River, 1859
Charcoal and white chalk on buff paper, 10½″ × 15¼″
LL: "Mouth of Milk River July 6th 1859"
Missouri Historical Society, Saint Louis (1950.116.2.24)

Two Landscape Sketches, 1859
Charcoal and chalk on brown paper, 10⅛″ × 15⅛″
LL: "July 8th"
Saint Louis Art Museum (70 : 1947)

July 8th Near Round Butte, 1859
Charcoal and white chalk on buff paper, 7⅜″ × 15″
LL: "July 8th near round Bute"
Missouri Historical Society, Saint Louis (1950.116.2.23)

Jim Birche's Grave, Upper Missouri River, 1859
Charcoal on paper, 10″ × 14¾″
"July 8th 1859 Jim Birches Grave"
Mongerson-Wunderlich Galleries, Chicago

July 9th, 1859
Pencil and highlights on buff paper, 9″ × 14″
LL: "July 9th"
Mr. Samuel Grant, Jr., Saint Louis

Buttes, Upper Missouri River, July 9, 1859
Charcoal with white on paper, 10½″ × 15½″
LL: "July 9th 1859 haute Bute"
Mongerson-Wunderlich Galleries, Chicago

July 9th Round Butte, 1859
Charcoal on paper, 10⅛″ × 15″
LL: "July 9th round Bute"
Missouri Historical Society, Saint Louis (1950.116.2.22)

July 9th Above Round Butte, 1859
Charcoal and white chalk on paper, 9½″ × 14⅝″
LL: "July 9th above round Bute"
Missouri Historical Society, Saint Louis (1950.116.2.15)

Two Studies of Buttes, 1859
Charcoal and chalk on brown paper, 10⅛″ × 15⅛″
LL: "July 9th above round Bute"
Saint Louis Art Museum (69 : 1947)

Buttes, 1859
Charcoal and chalk on brown paper, 10¹⁄₁₆″ × 15″
LL: "July 12th"
Saint Louis Art Museum (67 : 1947)

Two Studies of Rock Formations, 1859
Charcoal and chalk on brown paper, 9¹⁵⁄₁₆″ × 14⅞″
LL: "July 12th"
Saint Louis Art Museum (79 : 1947)

Two Landscape Studies, 1859
Charcoal on brown paper, 9¹⁵⁄₁₆″ × 15″
LL: "July 12th"
Saint Louis Art Museum (81 : 1947)

Two Studies of Rock Formations, 1859
Charcoal and chalk on brown paper, 10″ × 14¾″
CL: "July 13th"
LL: "July 16th"
Saint Louis Art Museum (76 : 1947)

The Missouri River, 1859
Charcoal and chalk on brown paper, 10″ × 14¹⁵⁄₁₆″
LL: "July 14th"
Saint Louis Art Museum (65 : 1947)

Study of Curious Rocks, Mouth of the Judith River, 1859
Charcoal with white on paper, 9¾″ × 14¼″
LL: "July 15th—Mouth of Judith"
Mongerson-Wunderlich Galleries, Chicago

Studies of Buttes, Upper Missouri River, July 16, 1859
Charcoal with white on paper, 10″ × 14¾″
LL: "July 16th"
Mongerson-Wunderlich Galleries, Chicago

Buttes on the Upper Missouri, 1859
Charcoal and chalk on brown paper, 10″ × 14¹³⁄₁₆″
LL: "July 16th"
Saint Louis Art Museum (72 : 1947)

Buttes, Upper Missouri River, July 16, 1859
Charcoal with white on paper, 10″ × 14¾″
LR: "July 16th, 1859"
Mongerson-Wunderlich Galleries, Chicago

Eroded Rock Formations Along the Upper Missouri, 1859
Charcoal and chalk on brown paper, 10″ × 14¾″
LL: "July 16th"
Saint Louis Art Museum (75 : 1947)

Two Studies of Eroded Rock Formations, 1859
Charcoal and chalk on brown paper, 10″ × 15″
LR: "July 16th"
Saint Louis Art Museum (77 : 1947)

July 16th Near Round Butte, 1859
Charcoal and white chalk on paper, 5⅜″ × 14⅝″
LR: "C. Wimar"
LL: "July 16th"
Missouri Historical Society, Saint Louis (1950.116.2.20)

Eroded Rock Formations/ The Pinnacles, Upper Missouri River, 1859
Charcoal on brown paper heightened with white, 10″ × 14¾″
LL: "July 16th"
Amon Carter Museum, Fort Worth (1988.26)

White Castles on the Missouri, 1859
Charcoal on brown paper, 9½″ × 14¾″
LR: "C. Wimar"
LL: "July 16th"
Missouri Historical Society, Saint Louis (1950.116.2.21)

Studies of White Cliffs, Near Judith River/ July 9th Above Round Butte, 1859
Charcoal and white chalk on buff paper, 9¹¹⁄₁₆″ × 15³⁄₁₆″
LR: "C. Wimar 1859"
Upper Scene LL: "July 16th"
Lower Scene: "July 9th above round Bute"
Missouri Historical Society, Saint Louis (1950.116.2.10)

Bluffs in the Vicinity of Fort Benton, 1859
Charcoal and white chalk on gray paper, 9¾″ × 15¼″
LR: "C. Wimar below Fort Benton July 17th"
Missouri Historical Society, Saint Louis (1950.116.2.16)

Bear Lake, 1859
Charcoal and chalk on brown paper, 10″ × 14¾″
LL: "Bear Lake on July 18th"
Saint Louis Art Museum (71 : 1947)

July 21st Round Butte, 1859
Charcoal and white chalk on gray paper, 9½″ × 15⅛″
LL: "July 21th Round Bute"
Missouri Historical Society, Saint Louis (1950.116.2.18)

Citadel Butte, Upper Missouri River, 1859
Charcoal with white on paper, 9¾″ × 15″
LR: "Citadel July 1859"
Washington University Gallery of Art

Buffalo Hunt, 1859
Pencil and charcoal on paper, 4½″ × 8⅛″
LL: "C. Wimar/59"
Missouri Historical Society, Saint Louis (1950.116.2.2)

Buffalo Hunt, 1859
Pencil on paper, 4½″ × 8⅛″
Missouri Historical Society, Saint Louis (1950.116.2.1)

Natural Fort, 1859
Charcoal and white chalk on buff paper, 9¾″ × 15″
LL: "Natural Fort 15 Miles blw. Fort Randle"
Missouri Historical Society, Saint Louis (1950.116.2.17)

Cloud Formation at Sunset, 1859
Pastel on paper, 9¼″ × 12¾″
LL: "C. Wimar. 1859"
Missouri Historical Society, Saint Louis (1950.116.2.40)

Indian Burial, Fort Pierre, 1859
Pencil, 14½″ × 9½″
LR: "Fort Pierre 1859"
The Dietrich American Foundation, Philadelphia

Missouri River Below Fort Stuart—View of Fort Kipp, July 1859
Charcoal on buff brown paper, 10″ × 15¾″
Wunderlich Gallery, New York

Studies of Eroded Rock Formations, Upper Missouri River, 1859
Charcoal on buff paper, 10″ × 14¾″
Wunderlich Gallery, New York

Indian Group and Portrait Studies, 1859
Pencil on paper, approx. 9″ × 14″
LL: "C. Wimar. 1859"
Missouri Historical Society, Saint Louis (1959.116.2.3)

View of La Framboise Island/ Mouth of the Bad River, 1859
Charcoal on tan paper heightened with white, 10⅝″ × 15⅝″
"[Illegible], Bad River 1859"
Amon Carter Museum, Fort Worth (1988.27)

Two Landscape Views, Upper Missouri River, 1859
Charcoal with white on paper, 10½″ × 15½″
Mongerson-Wunderlich Galleries, Chicago

Two Landscape Studies, Upper Missouri River, 1859
Charcoal with white on paper, 10½″ × 15½″
LL: "W."
Mongerson-Wunderlich Galleries, Chicago

Scenery on the Missouri River, Two Views, 1859
Charcoal on paper, 10½″ × 15″
Mongerson-Wunderlich Galleries, Chicago

Mouth of the Vermillion River, 1859
Charcoal with white on paper, 10½″ × 15½″
LL: "Mouth of Vermillion River"
LR: "Missouri"
Mongerson-Wunderlich Galleries, Chicago

Table Rock, 1859
Pencil and highlights on buff paper, 9″ × 14″
LL: "July 12"
Mr. Samuel Grant, Jr., Saint Louis

Landscapes, Upper Missouri River—Two Views, 1859
Charcoal with white on tan paper, 10⅝″ × 15⅝″
Amon Carter Museum, Fort Worth (1988.24)

Ein Amerik Buffelochse, 1859
Lithograph
LL: "Drawn from nature by C. Wimar"
Glenbow Museum, Calgary

Indians Approaching Fort Union, c. 1859
Oil on canvas, 24⅛″ × 48½″
Washington University Gallery of Art, Saint Louis

Reconnoitering, c. 1859
Oil on canvas, 10″ × 14″
LR: "C. Wimar"
Private collection

Portrait of a Half-Breed Indian, c. 1859
Oil on canvas, 11¾″ × 10″
CL: "C. Wimar"
Nancy Grant Corrigan, Tustin, California

Head of a Half-Breed Indian, c. 1859
Oil on canvas, 9″ in diameter
LR: "C. Wimar"
Formerly Wunderlich Gallery, New York

Portrait Study of Iron Horn, c. 1859
Oil on canvas, 7¼″ × 4¼″
LC: "C. Wimar"
LC: "Iron Horn"
Sotheby's Sale 5721 (May 25, 1988, lot #85)

Foraging Party on the Missouri, c. 1859
Oil on board, 5″ × 11″
LL: "CW"
Prof. and Mrs. Thomas Hall, Saint Louis

Squall, c. 1859
Oil on canvas, 5″ × 13½″
Missouri Historical Society, Saint Louis (1950.116.2.39)

Indian Clothing and Weapons, c. 1859
Oil on canvas, 7⅜″ × 11⅛″
LL: "C. Wimar"
Missouri Historical Society, Saint Louis (1950.116.2.33)

On the Alert, c. 1859
Oil on canvas, 10″ × 14″
Martin Kodner, Saint Louis

River Scene at Dawn, c. 1859
Oil on paper, 6½″ × 9⅝″
Missouri Historical Society, Saint Louis (1950.116.2.38)

233

Monarch of the Plains, c. 1859
Oil on academy board, 9¾″ × 14″
Kennedy Galleries, New York (#9431)

Cottonwoods on the Missouri, c. 1859
Charcoal and white chalk on gray paper, 9¾″ × 15″
Missouri Historical Society, Saint Louis (1950.116.2.13)

Indian Portrait Studies, c. 1859
Charcoal on paper, 14¹¹⁄₁₆″ × 9½″
Missouri Historical Society, Saint Louis (1950.116.2.29)

Indian Portrait Studies, c. 1859
Charcoal, white, red, yellow, and orange chalk, 10¾″ × 15⅜″
C: "[Illegible] Nia-to-a-Safa"
Missouri Historical Society, Saint Louis (1952.101.1)

Indian Encampment, c. 1859
Charcoal and white chalk on paper, 5″ × 14¾″
LR: "C. Wimar"
Missouri Historical Society, Saint Louis (1950.116.2.19)

Indian Running, c. 1859
Pencil on paper, 6¾″ × 6⅛″
Missouri Historical Society, Saint Louis (1950.116.2.4)

Indians in Ceremonial Dress, c. 1859
Pencil and ink wash on paper, 6¾″ × 6¼″
LR: "C. Wimar"
Missouri Historical Society, Saint Louis (1950.116.2.5)

Two Frontiersmen with a Bear, c. 1859
Pencil, ink wash, and white watercolor on paper, 10½″ × 8½″
Missouri Historical Society, Saint Louis (1950.116.2.9)

Ma-Sai-To, c. 1859
Charcoal and white chalk on paper, 14″ × 10″
C: "Ma-sai-to"
Missouri Historical Society, Saint Louis (1950.116.2.32)

Ree & Mandan Indians, c. 1859
Charcoal and white chalk on paper, 14⅝″ × 10″
LR: "C. Wimar"
C: "Ree"
LC: "Mandan"
Missouri Historical Society, Saint Louis (1950.116.2.31)

Indian Group, c. 1859
Charcoal and white and yellow chalk on gray paper, 7″ × 14″
Missouri Historical Society, Saint Louis (1950.116.2.25)

Two Studies of Cedar Island, c. 1859
Charcoal and chalk on brown paper, 10⁹⁄₁₆″ × 15⁹⁄₁₆″
CR: "Cedar Island"
Saint Louis Art Museum (66:1947)

Two Studies of River Banks, c. 1859
Charcoal and chalk on brown paper, 10¹¹⁄₁₆″ × 15⅝″
Saint Louis Art Museum (68:1947)

Western Landscape and Study of Mouth of Scalp Creek, c. 1859
Charcoal and chalk on brown paper, 10⅝″ × 15⁹⁄₁₆″
LR: "Mouth of Scalp Cr."
Saint Louis Art Museum (73:1947)

Two Landscape Sketches, c. 1859
Charcoal on brown paper, 10¹¹⁄₁₆″ × 15⅝″
CR: "Below March River"
Saint Louis Art Museum (74:1947)

Two Landscape Studies, c. 1859
Charcoal and chalk on brown paper, 10½″ × 15⅝″
LL: "Above Fort Randle"
Saint Louis Art Museum (78:1947)

Study of Dying Buffalo Cow, c. 1859
Pencil on brown paper, 7⅞″ × 10³⁄₁₆″
Verso: "Study of Dying Buffalo Cow"
Saint Louis Art Museum (89:1947)

View of the Missouri River, c. 1859
Charcoal on buff paper, 9⅝″ × 29¾″
Missouri Historical Society, Saint Louis (1950.116.2.11)

Mounted Indians Running Buffalo, c. 1859
Wash on paper, 9½″ × 15″
LR: "CW"
Bushnell Collection, Peabody Museum, Harvard University

Portrait of a Blackfoot Indian, c. 1859
Black crayon, 9½″ × 15″
Bushnell Collection, Peabody Museum, Harvard University

234

Two Landscape Views, Upper Missouri River, c. 1859
Charcoal on paper, 10½″ × 15¼″
Mongerson-Wunderlich Galleries, Chicago

Study of Trees, Landscape, Upper Missouri River, c. 1859
Charcoal with white on paper, 10″ × 15″
Mongerson-Wunderlich Galleries, Chicago

Two Views, Study of Buttes, Upper Missouri River, c. 1859
Charcoal with white on paper, 10″ × 15″
Mongerson-Wunderlich Galleries, Chicago

Abandoned Shelter, c. 1859
Pencil on buff paper, 9″ × 14″
Mr. Samuel Grant, Jr., Saint Louis

Fort Clark, c. 1859
Pencil on buff paper, 9″ × 14″
CL: "Fort Clark"
Mr. Samuel Grant, Jr., Saint Louis

Two Indians, c. 1859
Pencil on paper, 15″ × 10″ approx.
Nancy Grant Corrigan, Tustin, California

Indian, c. 1859
Pencil on paper, 15″ × 10″ approx.
Nancy Grant Corrigan, Tustin, California

Little Soldier and Man, c. 1859
Pencil on paper, 15″ × 10″ approx.
CR: "Little Soldier/Akichitha Chiga/Yanktonee"
LR: "Yanktonee/Man"
Nancy Grant Corrigan, Tustin, California

Mounted Indian and Indian Head, c. 1859
Pencil on paper, 15″ × 10″ approx.
Nancy Grant Corrigan, Tustin, California

Indians Crossing the Upper Missouri River, c. 1859–60
Oil on canvas, 24¼″ × 48⅛″
LR: "C. Wimar"
Amon Carter Museum, Fort Worth (1971.61)

Studies for "Indians Approaching Fort Benton" and "Laclede", c. 1859–62
Pencil on brown paper, 10⅜″ × 6⁵⁄₁₆″
Verso: "Capture of Buffalo"
Saint Louis Art Museum (82:1947)

Buffalo Dance, 1860
Oil on canvas, 24⅞″ × 49⅝″
LL: "Charles Wimar 1860"
Saint Louis Art Museum (164:1947)

Indian Encampment on the Big Bend of the Missouri River, 1860
Oil on canvas, 25″ × 49″
LR: "C. Wimar.1860"
Thomas Gilcrease Institute of American History and Art, Tulsa

Buffalo Hunt, 1860
Oil on canvas, 35¼″ × 60″
LL: "C. Wimar 1860"
Washington University Gallery of Art, Saint Louis

Indians on the Prairie, 1860
Oil on canvas, 8½″ × 12″
LC: "C. Wimar 1860"
Bronson-Rollins Gallery, Los Angeles

War Party, 1860
Oil on academy board, 10″ × 13″
LL: "C. Wimar 1860"
Private collection, Chicago

Head of a Dog, c. 1860
Oil on canvas, 10″ × 14″
LL: "Charles Wimar"
William Harmsen, Denver, Colorado

Council Fire, 1860
Pastel, 15″ × 19″
LL: "C. Wimar 1860"
Private collection

Buffalo Approaching Water Hole, 1860
Pastel, 18″ × 24″
LR: "C. Wimar 1860"
Lyle S. and Eileen E. Woodcock, Saint Louis

235

Buffalo Hunt, 1860
Pastel on canvas, 15″ × 19½″
LL: "C. Wimar. 1860"
National Cowboy Hall of Fame, Oklahoma City

After Carl Wimar
On the Prairie, 1860
Lithograph, 21⅞″ × 29⅞″ (paper)
LR: "Chas. Wimar, Pinixt."
LC: "On Stone by L Grozelier", "Printed at J.H. Bufford's"
Saint Louis Art Museum (39 : 1950)

Study for "The Buffalo Dance", c. 1860
Pencil on brown paper, 6¼″ × 8⁹⁄₁₆″
"Buffalo Dance"
Saint Louis Art Museum (83 : 1947)

Study for "The Buffalo Dance", c. 1860
Pencil on brown paper, 6⅜″ × 9¹⁄₁₆″
Verso: "Buffalo Hunt no. 1"
Saint Louis Art Museum (90 : 1947)

Portrait of an Indian (Bear Rib), c. 1860
Oil on canvas mounted on cardboard, 9½″ × 7¾″
LL: "C. Wimar"
Mr. and Mrs. Gerald P. Peters, Santa Fe

Buffalo Hunt, 1861
Oil on canvas, 89″ × 54″
LR: "C. Wimar 1861"
Missouri Historical Society, Saint Louis (1941.35.1)

Chief Billy Bowlegs (Holatamico), 1861
Oil on canvas, 25¼″ × 30¼″
LL: "C. Wimar 1861"
Saint Louis Art Museum (9 : 1938)

Portrait of Captain Constantin Blandowski, 1861
Oil on canvas, 24″ × 19⅞″
Saint Louis Art Museum (179 : 1946)

Buffalo Bull Pursued by Wolves, 1861
Oil on canvas, 12³⁄₁₆″ × 18⅛″
LR: "C. Wimar 1861"
Saint Louis Art Museum (144 : 1977)

Buffalo Hunt by Indians, 1861
Oil on canvas, 36″ × 61″
LL: "C. Wimar Saint Louis, Mo. 1861"
Thomas Gilcrease Institute of American History and Art, Tulsa

Portrait of August H. Becker, 1861
Oil on paperboard, 24″ × 20″
LR: "C. Wimar/1861"
Mrs. Samuel Grant, Saint Louis

Colonel Sigel, General Frémont, and Captain Blandowski, 1861
Oil on canvas (grisaille), 29¼″ × 24¼″
LL: "C. Wimar Saint Louis, Mo./1861"
Private collection, Saint Louis

Head of Buffalo, 1861
Oil on canvas, 23¾″ × 20″
LR: "C. Wimar/1861"
Formerly Mr. L. S. Dennig, Saint Louis

Buffalo, 1861
Oil on canvas, 20″ × 24″
LR: "C. Wimar 1861"
Private collection

Buffalo, 1861
Gouache, pastel on paper, 10¾″ × 14½″
LR: "C. Wimar 1861."
Private collection, Ohio

Buffaloes Drinking, c. 1861
Oil on canvas, 12″ × 18″
LR: "C. Wimar"
Phoenix Art Museum

Billy Bowlegs, c. 1861
Oil on canvas, 30″ × 25″
Private collection, New York

Billy Bowlegs, c. 1861
Oil on canvas, 30″ × 25″
Thomas Gilcrease Institute of American History and Art, Tulsa

A Study for the Indian in "Buffalo Hunt by Indians", c. 1861
Oil on paper mounted on canvas, 14″ × 12″
Verso: "Sketch made by Carl Wimar. Anna Schleifarth."
Indianapolis Museum of Art

236

Eagle (recto), *General Frémont* (verso), 1861
Pencil on paper, 10″ × 6¼″
Missouri Historical Society, Saint Louis (1986.73.3)

Studies for the "Buffalo Hunt" and "Billy Bowlegs", c. 1861
Pencil on brown paper, 10⅜″ × 6⁵⁄₁₆″
Verso: "Buffalo Hunt No. II"
Saint Louis Art Museum (84:1947)

De Soto Discovering the Mississippi, 1862
Mixed media, 7′ 1¼″ × 22′ 1¼″ × 24′ 8¾″
Old Courthouse, 11 North Fourth Street, Saint Louis

Indians Attacking the Village of Saint Louis, 1862
Mixed media, 7′ 1¼″ × 22′ 1¼″ × 24′ 8″
Old Courthouse, Saint Louis

The Landing of Laclede, 1862
Mixed media, 7′ 1¾″ × 22′ 3¾″ × 24′ 7½″
Old Courthouse, Saint Louis

Westward the Star of Empire Takes Its Way (The Cochetope Pass), 1862
Mixed media, 7′ 2″ × 9″ × 24′ 8¼″
Old Courthouse, Saint Louis

Portrait of Edward Bates, 1862
Oil on plaster
Old Courthouse, Saint Louis

Portrait of George Washington, 1862
Oil on plaster
Old Courthouse, Saint Louis

Portrait of Martha Washington, 1862
Oil on plaster
Old Courthouse, Saint Louis

Portrait of Senator Thomas Hart Benton, 1862
Oil on plaster
Old Courthouse, Saint Louis

Allegorical Figure of Law, 1862
Oil on canvas, 12¹¹⁄₁₆″ × 7⅜″
LL: "C. Wimar 1862"
Missouri Historical Society, Saint Louis (1950.116.2.36)

Allegorical Figure of Justice, 1862
Oil on canvas, 12¾″ × 7⅜″
LR: "C. Wimar 1862"
Missouri Historical Society, Saint Louis (1950.116.2.37)

Allegorical Figure of Liberty, 1862
Oil on canvas, 12¼″ × 5⅞″
LR: "C. Wimar"
LL: "_____ Hour 10th/62"
Missouri Historical Society, Saint Louis (1950.116.2.35)

Allegory of the Reconciliation of North and South by Liberty [*Symbolic Group*], 1862
Pencil and Gray wash on paper, 5″ × 7¾″
Missouri Historical Society, Saint Louis (1950.116.2.8)

Study for the Old Courthouse Murals (Justice and Draco), 1862
Pencil on brown paper, 10⅝″ × 15⅝″
Saint Louis Art Museum (63:1947)

Buffalo Stampede: Study for Old Courthouse Murals, 1862
Pencil on brown paper, 6⁵⁄₁₆″ × 10¼″
Verso: "A Buffalo Stampede"
Saint Louis Art Museum (86:1947)

The Landing of Laclede: Study for Old Courthouse Murals, 1862
Pencil and wash on brown paper, 5⁷⁄₁₆ × 9⅞″
Verso: "First setler! The Landing of La Clede on the western shore of the Mississippi river, where now stands the great city of St. Louis."
Saint Louis Art Museum (92:1947)

Portrait of a Man Wearing a Colletin, c. 1862
Oil on canvas, 30″ × 25″
Verso: "No. 2"
Formerly Charles C. Crecelius, Miss Frances Crecelius, Saint Louis

Indian Raid, n.d.
Oil on canvas, 14″ × 20″
Verso: "C. Wimar"
Verso: "Indian Raid-Louisville, Ky."
Lee Anderson, New York

Study of Trees, Mississippi, n.d.
Oil on wood, 7″ × 10″
Kennedy Galleries, New York (#9436)

237

Self Portrait, n.d.
Oil on canvas, 20″ × 16″
National Portrait Gallery, Washington, D.C.

Studies of a Quartered Buffalo, n.d.
Oil on paper mounted on cloth, 8″ × 11⁹⁄₁₆″
Saint Louis Art Museum (55 : 1947)

Studies for a Painting of a Half-Breed Indian and an Indian Woman, n.d.
Oil, 15″ × 18″
Saint Louis Art Museum (59 : 1947)

Miscellaneous Studies, n.d.
Oil, 7⅞″ × 11″
Saint Louis Art Museum (50 : 1947)

Sketch of a River Bank, n.d.
Oil on canvas, 6½″ × 12½″
Saint Louis Art Museum (65 : 1941)

Study for a Wounded Buffalo, n.d.
Oil on canvas, 8″ × 12″
Saint Louis Art Museum (53 : 1947)

Study of Hands, n.d.
Oil on cardboard, 8⅝″ × 15½″
LL: "Carl Wimar"
Saint Louis Art Museum (54 : 1947)

Landscape, n.d.
Oil on paper, 6¹⁵⁄₁₆″ × 9¹⁵⁄₁₆″
LR: "C. Wimar"
Saint Louis Art Museum (57 : 1947)

Study of Western Landscape (The Citadel ?), n.d.
Oil on paper, 8⅝″ × 12¼″
Saint Louis Art Museum (58 : 1947)

Sketch of Rock Formation, n.d.
Oil on paper, 10⁵⁄₁₆″ × 12⅞″
Saint Louis Art Museum (56 : 1947)

Indian Campfire by Moonlight, n.d.
Oil on canvas, 12″ × 14″
LR: "C. Wimar"
Thomas Gilcrease Institute of American History and Art, Tulsa

Turf House on the Plains, n.d.
Oil on canvas, 5¾″ × 12″
Bancroft Library, University of California, Berkeley

Attributed to Wimar
Fleeing a Prairie Fire, n.d.
Oil, 6½″ × 8½″
Bancroft Library, University of California, Berkeley

Study of an Indian Head, n.d.
Oil on canvas, 10″ × 8″
LR: illegible inscriptions
Lee Anderson, New York

Medicine Bag, n.d.
Oil on canvas mounted on pulpboard, 12⁵⁄₁₆″ × 9″
Saint Louis Art Museum (49 : 1947)

Portrait of Mandan Man, n.d.
Oil on canvas, 35″ × 28″ (oval)
Thomas Gilcrease Institute of American History and Art, Tulsa

Study for "The Lost Trail," n.d.
Pencil on paper, 6″ × 9⁹⁄₁₆″
Missouri Historical Society, Saint Louis

Landscape with Bear/Buffaloes in the Cochetope Pass, c. 1862
Pencil on buff paper, 7″ × 9⅝″
Missouri Historical Society, Saint Louis (1950.116.2.7)

Buffalo Head, n.d.
Chalk on grey laid paper, 16″ × 10″
Saint Louis Art Museum (63 : 1941)

Golden Shell, n.d.
Chalk on grey laid paper, 16″ × 10″
Saint Louis Art Museum (64 : 1941)

Indian Village, n.d.
Crayon on paper, 10⅛″ × 15⅝″
Saint Louis Art Museum (51 : 1947)

Below Fort Clark, n.d.
Charcoal and chalk on brown paper, 10⅜″ × 15½″
LL: "Below Fort Clark"
Saint Louis Art Museum (52 : 1947)

238

Black Bird Hills, n.d.
Charcoal on brown paper, 5⁵⁄₁₆″ × 15⁵⁄₈″
LR: "Black Bird Hills"
Saint Louis Art Museum (60 : 1947)

Studies of Indian Heads, n.d.
Charcoal, chalk, sanquine on brown paper, 15⁹⁄₁₆″ × 10⁹⁄₁₆″
Saint Louis Art Museum (61 : 1947)

Two Studies of Indians, n.d.
Charcoal on brown paper, 10⁵⁄₁₆″ × 15½″
UL: "Rant-Che-Way-Me/Female Flying Pigeon"
LR: "Young Ma-Has-Kah Joway Chief/White Cloud"
Saint Louis Art Museum (62 : 1947)

Western Rock Formation along the Yellowstone, n.d.
Charcoal and chalk on brown paper, 9¹³⁄₁₆″ × 15¹⁄₁₆″
Saint Louis Art Museum (64 : 1947)

Study of Cottonwood Trees and Gulch, n.d.
Charcoal and chalk on brown paper, 10⁹⁄₁₆″ × 15⁹⁄₁₆″
Saint Louis Art Museum (80 : 1947)

Buffalo Wading, n.d.
Pencil on brown paper, 6⅛″ × 10½″
Saint Louis Art Museum (85 : 1947)

Indian Burial, n.d.
Pencil on brown paper, 15.8″ × 24.9″
Verso: "Indian Burial"
Saint Louis Art Museum (87 : 1947)

Hunter with Dog, n.d.
Pencil on brown paper, 7″ × 9¹⁵⁄₁₆″
Saint Louis Art Museum (88 : 1947)

Study of an Indian, n.d.
Black chalk on paper, 8¾″ × 10½″
Saint Louis Art Museum (81 : 1971)

Indian Ceremony, n.d.
Pencil on tan paper, 6¼″ × 9¹⁵⁄₁₆″
Saint Louis Art Museum (82 : 1971)

Sketch of a River Bank, n.d.
Pastel on sandpaper, 7⅛″ × 12½″
Saint Louis Art Museum (66 : 1941)

Study of an Indian with Feathered Cap, n.d.
Pencil on paper, 7⅞″ × 12¾″
Formerly Wunderlich Gallery, New York

Study of an Indian on Horseback, n.d.
Pencil on paper, 12¼″ × 7⅞″
Mongerson-Wunderlich Galleries, Chicago

Study of Indians and Horses, n.d.
Pencil on paper, 8¼″ × 12½″
Martin Kodner, Saint Louis

Study of a Buffalo, n.d.
Charcoal, 9¼″ × 13¾″
Formerly Kennedy Galleries, New York

Portrait of a Nude Man, n.d.
Oil on canvas, 25″ × 13″
LL: "C. Wimar"
Private collection, Saint Louis

Indian Head, n.d.
Charcoal on paper, 7″ × 9½″
Private collection, Pennsylvania

Bison Herd, n.d.
Pencil on paper, 6½″ × 10½″
Kennedy Galleries, New York (#9432)

Sketches of an Indian and Trapper, n.d.
Pencil on paper, 8″ × 10½″
Kennedy Galleries, New York (#9434)

Study for an Indian Guide, n.d.
Charcoal on paper, 13½″ × 10″
Kennedy Galleries, New York (#9435)

The Different Forts of P. Chouteau Sr. & Co. Fur Company, n.d.
Photographic print of drawing
LR: "C. Wimar"
Missouri Historical Society, Saint Louis (1986.73.4)

Three Indians, n.d.
Pencil on white paper, 8″ × 12¾″
Dr. and Mrs. John M. Grant

Pawnee Brave, n.d.
Pencil and wash on buff paper, 10½″ × 15½″
LR: "Petalsharoe Pawnee Brave"
Dr. and Mrs. John M. Grant, Saint Louis

Four Indians, n.d.
Pencil on white paper, 10″ × 14″
Dr. and Mrs. John M. Grant, Saint Louis

Three Figures, n.d.
Pencil, 10½″ × 14¼″
Mrs. Samuel Grant, Saint Louis

Campfire/Landscape in Moonlight, n.d.
Pastel, 14″ × 34″
Zaplin-Lampert Gallery, Santa Fe

Study of an Indian, n.d.
Pencil, 7½″ × 11½″
Zaplin-Lampert Gallery, Santa Fe

Indians Hunting Buffalo, n.d.
Pencil, 10″ × 14″
LL: "C. Wimar"
Zaplin-Lampert Gallery, Santa Fe

Selected Bibliography

UNPUBLISHED SOURCES

Lewis, Henry. Papers. William L. Clements Library, University of Michigan, Ann Arbor.

McDermott, John Francis. Papers. Southern Illinois University, Edwardsville.

Miller, Angela. "The Imperial Republic: Narratives of National Expansion in American Art, 1820–1860." Ph.D. diss., Yale University, 1985.

Mitgliederliste des Kunstlervereins Malkasten, December 1852-September 1856. Malkasten Archives, Hauptstaatarchiv, Düsseldorf.

Neilson, Reka. "Charles F. Wimar." Master's thesis, Washington University, Saint Louis, 1943.

Wimar, Carl. Correspondence with family, 1857–59. Thomas Gilcrease Institute for American History and Art, Tulsa, Oklahoma.

———. Papers. Missouri Historical Society, Saint Louis.

PUBLISHED SOURCES

Ankeney, J.S. "A Century of Missouri Art." *Missouri Historical Review* 16 (1922): 481.

Artists of the Western Frontier. Omaha: Joslyn Art Museum, 1976.

Audubon, Maria R., and Elliott Coues. *Audubon and His Journals.* 2 vols. New York: Charles Scribner's Sons, 1897.

Barsness, Larry. *The Bison in Art.* Fort Worth: Amon Carter Museum, 1977.

Barter, Judith A., and Lynn E. Springer. *Currents of Expansion: Painting in the Midwest, 1820–1940.* Saint Louis: Saint Louis Art Museum, 1977.

Becker, Wimar A., and William R. Hodges. "Carl Wimar." *Student Life* (Washington University in Saint Louis) 14 (January 1890): 68–70; (February 1890): 85–87; (March 1890): 103–5.

Boller, Henry A. *Among the Indians: Eight Years in the Far West, 1858–1866.* Edited by Milo M. Quaife. Chicago: R.R. Donnelly and Sons Company, 1959.

Born, Wolfgang. "The City of St. Louis in the History of American Art." *Gazette des Beaux Arts* 30 (October–December 1946): 301.

"Buffalo Hunt by Indians Given to Historical Society." *Saint Louis Daily Post-Dispatch*, February 20, 1941.

"Career of Carl Wimar." *Saint Louis Republic*, November 18, 1894.

Catalog of Paintings on Permanent Exhibition. Saint Louis: Museum of Fine Arts, 1901.

241

Catalogue of the First Annual Exhibition of the Western Academy of Art. Saint Louis: The Missouri Democrat Book and Job Office, 1860.

Catlin, George. *Letters and Notes on the Manners, Customs, and Conditions of the North American Indians.* London: Published by the Author, 1841.

"Charles Wimar 1828–1862." *Montana: The Magazine of Western History* 22 (Spring 1972): 8.

Chittenden, Hiram M. *Early Steamboat Navigation on the Missouri River.* New York: Francis P. Harper, 1903.

"The City's Historical Paintings on Verge of Ruin." *Saint Louis Post-Dispatch*, February 22, 1903.

Coen, Rena N. "David's *Sabine Women* in the Wild West." *Great Plains Quarterly* 2 (Spring 1982): 67–76.

———. "Last of the Buffalo." *American Art Journal* 5 (November 1973): 83–94.

Cowart, Jack. "Recent Acquisition: *Buffalo Pursued by Wolves* (1861)." *Saint Louis Art Museum Bulletin* 12 (November 1977): 199–200.

deLagerberg, Lars Gaston. "The Life Story of a St. Louis Merchant: James Gaston Brown." *Missouri Historical Society Bulletin* 7 (April 1951): 306, 309; 8 (October 1951): 6–7.

Dippie, Brian W. "Two Artists From St. Louis: The Wimar-Russell Connection." In *Charles M. Russell: American Artist*, 20–34. Saint Louis: Jefferson National Expansion Historical Association, 1982.

"The Director's Notebook: The Blow Library." *Missouri Historical Society Bulletin* 24 (January 1968): 181.

"Domestic Art Gossip." *Crayon* 5 (December 1858): 353–54.

Dosch, Donald F. *The Old Courthouse.* Saint Louis: Jefferson National Expansion Historical Association, 1979.

Drumm, Stella M., and Charles Van Ravenswaay. "The Old Courthouse." *Missouri Historical Society Glimpses of the Past* 7 (January 1940): 40.

"Early Navigation up the Missouri River: Report of Charles P. Chouteau to the Secretary of War of a Steamboat Expedition from St. Louis to Fort Benton, 1859." *Contributions to the Historical Society of Montana* 7 (1910): 253–56.

"Ein beruhmter Akademie-Student." *Rheinische Post* (Düsseldorf), January 22, 1975.

Englaender, Alfred. "Der Sohn einer Wascherin." *Kenkel Zeitschrift* (Düsseldorf), March 1954.

———. "Der Indianermaler Wimar in Heidelberg." *Heidelberger Fremdenblatt*, July 15, 1960.

———. "Der Malerfreund der Rothaute." *Rheinische Post* (Düsseldorf), December 16, 1959.

"Erinnerung an Charles Wimar." *Neue Rhein-Zeitung* (Düsseldorf), August 14, 1963.

Ewers, John C. "Fact and Fiction in the Documentary Art of the West." In *The Frontier Re-examined*, edited by John F. McDermott. Urbana: University of Illinois Press, 1967, 79–95.

———. "Not Quite Redmen: The Plains Indian Illustrations of Felix O. C. Darley." *American Art Journal* 3 (Fall 1971): 88–98.

———. *Artists of the Old West.* Garden City, N.Y.: Doubleday, 1973.

"The Fair." *Daily Countersign* (Saint Louis), May 28, 1864.

Fleming, Paula Richardson, and Judith Luskey. *The North American Indians in Early Photographs.* New York: Harper and Row, 1986.

Gachtgens, Barbara. "Amerikanische Kunstler und die Düsseldorfer Malerschule." *Bilder aus den Neuen Welt.* Munich: Prestel-Verlag, 1988.

Gerdts, William H., and Mark Thistlethwaite. *Grand Illusions: History Painting in America*. Fort Worth: Amon Carter Museum, 1988.

"German Immigrant Portrayed Indian Life." *Saint Louis Globe-Democrat*, June 25, 1955.

Glanz, Dawn. *How the West Was Drawn: American Art and the Settling of the Frontier*. Ann Arbor: UMI Research Press, 1982.

Goetzmann, William H. *Army Exploration in the American West*. New Haven: Yale University Press, 1959.

Goetzmann, William H., David C. Hunt, Marsha V. Gallagher, and William J. Orr. *Karl Bodmer's America*. Omaha: Joslyn Art Museum and the University of Nebraska Press, 1984.

"A Great but Forgotten Painter." *Saint Louis Globe-Democrat*, March 3, 1899.

Groseclose, Barbara. *Emanuel Leutze, 1816–1868: Freedom is the Only King*. Washington, D.C.: Smithsonian Institution Press, 1976.

Hartmann, Horst. *George Catlin und Balduin Möllhausen*. Berlin: Dietrich Reimer Verlag, 1963.

Helmuth, William Tod. *Arts in Saint Louis*. Saint Louis, 1864.

Hewitt, J.N.B., ed. *Journal of Rudolph Friedrich Kurz*. Lincoln: University of Nebraska Press, 1970.

Hills, Patricia. *The American Frontier: Images and Myths*. New York: Whitney Museum of American Art, 1973.

"Historical Society Gets Four Portraits." *Saint Louis Globe-Democrat*, March 13, 1953.

Hodges, William Romaine. "Charles Ferdinand Wimar." *American Art Review* 2 (1881): 175–82.

———. *Carl Wimar*. Galveston, Tex.: Charles Reymershoffer, 1908.

Hoopes, Donelson. *The Düsseldorf Academy and the Americans*. Atlanta: The High Museum of Art, 1972.

Hopewell, M., M.D. *Report of the Fourth Annual Fair of the St. Louis Agricultural and Mechanical Association of September 1859*. Saint Louis: George Knapp and Company, 1859.

———. *Report of the Annual Fair of the St. Louis Agricultural and Mechanical Association, of September 1860*. Saint Louis: George Knapp and Company, 1861.

The Hudson and the Rhine. Düsseldorf: Kunstmuseum, 1976.

Hynds, Reed. "First All Wimar Exhibit Opens at City Art Museum." *Saint Louis Star-Times*, October 1946.

"Indian Portraits by Carl Wimar." *Missouri Historical Society Bulletin* 6 (April 1950): 416.

"Indianermaler studierte am Rhein." *Rheinische Post* (Düsseldorf), January 1, 1969.

"Journal of Dr. Elias J. Marsh, Account of a Steamboat Trip on the Missouri River, May-August 1859." *South Dakota Historical Review* 1 (January 1936): 79–127.

"Karl Wimar." *Westliche Post* (Saint Louis), December 2, 1894.

Kate, Herman Ten. "On Paintings of North American Indians and Their Ethnographical Value." *Anthropos* (Vienna) 6 (1911): 521–45.

"Keep It in St. Louis." *Saint Louis Post-Dispatch*, June 29, 1936.

Kemp, Fred. "Ein Sieburger malte die Indianer." *General-Anzeiger*, November 29, 1962.

Kennerly, Maj. William Clark. "Early Days in St. Louis From the Memoirs of an Old Citizen." *Missouri Historical Society Collections* 3 (1911): 420.

Kinealy, Lily Marie Coale. "Charles Ferdinand Wimar." *Mirror*, February 18, 1909.

Koch, Ekkehard. *Karl Mays Vater: Die Deutschen im Wilden Westen*. Huesuem: Hansa Verlag, 1982.

"Kopie fur Siegburger Museum." *Rheinische Post* (Düsseldorf), August 8, 1963.

Luft, Martha Levy. "Charles Wimar's *The Abduction of Daniel Boone's Daughter by the Indians*, 1853 and 1855: Evolving Myths." *Prospects* 7 (1982): 301–14.

Matthey, Horst. "Ein Deutscher Maler: Karl Ferdinand Wimar (Siegburg 1828–1862 St. Louis)." *Ethnologia Americana* (Düsseldorf Institut für amerikanische Völkerkunde) 14 (September-October 1977): 788–791; (November-December 1977): 800–3.

———. "Indianermaler und posthumer Botschafter: Charles Wimar." *Zeitschrift fur Kulturaustausch* (Institut fur Auslandsbeziehungen, Stuttgart) 19 (July-September 1969): 250–52.

———. "Der 'untbekannte' Indianermaler Charles Wimar." *Kalumet* (Interessengemeinschaft fur Indianerkunde, Frankfurt/Main) 18 (May-June 1969): 16–22.

Mattison, Ray H. "Henry A. Boller, Upper Missouri River Fur Trader." *North Dakota History* 33 (Spring 1966): 106–219.

Maximilian, Prince of Wied-Neuwied. "Travels in the Interior of North America." In *Early Western Travels, 1748–1846*, edited by Reuben G. Thwaites. Vols. 22–24. Glendale, Cal.: The Arthur H. Clark Company, 1966.

Mittler, Max. *Die Erobung eines Kontinents*. Zurich: Atlantis Verlag, 1968.

Moulton, Gary E., ed. *The Journals of the Lewis and Clark Expedition*. 4 vols. Lincoln: University of Nebraska Press, 1986–87.

"Museum Gets Painting by Early City Artist." *Saint Louis Post-Dispatch*, September 5, 1946.

Musick, J. B. "*Billy Bowlegs* Acquired by Saint Louis Art Museum." *Saint Louis Art Museum Bulletin* 24 (January 1939): 8.

Musick, James B. "Three Sketch Books of Carl Wimar." *Bulletin of the City Art Museum of Saint Louis* 27 (May-June 1942): 10–14.

Napton, William Barclay. "Lewis and Clark's Route Retraveled. The Upper Missouri in 1858." In *Over the Santa Fe Trail, 1857*. Kansas City: Franklin Hudson Publishing Company, 1905.

Novak, Barbara. *The Thyssen-Bornemisza Collection: Nineteenth-Century American Painting*. New York: The Vendome Press, 1986.

"Old Courthouse Murals to be Restored Again." *Saint Louis Post-Dispatch*, June 21, 1942.

"Painting by Pioneer Artist of St. Louis is Presented to the City Art Museum." *Saint Louis Post-Dispatch*, November 6, 1925.

"Painting of a Painter." *Saint Louis Globe-Democrat*, December 30, 1938.

"Paintings by Wimar: Exhibit at Saint Louis Art Museum." *Antiques* 50 (December 1946): 398.

"Paintings Typical . . . To Be Preserved." *Saint Louis Republic*, February 5, 1905.

Parrish, William E. *Turbulent Partnership: Missouri and the Union, 1861–1865*. Columbia: University of Missouri Press, 1963.

"The Pioneer Artist of the West Has Laid Aside His Palette and Brush." *Saint Louis Globe-Democrat*, May 26, 1903.

Powell, Mary. "Three Artists of the Frontier." *Missouri Historical Society Bulletin* 5 (October 1948): 40.

Rathbone, Perry T. *Charles Wimar 1828–1862: Painter of the Indian Frontier*. Saint Louis: City Art Museum, 1946.

———. "Indian Frontier Artist." *Magazine of Art* 40 (December 1947): 315–19.

———, ed. *Mississippi Panorama*. Saint Louis: City Art Museum, 1950.

———, ed. *Westward the Way*. Saint Louis: Van Hoffman Press, 1954.

Saint Louis Agricultural & Mechanical Association. *Fine Art Department* (1858): 96–110; (1859): 121–136; (1860): 94–106; (1866): 80–84; (1867): 92–109; (1869): 59–72; (1870): 70–91; (1871): 74–79; (1872): 44–51.

"A St. Louis Artist's Story." *Saint Louis Daily Globe-Democrat*, November 20, 1887.

Saint Louis Exposition and Music Hall Association. *Catalogue of the Fine Art Department. First Annual Exhibition*. Saint Louis: Nixon-Jones Printing Company, 1884.

Samuels, Peggy, and Howard Samuels. *The Illustrated Encyclopedia of Artists of the American West*. Garden City, New York: Doubleday, 1976.

"Says Wimar Paintings Were Done By $20-a-Week Sign Painter About 1865." *Saint Louis Daily Post-Dispatch*, February 12, 1922.

Scharf, Thomas J. *History of Saint Louis City and County, from the Earliest Periods to the Present Day*. Philadelphia: Louis H. Everts and Company, 1883.

Schmutterer, Gerhard M. *Tomahawk and Cross: Lutheran Missionaries Among the Northern Plains Tribes, 1858–1866*. Sioux Falls, S.D.: The Center for Western Studies, Augustana College, 1989.

Schulte, E. "Die permanente Kunstausstellung." *Correspondenz-Blatt, des Kunstvereins fur Rheinlande und Westphalen zu Düsseldorf* 10 (March 1855): 12.

Shoemaker, Floyd C. *Missouri and Missourians*. Chicago: Lewis Publishing Company, 1943.

———. "Missouri Miniatures." *Missouri Historical Review* 37 (October 1942-July 1943): 208–13.

Sonntag. "Carl Ferdinand Wimar: Liebensbild eines St. Louiser deutschen Kunstlers." *Deutschen Pionier* (Saint Louis) 13 (July 1881): 130.

Spiess, Lincoln Bunce. "Carl Wimar's Trip Up the Missouri River." *Westward* 4 (May 1975): 16.

———. "Carl Wimar: The Missouri Historical Society's Collection." *Gateway Heritage* 3 (Winter 1982–83): 16–29.

———. "Some Little-Known—and Unknown—Portraits by Carl Wimar." *Missouri Historical Society Bulletin* 34 (January 1978): 83–88.

Sunder, John E. *The Fur Trade on the Upper Missouri, 1840–1865*. Norman: University of Oklahoma Press, 1965.

Taft, Robert. *Artists and Illustrators of the Old West*. New York: Charles Scribner's Sons, 1953.

Taussig, Dr. William. "Carl Wimar." *Westliche Post* (Saint Louis), September 29, 1886.

Truettner, William H. "The Art of History: American Exploration and Discovery Scenes, 1840–1860." *American Art Journal* 14 (Winter 1982): 4–31.

Tyler, Ron, et al. *American Frontier Life: Early Western Painting and Prints*. New York: Abbeville Press, 1987.

Wagner, Oswald F. "Lutheran Zealots Among the Crows." *Montana: The Magazine of Western History* 21 (January 1972): 2–19.

The West Explored. Santa Fe: Gerald Peters Gallery, 1988.

"Wimar Drawing: The Abduction of Daniel Boone's Daughter," *Antiques* 69 (May 1956): 450.

"Wimar Paintings to be Restored." *Saint Louis Globe-Democrat*, February 19, 1941.

"Wimar Rediscovered in St. Louis Show." *Artnews* 45 (October 1946): 8.

"Wochentlicher Kunstbericht. Bildende Kunst. Die Kunstvereins-Ausstellung." *Düsseldorfer Journal und Kreis-Blatt*, August 3, 1854.

"Works of Carl Wimar at City Art Museum." *Saint Louis Post-Dispatch*, October 13, 1946.

Index

Abduction of Daniel Boone's Daughter
by the Indians, 1, 5, 44, 48, 49–54, 55,
56, 62–64, 67, 68, 74 n.97, 75 nn.98,
104
Academy of Science of Saint Louis,
115–16, 177 n.76
Achenbach, Oswald, 44, 58, 59
American Fur Company, 26, 33, 83, 84,
91, 95, 97, 100, 104, 114–115, 128, 139,
144–145, 174 nn.48, 49; 175 n.55, 183
n.109
Arikara, 95–96, 97, 98, 124, 125, 141,
142, 164, 165, 173 nn.41, 42; 174 n.48,
179 n.89
Art education, in America, 33–34, 37,
38–39, 40, 58
in Düsseldorf, 40, 58–62
Assiniboine, 99, 100–101, 102, 103, 104,
105–106, 110, 128, 154, 175 n.51, 176
n.57
Attack on an Emigrant Train, 6, 55–56,
57–58, 62, 65–67, 68–69, 74 n.97, 75
n.104
Audubon, John James, 124, 125, 147, 153,
169 n.11, 174 n.46, 176 n.63, 177 n.68,
178 n.82, 185 n.125

Badlands, 97, 122, 131
Bad River, 119
Bates, Edward, 20, 210, 211, 224 n.80,
226 n.110
Beale survey, 204, 205, 222 nn.45, 47, 224
n.74
Bear Paw Mountains, 139–140
Bear Rib, 17, 89, 120–121, 179 nn.83, 84
Becker, August, 81, 191, 192, 218, 220
n.15
Becker family, 31, 32, 33, 72 n.39

Beeson, Henry W., 111
Bellevue, 83, 169–70 n.11
Benton, Thomas Hart, 21, 190, 202, 204,
205, 206, 208, 210, 211, 212, 220 n.9,
222 nn.40, 47; 223 nn.52, 53; 224 n.73,
224 n.84, 226 n.110
Bierstadt, Albert, 42, 43, 59, 198, 207,
208–209, 221 n.32
Big Head, 93, 94, 123–124, 173 n.40
Billy Bowlegs, 19, 167–68
Bingham, George Caleb, 38, 43, 48, 52, 54,
58, 60, 69, 184 n.119, 212, 224 n.79
Blackfeet, 84, 86, 114, 133, 185 n.125
Blackbird Hills, 116, 178 n.78
Blandowski, Constantin, 84, 106, 109, 111,
225 n.84
Blow, Henry T., 149, 150, 161, 184 n.119,
185 n.129, 186 n.132
Bodmer, Karl, 25, 37, 38, 46, 69, 110, 135,
136, 147, 151, 152, 154, 155, 157, 160,
165, 169 n.11, 182 n.101
Boller, Henry A., 82, 85, 88, 92, 94, 97,
99, 101, 110, 169 nn.5, 6; 175 n.55, 178
n.78, 179 nn.85, 89
Bonn, 41
Boone, Daniel, 44; representations in art,
44, 45–49
Boone, Jemima, 44, 45–46, 53–54, 62,
63–64
Braeuninger, Moritz, 82, 86, 105, 109,
113, 177 n.73
Bridger, Jim, 116, 178 n.77
Broken Arm, 101, 102
Brownlee, John A., 113, 177 n.73
Brulé, 84, 89
Brulé Bottom, 139, 140
Brumidi, Constantino, 213–214
Buffalo, 26, 27, 99, 107, 108, 114,
126–127, 144, 145, 147, 148, 157, 158,
159–60, 176 n.63, 205, 209, 224 n.74
Buffalo Crossing the Platte, 11, 146,
147–149
Buffaloes Crossing the Yellowstone, 10,
145, 146–147, 151, 209, 224 n.75
Buffalo Dance, 14, 164–65, 166

Buffalo Hunt, 16, 18, 156–164, 209
Burial scaffolds, 92–93, 122, 125, 173
n.36, 179 n.89, 185 n.130

Calling of Cincinnatus from the Plow,
213, 214
Calling of Putnam from the Plow to the
Revolution, 213, 214
Capt. John Smith and Party Landing at
Jamestown, 199
Captive Charger, 4, 60–62, 61
Captivity narratives, 49–54, 56
Captured by the Indians, 52, 54
Castle of Heidelberg, 41–42
Catlin, George, 25, 37, 38, 67, 89, 110,
156–58, 159, 160, 165–66, 170 n.11,
172 n.32, 177 n.68, 178 n.82
Cedar Island, 118, 119, 178 n.81
Chapman, John Gadsby, 198, 199, 221
n.32
Charlemagne, representations in art, 216,
225 nn.99–100
Chicago, 188, 202, 207
Chief Billy Bowlegs (Holatamico), 19, 167
Chippewa (steamboat), 115, 116, 126,
128–143 passim., 183 n.109
Chouteau, Charles P., 115, 116, 127–128,
129, 131, 133, 138, 140, 142, 144, 145,
177 n.76, 184 n.119
Chouteau, Pierre Jr., 81, 91, 114
Citadel Rock, 136, 137, 182 n.102
Civil War, 27, 189, 191–192, 206, 210,
224 n.68
Cochetope Pass, 202, 205, 206, 207, 209,
222 nn.47–49, 223 n.53. See also
Westward the Star of Empire.
Cole, Thomas, 47, 49, 51, 53, 224 n.72
Columbus, representations in art, 48, 193,
196, 197, 221 nn.31–32
Coming from the Fair, 151
Concealed Enemy, 49, 51
Coo-Che-To-Pa Pass View Looking up
Sahwatch Creek, 204, 205

Cooper, James Fenimore, 25, 27, 32, 33, 45, 110, 111, 156, 184 n.122
Crapster, M. H., 115, 127
Crawford, Thomas, 63
Crow Indians, 82, 101, 110, 112–113, 177 n.68
Culbertson, Alexander, 104, 105, 106, 109, 115, 116, 139, 174 n.48
Curly Hair, 91, 92
Cushing, Caleb, 155

Daniel Boone and His Cabin on the Great Osage Lake, 47, 49
Daniel Boone Escorting Settlers Through the Cumberland Gap, 48, 50
Daniel Boone's First View of the Kentucky Valley, 47–48, 50
Darley, Felix O. C., 38, 39, 56, 67–68, 161, 185 n.127
Dauphin's Rapids, 132–133, 140, 181 n.98
David, Jacques-Louis, 50
Deas, Charles, 38, 54, 56, 69, 184 n.119
DeBry, Theodore, 197
de la Tour, Georges, 53
Deppe, Henry, 35
De Smet, Pierre-Jean, 153, 181 n.99
De Soto, 193–197, 198, 220–221 n.20
De Soto Discovering the Mississippi, 20, 193, 194–196
Discovery of Boone's Encampment by the Indians, 44, 49–50, 51
Discovery of the Mississippi by De Soto, 193–194
Duden, Gottfried, 32
Düsseldorf, Academy, 59–60, 217, 225 n.97
    as art center, 30, 40, 42–44, 58–63, 67, 69, 73 n.59, 207, 215–217
    Gallery, New York, 39, 40
    Wimar in, 42–47, 52–70
Dying Gaul, 63
Dying Indian Chief, Contemplating the Progress of Civilization, 63

Eads, James B., 150, 188
Eagle Rock, 136, 137
Easterly, Thomas M., 85
Eastman, Seth, 184 n.119, 193, 221 n.20
Elberfeld, 59, 216, 226 n.103
Emigrants Attacked by Indians, 67
Emil Becker and His Dog Dash, 35, 36
Entrance to the Jeddo River, 35, 36
Eye of the Needle, 137, 138, 182 n.102

Fay, Joseph, 58, 59, 216, 226 nn. 102–103
Ferry, Gabriel, 65, 75 n.101
Fitzgibbon, John, 85, 170 n.17
Flatboatmen on the Mississippi, 3, 58, 59
Fort Atkinson, 97, 99, 174 n.48
Fort Benton, 25, 80, 114–115, 127, 130, 138, 139, 144, 145, 175 n.55, 182 n.104, 183 n.109
Fort Berthold, 97, 99, 141, 144, 173 n.43, 174 n.48, 185 n.130
Fort Clark, 94, 95–96, 124, 125, 141, 144, 165, 173 nn.41, 43; 174 nn.45, 46; 179 n.89
Fort Kipp, 128, 144
Fort Lookout, 88, 89, 171 n.24, 172 n.28
Fort McKenzie, 139
Fort Pierre, 91, 92, 119, 120, 121, 142, 144, 172 n.32, 173 n.43
Fort Randall, 86, 87, 89, 91, 114, 119–120, 142, 165, 171 nn.21, 24; 172 n.28
Fort Sarpy, 109, 111, 177 n.68
Fort Stuart, 101, 104, 128, 175 n.55
Fort Union, 81, 100–101, 104, 105–106, 111, 127, 140, 144, 154, 155, 167, 175 n.54, 176 n.57, 182 n.104, 184 n.122
Fort William, 99, 154, 155, 175 nn.51, 52, 54
Fortress Butte, 132
Frémont, John C., 204, 205, 222 n.47, 225 n.84
Frémont expedition, 183 n.114, 204–205, 222 n.48

Fresco decoration, in Germany, 215–217, 225 nn.95, 97, 99–100, 226 n.106
    in Italy, 214, 216
    in United States, 209–211, 212–215
    See also Saint Louis Courthouse, Wimar mural cycle
Frost, Todd and Company, 81, 82, 87, 91, 97, 101, 114, 119, 128, 145, 169 n.6, 174 nn.48, 49; 175 n.55
Funeral Raft of the Dead Chieftain, 7, 64, 65
Fur trade, 25, 81–82, 114–115, 144–145, 155, 174 nn.48, 49; 197

Gamble, Governor Hamilton R., 67, 192, 212, 224 n.83
Géricault, Theodore, 62–63
German,
    interest in the American West, 25, 32–33
    migration to the United States, 31–32
    mural movement, 193, 215–217, 225 n.97, 226 nn.99–100, 103, 106
Good Times in the New World (The Hope of Jamestown), 198, 199
Golden Shell, 126
Great Bend of the Missouri, 89–91, 119, 152, 153, 172 n.31, 178 n.82
Gros Ventre (Hidatsa), 95, 97, 98, 99, 100, 141, 164, 174 nn.48, 49
Grozelier, Leopold, 67
Grünewald, Matthias, 53
Gunnison survey, 202, 204, 205, 222 n.43, 223 n.52

Hart, James M., 43
Haseltine, William S., 43, 59
Hayden, Ferdinand, 115–116, 171 n.23, 174 n.45, 176 nn.57, 63; 178 n.81
Hegelian logic, 217, 226 n.108
Hill, Thomas, 68

History painting, 39, 40, 189, 192–201, 207–218
Hitchcock, Charles, 198, 199
Hole in the Wall, 136, 182 n.102
Hudson, Henry, representations in art, 197–198, 221 n.32
Hunkpapa, 84, 86, 89, 121

Indian and Captive, 68, 70
Indian Encampment on the Big Bend of the Missouri River, 15, 152, 153
Indians Abducting Woman, 56
Indians Approaching Fort Union, 12, 153–155
Indians Attacking a Wagon Train, 68, 69
Indians Crossing the Upper Missouri River, 13, 151, 152
Indians Pursued by American Dragoons, 2, 62, 64, 65
Indians Stealing Horses, 9
Indians, depictions in literature, 32–33, 45, 110–111
    depictions in art, 44–58, 60–70, 75 n.102, 110
    German interest in, 32–33, 44, 73 n.54
    photographs of, 80, 85, 88, 92, 98–99
Iron Horn, 89
Iron Nation, 89
Irving, Washington, 158
Isenheim Altarpiece, 53, 55

Johnson, Eastman, 43
Jolly Flatboatmen, 58, 60, 74 n.86
Judith River, 133, 140, 152, 181 n.99

Kansas City, 82–83, 169 n.10
Kate Howard (steamboat), 143
Kern, Richard H., 204, 205
Kurz, Rudolph, 147, 163–164, 170 n.11, 174 nn. 48, 50; 176 n.63, 177 n.68

LaBarge, Captain John, 115, 122, 128, 133, 139, 140, 141
LaBarge Rock, 137, 138, 183 n.104
Laclede, Pierre, 190, 193, 196–197, 198, 221 nn.28, 30
La Framboise Island, 119
Landing of Columbus at the Island of Guanahani, West Indies, 198
Landing of Henry Hudson, 1608, at Verplanck Point, 198
Landing of Laclede, 21, 193, 195, 196–198, 218
Landing of Roger Williams at State Rock, 198, 199
LaSalle, representations in art, 196, 221 n.20
Last of the Mohicans, 45, 51, 53
Leutze, Emanuel, 39–40, 42, 43–44, 46–47, 48, 55, 58, 59, 61, 207, 208, 209, 215, 216, 224 nn.70, 76
Lewis, Henry, 34, 42–43, 44, 59, 67
Like-a-Fishhook village, 97, 164, 174 n.48
Little Soldier, 122, 123
Lodges, Indian, 123, 124–125, 174 n.45, 181 n.99
Lost Trail, 8, 64
Long Jakes, 64, 65
Lyons, Lord, 151, 156

Malkasten, 44
Mandan, 95, 97–98, 124, 125, 126, 164, 165, 166, 173 n.41, 174 n.48, 179 n.89
Marias River, 138, 182 n.103
Marsh, Dr. Elias J., 116, 119, 122, 123, 127, 128, 130, 131–132, 133, 140, 141, 142, 147, 178 n.80
Mary Magdalen, images of, 52–53
Ma-Sai-To, 126
Maximilian, Prince of Wied-Neuwied, 32, 37, 110, 130, 132, 135, 136, 155, 169 n.11, 171 n.24, 181 nn.97, 98
Medicine Cow, 88
Meldrum, Robert, 105–106, 109, 176 n.59

Michelangelo, 56, 57
Milk River, 129–130, 180 n.93
Millet, Jean-François, 46
Miniconjou, 84, 86, 89, 172 n.28
Miragoli, 218, 226 n.110
Missouri River frontier, 25–27, 78–79, 80–81, 82–106, 116–145
Möllhausen, Balduin, 32
Mullan, Lieutenant John, 127–28
Murder of Jane McCrea, 50–51, 52

Napton, William, 85, 91, 92, 178 n.81, 183 n.114
Nazarenes, 217, 225 n.97
Nebraska City, 114
Niobrara, 142

Omaha, 114, 116, 143
Omaha (steamboat), 111–112
On the Prairie, 67, 68
One Horn, 89
Oregon Trail, The, 208–209
Osage Scalp Dance, 51, 53

Pacific railroad. *See* Transcontinental railroad.
Panoramas, 33–34, 71 n.21
Park/Pope survey, 204
Paris, as art center, 40, 62
Pawnees, 83, 116, 163
Pearsall, John, 116
Persephone myth, 50, 64
Phelps, John S., 205–206, 223 nn.56, 59
Photography. *See* Indians, photographs of
Pietà, 56–57
Pinnacles, 136
Pomarede, Leon, 33–34, 42, 209, 214–215, 225 nn.88–89
Powell, William H., 193–194, 196
Poussin, Nicolas, 50
Prairie fires, 112, 146, 148

Prairie Fire, 54, 56, 62, 66
Primm, Judge Wilson, 192, 196–197, 198, 200, 224 n.80
Prince of Wales, 151, 156

R*aft of the Medusa*, 62–63
Railroad surveys, 203
Ranney, William T., 39, 47, 66, 69, 193
Rape of the Sabine Women, 50, 74 n.71
Raynolds, Captain W. F., 116, 119, 120, 122, 127, 139, 171 n.23, 177 nn.68, 76; 179 n.84, 182 n.103, 185 n.130
Reconciliation, 191, 192
Recontre, Zephyr, 94, 178 n.77
Redfield, Alexander, 82, 84, 88, 92, 94, 95, 97–98, 101, 104–105, 106, 109, 111, 116, 118, 142, 170 n.14, 173 n.42, 176 nn.61, 62
Religious iconography, in western themes, 48, 52–53, 57–58, 73 n.66, 207, 224 n.73
Reni, Guido, 57
Richards, William Trost, 43
Rindesbacher, Peter, 157, 158
Round Butte, 130, 180 n.94
Rowlandson, Mary, 49–50

S*abine Women*, 50
Saint Helena, 83
Saint Louis, 24, 26–27, 31, 32, 33–35, 37–38, 77, 81, 143, 168, 190–191, 192–193, 196–197, 198, 200–202, 205–207, 217–219, 221 nn.25, 28; 222 n.47, 223 n.68
Saint Louis Agricultural and Mechanical Fair, art exhibition of 1858, 113, 183 n.112
art exhibition of 1859, 146–151
Saint Louis Courthouse, 26, 187, 188–189, 190–191, 192–193, 196–198, 200–202, 206–208, 209–212, 217–219, 220 nn.6, 14, 15, 18; 224 nn.75–78, 226 n.113

Saint Louis Merchants Exchange, 215
Saint Mary Magdalen Meditating, 53
Scalp Creek, 118, 119, 178 n.81
Schadow, Wilhelm von, 59, 217
Schmidt, Jakob, 82, 88, 93, 104–106, 107, 108, 109, 110, 113–114, 149, 155, 170 n.15, 173 n.40, 177 n.73
Scholton, John A., 144, 183 n.111
Schoolcraft, Henry Rowe, 155, 221 n.20
Schoonover, Bernard S., 116, 120, 123–124
Sealsfield, Charles, 32–33
Sectional crisis, 189, 190–192
Sevier, Mr., 106, 108, 109, 149
Shaw, Captain John, 81, 82
Siegburg, 30–31, 41
Sioux, 84, 86, 92, 95, 99, 116, 120–121, 123, 126, 141, 164, 173 nn.42, 43; 179 nn.83, 89. *See also* Yanktons, Hunkpapa, Brulé
Slaughter of the Innocents, 57
Smith, John, representations in art, 197, 198
Smithsonian Institution, 115–116, 159, 160
Smutty Bear, 87–88, 118, 178 n.80
South-West Branch railroad, 203, 206, 223 n.64
Spanish Island, 138
Spread Eagle (steamboat), 115–128 passim., 140–143, 175 nn.54, 55
Stanley, John Mix, 38, 41, 101, 130, 154, 155, 170 n.16, 176 n.57, 198, 199, 204
Steamboat Rock, 135, 136, 182 n.101
Stereochromy, 215, 225 n.95
Struck By the Ree, 87–88, 171 n.23

T*aussig*, William, 192–193, 208, 220 nn.14, 15, 18; 224 nn.76, 78; 225 n.96
Thomas Jefferson, Secretary of State, 214
Three Children Attacked by a Wolf, 36, 37
Transcontinental railroad, 188, 190, 202–207, 212, 220 nn.5, 9; 222 nn.42, 43, 53; 223 nn.58, 59, 62, 66; 224 nn.67, 81

Trumbull, John, 212
Twilight (steamboat), 81–83, 91, 101, 169 n.7, 175 n.55
Two Bears, 89, 173 n.40
Two Shepherd Boys With Dogs Fighting, 36, 37

U*nited States* Capitol building, 189, 207, 212–214, 221 n.32, 224 n.70, 225 n.96

V*alley of the Mississippi Illustrated*, 38
Vanderlyn, John, 50–51, 197, 198
Van Zandt, William, 156
Vaughan, Alfred J., 82, 104–105, 114, 116, 120, 123, 130
Vermillion River, 116–117, 178 n.79
Vikings First Landing in America, 46–47, 48

W*ashington*, George, 24, 211, 226 n.110
Washington, Martha, 23, 211, 226 n.110
Washington and Delaware Indians at a Council Fire, 62
Washington Crossing the Delaware, 39–40, 43
Weir, Robert Walter, 197–198, 221 n.32
Western Academy of Art, 150–152, 153, 156, 164, 168, 184 nn.117, 119; 185 n.129, 186 n.132
Westward the Course of Empire Takes Its Way, 48, 207–208, 215, 225 n.96
Westward the Star of Empire, 23, 193, 201, 207–209, 222 n.39, 224 n.75
Whipple survey, 202–204
White Cliffs, 130, 131, 152, 181 n.97
White Parflesh, 96
Whitman, Walt, 27
Whitney survey, 202, 203
Whittredge, Worthington, 42, 43, 44, 59, 73 n.54
Wild, J.C., 11

250

Williams, Roger, representations in art,
    197, 221 n.33
Wimar, Carl Ferdinand, frontispiece, 29,
    34, 17, 150
    collection of Indian artifacts, 61, 66, 94,
        112–113, 177 n.72
    Düsseldorf paintings, 25, 44–47, 52–70,
        74 n.79
    early years in Germany, 30–31, 74 n.95
    family background, 30–31
    in Düsseldorf, 40–47, 52–70, 72 n.53,
        216–217, 226 nn. 102–103
    in Saint Louis, 26–27, 30, 31, 33–38,
        66, 70, 93, 112–114, 146–168, 188,
        191–202, 206–208, 209–212,
        214–215, 217–218
    mural cycle for Saint Louis Courthouse,
        26, 188–219, 220 n.15, 224
        nn.75–77, 226 n.112
    photography by, 83, 92, 96, 98–99, 111,
        112, 113, 169 n.5
    trip up Missouri River (1858), 80–112,
        169 n.5, 171 nn.19, 25; 175 n.55
    trip up Missouri River (1859), 114–144,
        179–180 n.90, 181 nn.97, 99; 182
        nn.101–102, 104
Wood Boatmen on a River, 58, 60, 74 n.86
Wounded Buffalo, 148, 149–150, 209

Yanktons, 84, 88, 89, 92, 93–94, 110,
    116, 118, 122, 142, 159, 165, 172 n.29
Year of the Blow, 22, 193, 198, 200–201
Yellowstone River, 81, 82, 99–100,
    106–110, 116, 120, 155, 176 n.61

CARL WIMAR

Edited by Nancy Stevens
Designed by James A. Ledbetter, Dallas
Typeset by G & S Typesetters, Austin
Printed by South China Printing Co., Hong Kong